# DE GAULLE

# DE GAULLE

BERNARD LEDWIDGE

St. Martin's Press
New York

DE GAULLE. Copyright © 1982 by Bernard Ledwidge. All rights
reserved. Printed in the United States of America. No part
of this book may be used or reproduced in any manner
whatsoever without written permission except in the case of
brief quotations embodied in critical articles or reviews.
For information, address St. Martin's Press, 175 Fifth
Avenue, New York, N.Y. 10010.

ISBN 0-312-19127-8

Library of Congress Cataloging in Publication Number: 82-61701

First published in Great Britain by George Weidenfeld and
Nicolson Ltd.

First U.S. Edition
10 9 8 7 6 5 4 3 2 1

# Contents

# Illustrations

# Acknowledgements

I have been greatly helped in writing this book by the kindness of many people who knew General de Gaulle well and have been ready to talk to me about the man, his character, and his work.

My grateful thanks are due, in the first place, to his son Admiral Philippe de Gaulle, his niece, Madame Anthonioz (née Geneviève de Gaulle), his sister-in-law, the late Madame Jean-Henry Rérolle, and her daughter, the Comtesse de Guitaut, all of whom received me. The General's sister, the late Madame Cailliau, was also good enough to reply to some enquiries about the family history; and the Comte and Comtesse de Guitaut have kindly allowed me to select photographs of the General from their collection for use among the illustrations. Madame Anne MacKean also helped with family history.

I have also to record my gratitude to President François Mitterrand who did me the honour of receiving me at the Elysée and discussing his illustrious predecessor; and to Messieurs Maurice Couve de Murville, Michel Debré, Louis Joxe, Gaston Palewski, René Massigli, Roger Frey, Olivier Guichard, Jacques Foccart, Hervé Alphand, Geoffroy de Courcel, Etienne Burin des Roziers, Bernard Tricot, Roger Vaurs and Pierre-Louis Blanc, all of whom gave me interviews, as did General Jacques Massu. My thanks go also to Monsieur Alfred Fabre-Luce, who gave me another point of view.

In Britain Sir Harold Wilson, Lady Soames, Lord Soames, Sir John Colville, Sir Patrick Reilly and Sir John Balfour were kind enough to talk to me about their encounters and dealings with the General. I am most grateful to them all.

I should also like to thank the directors and officials of the various archives and libraries which I consulted for their unfailing help and courtesy. These include the Public Record Office and the Foreign and Commonwealth Office Library in London, the Churchill College Archive Centre at Cambridge, the Quai d'Orsay in Paris, the National

Archives in Washington and the Princeton University Library. My thanks go also to Monsieur Pierre Lefranc, Director of the Charles de Gaulle Institute in Paris, and to his library staff for all their help.

Quotations from printed books are acknowledged in the Notes as they occur. I am grateful to the authors and publishers who authorized quotation; particularly to Plon, who have allowed me to quote from de Gaulle's Memoirs (in my own translation), and to Cassells, the publishers of Churchill's Memoirs.

I am also most grateful to the Master and Fellows of Pembroke College, Cambridge, for their kind hospitality at the time when I began writing this book in the summer of 1980, to Philip Cerny of York University for reading the manuscript and offering many valuable suggestions, to Dr Martin Gilbert of Oxford University for advice and encouragement, and to Martin Hillenbrand, Director of the Atlantic Institute in Paris, for help in obtaining the release under the Freedom of Information Act of State Department records and to Walter Eytan, formerly Israel Ambassador in Paris, for reminiscences. Finally I should like to thank Elizabeth Burke and Sally Mapstone of Weidenfeld and Nicolson for all the aid they have given me by reading my manuscript and generally guiding my footsteps.

# PREFACE

A passage in Polybius impressed me in my schooldays which describes a warrior dying in the dust of battle but still aiming a last blow at the enemy horseman riding him down. The warrior was a Gaul, and I thought of his courage when I first heard of de Gaulle in 1940. For me he was the dying Gaul who refused to die, and I took an immediate liking to him because I very much wanted to believe that France would not die.

His subsequent destiny in the war years was of a piece with this beginning. He was like a legendary hero sustaining his cause against great odds, and I think that was why so much of British and American public opinion persisted in sympathizing with him even when he was quarrelling with Churchill and Roosevelt. His consecration as a hero by the French people when he walked down the Champs Elysées in liberated Paris seemed to me so right artistically that it could not be wrong politically.

I followed de Gaulle's fortunes from afar during the war and had nothing to do with Free France. But, as a British diplomat, I had a great deal to do with the Fifth Republic. When de Gaulle returned to power, I was in Berlin as Political Adviser to the British Military Government, and I remained there in close liaison with the French and Americans until after the Berlin Wall was built. I was well placed to appreciate how much difference his firmness made to the posture of his more flexible Allies. Without him the West would not have come out of the Berlin crisis as well as it did.

Subsequently I was head of Western Department in the Foreign Office and then went to Paris as Minister at the British Embassy, arriving on the day de Gaulle announced he would stand for a second term as President, and remaining until after his final resignation. During all this time I was closely concerned with Anglo-French relations, and in Paris I was able to observe from a privileged position the whole sweep of the General's policy, foreign and domestic. I met de Gaulle from time to time and came to know many of those who worked for him.

It is on my experience during the years of the Fifth Republic that my claims to write a book about de Gaulle are chiefly based. But my desire to write about him certainly derives in part from what he achieved and what he symbolized during the Second World War.

I have said enough to show that I began writing this book as an admirer of its subject. In the course of producing it I have learned a great deal about the man that I did not previously know, and I remain as admiring as before. I do not think it is possible today to sustain the view, once so popular, that de Gaulle did grave harm to the Western world. On the contrary it is remarkable how much vitality his ideas have displayed since he departed from the scene. His advice to the Americans, for instance, to leave Vietnam, to recognize China, and to allow the price of gold to find its own level, was rejected when he gave it, but it has long since won acceptance; and Washington is still trying to find a wholly satisfactory answer to the question he put successively to Presidents Eisenhower, Kennedy, and Nixon about how far the Europeans could safely rely for their security on the American nuclear deterrent. As to Britain, in the light of what has happened since she joined the EEC, nobody can deny any longer that he had reason to be dubious about the effect her entry would have both on her partners and herself.

It is the same with de Gaulle's advice to the Europeans to be more self-assertive *vis-à-vis* their American allies. In his day when France expressed disagreement with Washington's views, she did so in isolation. But in the current disputes over the Siberian gas pipeline, and over the steel trade, France has the support of Britain, Germany and Italy in resisting American demands. A kind of European Europe may be coming to birth whether or not Britain stays in the Common Market. Perhaps the day will even arrive when the Russians have to admit that they would have done better to accept the advice de Gaulle gave them to allow their allies more freedom. He was also the first statesman to advocate the abandonment of 'power bloc' politics, and there have been many responsive echoes to his call. Nor has his cherished belief that nations outlast ideologies been invalidated by what has happened since his death.

In fact the voice of the prophet de Gaulle is still audible in many lands, particularly of course in France, where a socialist régime under the direction of his principal political opponent, François Mitterrand, continues to follow the main lines of his foreign and defence policies and functions happily enough under the presidential system of government he introduced in 1958.

On the other hand de Gaulle the hero is less in vogue at the moment than de Gaulle the prophet because of the wide circulation of a story that he nearly went into exile during the disturbances of May 1968 and was only dissuaded from doing so by the valiant General Massu. The essence of this story was in fact already known and I had had the advantage of discussing it with General Massu. I think my account puts things in perspective. The great point of it is that de Gaulle overcame his discouragement, returned to the battlefield and gained the day. It is a recognized heroic procedure.

Oddly enough this is the first biography of Charles de Gaulle to appear for nearly ten years. None has appeared in French since 1969, none in English since 1973. Much new material relating to his career has become available since then in governmental archives and elsewhere, and I have made use of a great deal of it in preparing my account of the life of this extraordinary human being.

# 1 THE END AND THE BEGINNING

Solon in his wisdom taught King Croesus to consider no man happy until he was dead; however fortunate a living man appeared, a tragic fate might lie in wait for him. Judgement had to be reserved until he had ended his days blessed by the gods and honoured by his fellow citizens.

By the criterion of Solon, Charles de Gaulle might be judged to have achieved happiness when he died tranquilly under his own roof in his own land of France on 9 November 1970, at the age of seventy-nine. A tragic fate had indeed come very near to overtaking him in May 1968, when civil disturbances suddenly blew up into a storm which almost swept him away to political shipwreck. But he had contrived to escape the clutches of those demons of disaster who so often beset the last days of great French leaders. Joan of Arc and Napoleon had died in the hands of their enemies. Charles de Gaulle, who had done as much as they in life, did better in death.

His end was not merely tranquil, it was elegant. One autumn evening, after a day spent working on his Memoirs, the General collapsed unconscious in his chair at the card-table where he had been playing patience (*réussite*, or success, as the French call the game) in the library at his home at Colombey-les-Deux-Eglises. He remained alive just long enough to receive the last rites of Holy Church, as befitted one who had always practised his religion, and then he died. The process had taken less than thirty-five minutes and had, in the judgement of the doctor who arrived at the same moment as the priest, been virtually painless.[1]

Had the General wished, his mortal remains would have received the most splendid of State funerals, but his last directions declined that honour and laid down that he should be buried simply at Colombey in the presence of his family and close wartime companions. His wishes were of course respected, and his body was laid to rest at Colombey on 12 November. On the same day, Georges Pompidou, the second

President of the Republic which de Gaulle had fashioned, invited the great of the world to a service of commemoration at Notre Dame, and a gathering of the General's friends and enemies assembled to do him honour in the Paris which he had conquered more than once.

His incomparable services to France acknowledged even by his opponents, his country widely respected and more prosperous than ever before in its history, the State of his fashioning in the political control of his supporters, public honours paid to him on his death, in outward appearance de Gaulle corresponded closely to the Athenian philosopher's definition of the happy man.

But there was another and darker side to the picture. De Gaulle had not emerged unscathed from his brush with disaster in 1968. His prestige and his confidence had suffered. In April 1969, defeated for the first time in a referendum, he had resigned from the Presidency, judging that the mystical rapport with the French people in which he had placed such faith ever since 1940 was no longer to be counted on. His successor and former friend, Georges Pompidou, was pledged to adhere to Gaullist policies, but it was no secret that he had contributed to de Gaulle's downfall. No member of the General's family attended the service of commemoration arranged by Pompidou at Notre Dame. De Gaulle's life ended in a shadow of melancholy. 'He has suffered so much in these last two years,' said his widow.

Still the balance of even those two final years was positive. The General had been spared his own particular nightmare, the decline into failing judgement and dwindling powers, that 'shipwreck of old age' in which his one-time mentor, Marshal Pétain, had foundered. De Gaulle had indeed grown both weary and impatient, but his mind remained clear to the end. He had proved that by the way in which he laid down his power the year before his death. By showing that he did not cling to office he saved the political edifice he had constructed and the personal image he had created, when both were under menace. His legacy to France and to the world is far richer for that final act of renunciation.

The life which ended in triumph and melancholy in the forests of Lorraine had begun in another frontier region of France on 22 November 1890 when a son was born, at 9 rue Princesse in Lille, to Jeanne (née Maillot) and Henri de Gaulle. They lived in Paris, where Henri was a teacher at the College of the Immaculate Conception, a well-known Jesuit school, but in accordance with the custom of French middle-class families at that time, Jeanne returned to her parents' home to have her children.

The baby was baptized the following day and christened Charles André Marie Joseph. He was the third child of his parents, who produced five in all: Xavier, Marie-Agnès, Charles, Jacques and Pierre.

Both the de Gaulles and the Maillots belonged to the considerable section of the bourgeoisie which, along with almost the whole of the aristocracy, had never accepted the values of the great Revolution of 1789 and remained loyal to the monarchy and the Church. They were divided politically between Legitimists, who favoured the return of the ancient Bourbon line, and Orleanists, who preferred the junior Orleans branch which had ruled from 1830 to 1848. But they were united in blaming the philosophy summed up in the slogan 'Liberty, Equality and Fraternity' for the misfortunes that had overtaken their country since 1789, from the Terror to the Commune, from Waterloo to Sedan. Some of these traditionalists worked actively against the Third Republic which had replaced the régime of Napoleon III in 1870 during the disasters of the Franco-Prussian War; others accepted the system of the day in practice, while hoping that events would lead to the restoration of the monarchy. Henri de Gaulle was of this more moderate kind. In principle he was a Legitimist, but by the time of Charles's birth he was not active in the cause. Above all, Henri and Jeanne were ardent patriots and devout Catholics. However France might be governed, they desired her glory and her grandeur, and they suffered acutely from the consequence of her defeat by Prussia in the war of 1870–1.

The existence of an influential and educated class for whom the golden age of their country lay in the past was a feature of French society which had no counterpart elsewhere at the time. The ruling classes in Britain and Germany, the traditional rivals of France, looked to the future with relative confidence, while in America optimism was boundless. A more critical and nostalgic spirit prevailed in the circles in which Charles de Gaulle was brought up, and had a profound influence on his character and view of life. Henri and Jeanne de Gaulle were by no means rich, but they were members of a class which could afford mobility, space and servants. As Henri rose in his profession, their circumstances improved. At first they lived in accommodation in the rue de Vaugirard at the school where Henri taught, but later they moved to the Place St François-Xavier, near the Invalides, in the fashionable seventh *arrondissement*. Summer holidays on the Channel coast, often in houses rented jointly with members of the Maillot family, were also part of their pattern of life, until they were able to buy a modest country property of their own, 'La Ligerie' in the Dordogne.

One of the principal concerns in life of Henri and Jeanne was to pass their beliefs on to their children. The young Charles was an apt pupil, as is shown by the tribute he paid to the influence of both of his parents at the beginning of his Memoirs. His mother, he says, 'had an uncompromising passion for her country equal in strength to her religious devotion'.[2] Charles inherited this uncompromising passion for France – both the adjective and the noun should be given their full weight – no doubt because his mother transmitted it with love. He and his mother always remained very close. He was in his fiftieth year and had 'assumed' France, as he put it in his Memoirs, before she died in July 1940.

Of his father, who had university degrees in philosophy, literature and mathematics and had gained a high reputation as a gifted teacher, Charles says: 'My father was filled with a feeling for the dignity, the worth, of France. Through him I discovered her history.'[3]

These influences combined with the promptings of his own nature to inspire the boy's own special vision of France. He described it in words that have become famous:

All my life I have cherished a certain vision [*idée*] of France, inspired by feeling as well as by reason. The emotional side of me imagines France, like the princess in a fairy tale or the Madonna in a fresco, as vowed to a unique and spectacular destiny. My instinct tells me Providence has created her for triumphs and disasters. If France happens to behave in a mediocre fashion, I feel that there has been a ridiculous error, due to the mistakes of the French people rather than the character of the country. My practical side is convinced that France is true to herself only when she stands in the front rank; that only great enterprises can neutralize the poisons of disunity which her people carry in their veins; that our country, such as it is, in the world as it is, must hold itself erect and look to the heights, if it is not to fall into mortal peril. To sum it up, France cannot be France for me without grandeur. France is not France unless she is great.[4]

This creed grew up in me as I myself grew up in my family atmosphere ...

The fate of France . . . interested me above all else . . . The more so because with the new century came the first signs of war. I must admit that my youthful spirit faced the prospect without fear and dramatized beforehand the venture into the unknown. I was sure that France would have to undergo immense trials; that the whole point of life lay in doing her some great service which would win acclaim; and that I should have the chance to perform such service.[5]

These famous opening paragraphs of his War Memoirs represent the adult's vision of what the child was like, but all the evidence suggests that the vision was accurate. From his earliest years this remarkable boy was in love with France and imbued with a sense of his mission in her cause.

The de Gaulles were interested in their family history as well as that of France, and Henri wrote a memoir on the subject for his children to read.[6] The clan came from the northern marches of France and ranked among the minor nobility before the Revolution. Charles's direct forebears had been in the legal profession from the sixteenth century until the Revolution, first in Dijon in Burgundy, and then in Paris.

The Revolution brought ruin to the de Gaulles, and the head of the family, Jean-Baptiste Philippe de Gaulle, who had been a legal counsellor to the Parliament of Paris, was imprisoned during the Terror. After his release he managed to restore his fortunes to some extent as a director of the mail services of Napoleon's armies. With the return of peace, his son Julien-Philippe became a teacher in the north and married Joséphine Maillot of Dunkirk. The youngest of their three sons was Henri de Gaulle.

Joséphine was an exceptional personality, energetic and intelligent, a prolific writer and the editor of a magazine. She wrote both romantic novels of a high moral tone – one of them, *Adhémar de Belcastel*, was a bestseller – and biographies, including one of Daniel O'Connell, entitled *The Liberator of Ireland*, praising him for having achieved Catholic Emancipation within the law. The young Charles read her book and became an admirer of O'Connell. Joséphine seems to be the one ancestor further back than Henri and Jeanne who contributed something of herself to Charles's make-up.

Henri had only been able to afford to marry at the age of thirty-eight after the death of an invalid brother, a Breton poet named Charles, to whose upkeep he contributed. He had then chosen a wife from his mother's family, an acknowledgement perhaps of her powerful influence. Jeanne Maillot was in fact a second cousin, twelve years younger than Henri. The young Charles was therefore doubly a Maillot. He was always very conscious of his northern ties and described himself in his Memoirs as '*petit Lillois de Paris*'. His mother brought strains of Irish, Scots and German blood into the family. Charles was conscious of them all, and always felt an interest in Ireland.

As the children grew up, Charles soon asserted a strong character. In later years his niece Geneviève de Gaulle was told by his mother that Charles had been the roughest and the least hard-working of her children.[7] He was not the eldest but before long he was the biggest, and determined to have his own way. His elder brother Xavier complained that he must have been dipped in ice at his birth, so coldly stubborn could he be.[8] One or two family stories illustrate his character. A favourite game of the de Gaulle children was playing with toy soldiers of different nationalities. Charles always insisted on having command of the French forces. One day Xavier suggested a change. 'Never,' said Charles. 'I only want to be France.' He had his way as usual. During the summer holidays in the Dordogne he organized war games in which he directed his brothers and the local farmers' sons. He insisted on a high standard of realism, and once when his brother Pierre was captured by the enemy and failed to swallow the message he was carrying he vigorously smacked the culprit's head.[9] What he always wanted was to be in command.

# 2 SCHOOLDAYS

Charles, like his brothers, was sent to the College of the Immaculate Conception. He had all his school education, except the final year, from the Jesuits, whom he admired, like his father, for their discipline and scholarship, and received a solid grounding in classics, mathematics, and French history and literature, with German and English as supporting subjects. The root and basis of all else was of course the teaching and practice of the Catholic faith.

Charles seems in general to have been well liked by his classmates, whom he impressed by his height and strength and his talent for learning by heart. He was not particularly talkative, but he made friends in a normal way and also used his strength to protect the weak against bullying. He was a fairly good scholar, though never the equal of his brother Xavier. Outside interests distracted him, including 'the unending serial of public events' referred to in his Memoirs. But because Charles went to a day school, according to French custom, and was in constant contact with his parents – his father was one of the most eminent teachers at the school – his home remained the main influence throughout his formative years.

The de Gaulles were a loving and united family. Their father added education to every activity. When he took the children for walks in Paris he told them the stories of the great men and events that had given their name to the streets. Acting at home was one of their amusements, and every year on their mother's name-day – the feast of St Jeanne, 21 August – the children dressed up and acted scenes for her from a suitable play.[1]

There were family visits to the theatre as well. Of these the most memorable took place on Charles's tenth birthday, when his father took him to see *L'Aiglon*, Rostand's famous play about the tragic life and death of the son of Napoleon and his second wife Marie-Louise, daughter of the Austrian Emperor. Rostand describes how in Austria after Waterloo the young man rejects all the influences brought to bear on him to forget France and his father. He maintains his resistance to the end and dies in exile dreaming of France and her grandeur. According to George Cattaui, an early biographer who knew de Gaulle and his family, the play so moved Charles that he decided there and then to become a soldier when he grew up.[2]

Charles was a voracious reader, with a remarkable memory, a gift that he inherited from his father and retained throughout his life. He learned verse and prose with ease and was reputed in the family to be able to recite the whole of Rostand's *Cyrano de Bergerac*. He devoured newspapers and novels as well as the standard classics in French, Latin and Greek. He liked the early Greek lyric poets, Lucretius and Virgil among the Latins, and of course Racine and Corneille. The uncompromising devotion of the typical Cornelian hero made a natural appeal to him. The sermons and essays of Bossuet and the works of Chateaubriand were also favourites of his, while among the moderns he had a particular liking for Paul Déroulède, the poet of the war of 1870, Edmond Rostand and Charles Péguy. The newspaper that influenced him was the royalist *L'Action Française*, edited by Charles Maurras. He naturally disapproved of Maurras's atheism, but many of his political and social judgements are echoed in de Gaulle's own writings.

His English was never as good as his German, but he knew enough to read the language. He admired Shakespeare and Kipling and a quotation from Oscar Wilde – 'Each man kills the thing he loves' – is to be found in an early notebook. His knowledge of German literature was wider, and he had a taste for the philosophers whose works he met in the later years of his school career. He read Goethe and Heine and was interested by Kant and Hegel. But it was Nietzsche who exercised a kind of fascination. Charles was always attracted by the Nietzschean view of the ultimate emptiness of life. It was a philosophy which represented a standing challenge to his own Catholic beliefs and perhaps a temptation in moments when he was assailed by the streak of melancholy which was part of his nature.

The philosopher who appealed to him in his more normal and hopeful frame of mind, however, and who seems to have influenced him most, was Henri Bergson. Both his readiness to accept the spiritual side of life and his pragmatism were congenial. Other writers whose ideas attracted him were Maurice Barrès, an ardent monarchist, and Ernest

Psichari, a young philosopher from a liberal background who returned to his religion and joined the Army as a private soldier.

Even more important to the young Charles than poetry or philosophy was the study of history. He read Thucydides, Livy and Caesar as well as Froissart and the moden writers. His knowledge of the history of France and her great continental rivals, the Habsburg Empire and Prussia, was voluminous. But Charles looked forward as well as back; and hoped that the future would treat France better than had the recent past.

Charles grew up at a melancholy time for French patriots. The country had never recaptured the position in the world which it had held in Napoleon's years of triumph: the defeat of Waterloo had ended that chapter and ushered in a period of relative weakness. Napoleon III's effort to revive imperial glories had ended in disaster, the loss of Alsace and Lorraine, and the creation of a unified German Empire. The Third Republic was at first sustained by hopes of an early revenge on Germany, but these were dashed by the enemy's rapidly growing strength. In 1870 the populations of France and Germany had been approximately the same, 38 million. By 1890 France still had about that number, while Germany had grown to 50 million. France could not reasonably hope to defeat her without the help of allies, and began to fear that she might be attacked. She succeeded in concluding an alliance with Russia in 1893, but it was defensive in character.

If Germany was the danger in Europe, Britain was the rival elsewhere. She and France were engaged in colonial expansion in Africa and southern Asia, and their interests clashed. In the 1870s Britain took over from France the leading role in Egypt and consolidated it when her forces occupied that country in 1881.

The de Gaulle children heard much of these misfortunes past and present. Their father took them to see the positions his regiment had occupied during the siege of Paris in 1870–1 and told them of the vain sortie against the Prussians in which he had been wounded. They were deeply moved when their mother related how she had found her parents in tears at the news of the surrender of Marshal Bazaine and his army at Metz. The young Charles, as he tells us at the beginning of his Memoirs, was inspired by the sight of the past splendours of France – Versailles, the Arc de Triomphe and the captured enemy standards displayed in the chapel of the Invalides – while 'nothing made me sadder than our errors and our failings revealed to me by the looks and the

9

words of my elders, the retreat from Fashoda, the Dreyfus affair, social conflict, religious discord'.[3]

Charles was approaching his eighth birthday at the time of the Fashoda crisis in the autumn of 1898. It was perhaps the first question of current foreign policy to make an impression on him. The world held its breath during this confrontation, at a small fort on the Upper Nile, between a French expeditionary force from West Africa under Captain Marchand, which had hoisted the Tricolour, and British forces sent from the Sudan by General Kitchener to warn them that they were on territory claimed by Egypt and must withdraw. The French government, unwilling to risk hostilities with Britain when Germany was the real enemy, ordered a retreat from Fashoda and managed to survive the subsequent outcry at home.

On the outbreak of the South African War in 1899 they adopted the same prudent policy, despite the strength of anti-British sentiment in France. Henri de Gaulle was deeply shocked by what he saw as an unjustified attack prompted by British greed for the gold of the Transvaal. He declared that *'perfide Albion'* had become too mild a term for Britain. The final words of the obituary he pronounced to his class at school when Queen Victoria died were: 'I hope Her Majesty was able to compose her soul before she faced God's judgement.'[4] Hearing such views from such a source must have caused the young Charles to form *une certaine idée de l'Angleterre* to set against his famous *idée de la France*.

In 1904, France and Britain succeeded in agreeing on their respective spheres of interest outside Europe, but this *Entente Cordiale* did not change the nature of the British in French eyes. When Maurras described the *Entente* in *L'Action Française* as 'a marriage of convenience' he was not speaking exclusively for royalist opinion. For many Frenchmen there was respect for Britain's power behind the *Entente*, but no affection.

The France that lived dangerously abroad was deeply divided at home. The civil strife and religious discord which de Gaulle lamented had been endemic ever since 1789. Under the Third Republic new causes of dissent were added to the old. Monarchists and republicans, anti-clericalists and supporters of the church were as much at loggerheads as ever, while the struggles between the gradually organizing forces of labour and the owners of industry grew more violent. The atrocities of the Commune and of its crushing in 1871 left a legacy of bitterness between Right and Left. The universal desire for revenge on Germany dominated other passions in the 1870s, but the failure to fulfil that desire thereafter began to provoke impatience with the régime among right-wingers who condemned it for being too weak to be able to prepare the nation for war. General Boulanger, a military man who had won political popularity, tried to mount a coup d'état in 1889 with the help of the Right. He failed and fled abroad leaving a legacy of distrust between the military leadership and left-wing Republicans, who began to call for reform of the officer class. Some Socialists even challenged the philosophy of *la revanche* and talked of pacifism.

These divisions in French society explain why the Dreyfus affair aroused such passions and dragged on for so long, with Left and Right fighting over the question of whether or not the Army chiefs had fabricated the evidence against Dreyfus in 1894 and suppressed what was favourable. Henri de Gaulle began by believing in the guilt of Dreyfus, but he soon changed his mind and said so to the resentment of many of his friends.[5] In later years Charles was proud of the position his father had taken. Neither of them of course, regarded the affair as a reason for turning against the Army, whose importance to the nation remained as great as ever in their eyes. Others however disagreed, and by the time the verdict against Dreyfus was quashed in 1906, the affair had done infinite harm to France.

Through these years of strife and anxiety Charles kept to his choice of a soldier's career. He decided to prepare for the entrance examination for the famous military academy at St Cyr and to aim at a commission in the infantry. Henri welcomed his decision but warned him that he would have to work harder at school. Charles did so from the age of fourteen onwards and quickly rose to the top of his class.[6]

A curious incident at this period showed how Charles's imagination was at work on his future career. One night his family received a message that a distinguished military visitor was about to call on them. Soon there was a knock on the front door and the card of General Faidherbe was sent in. At the door was Charles in uniform masquerading as his hero. Faidherbe, born in Lille like Charles, had been the most successful French commander in the war of 1870–1. Charles was already identifying himself with the General who had never lowered the flag, already playing the game of make-believe.

Charles's preparations for St Cyr were made more difficult by an intensification of the struggle between Church and State. In 1905 the anticlerical government of the day finally passed the long-threatened law disestablishing the Church. The Jesuits were expelled from France and the College of the Immaculate Conception ceased to exist. Henri de Gaulle founded his own teaching establishment, the Ecole Fontanes, but decided that Charles should be sent to study mathematics, an important subject at St Cyr, at the Jesuit school at Antoing in Belgium where some of his teachers were going.

During his summer holidays before Antoing, Charles served for a spell as a volunteer stretcher-bearer at Lourdes. After his first day's service he duly wrote to his mother that it had been pretty hard work, but not as bad as one might think. He added that he had seen a paralysed Italian girl cured during the procession of the Blessed Sacrament.[8] His faith had been unshaken by the atmosphere in France.

Charles did outstandingly well at Antoing. His marks in the mathematics examination were so high that his teachers urged him to change his plans and try for the Ecole Polytechnique in Paris, which had the highest standards in mathematics and science and prepared boys for commissions in the technical branches of the Army. A degree from the 'X', as it is still called, conferred great prestige and opened the way to careers in administration or business, as well as in the Army. But Charles replied that he preferred St Cyr. In the infantry, he explained, 'the scope for action is infinitely larger'.[9] Most of the highest commands in the Army went to infantry generals. As always, Charles was aiming at the top. He gave further proof of that when chosen as class orator for the ceremonies that followed the final religious retreat of the school year. 'The pupils of the Jesuits,' he said, 'are criticized for lacking personality. We shall prove that the charge is false.' A dramatic pause followed. Then: 'As to the future, it will be immense – because it will be shaped by our achievements.'[10]

That summer Charles paid his first visit to Germany. St Cyr attached importance to knowing the enemy's language. He lodged with the parish priest of Riedern, a village in the Black Forest, and took a lively interest in everything military. He wrote to his father that the German press were sharply criticizing French policy in Morocco: 'It makes me think of the troubles which go before great wars, in particular that of 1870. I hope our roles will be reversed this time.'[11]

A year at the Collège Stanislas in Paris followed Antoing. There he made his final preparations for the entrance examination to St Cyr. According to the well-informed Jean-Raymond Tournoux, who has written much about de Gaulle, he indulged in practices of mortification while at Stanislas in order to strengthen his self-discipline and will-power. He was emerging from a moral crisis provoked by the misbehaviour of a Jesuit priest he had admired. His father, feeling perhaps that sound theology made up for a little misbehaviour, was deeply anxious. 'I'd rather Charles had three mistresses than see him lose his faith,' he sighed.[12]

Charles did not lose his faith, but perhaps because of this crisis he did not do very well in his entrance examination for St Cyr. He passed, but was only placed 111th out of an intake of 212 – not a brilliant result after he had done so well at Antoing.

But that was a minor matter. St Cyr had accepted him, and in October 1909 his military career began.

# 3 THE YOUNG WRITER

At the age of fifteen or earlier, years before becoming a soldier, Charles de Gaulle was already a creative writer. In his later life his talents as a writer were harnessed to the requirements of his military and political career. But this was not so at first. He began to write because he had a natural, no doubt hereditary, gift for doing so. His earliest poetic efforts have not been published but a few other works dating back to his schooldays reveal a good deal about the way he saw the world. The earliest to come to light so far was published only in 1980, in a volume of his miscellaneous letters and other writings, *Lettres, Notes et Carnets*. Entitled 'The German Campaign' and written in 1905 while Charles was at the College of the Immaculate Conception, it is the story of a war declared by Germany on France in 1930. The Commander-in-Chief of the French armies is General Charles de Gaulle, who succeeds in a few weeks in bottling up a German army in Metz and defeats them when they try to break out. It is an imaginary revenge for the surrender of Metz by Marshal Bazaine in 1870, which had reduced Jeanne de Gaulle's parents to tears; his first theme is *la revanche*.

Certain other revealing works survive from Charles's schooldays. In 1906 he wrote a short play in verse, *Une mauvaise rencontre*, which won a competition in a magazine. Invited to choose between a money prize and publication, Charles characteristically opted for the latter. The piece is very much in the style of Edmond Rostand; its interest is not in any claim to originality but in the fact that the theme appealed to Charles sufficiently for him to adopt it as his own in public. The play tells the story of a traveller, alone and defenceless, who meets an armed robber in a forest by night. The brigand strips his victim of his possessions one by one, pretending at each stage that the present exaction is his last, and then immediately proceeding to the next. He is unfailingly polite, but always produces his pistols at the critical moment. There is no happy ending for the luckless traveller. The robber departs with his loot rejoicing, after a cordial farewell.

In its modest way the piece is a black comedy. The strong, it seems, can do what they like to the weak, but certain conventions should be observed. The negotiating technique of César-Charles Rollet, the robber, a mixture of formal courtesy and brutal action, rather resembles that of de Gaulle with General Giraud in the war years. When *Une mauvaise rencontre* was staged *en famille* among the de Gaulles, Charles naturally played the part of the brigand.

Another surviving work of interest is an essay written at Antoing in 1907, entitled 'The Congregation in France', on the subject of the efforts of the Jesuits to revive religion in France after 1815. In the face of political opposition they abandoned their chosen instrument, a society of devout laymen known as the Congregation. Charles's verdict is characteristic. 'In the long run,' he says, 'these men would have been able to instil moral values into the people and produce a Catholic reaction.'[1] Like his Jesuit teachers he always tended to think of desirable change as a counter-reformation, the restoration, with improvements, of a previously existing state of affairs.

Finally there is a short story and a poem dating back to 1908 which have been published in the same collection and reveal a decided vein of melancholy. 'Zalaina', the short story, treats the theme of renunciation. It is about a young French army officer in New Caledonia who falls in love with a beautiful Polynesian girl. They live together for a time and then he is told by his superiors that, for the sake of his career, he must give her up. He does so, and Zalaina in her grief tries to kill her lover and herself with a drug of which she has the secret. She dies, but he survives to serve France. In old age he retires to the island of his romance. He left Zalaina, but he can never forget her.

The poem, which echoes the melancholy tones of Sully Prudhomme, is even more concerned with death. Charles says that he would choose to die in the evening at the end of a victorious battle, and 'as Lethe's river folds me in its icy flow, to feel the kiss of Glory burning on my brow'. He was thinking much of death at this time, because he had a premonition that he would die young in battle against the Germans.[2] It was not an unreasonable expectation for a St Cyrian; this was the fate of 98 of the 212 among whom Charles graduated from the Academy.

# 4 THE YOUNG OFFICER

De Gaulle says in his Memoirs: 'When I entered the French Army, it was one of the greatest things in the world.'[1] That was certainly true inasmuch as no Frenchman doubted that the security of the nation depended upon the capacity of the Army to protect it, and that revenge on Germany would only be possible if the Army could achieve it. But the old sense of solidarity between the left-wing political parties and the Army had been destroyed by the Boulanger and Dreyfus affairs. The officer corps was politically suspect to the Left.

De Gaulle felt the effects. Under a new regulation designed to counteract the élitist mentality of the past, officer cadets had to spend a year in the ranks before entering St Cyr. De Gaulle was attached to the 33rd Infantry Regiment, stationed at Arras in Northern France, for his preliminary year. He did not enjoy the experience, which he regarded as a waste of time from the point of view of military training, but he stood up to it well enough both physically and psychologically. He seems to have liked the rugged peasants and miners who formed the bulk of the regiment's conscripts and he made his mark as somebody exceptional. Soon he was writing home to announce that he would be giving a lecture to the whole of his battalion which might be attended by the commanding officer.[2] His company commander, Captain de Tugny, was asked one day why he did not give this very able recruit accelerated promotion. 'What's the point of making a sergeant out of a young man who would only be satisfied as Commander-in-Chief?' was the reply.[3] Charles was nevertheless promoted to corporal and sergeant in due course before he went on to St Cyr in October 1910.

De Gaulle did well at St Cyr. The potential hazard for him was not the work but relations with his fellow cadets. Shy, intelligent, more than a little arrogant, he was an obvious target for teasing. Jokes were made about his nose and his height (six feet five inches); he was called

'The Cock', 'Cyrano' and 'Double Metre'. At the initiation of the new entrants, he had to climb on a table and recite Cyrano de Bergerac's speech about the immensity of his nose, and the next year he had to play the part of a circus clown. The roles were chosen with cruel skill, but he had the sense to take his treatment in good part, and he did make friends – one of them, Ditte, was best man at his wedding. Alphonse Juin, the future marshal, was one of the stars of the class. They always called each other '*tu*' in later years, even when quarrelling about policy in Algeria after 1958.

He passed out in 1912 the thirteenth in his class, having climbed nearly a hundred places since his entry, high enough to choose the arm of the service which he preferred. He could have opted for the fashionable cavalry or the colonial army, but he remained true to his original choice of the infantry and asked to be sent back to the 33rd Regiment at Arras. During Charles's absence a new Commanding Officer had taken over: Philippe Pétain, the only other individual in all the immense army of France for whom a destiny comparable to his own was in store. It was an extraordinary stroke of chance.

In 1912 nothing seemed less likely than a brilliant future for Philippe Pétain. He was fifty-six years old and approaching the end of a long career during which he had never heard a shot fired in anger. His battles had been waged not with the enemy but with his superiors. He had never been willing to accept the theory of war which became the orthodox doctrine of the French General Staff in the wake of the defeat of France by Prussia in 1870–1: the doctrine that attack, the seizing and holding of the initiative on the battlefield, was the one infallible means of achieving victory. This was inculcated into all ranks of the French Army in Pétain's day, but he himself refused to set unconditional aggression so high. He did not erect a rival military theory of his own, but argued that the key fact of modern war was 'Fire power kills'. He stressed the importance of artillery and of strong defensive positions, and developed his theme in the lectures he gave at the Ecole de Guerre. This was enough to earn him the disapproval of the military Establishment. He was marked out as a man not to be entrusted with high command. Pétain served only in France, and now he was not far from retirement.

In 1912, therefore, Pétain was a disappointed man. But this did not prevent him from doing all he could to bring his regiment to a high standard. He appreciated de Gaulle's quality and gave him excellent reports. On 1 October 1913, de Gaulle was promoted to lieutenant. Pétain's assessment was: 'Very intelligent, intensely keen on his work . . . Deserves the highest praise.'[4]

There is one story from the period of a personal encounter between de Gaulle and Pétain. Apparently the Colonel was irritated one day when part of the regiment marching back through Arras blocked the traffic and caused a bottleneck. Pétain felt that this happened because his instructions had not been obeyed, and he ordered those responsible, of whom de Gaulle was one, confined to barracks. At the weekend, however, he relented and revoked his order just before leaving for Paris. In the train he was surprised to see de Gaulle climb in at the last minute and sit down opposite him. He had hardly had time to prepare for the journey since hearing that his detention was cancelled. 'Did you arrange to go on leave this weekend?' asked Pétain. 'Yes, Colonel,' de Gaulle replied. 'But you were confined to barracks, young man.' 'Yes, Colonel,' he answered. 'But, as the sentence was unjust, I was sure you would cancel it.'[5] It seems that Pétain accepted this left-handed compliment without demur, and this extraordinary couple travelled together to the city whose defence was to involve them both in such dramatic adventures in later years.

As de Gaulle learned his trade, crisis followed crisis between the great powers. In 1911 Germany challenged the special position of France in Morocco, as she had done in 1905, but was frustrated by the support which Britain gave to her partner in the Entente Cordiale. Then came the Italo-Turkish conflict, and wars in the Balkans. Of these years he wrote: 'The Army . . . felt the moment approaching when everything would depend upon it. The prospect was faced with calm, even with a quiet hopefulness.' When in April 1914 de Gaulle was detailed to give a talk on the German Army to the officers and NCOs of his regiment, his speaking notes ended: 'So France has no cause for anxiety. The value of an Army depends on the strength of its morale. It is up to us to build that strength.'[6]

In the summer of 1914 the moment arrived. On 28 June the heir to the Austrian throne, the Archduke Francis Ferdinand, was assassinated at Sarajevo by a Serb. On 28 July Austria declared war on Serbia, and the rival systems of interlocking alliances drew all the major European powers, except Italy, into the conflict in the next seven days. France, Britain and Russia were arrayed against Germany and Austria.

# 5  THE GREAT WAR, 1914–18

De Gaulle and Pétain were still with their regiment at Arras when war began. The Germans had made the first move by declaring war and invading Belgium. The French, true to their doctrine of attack, hastened to try and wrest the initiative from the invader. The 33rd Regiment was among the forces that were ordered forward into Belgium as part of the Second Army under General Lanrezac. It left Arras on 5 August. De Gaulle had the reflex of the true writer. He began a diary on 1 August and scribbled a few lines every day despite all the demands on his time. On 5 August he noted: 'Everybody is united. This is the controlled enthusiasm I dreamt of.'[1]

On 15 August, at Dinant in Belgium, the 33rd met the advancing Germans and both Pétain and de Gaulle had their baptism of fire. It was precisely the date on which de Gaulle had had a premonition that he would die. At first his company was in reserve. Then, as the Germans forced the French back from the far side of the Meuse which divides Dinant, it was ordered forward with bayonets fixed to hold the bridge against an enemy crossing. Charles led the way through the streets at the double under German fire. This is how he described in his journal what happened:

I felt I was two people: one running like a machine, the other anxiously looking at him. I had just covered the last twenty metres to the bridge when I felt what seemed like a whiplash on my knee and missed my footing. The four who were with me were all brought down in the same instant. Sergeant Debout fell on top of me. A hail of bullets smacked the pavement and the walls around us and thumped with a duller sound into the dead and wounded on the ground.[2]

His leg useless, Charles was taken off to hospital in Arras, complaining bitterly that the French artillery had let their infantry down by appearing on the scene too late. He had learned in his own person the truth of Pétain's dictum 'Fire power kills'. On his first day in battle after five years of preparation he was put out of action; but contrary to his premonition, he had survived. From Arras he was moved to Paris for an operation and then on to Lyons for further treatment to his damaged leg. According to his chronicler Jean-Raymond Tournoux, he arranged these transfers himself in order to avoid the risk of being captured by the advancing enemy.[3]

His enforced leisure enabled him to comment on the course of the war in letters to his parents. As always, he surveyed the scene with the eye of a Commander-in-Chief. He had nothing but praise for the French troops and blamed the setback of August on tardy mobilization and inadequate generalship. 'Finally the British government bear a heavy responsibility for not making up their minds to go to war until the last minute and having their army very ill prepared. Their forces arrived considerably later than promised, at the decisive point on our extreme left. I say nothing of their very limited numbers...' He repeated these strictures on the British 'auxiliaries' as he called them in another letter, and placed more hope in the Russians, whom he acknowledged as 'allies'. He wrote to his mother on 18 September: 'Our own best interests require us not to lay down our arms until we have linked up with the Russians across Germany. Otherwise we'll have to start again in ten years' time.'[4] That link-up was not to take place until 1945, and, when it did, the Russians were to meet not Frenchmen but Americans coming from the West.

During his days in Lyons Charles thought of love as well as war. He wrote a short story entitled 'Baptism', published for the first time in 1980,[5] which was a variation on the theme of 'Zalaina'. It begins in a garrison town in France at the outbreak of war. The regiment hurries to the front. Before the battle Captain Bertaud tells Lieutenant Langel, a young officer aged twenty-three, like de Gaulle, that he knows he will be killed. He hands Langel his wallet and asks him to give it to his wife. Langel, who has been having an affair with her – 'savouring all the sensual and intellectual delights of love' as Charles puts it – realizes that Bertaud knows his secret. He takes the wallet, 'his heart torn by a remorse he would never forget'.

In the battle Bertaud dies and Langel is wounded. In hospital at Lyons he is visited by the widow. He hands her the wallet and explains that, after what has passed between him and Bertaud, he must give her up. She understands. Sadly they say goodbye. The next morning news arrives of 'The Miracle of the Marne', the victorious French counter-attack when Paris seemed lost. The men in the hospital forget their wounds and rejoice. 'Langel tried to soothe the pain of his lost love with the balm of victory. So many sacrifices had gone to its winning. Who knows if his own had not weighed in the balance?'

Is this an improving tale, such as his grandmother Joséphine might have written, or the souvenir of a love affair? Apart from the romantic element it can be seen from de Gaulle's diary that the background of the story corresponds closely to his own experience in August and September 1914. And Langel is an anagram of Gaulle, with the letter 'u' inverted into an 'n'. Charles had an odd taste for reshuffling his name in this way, and signed some of his writings in these years with anagrams such as 'C. de Lugal'. There are the faintest indications of a possible romance in Arras in his recently published writings. One is in his diary, under the date of 4 August: 'In the evening a very gay dinner at our lodgings. Then we put our affairs in order. Papers burnt. I am ready to go.'[6] It is hard to imagine what papers a subaltern might have for burning except love letters.

Towards the end of the year he was able to rejoin his regiment, now in Champagne. Pétain had left the 33rd to take command of a brigade. His successor, Colonel Claudel, made de Gaulle his adjutant. During his months of absence the nature of the war had completely changed. Both sides were dug in, and two systems of trenches confronted each other from the Channel coast to Switzerland. On 20 January 1915 de Gaulle was mentioned in dispatches for the successful completion of a series of dangerous reconnaissance missions which brought back valuable information. On 18 February he was appointed a temporary captain, but continued as adjutant with the regiment's new colonel, Boud'hors. He was passing with flying colours the soldier's supreme test – to function efficiently under fire. There is no examination which gives more confidence to those who pass it. Before long, however, he was wounded again and back in hospital. Fragments of a mortar had torn his left hand during an engagement near the village of Mesnil-le-Hurlus in Champagne. The damage done was permanent. In later life he had to wear his wedding ring on his right hand.

In June he was back with his regiment. The war did not go as well for France in 1915 as de Gaulle had expected. In letters home he blamed the government and the parliamentary system. Writing to his mother on 23 December 1915 he said:

Parliament is growing more and more odious and stupid. Literally the whole time of ministers is taken by sittings of the Chamber, the Senate, or the committees . . . Even if they wanted to, they couldn't possibly find the time to administer their departments . . . We shall conquer when we've got rid of all that rifraff, and every Frenchman, above all those who are doing the fighting, would shout with joy. The idea is making headway, and I should be very surprised if this régime survives the war.[7]

The régime did survive the war, but so did his profound distaste for it. His Constitution of 1958 forbade ministers to sit in Parliament.

The supreme trial of the French Army was now at hand. As the year ended, the Germans, under General Falkenhayn, launched their great offensive at Verdun. General Pétain, who had made his reputation in the battles of 1915, was in command of the French defence. The 33rd Regiment were soon thrust into the fiery furnace. In February 1916 they were sent from Champagne to Verdun, and they moved into the front line on 1 March in the sector of Fort Douaumont, just captured by the Germans. Colonel Boud'hors selected de Gaulle to lead the advance party and arrange the takeover from the departing 110th Regiment. The Colonel later recorded: 'I found everything as it should be, thanks to Captain de Gaulle . . .'

The next day marked the end of de Gaulle's war. The Germans attacked and overran most of the positions of the 33rd, including that held by de Gaulle, who resisted desperately to the last. The official citation of what he did was ordered by General Pétain, who is said to have put the finishing touches to it himself:

Captain de Gaulle, company commander, reputed for his great intellectual and moral worth; as his battalion was decimated by a frightful bombardment and the enemy reached its lines on a broad front, led his men in a fierce attack and savage hand-to-hand fighting – the only solution that met his sense of military honour. He fell in the fighting. A peerless officer in all respects.[8]

Pétain thought he was writing de Gaulle's epitaph, because at first he was reported dead. In fact, he had collapsed after receiving a bayonet thrust. Instead of administering the *coup de grâce*, one of his German assailants saved his life; still unconscious he was taken prisoner, and in due course the news reached his parents, who had at first been told through private channels that he was dead.

Until recently the official citation remained the authorized version of de Gaulle's capture. But in 1981 his own personal account was published for the first time. De Gaulle sent it to Boud'hors as soon as he returned from captivity. The tone is defensive, as if, without admitting it in so many words, he were trying to justify the failure of his men to hold their positions. He calls the day's fighting '*une mauvaise affaire*', refers to the 'defeatism' of some of those involved, and relates how, after heavy bombardment, his company and its neighbours suddenly found themselves attacked from both sides.

'Two islands of resistance still held out,' de Gaulle says. 'Mine to the west of the church, Averlant's [his second lieutenant] to the east.' He decided to lead the few survivors still with him to join Averlant and they crawled along a communications trench.

I had hardly gone ten metres when I came on a group of Boches crouching in a shellhole. They saw me at the same moment and one of them ran his bayonet into me. The thrust went through my map-case and wounded me in the thigh. Another Boche shot my orderly dead. Seconds later a grenade exploded literally in front of my face and I lost consciousness.[9]

Boud'hors (now a general), to whom de Gaulle had written an account of this incident, exerted himself on de Gaulle's behalf, and in July 1919 he was made a Chevalier of the Legion of Honour for his services at Douaumont. The accompanying citation, signed by Marshal Pétain, was a slightly diluted version of the one issued in 1916. De Gaulle was delighted but had no illusions. 'The citation much exaggerates the facts,' he wrote to his father, and repeated it in his letter of thanks to Boud'hors. If he had not taken the initiative of writing to Boud'hors when he returned to France, he would probably not have received a decoration. This was not the last time that his career was helped by a well-directed letter.

It was as a prisoner in Germany that he lived out the remaining thirty-two months of the war. He made five attempts to escape, but his height made him too easily identifiable. Finally he was sent to the punishment camp of Ingolstadt in Bavaria where he underwent a total of 120 days of solitary confinement, in a darkened cell, as punishment for his efforts at escape. At other times he had the consolation of being able to read widely and of meeting a number of remarkable characters among his fellow-prisoners. Among the friends he made at Ingolstadt

were Georges Catroux, the only officer senior to him who joined the
Free French in 1940, Berger-Levrault, who was to be his publisher,
Rémy Roure, the journalist, and the future Marshal Tukhachevsky,
who after the war became a commander of the Russian armies which
de Gaulle helped the Poles to fight. Tukhachevsky perished in one of
Stalin's purges before he and de Gaulle could become allies once more.

De Gaulle made voluminous notes during his captivity which show
that the Germans allowed him access to well-stocked libraries, and
although these are mainly jottings on history, literature, politics
and war, written to aid his memory, a few of them have a bearing on
his future. There is, for instance, a passage on character which lays
down rules to which he tried to remain faithful throughout his career:

> One must be a man of character.
> The way to succeed in action is to be capable of self-mastery at all times. To
> be more precise, it is an indispensable condition of success.
> Self-mastery should become a kind of habit, a reflex created by constant
> exercise of the will, in small matters as well: dress, conversation, direction of
> thought, a methodical carefully worked out approach in everything, particu-
> larly in one's work.
> To talk little is an absolute necessity . . . And in action one must say
> nothing. The leader is the man who does not talk.[10]

De Gaulle, who studied the German language and followed the
course of events in the German newspapers, gave talks on the war to
his fellow prisoners, and so impressed them by his patriotic ardour and
confidence in victory that they gave him the nickname '*Le Connétable*', which for many centuries under the monarchy had been the title
of the commander-in-chief of the French armies.

From this time onwards the Germans always exercised a kind of
fascination on de Gaulle. The idea that one day the Gauls and the
Germans might stop fighting and find it possible to work together to
reconstitute the Europe of Charlemagne was perhaps implanted in de
Gaulle's mind by his time as a prisoner of war. In a letter to his mother
dated 17 September 1916, he says: 'This will make you laugh, but
there are a lot of people among the Germans here – educated men for
the most part – who have the nerve to come and talk to us from time to
time of an alliance between our two races after the war!'[11] Emo-
tionally engaged as he was in the battle that was remodelling the

world, he could not accept such ideas at the time. But they may have taken root nonetheless.

His period of captivity was frustrating, but not without its compensations. While he missed the chance of distinguishing himself further in battle and gaining more honours and promotion, he also escaped the terrible attendant risks. Death was not the only one. He was spared more experience of what had already shocked him, it is said, in Champagne in 1915, the squandering of French lives in vain attacks; and he did not have to live through the desperate days of 1917 when the sorely tried French Army came so near to collapse. De Gaulle, a combatant for only the first twenty months of the war, preserved a certain freshness of spirit, a certain innocence, which was lost by many of the Frenchmen who went through the whole ordeal. He was less war-weary than most of those who had to conduct the affairs of France, military and political, in the 1920s and 1930s. Perhaps this helps to explain why he so often saw matters differently from others, and why his confidence in French capacities remained so high.

Yet these advantages were not apparent to him while he languished in Ingolstadt. It was bitter to reflect that he had missed all the chances presented by the war of performing those signal services to France of which he had dreamt. As victory drew near, he wrote to his parents that his joy was mingled with 'indescribable regret at not having played a worthier part'. At the end of November 1918, when he returned to France, he was eager to make up for lost time.

# 6 BUILDING A CAREER

De Gaulle, full of energy in an exhausted land, was no sooner back in France than he was seeking a chance of active service in which he could distinguish himself. After a reunion at La Ligerie where the family celebrated the return from the war of all four sons, he went to see his former chief, General Philippe Pétain, whose successful defence of Verdun had made him a national hero. The great man, Commander-in-Chief since 1917, received him kindly and a friendship was born between them.

In the spring of 1919 de Gaulle took service with the French Military Mission sent to Poland to help the newly independent republic build up its armed forces, which were in sporadic conflict with Soviet armies across the great eastern plain that was now without fixed frontiers. He taught in the summer of 1919 at the officers' training school at Rembertow, and wrote to his father that the French were doing useful work but that the Americans, British and Italians had sent 'vague Missions' which were really just out to make money. 'Like most of my countrymen', he said, 'I finish the war brimming over with sentiments of generalized xenophobia and convinced that, in order to make ourselves respected, we must make a rational use of our military power, which is today the first in the world.'[1]

In other letters de Gaulle made clear how he thought the military power of France should be used. He wanted France to exact a huge indemnity and retain her hold on German territory on the left bank of the Rhine. In this he was disappointed. The Treaty of Versailles created the League of Nations and imposed reparations and arms restrictions on Germany, but it did not give the left bank of the Rhine to France. De Gaulle saw a possible use for military power on the home front too: writing to his mother after the strike wave of June 1919, he expressed confidence that 'our marshals have so much authority over the Army that any revolutionary movement would be stifled at once'.[2] Politically he was a man of the Right.

He left Poland in April 1920 on transfer to France, but was sent back in June, because crisis was at hand. The Russians were advancing on Warsaw. French officers were authorized by their government to go further than merely training the Poles and to join combat units. De Gaulle saw some action as a battalion commander in the Polish counter-attack planned by his compatriot, General Weygand, who had won fame as Marshal Foch's chief of staff in 1918. It forced the Russians back beyond the Curzon Line and made peace possible. He was invited to become an instructor at the new Ecole de Guerre which was to be set up in Poland, but the French High Command wanted him at home, and he was appointed Assistant Professor of History at St Cyr – a post he had requested. He thought it would give him time to prepare for entering the Senior War School (Ecole Supérieure de Guerre), where he was on the waiting list.

Charles, encouraged by his mother, had been wanting to get married ever since his return from captivity in Germany. He is said to have had a romance with a Polish princess and to have fought a duel on her account,[3] but, when it came to marriage his thoughts turned to France. In December 1919 he told his mother what he hoped the next year would bring him: 'A family, the tranquillity which comes with deep and blessed love, and the chance to give someone all the love a man can offer.'[4]

In fact he had already met his 'someone' in Paris in the autumn of 1919. She was Yvonne Vendroux, a shy pretty girl of nineteen, who came from a background similar to his own, northern, Catholic and conservative. Her family were prosperous biscuit manufacturers in Calais, where they had been prominent local citizens for many generations. Tradition has it that Charles first made an impression on Yvonne by spilling a cup of tea over her dress at a party. Soon they were in love. Their engagement was delayed by his absences in Poland during 1920, but on 11 November of that year it was announced. He had to leave immediately afterwards on a final brief tour of duty in Poland, but by February he was home again, and on 6 April 1921 he and Yvonne were married at the church of Notre Dame de Calais.

It turned out that Charles and Yvonne had chosen well. They were always together, as far as war and politics would allow, and she was with him when he died forty-nine years later. Yvonne was self-effacing in public but a strong personality in the home which she made a place where her husband could relax from the tensions of his stormy life outside.

Three children were born to Yvonne and Charles: one son, Philippe (born in December 1921), and two daughters, Elisabeth (born in 1924) and Anne (born in 1928), who was a victim of Down's syndrome.

Yvonne's approach to marriage corresponded very well with de Gaulle's view of women's mission in life, which seems to have been based on a mixture of biological theory and romanticism. According to what he said *en famílle*, he felt that women had charge of humanity. It was their business to ensure the continuity of the race and to look after men and children. They had to fulfil this function in order to fulfil themselves, even though they might pursue a career as well. The business of men was to be adventurers and discoverers, looked after by women. These orthodox conservative views where political rights were concerned did not prevent de Gaulle moving with the times and giving women the vote in 1945 for the first time in French history.

Family life meant a great deal to de Gaulle. He was still very close to his parents, as can be seen from the letters he wrote them from Poland. His father retired from being headmaster of the Ecole Fontanes in 1920 but remained active and mentally alert, as did his mother. Now he added the Vendroux to his family circle. He got on well with his wife's relatives, and he and Yvonne often spent holidays at Septfontaines, the Vendroux country house in the Ardennes. There Charles enjoyed solitary riding and more sociable rough shooting.[5] He struck up a friendship with Jacques Vendroux, Yvonne's brother.

At St Cyr Captain de Gaulle made a reputation for himself as a brilliant lecturer and a hard taskmaster who gave low marks and dealt out detentions liberally. Once a student researching a classic military problem which de Gaulle had set his class happened in the library on de Gaulle's own solution produced in his days as a cadet. He copied it and submitted it to de Gaulle as his own. He was given 7/20 and gated for the weekend. In protest he pointed out that it was de Gaulle's own answer and had been given top marks. 'I was aware of that,' replied the Captain coldly. 'But now it is out of date.' He was always against the idea that there were right and wrong answers in war; everything depended on circumstances.

One lesson he taught in his history course struck a prophetic note. 'Remember this,' he told his students:

History does not teach fatalism. There are moments when the will of a handful of free men breaks through determinism and opens up new roads. People get the history they deserve. When you lament a misfortune and fear that worse is to come people will tell you 'It's the law of history. It's the will of evolution.' They will explain it all very lucidly. Stand up, gentleman, against such clever cowardice. It's worse than stupidity. It's the sin against the Holy Spirit.[6]

These words distil the essence of de Gaulle's philosophy. This was the faith that guided him across the sea to England when France fell in 1940 and made him stand up for the independence of France in the two-power world of the 1960s.

De Gaulle was only at St Cyr for a year. The Ecole Supérieure de Guerre in Paris had resumed its courses in 1920, and in November 1922 he became a member of the third postwar class to embark on the two-year course. It was a compliment to be chosen. Since the School had not functioned during the war, there was a long waiting list, and priority was given to those who had distinguished themselves in action. A first-class degree from the Ecole Supérieure was the recognized passport to senior appointments.

It was here that de Gaulle's career was to sustain its first setback. Since his capture in 1916 he had never served in an ordinary military unit in the normal chain of command. In Poland and at St Cyr it had been his function to teach and direct. Now, after an interval of six and a half years, he found himself in a subordinate position, a pupil answerable to a host of instructors who were also his superiors in the military hierarchy.

The man who had won the nickname '*Le Connétable*' from his fellow prisoners did not take kindly to this. He had to contend once more with the French tendency to construct general theories of warfare and to lay down rules held to be valid in all circumstances. The chair of military tactics at the school was held by a Colonel Moyrand, who based his teachings on the lessons the General Staff had drawn from the Great War. The emphasis had now switched back to the virtues of the strong defensive position which the enemy is forced to attack. De Gaulle could not accept such a doctrinaire approach, and he made his disagreement plain. He argued in favour of a free offensive use of tank units, and against the official thesis that tanks could not operate independently of infantry. This caused frictions which were increased rather than diminished by knowledge of his special relationship, of which he made no secret, with Marshal Pétain, who kept in touch with him and sent congratulations on the birth of the de Gaulles' first child in December 1921.

De Gaulle stood out among his classmates, metaphorically as well as literally. They were impressed by his intellectual powers, his knowledge of history, and his prodigious memory. One day one of them, the future General Chauvin, said to him: 'I believe you're destined for great things.' De Gaulle, without a trace of irony, replied: 'Yes, so do I.'[7] It was an attitude which, inevitably, made him enemies as well as friends. Some of his colleagues found Pétain's protégé far too self-assertive and arrogant. One of his instructors later described him as 'a monster of ambition who would sell his own mother to get ahead'.

Perhaps because the directing staff were still uncertain as to how to grade him at the end of the course, de Gaulle was assigned a vital role in the final tactical exercise which took place near Bar-sur-l'Aube. For a full day he was made commander of an Army corps. He dealt with the problems posed in accordance with his own pragmatic approach, never applying the School doctrine of the need to establish a strong central position sustained by ample firepower and supplies of all kinds. At the post mortem that evening, attended by the whole class, Colonel Moyrand asked him a technical question: 'Where are the supply trains of the regiment on the left of your right-flank division?' De Gaulle turned to his chief of staff. 'Chateauvieux, please answer.' 'I want the answer from you, de Gaulle,' interjected Moyrand. '*Mon Colonel*,' was the reply, 'you have entrusted me with the responsibilities of a corps commander. If I had to do my subordinates' jobs as well, I wouldn't have my mind free to do my own properly. "*De minimis non curat praetor*"[8] . . . Chateauvieux, please answer the Colonel.' Colonel Moyrand kept his temper. 'Very good,' he said. 'We knew that you regarded many duties as beneath you. Now I've made my mind up.'[9]

Because of his undisguised contempt for orthodoxy, de Gaulle emerged from the school with only '*Mention bien*', equivalent to a second-class degree. It was a serious setback, because only those who received first-class honours, '*Mention très-bien*', were eligible for posts both in the coveted Directorate of Operations of the General Staff and on the teaching staff at the Ecole Supérieure. It is said that Pétain intervened on de Gaulle's behalf and that, if he had not, his protégé would have been placed in the third class, not the second. Even Pétain could not extract a First from the School Directorate for the man whom they summed up like this: 'An intelligent well-read officer, keen on his job: brilliant and resourceful qualities; a lot in him. Unfortunately he spoils his undoubted talents by his excessive assurance, his contempt for other people's point of view, and his attitude of a king in exile.'[10]

The 'Mention bien' was a hard and apparently unexpected blow. De Gaulle was furiously resentful. He felt he had been penalized for displaying precisely the qualities the School should have been trying to cultivate in the future military leaders of France – independent judgement and forceful character – and vowed vengeance against the Establishment at the Ecole Supérieure. Thanks to Pétain he was to have spectacular satisfaction.

# 7 UNDER A CLOUD

The immediate result of de Gaulle's setback was that he was posted not to Paris, with the stars of the course, but to Staff HQ at Mainz in Germany in the Supplies Branch. After a few months he found himself dealing with questions of cold storage. But Marshal Pétain soon rescued him from Moyrand's revenge. In 1925 he had de Gaulle recalled from Germany to Paris and appointed to his own staff with the Supreme War Council, of which he had been vice-president since 1921.

It had been some consolation to de Gaulle that his first book, *La Discorde chez l'ennemi*, had been published in 1924. It was a study of the errors of the German military leadership and owed much to observations he had made while a prisoner of war. The five chapters related incidents during the war of 1914–18 in which German military or naval commanders exceeded their authority with disastrous consequences. De Gaulle draws the conclusion that the cultivation of Nietzsche's ideals of the élite and the superman, 'craving for power, taste for risk, contempt for others', had played a major part in bringing Germany to discord and defeat; and that generals must leave the political direction of war to the government. They should form their character, he says, on the model of the French classical garden, in which no element seeks to monopolize admiration. These were surprisingly sober conclusions for one who was even then being accused of arrogance by his military superiors. But de Gaulle always accepted the distinction between political and military spheres of responsibility, and the supremacy of the political role. It was only after he had assumed political leadership in circumstances without precedent in European history that de Gaulle grew far taller than any other tree in the French garden.

The literary talent revealed in de Gaulle's book probably influenced Pétain in rescuing him from Germany. Much of the work assigned to him was connected with the preparation of written studies on various military topics. One such task was to work on a project which Pétain had been nursing since 1921 for a fresh study of the Army's past in order to chart its future course. Little had been done, however, before de Gaulle arrived and took matters in hand. At Christmas 1926 de Gaulle's name appeared on the list of officers to be promoted to the rank of major (*commandant*).

But his routine tasks were not taking up all his time. Pétain was preparing a spectacular revenge on the Establishment of the Ecole Supérieure de Guerre which had snubbed him before 1914 and flouted his protégé in 1924. He had decided that de Gaulle should give a series of lectures at the school, and that the entire staff, instructors as well as pupils, should be obliged to attend and listen to the ideas of the man whose talents had been so underrated. De Gaulle worked on the text of the three talks which he was to give, while Pétain laboured to overcome the opposition of the School. He was only successful when a new director, General Hering, was appointed.

On 7 April 1927 the first lecture took place. Pétain himself introduced the lecturer in flattering terms. Then de Gaulle appeared, immaculately turned out and wearing white gloves which were not part of prescribed Army uniform. He strode to the rostrum, unhurriedly took off the gloves, and began to address his captive audience. His argument was that France must prepare without delay the race of military leaders she would need if war came again. 'It is time,' he proclaimed, 'for the military élite to become conscious once again of their preeminent role. France must throw off the mood of self-doubt which assailed her after her costly victory in 1918.' He went on to discuss in detail the qualities required to make a great military leader, '*un chef*', in time of war. This was the theme of all his three talks, which were later to provide the matter for three chapters of *Le Fil de l'Épée*, 'The Sword's Edge', published in 1932.

The lectures are admirably composed and abound in literary and historical references, from Heraclitus to Marshal Pétain, who is held up as the model of *le grand chef*. The display of knowledge is formidable, but the substance sometimes reads like a justification of de Gaulle against his critics at the School, particularly when he talks of the character of the *chef*. Because of his superior talents, he says, the great captain is not an easy man to get on with in peacetime. His subordinates suffer from his rigour, his seniors are irritated by his

33

frankness. But, when the storm comes, his qualities are recognized. Everybody turns to him, and it is he who willingly accepts the supreme responsibilities. He acts but he does not always explain, because *le chef* must be surrounded by an aura of mystery. 'No prestige without mystery', says de Gaulle. The personality he describes has touches about him of the Nietzschean superman whom de Gaulle had rejected as a model for French military leaders in his first book. He was in fact proposing to the school a radically new approach to their task of training the military élite of France, an approach which would concentrate on developing personality rather than uniformity.

De Gaulle doubtless hoped that his ideas would make converts and lead to changes in the curriculum at the School. He had prepared a paper containing his proposals for liberalization, which included a sociology course, but it would have required systematic pressure by Pétain to create even a chance of overcoming the inevitable resistance of the Establishment; and the Marshal lacked the energy and conviction required for the task. For him the gesture of organizing the talks was enough of a rebuke to the school. It therefore had to suffice for de Gaulle too. It was a spectacular revenge, but it changed nothing and made him more enemies than friends in the Army.

Late in 1927 Pétain did de Gaulle another considerable favour. He arranged for him to repeat his three lectures to a distinguished historical society which met at the Sorbonne.[1] The audience mostly came from the great world of Parisian society, politicians, journalists and intellectuals included. This time the reception was rather more favourable, but again there were many who felt a disproportion between the lofty nature of the subject and the rank and youth of the speaker. Still, de Gaulle began to be known outside the army as a young soldier with ideas. This mattered to him more than promotion to Major. He said in a letter to his friend Lucien Nachin, who had been a brother officer in the 33rd Regiment: 'Promotion is fine, but the real question is elsewhere . . . One has to make one's mark.'[2]

Late in 1927 he left Pétain's staff to take command of the 19th Light Infantry Battalion at Trier and assume the rank of Major. It was at this point that a domestic tragedy overtook Charles and Yvonne de Gaulle. Their third child, born on 1 January 1928, proved to be incurably abnormal, mongoloid, an afflicting sight. There was no hope of her ever being able to lead an ordinary life. It was an abiding grief to both of them. 'Her soul was made for another body', said her father. They decided to bear the burden themselves and rejected any idea of putting Anne in a home. The de Gaulles gave her the affection she needed, at much cost to themselves. Inevitably the strain increased as Anne grew, but Yvonne and Charles did not change their minds. Anne was with them constantly until her sudden death from pneumonia in 1948.

The first recorded disagreement between de Gaulle and Pétain took place during 1928, when de Gaulle objected to Pétain's plan to publish de Gaulle's studies on the history of the French Army in his own name. Pétain bowed to his objections and continued to protect de Gaulle. But it is extraordinary that the younger man should have taken such umbrage when he owed so much to Pétain and still needed him.

In the troubled Germany of 1928, de Gaulle sensed the rise and the danger of the new nationalism. He confided his fears to Nachin: 'Irresistible forces are sweeping away such barriers as are still recognized in Europe. There is no doubt that the Anschluss is near. Next Germany will take back, by force if necessary, what she has lost to Poland. After that she will demand Alsace from us. It seems to me that it's all predestined.'[3]

His prophetic bent as well as his boredom with life in Trier must have contributed to the now famous remark de Gaulle made in another letter to Lucien Nachin: 'How hard it is to wear the military harness nowadays. But it must be done. In a few years they'll be grovelling to us to save the country . . . and the scum [*la canaille*] into the bargain.'[4] Some read the illegible text as saying 'grovelling to me' not 'to us', but there is no evidence that de Gaulle ever foresaw that he would have to act alone as he did in 1940 to save France. '*La canaille*' is probably a reference to the parliamentarians, whose behaviour he had condemned during the war and thought no better of now, rather than to his fellow citizens in general.

His statutory two years as battalion commander at an end, de Gaulle was posted at his own request late in 1929 to the headquarters of the Army of the Levant in Beirut as chief of operations and military intelligence. It was his first and only spell of service outside Europe, and he proved impervious to the charms of the Orient. He had no praise either for the inhabitants or the local French. Writing to Nachin he said, 'the inhabitants have never in history been satisfied with anything or anybody.' As for the French: 'We are scarcely having any impact . . . Nothing has ever been achieved in this part of the world without firmness. As I see it, our destiny must be either to make a real impression or to leave.'⁵ De Gaulle, imbued with the history of France's achievement in the Crusades and Napoleon's campaigns, would certainly have preferred France to make a real impression rather than to leave.

He travelled extensively in the British sphere of influence in the Middle East, visiting Jerusalem, Cairo and Baghdad. Anglo-French rivalry in the area was deeply rooted in the past, and had never been overcome by the influence of the Entente Cordiale. The spirit of Fashoda, which de Gaulle had been brought up in by his father, was still alive in both camps. It is certain that nothing he saw on his travels diminished his natural tendency to regard the British as adversaries in the Levant; some of the seeds of his wartime discord with Churchill over the affairs of Syria and Lebanon were sown in the years from 1929 to 1931.

Much of de Gaulle's strictly personal correspondence has been omitted from the four volumes of his miscellaneous writings already published. The first letter to his wife which is included dates from November 1929 and was sent while he was on a tour of inspection in Northern Syria a few weeks after taking up his new post. It begins, like all his letters to her, '*Ma chère petite femme chérie*'. An unexciting account of his travels follows, until the last paragraph, in which the letter comes to life:

> I love you with all my heart. Everybody here says to me: 'We hope your wife wasn't too upset by the opening of the campaign.' I reply with the truth, which is 'No'; but I think to myself that perhaps she *was* upset, but had the courage to pretend not to be . . . I shall never forget how you backed me up at a difficult moment.⁶

It is impossible to say what the difficult moment was, but this is a tender letter which shows how much de Gaulle valued that gift of unfailing support which his wife brought to him, and proves that he was capable of saying what he felt.

# 8 The Approaching War

De Gaulle returned to Paris late in 1931 to a post in the Secretariat-General of the Supreme Council for National Defence, where he became one of the team who kept the Army War Plan up to date. The emphasis in military policy was increasingly on a defensive posture. The principal fortifications on the northeastern frontier were put in hand in 1930, becoming known as the Maginot Line, after the War Minister of the day, André Maginot.

In the summer of 1932 Charles de Gaulle had to sustain a personal grief: his father died at the age of eighty-three. He had been mentally alert to the last, and had been able to help his son with *Le Fil de l'Épée*, which appeared in the course of this year. It consisted of the definitive version of his three lectures at the Ecole Supérieure in 1927, with two extra chapters on the evolution of strategic thought and relations between the politician and the soldier. The theme is still the nature of war and the qualities required in the great captain who is to direct it.

In fact, as emerges more clearly from the foreword than from the book itself, de Gaulle was advancing a proposition which had political as well as military implications. It was that the blend of internationalism and pacifism, the rejection of war as an instrument of policy, which was so powerful at the time was based on a fallacy:

International law would be worthless without soldiers to back it. Whichever way the world goes, it will not be able to do without weapons. In fact, is it possible to conceive of life itself without force?

De Gaulle goes on to draw the moral for France:

If those who make use of the force of France lose heart, not only will our country be menaced, but the very harmony of the general order of things will be shattered. If wise men give up the use of power, what madmen will seize it, what fanatics?

The conclusion which follows from accepting de Gaulle's thesis is that the leaders of France have the right and the duty to use force in the national interest and that they must prepare in peacetime the men and the philosophy that they will need if the hour comes – 'It is the man of character who confers nobility on an enterprise. Without him it is the dull task of a drudge; with him it becomes the divine sport of the hero.'[1]

*Le Fil de l'Épée* made a considerable impression on the few who read it, but provoked the same questions as de Gaulle's lectures five years earlier. What right had an officer of middle rank to be laying down the law about such high matters as if he were a new Clausewitz? And precisely what action was he calling for? As one military journal put it, 'It requires audacity to put forward ideas in so lofty and sweeping a manner.' The military Establishment did not like audacity in majors and had already seen too much of it in de Gaulle. It ignored his work, as did the political world.

But some less orthodox military thinkers admired the book. At about this time his old friend Lucien Nachin introduced de Gaulle to a group who met regularly to discuss the shape of things to come. Many of them were from the world of politics and journalism. The central figure was a retired officer of over eighty, Lt.-Col. Emile Mayer. A graduate of the Ecole Polytechnique and a first-class brain, Emile Mayer had irretrievably damaged his career by expressing unpopular opinions. A Jew himself, he had proclaimed his belief in the innocence of Dreyfus too early in the day. Later on he had shown interest in disarmament and admiration for the Germans. In retirement he became a much respected commentator on military matters and forecast, on the evidence of the Russo-Japanese war of 1904–5, that the defensive would prevail in the next great war in Europe.

De Gaulle was now turning his thoughts from the kind of leadership France would need in the next war to the weapons she would require. Talks in the Mayer circle nourished his long-standing interest in the possibilities of the tank, and in May 1933 he published an article in the *Revue militaire et parlementaire* outlining the case for the creation of an armoured and motorized army. Urgency was added to his theme by the fact that Hitler had become Chancellor of Germany in January 1933. Soon it became known that the Nazis were planning to build armoured divisions. De Gaulle began to write a book on the subject.

While he was at work, there was a dramatic deterioration in the political situation in France. In January 1934 a financier, Serge

Stavisky, disappeared and was found dying by the police. Investigation of his affairs suggested, but did not prove, that prominent left-wing politicians were involved in his dubious dealings. Public opinion was shocked. After demonstrations and counter-demonstrations Edouard Daladier's Radical administration gave way to a more conservative coalition headed by the veteran Gaston Doumergue.

With the formation of Doumergue's government, the hope of a more glittering prize than his post at the Secretariat-General of the Defence Ministry appeared fleetingly for de Gaulle. Marshal Pétain, who had retired from the Army in 1930, began his political career by becoming Minister of War under Doumergue and considered inviting de Gaulle to be his *Directeur du Cabinet*. But some of the Marshal's entourage warned him that his ex-protégé now had ambitions of his own which made his loyalty suspect. De Gaulle thought it best to resolve the dispute by stating that he did not wish to enter Pétain's *Cabinet*. Had he done so, it might have been impossible to publish the book he had nearly finished. As it was, he retained his liberty.

During these troubled times de Gaulle and his wife looked for a country property which they could make into a family home. In June 1934 they found a house outside a small village in Lorraine called Colombey-les-Deux-Eglises. It was not far from the garrison towns along the eastern frontier where de Gaulle was likely to be stationed in future. The house they purchased, La Boisserie, was an old brewery on the edge of the village. Colombey was surrounded by open countryside and great forests, and Anne could play in the quiet walled garden without risk of disturbance. It became the family home for the rest of Charles's days and most of Yvonne's widowhood. Here de Gaulle was to pass the years of his exile from power between 1946 and 1958, and the period of his final retirement in 1969–70; and here he wrote the Memoirs which earned him a second title to fame.

In May 1934, just before the purchase of La Boisserie, his book *Vers l'Armée de Métier* – 'Towards the Professional Army' – was published. This was not a technical work. The argument was general and in its implications political. De Gaulle recognizes the usefulness of fortifications but argues that France cannot rely on them alone. It is her policy to maintain a number of small allies in Eastern Europe to check German expansionism, and she must be able to go to their aid. Therefore, she needs to be able to take the initiative in self-defence, and this she can only do in existing conditions if she forms an armoured army in which every man is fully trained in peacetime, 'ready to march upon the hour'. Its strength should be 100,000 men, and it should be composed of six armoured divisions, one light armoured division, with supporting mobile artillery, infantry and technical services, and an air reconnaissance contingent with protective fighters.

De Gaulle attaches the highest importance to his army's capacity to achieve surprise:

> Surprise has to be organized, not only by secrecy . . . but by a heavy veil of deception . . . Provided one is prepared to mislead one's own side as to one's intentions . . . one can conceal the true behind the false, as Themistocles did before Salamis . . . To bear such treatment from one's leaders requires the highest military virtues, but a chosen force, hardened to take what comes, can endure being promised rest when they are destined for battle.[2]

Here de Gaulle is describing a political as well as a military technique, and one to which he was much addicted in his years of power.

*Le Fil de l'Épée* and *Vers l'Armée de Métier* should be read as two volumes of a single book. In them de Gaulle describes the man who can win the next war for France and the army he will need. The crucial passage comes in the last section of *Vers l'Armée de Métier* when he reverts to the philosophy of leadership. Leadership is, he says, 'as unchangeable across the centuries as human nature itself . . . It is to raise oneself above one's own level in order to dominate others and, through them, the course of events. The effort does not change in essence from age to age. It is the procedures that change radically.'[3] Then he turns to the qualities required in the leader who makes this great effort. France, he says, will have to train in peace the leaders she will need in war. 'If the professional army is to come to birth in future with the fresh resources and spirit that it must possess in order to be more than a disappointing triviality, then its master must appear.' At the end of a long list of the master's necessary attributes, de Gaulle puts these: 'A man with strength enough to impose his will, charm enough to secure his wishes, greatness enough to accomplish a great mission. Such will be the Minister, be he soldier or politician, to whom the country will be indebted for making good use of her force.'[4] He ends his book in fact by stressing the importance not of a '*corps d'élite*', but of a single leader.

By implying that the two characters who feature in the last chapter of *Le Fil de l'Epée*, the politician and the soldier, need to be merged into one if France is to find an ideal leader, de Gaulle is prefiguring his own destiny. It is as if he had to state the requirement in words before he could meet it in action.

Writing long afterwards in his Memoirs, de Gaulle described his long campaign for the *armée de métier* as, 'my great quarrel', a vital phrase in his vocabulary. He prefaces *Le Fil de l'Épée* with the quotation: '*Être grand, c'est soutenir une grande querelle*', or 'To be great is to sustain a great quarrel.' De Gaulle attributes these words to Shakespeare's Hamlet, but in fact he is misquoting. What Hamlet says is significantly different:

> Rightly to be great
> Is not to stir without great argument,
> But greatly to find quarrel in a straw
> When honour's at the stake.[5]

De Gaulle's misquotation of Hamlet is revealing; to Hamlet his 'quarrel', the mission thrust upon him by Fate, was unwelcome; whereas de Gaulle's mission, his 'quarrel', was essential to the pursuit of greatness for himself and for France. For once his astonishing memory played him false and allowed him to believe that Hamlet had expressed de Gaulle's philosophy. If de Gaulle had not had a great quarrel, he would have had to invent one or accept frustration. Hitler saved him from having to face that dilemma.

The reaction to *Vers l'Armée de Métier* was tepid. A few journalists praised it, but only 700 copies were sold in France; it aroused more interest in Germany and Russia than among policy makers in France. Of course, as de Gaulle himself acknowledged, his ideas about the use of tanks were not new or revolutionary. The concept had its advocates and opponents among the military experts of every important power.

The rejection of his thesis by the General Staff was not the end of the 'great quarrel' for de Gaulle, who had foreseen it, but the beginning. He cultivated journalists who had shown interest, and André Pironneau, chief editor of *L'Echo de Paris*, became an ally. Others raised the subject too, including Rémy Roure of the influential conservative newspaper *Le Temps*, who had been a prisoner of war with de Gaulle and remained a friend.

But above all de Gaulle needed to enlist the support of a politician of sufficient standing to be able to champion his ideas in Parliament with a chance of being heard. In this task valuable help was forthcoming from the hospitable Emile Mayer who encouraged his many friends to read *Vers l'Armée de Métier*. One who did so and admired it was a lawyer and writer on current affairs named Jean Auburtin, who happened to know the rising independent conservative member of Parliament, Paul Reynaud. Auburtin arranged the vital first meeting between de Gaulle and Reynaud, which took place on 5 December 1934 and was an immediate success. Reynaud agreed to sponsor the idea of a professional mechanized army in Parliament, and set his *Directeur du Cabinet* (the head of his private office) Gaston Palewski to work with de Gaulle in drawing up a project for him to table in the Assembly.

Reynaud was by far the most influential supporter de Gaulle was to acquire. He was a Deputy for Paris who had already held office in the Ministries of Tardieu and Laval between 1930 and 1932 and was widely respected as an economic expert with a political future. From this time onwards he treated de Gaulle as his military adviser and proved a faithful friend, as did Palewski and Auburtin.

On 15 March 1935 there was a defence debate of major importance in the Chamber of Deputies. The French government had reluctantly decided that in face of German rearmament they must seek parliamentary approval for the extension of national service from twelve months, at which it had been set after the victory of 1918, to two years. Reynaud chose this occasion to state the case for the *armée de métier* and to table an amendment providing for the creation of a 'motorized corps' of six armoured divisions, plus a light armoured division and supporting forces, composed of soldiers serving for six years on contract. The force was to be completed and ready for action by 15 April 1940 at the latest.

The Assembly approved the government's recommendation, but took no action on Reynaud's plan. The War Minister, General Maurin, decried it, asking 'When we have devoted so much effort to building a fortified barrier, does anybody think we should be mad enough to advance in front of that barrier on Heaven knows what adventure?' Nevertheless the occasion helped to make de Gaulle's name better known and to give increased stature to his project.

It was not only for the reasons advanced by General Maurin that the Assembly had rejected the idea of an armoured Army. The whole concept of a professional army was repugnant to the Left. In their eyes it could too easily become a Praetorian Guard that would intervene in politics at the order of its commander, as had the grenadiers of Napoleon I and Napoleon III. Reynaud realized this and considered, as he said in his Memoirs, that de Gaulle had made an error in giving his book such a provocative title. If he had stressed the mechanization rather than the professionalism of his army, his proposals might have aroused less suspicion.

Indeed de Gaulle did not attempt to deny that the creation of his new model Army would have political implications. In the last pages of his book he had stated that such an Army could only function effectively if the institutions of France made it easier to exercise authority, and he had gone on to predict that change in that direction was on the way. That had been imprudent, but de Gaulle's views were strongly held. He explained his thinking in a letter to Paul Reynaud, dated 28 June 1935:[6]

The crisis, economic, political and moral, is gradually bringing the question of public order to the front of the stage.

In the mounting tumult, how is anarchy, and perhaps civil war, to be prevented without adequate public force? . . .

Under all régimes the Army has had the role and the duty of siding in the maintenance of order. How can one ask this of an Army in which all units are basically composed of voters . . . or of natives [i.e. Africans]?

The creation of the specialized corps is required not only by the current situation abroad but also by approaching needs on the home front.

There was no chance of such an argument carrying conviction with the Left. They knew from experience that armies obeyed generals, not legislators. Germany went on building armoured divisions, but France did not follow suit.

On 7 March 1936 Hitler struck the final blow at the Treaty of Versailles by ordering his forces to reoccupy the Rhineland, and France and Britain tamely acquiesced. De Gaulle was appalled. 'We should have reacted with surprise, ruthlessness, speed', de Gaulle wrote to his friend Jean Auburtin after the débâcle. There would have been no question for him of waiting for British support. 'If we'd had my *armée de métier* and its tanks,' he lamented 'there would have been no need for mobilization. We should have advanced and the Germans would have withdrawn. If we had done our duty, peace would have been saved.'[7] All that was learned after the war about the situation in Germany at this time suggests that de Gaulle was right. This was the last moment at which France had the power to save peace and overthrow Hitler by resolute action.

But the West remained inert, and France's allies in Eastern Europe began to say to themselves that they could not rely on her to come to their defence against German expansionism. Even in Belgium confidence drained away: in October 1936 Belgium withdrew from her alliance with France, and defensive collaboration between the General Staffs came to an end. The northern flank of the Maginot Line, which protected the north-east frontier with Germany, was left exposed. There was no defence system to cover the high-road of invasion into France between the Line and the Channel coast. The French faced a new dilemma. To extend the Line to the sea was formally to abandon Belgium. They chose the easier course of doing nothing and hoping for the best. But the worst was happening. The balance of power was tilting away from France.

The elections of May 1936 were won by the Popular Front, a coalition of radicals, Socialists and Communists and Léon Blum became Prime Minister. The change was of no help to de Gaulle's campaign. In October 1936, however, thanks to the influence of Emile Mayer, Blum agreed to give de Gaulle a hearing. He was impressed by de Gaulle's intelligence, but could not see his way to making a major change in national defence policy, which he knew would be distasteful to his party.

In December 1936 de Gaulle suddenly faced a crisis in his career. He learned that the General Staff had recommended that he should not be listed at the year's end for the promotion to the rank of full colonel during 1937 for which he was due by seniority. Their attitude should not be attributed to mere malice. De Gaulle was after all actively and publicly campaigning against the official French policy which it was his duty to implement. Such conduct in a serving officer would hardly have been tolerated in the British Army. It can be argued that the General Staff showed forbearance in not telling him to shut up or resign his commission. In the event de Gaulle escaped their wrath by appealing to Reynaud, who intervened personally with the Minister, Edouard Daladier. Despite his disagreement with de Gaulle's ideas, Daladier wrote his name into the promotion list himself. But, when Reynaud renewed his plea for the *armée de métier* in a New Year debate, Daladier had the proposal voted down.

In the summer of 1937 de Gaulle was duly promoted Colonel commanding the 507th Tank Regiment at Metz. This meant that he had more or less to abandon his campaign in Paris and concentrate on regimental duties in Metz.

In the late summer General Gamelin, the new Chief of the General Staff, included him in a group that toured defences on the Franco-Italian frontier. On the way he dined one night with his brother-in-law, Jacques Vendroux, who was holidaying in Haute Savoie, and confided in him his fears that war was coming soon. This, he said, might be their last summer of peace. He lamented the feebleness of Western politicians in face of Hitler and the folly of Gamelin's defence doctrine that 'concrete was king'. France would pay the heaviest price for Allied unpreparedness, he forecast, because she was in the front line. 'The British aren't ready; it's not at all sure we can count on the Russians; as to the Americans, they're always hesitant. They'll stay on the sidelines at first, cheering us on.' Of course, he said, the Allies would win in the end, but only after heavy losses. Paris would fall to the invader in a matter of days and the counter-attack would have to come from Brittany or Algeria.[8] De Gaulle was in his best prophetic vein that summer's night. Training at Metz convinced him more than ever of the soundness of the military doctrine he had been preaching. The day of the tank had arrived, and it was in the armoured corps that he would now seek to become *le chef*, the great captain.

His political ideas had also somewhat changed. Perception of the German menace had caused him to abandon some of his earlier Maurrassian sentiments.[9] *L'Action Française* advocated an understanding with the dictators, and he did not agree. In his campaign in favour of the mechanized army he had found sympathizers on the Left as well as the Right, and the experience had broadened his political horizons. He still disliked the irresolute unstable parliamentary régime of the day, but he saw no acceptable solution in Fascist methods. 'How could we accept the death of liberty as the price of social stability?' he wrote to his friend Jean Auburtin in November 1937 from Metz.[10] There is no evidence that he was among those extremists who hoped to see the existing political order overthrown by a coup d'état. By 1937 he might have been defined as a right-wing Republican whose aim in life was to modernize his country's system of defence and who was willing to seek allies in any political camp.

# 9 DISASTER .

When de Gaulle arrived in Metz, it was eight years since he had last commanded troops. Then it had been light infantry; now it was an armoured regiment. The parting words of the War Ministry had been: 'You've given us enough trouble with your tanks on paper. Now let's see what you make of real tanks'.[1] De Gaulle accepted the challenge, and set about raising the level of efficiency of his unit. He worked the men and their material so hard that the Directorate of Material raised their eyebrows at the 507th's rate of equipment wastage. But he escaped censure. He was delighted with the tanks and wrote about them not only to Lucien Nachin but to Paul Reynaud, who became Finance Minister in the government formed by Edouard Daladier in April 1938 when the Popular Front broke up.

The idea of the armoured unit was gradually becoming more respectable even with the most conservative military minds. In December 1938 the French High Command decided on the creation of two armoured divisions to be ready early in 1940, but they were not designed to operate independently. The Maginot Line and the mass conscript army retained their place as the essential elements in the French war plan.

De Gaulle was no longer writing about tanks, but another work of his, *La France et son Armée* was published in September 1938. This was a revised and expanded version (on which Emile Mayer helped him) of the historical study on the French Army which he had prepared at Pétain's order in 1925–7 and had prevented the Marshal publishing under his own name in 1928. Now Pétain retaliated by raising objections to de Gaulle appropriating work based on a staff study which Pétain had initiated. De Gaulle had to make a personal call on him at his apartment in Paris before Pétain agreed to the book appearing under his name, on condition that it bore a suitable dedication to himself.

*La France et son Armée* was well received by the critics but sold less well than expected, perhaps because it came out during the Munich crisis. It also provoked the wrath of Pétain because de Gaulle had slightly altered the draft dedication the Marshal had sent him, without obtaining his agreement. De Gaulle promised that the second edition would bear the dedication in the form desired by Pétain, but the old man was not appeased. He felt de Gaulle had let him down; de Gaulle on the other hand felt Pétain was making a fuss about nothing out of senile irritability. There was no formal rupture, but in fact the long friendship between the two men was now at an end. In March 1939 Pétain left for Madrid to become French Ambassador to General Franco, finally victorious over the Republicans in the Spanish Civil War.

While Pétain and de Gaulle had been arguing, the Munich crisis had once more exposed the feebleness of British and French leadership. Czechoslovakia was lost to the West, and the other small countries of Eastern Europe could have no further hope of French protection. France, no longer capable of independent political action in Europe, had to look for a British lead in everything; and Britain's leader was Neville Chamberlain. In September 1938 de Gaulle, who had been ready and eager for battle, wrote bitterly to his wife: 'As usual, we surrender without a fight to the insolent demands of the Germans and deliver our allies, the Czechs, to the common enemy . . . This surrender will win us a brief respite. We are like Madame du Barry with her head on the block begging: "Please give me a few more seconds, Mister Executioner."'[2]

In November 1938 Emile Mayer, who had been de Gaulle's constant ally and adviser since they first met in 1932, died. De Gaulle was so absorbed in military affairs that he could not come to Paris from Metz for the funeral. But he remembered the old Colonel's aid and spoke of him long after the war to his assistant, Olivier Guichard, with 'a certain emotion' which showed that he had a special place in his recollections.[3] In 1939, as the German menace grew with the occupation of Prague, and the crisis over Poland took shape, de Gaulle seems to have done no writing. His energies were absorbed in preparing his armoured regiment for war. He was rewarded by being placed on the list of those qualified for promotion to the rank of general. When war came in September 1939, de Gaulle was posted from Metz to Lower Alsace to be tank commander of the Fifth Army, but his tanks were broken up into units tied to infantry formations. The French Army by now had considerable numbers of modern tanks at its disposal, but even the two newly born armoured divisions which entered into the order of battle in September and October 1939 were not equipped to operate independently of other arms.

France was mobilized and the Maginot complex was packed with men. Between the end of the Line and the Channel coast the French and the British Expeditionary Force of 250,000 fighting troops laboriously prepared new defences along the frontier of neutral Belgium. The defensive mentality was dominant. No serious thrust was made into German territory while the bulk of Hitler's forces were in the east in October, destroying Poland by blitzkrieg and partitioning it with the Red Army. It was the period of what an American Senator called 'the phony war'. In the inactive tedium of life in the Maginot Line, the morale of the French troops began to suffer.

It was evident that there was no enthusiasm for the war in France. The situation was utterly different from that of 1914. Then Germany had declared war on France. The French had no alternative but to fight, and they had a clear war aim: the return of Alsace and Lorraine. Now it was France that declared war on a Germany that protested peaceful intentions towards her, and she did so less of her own initiative than because Britain gave the lead. Yet it was France that had to mobilize a hundred divisions and face the German Army. This inequality added to the distaste for the war felt by many right-wingers, who had come to regard the Popular Front as more of a menace to their society than Hitler. Pierre Laval was their political leader. The Left meanwhile was split by the Nazi-Soviet Pact. The Communists turned against the war overnight, and when their leader, Maurice Thorez, was called up, he deserted and fled to Russia.

The Allies concentrated on blockade. German territory was not bombed, in the hope that British and French territory would be similarly spared by the Luftwaffe. Daladier encouraged the formation of an Anglo-French force to go to the aid of Finland, which the Red Army invaded in November. The idea behind this was that the force would establish itself in neutral Scandinavia and cut off the supplies of iron ore from Northern Sweden on which the German war industry partly depended.

Meanwhile de Gaulle took up his pen again to attempt a final warning. On 26 January 1940 he addressed a memorandum to eighty political and military leaders entitled 'The Arrival of the Mechanized Force'. It drew on the lessons of the devastating German victory in Poland to make its point:

In this war to be immobile is to be beaten . . . The French people must not at any price succumb to the illusion that the present military lull corresponds to the nature of the present war. On the contrary, the motor gives modern means of destruction such power, speed and range that the present conflict will sooner or later be marked by developments . . . far exceeding those of the most devastating events of the past.

The conflict which has just begun could well be the most widespread, complex and violent of all . . . The political, social and moral crisis which gave rise to it is so profound and widespread that it will inevitably lead to a complete upheaval of peoples and states. The mysterious harmony which rules great events has produced in the mechanized army a military instrument exactly in proportion to this colossal revolution. It is high time that France drew the necessary conclusions.[4]

As usual, the Generals rejected his recommendations, but at least the memorandum was a timely reminder to Paul Reynaud of de Gaulle's existence and his talents. For on 21 March, after the conclusion of peace between Finland and the Soviet Union, there was sharp criticism in the Assembly of the government's inertia, and Daladier was obliged to resign. On the same day President Lebrun invited Reynaud to form an administration. This was no easy task because Reynaud, being an independent, lacked a solid block of party votes to provide the core of his support. When he presented his government to the Assembly on 23 March, he received a majority of only a single vote. De Gaulle, whom Reynaud had immediately summoned to Paris, was in the gallery for the debate, which he described as 'frightful'. It was dominated by partisan disputes and must have increased his distaste for parliamentary government as practised in France.

He became himself a victim of Reynaud's weak position. The Premier had wanted to appoint him secretary of the new War Cabinet which he was setting up on the British model, but Daladier, now Defence Minister, objected to de Gaulle as a 'belliciste' – warmonger – a term of disparagement invented by the advocates of inertia. So the post was given to Paul Baudouin, an ex-banker with no enthusiasm for the war. Instead of a place at the centre of power de Gaulle had to content himself with being named future commander of the Fourth

Armoured Division, which was due to be formed by 15 May. Meanwhile he returned to Alsace, aware that there were influential groups in Paris openly in favour of putting an end to the war.

Early in April Reynaud, trying to pursue a more active war policy, prevailed on the British to revive the plan for mining Norwegian waters and thus cutting the main supply route of Swedish iron ore to Germany. But the Germans moved faster, occupying key points in Norway while the Allies were still on their way, and taking Denmark as well for good measure. In the battles which followed, German tanks and aircraft again proved their superiority. Soon the only foothold left to the Allies was at Narvik in the far north, where they inflicted a naval defeat on the Germans.

Shaken by the failure in Norway, Reynaud was finding his task as Premier almost impossible. He was at odds with Daladier, and the peace party was growing stronger. On 9 May he offered the President his resignation. The next day everything changed. At dawn the Germans began a great offensive. Reynaud had to withdraw his resignation, while in London Churchill replaced Chamberlain as Premier and formed a coalition government.

When the Germans invaded the Low Countries, the Allies left their winter defence lines and moved forward into Belgium. In reply the Germans punched through the Ardennes just north of the Maginot Line with ten massed armoured divisions and six more of motorized infantry, destroyed the Ninth and Tenth French armies in three days and began a sweep across northern France. By 15 May they were in a position either to advance on Paris or to cut the Allied armies in two by thrusting on to the Channel coast. The Allied war plan was in ruins.

On 11 May de Gaulle was ordered to take command of his armoured division, which was gathering at Le Vésinet, near Paris. On 15 May he was directed to move northeastwards to the region of Laon to stem the German flood and gain time while a defensive position was established along the Aisne barring the route to Paris. The next day, reconnoitring around Laon, he saw for the first time the long columns of civilian refugees fleeing from the battle. Mixed in with them he saw the sight, still more terrible to him, of bands of disarmed soldiers in disorganized retreat.

His tank units, coming from various rallying-points, began to arrive on 16 May. At dawn the next morning, the division, still incomplete, was ordered into action from Laon towards Montcornet. At once de

Gaulle's untried men in their unfamiliar tanks had to confront the seasoned 19th Corps under General Guderian, one of the most brilliant exponents of the *Blitzkrieg*. In three days of fierce and confused fighting, they showed an ability to attack, occupying Montcornet for a while on the 17th, and took 120 prisoners. It was an honourable début. By the time de Gaulle had to order a withdrawal south of the Aisne, the river line was firmly held by the French. The Germans pressed on not for Paris but westwards to the coast, as had always been their intention.

French morale, already frail, sustained a shattering blow from this utterly unexpected German breakthrough into the heart of the country. Reynaud, with defeat staring him in the face, strove to restore the situation by appeals to Churchill and Roosevelt, and by calling to his aid men whose names evoked the victory of 1918. On 18 May he reconstructed his government, summoning Pétain back from Madrid to become vice-president of the Council of Ministers and appointing Georges Mandel, the distinguished Jewish statesman who had been Clemenceau's *Directeur du Cabinet* in 1917–18, Minister of the Interior. He also named Weygand, Foch's Chief of Staff, as Commander-in-Chief in place of Gamelin and took over the Defence portfolio himself from Daladier, who became Foreign Minister. It was a courageous effort but misguided, because Pétain was already profoundly defeatist, as Reynaud should have known, and Weygand soon became equally so.

In the succeeding days, while Paris enjoyed a brief respite, the Fourth Armoured Division regrouped and moved to the Somme. There from 28 to 30 May de Gaulle and his men fought their second battle and did better. Their mission was to reduce the bridgehead across the Somme which the Germans had established south of Abbeville. De Gaulle attacked in the late afternoon on the 28th and took the enemy by surprise. The first day's objectives were attained, prisoners were taken, and the tablecloth of the officers' mess that night was a captured swastika flag. On the 29th the advance continued, but resistance stiffened and losses were heavy. On the afternoon of the 30th a final thrust was made against the remaining part of the Abbeville bridgehead, but, after initial success, it failed.

On the 31st, neighbouring British forces (whose determination impressed de Gaulle)[5] relieved the battle-scarred division (seventy tanks lost out of 140), who were pulled into reserve to reform. They had not attained their objective but they had considerably reduced the size of the Abbeville bridgehead, prevented its use for offensive operations, and captured 500 prisoners and some war material. In a catastrophic situation their achievement stood out and brought credit to de Gaulle. He was mentioned in dispatches by General Weygand on 1 June and praised in the press. But the battle was lost. The armies in Belgium were cut off and forced to surrender, except for the British, who escaped at Dunkirk with some of the French.

These battles provided de Gaulle with the only opportunity that was to come his way as a soldier of applying the maxims of leadership laid down in *Le Fil de l'Épée*. By all accounts he lived up to his precepts. He was indefatigable, and frequently up with his leading troops in positions of danger. Talking little, impatient of questions, constantly smoking, he thought of nothing but the battle. When told an officer was killed, his only remark was: 'Who's replacing him?' He was pitiless with officers who fell short of his standards. The penalty was dismissal to safety at the regimental depot. To an ineffectual subaltern hastening from his officer to repair an oversight, he thundered a characteristic word of advice: '*Existez, Jourdain, existez.*'[6]

De Gaulle was suffering from shock and from shame. He had expected the French Army to sustain reverses, but he never foresaw anything like the débâcle of May 1940. On the contrary he had said repeatedly to Reynaud and others that he was confident the French would throw back an all-out German attack. Now he had to face the fact that he was wrong and that the cause of his miscalculation was not only the force of the German attack but the feebleness of the French defence. In some units there had been a collapse of morale, '*cette déroute militaire*' as he calls it in his Memoirs. That was what made him swear to fight on 'wherever I have to and as long as I have to, until the enemy is beaten and the stain on our national honour is wiped out. Whatever I was able to do afterwards stemmed from the resolution I took on that day.'[7]

On 1 June de Gaulle assumed the rank of brigadier-general and drove to see General Weygand. The Commander-in-Chief received him warmly but shocked him by his gloom. Weygand asked for advice on how to use the 1,200 modern tanks still at his disposal, and de Gaulle urged that they be allowed to operate independently in the German style. He followed up his words by a letter the next day, recommending that all available tanks should be massed in a corps of three divisions coming directly under Weygand's orders. He added: 'Without any modesty but in knowledge that I can do it, I propose myself as Commander of the Corps.'[8] Weygand did nothing.

Throughout his battles de Gaulle had kept in touch with his wife. As early as 15 May he warned her that she might possibly have to leave Colombey, and told her: Make sure, *very discreetly*, that you have transport available.' On her birthday, 22 May, he wrote: 'I spent your birthday in the thick of the fight, and it turned out well for our side – a rare thing in this war. I thought of you and sent you my most loving wishes, Yvonne.'[9] He was eager to receive letters too and complained to her when the two elder children, away at school, did not write to him. Yvonne, taking Anne with her, went first to the Loiret and then on to Brittany, where Philippe and Elisabeth joined them as the German threat to Paris grew. De Gaulle did not try to guide their movements precisely, but made suggestions and laid it down as a rule that they should not allow the Germans to outflank them.[10]

Early on 6 June he received a telephone call. A neighbouring general had heard in a news bulletin that de Gaulle had been appointed Under-Secretary of State for National Defence by Prime Minister Reynaud. Official confirmation was soon forthcoming. He had been included in what was to prove the last readjustment of the last legitimate administration of the Third Republic. He handed over his Division the same morning and took off for Paris, just as the new German offensive was spreading along the line of the Somme. Having participated in the failure of the military élite, he was now to live through the expiring moments of the political élite.

# 10 DE GAULLE REFUSES TO DESPAIR OF THE REPUBLIC

Nothing in de Gaulle's extraordinary career is more extraordinary than the style of his début as a minister. In rank he was a modest Under-Secretary of State, the lowest grade in the French ministerial hierarchy, but in fact he immediately began to behave, and to be accepted by Reynaud and Churchill, as a major personality.

His first talk as a minister with Paul Reynaud ended with him being entrusted at his own suggestion with a most important mission to Churchill, and as early as 12 June Churchill was singling him out from the rest of the French ministers for praise in a telegram to President Roosevelt. It was the considerable achievement of so impressing Britain's leader after only two meetings that paved the way to the welcome he received in London on 17 June.

Reactions to de Gaulle's appointment were mixed. The French press praised his achievements in battle, while *The Times* described him as 'rather aggressively "right-wing" . . . a man of action as well as a man of dreams and abstract ideas'. Pétain, who had joined Reynaud's Ministry on 16 May, and Weygand were frankly hostile. Both of them protested to Reynaud. Pétain told the story of how he had appropriated the manuscript of *La France et son Armée*, presumably to illustrate his untrustworthiness. Weygand simply said '*C'est un enfant.*' It was true that de Gaulle, at forty-nine, was the youngest general in the French Army, but as Reynaud observed in his Memoirs, it was a curious reason for objecting to him.[1]

The aim of this final reshuffle of Reynaud's Cabinet was to strengthen his personal authority and rebuff defeatism, but the effect was limited. He was able to drop the halfhearted Daladier but he dared not dismiss the principal defeatists Pétain and Weygand.

When Reynaud received him on 6 June, de Gaulle urged that preparations should be put in hand at once for the move of the government to North Africa and asked to be employed on the task himself. Reynaud agreed and told him to go to London as soon as possible. 'Our aim at this point must be to persuade the British that we will carry on whatever happens, even overseas if necessary,' he said. 'See Churchill and tell him that the changes in my government and your presence in it at my side are proofs of our determination.'[2] De Gaulle was also to press for more British aid, air force and military, to be sent to France with all possible speed.

Reynaud's words have an equivocal ring, like so much of what he says and does from now on. He does not say unambiguously that the impression he wishes to give the British corresponds to his true intentions. Perhaps he was no longer sure by this time what his true intentions were. He had to contend with the pressures of defeatism in his private as well as his public life. His mistress, Hélène, Comtesse de Portes, who had a great deal of influence on him, was well known to have friends in pro-German business circles, and had been against the war from the beginning. Her opposition intensified as the news grew worse. The unfortunate Reynaud's nights were, therefore, as grim as his days.

In preparation for his mission to London de Gaulle went to see General Weygand on 8 June. The Commander-in-Chief was even more defeatist than he had been a week before. He said his armies were outnumbered and could not hold the new German offensive; the battle of France, and in consequence the war, was irretrievably lost. He dismissed de Gaulle's argument that France could fight on in her Empire and throughout the world. 'When I've been beaten here, Britain will not wait a week before opening negotiations with the Reich.'[3]

De Gaulle went back to Paris and told Reynaud that the government ought to replace Weygand, who had lost the will to fight. He recommended General Huntziger as a successor. Reynaud agreed in principle, but said it was impossible to dismiss Weygand at once. He did not explain why, but the reason was evident: he could not face the open break with Pétain which would immediately ensue.

On 9 June de Gaulle flew to London and had his first meeting with Churchill. He delivered Reynaud's message that his government meant to fight on from overseas if necessary and made his plea for more British troops and planes. His determination made an excellent impression on the British who met him. Churchill heard him out sympathetically, but did not conceal either his belief that the battle of France was lost or his doubts whether the French government would truly move to Africa. His hope was that the battle of France would be continued as long as possible. To that end he promised to hurry to France such troops as were equipped and trained, while refusing to send any more of the RAF fighter force. That must be held in reserve, he said, for the battle of Britain which would surely follow the battle of France.

As de Gaulle was leaving Churchill, he turned back at the door and said: 'Mr Prime Minister, I think you are right.'[4] Thus in a few words he put himself in a different category from Reynaud and the rest, who went on urging the total commitment of the RAF to a lost battle. Unlike them, de Gaulle accepted that it was in the ultimate interest of France for the RAF now to concentrate on winning the battle of Britain, and he wanted Churchill to know it. So he seized the fleeting opportunity and made his mark. Churchill saw that there was at least one French minister who seriously intended to carry on the war even if France was lost; de Gaulle realized that he was in the presence of a man who might make it possible for him to keep the vow he had made among the fleeing soldiers around Laon to fight on to victory whatever the cost.

De Gaulle returned to Paris to find that the situation at the front had still further deteriorated. During the night of 9/10 June he was summoned to Reynaud's office for urgent consultations. The Premier announced that Italy was about to declare war on the Allies and that the Germans were approaching Paris against crumbling resistance. De Gaulle urged that the city should be resolutely defended and that the government should firmly commit itself to carrying on the war in coalition with Britain by withdrawing to North Africa as soon as possible. Reynaud knew, however, that either of these decisions would involve him in a confrontation with the peace party. He confined himself to directing that the government should move southwards to the Loire valley.

'10 June,' wrote de Gaulle, 'was a day of agony.' Weygand appeared unbidden in Reynaud's office to plead for an immediate armistice. Reynaud refused, with strong support from de Gaulle, and the interview closed in an unfriendly atmosphere. Just before departing from Paris at 11 pm Reynaud, who was accompanied by de Gaulle, was asked by a delegation of municipal councillors if the city would be defended by the Army. No clear pronouncement on the subject had been made. Reynaud did not reply himself but turned to Weygand, who was present once more. 'Paris is an open city,' said the Commander-in-Chief. In the following days the decision was made public and at Reynaud's request the Americans interceded for Paris with the Germans through diplomatic channels. When German troops moved into the city on 14 June there was not a single untoward incident.[5]

So the beauty and history of Paris was saved. It might not have been. The Germans pulverized Warsaw and Rotterdam, and could have done the same to Paris if they had met with resistance. The material consequences of defence would have been far more shattering than they were in 1870–1 or would have been in 1914. De Gaulle knew this, but he was willing to make the sacrifice even though it could not have changed the result of the battle of France. The *'certaine idée de la France'* which he cherished put resistance to the enemy above the conservation of monuments of the past, however precious. As we shall see, he was ready to apply the same principle when the time to liberate Paris came in 1944.

On the morning of 11 June Reynaud first sent de Gaulle from Orléans to General Huntziger's HQ to ask him if he would take over command from Weygand. Huntziger agreed, but when de Gaulle returned to Weygand's headquarters at Briare for the meeting of the Anglo-French Supreme War Council which Churchill had demanded, he found that Reynaud had changed his mind and resolved to keep Weygand despite his defeatism. Other influences had been at work in de Gaulle's absence. From this point onwards until his resignation on 16 June Reynaud became more equivocal than ever. He had decided to avoid at all costs a rupture between the rival factions in the Council of Ministers. The effect was to play into the hands of the peace party, which, helped by the inexorable German advance, grew steadily stronger and bolder.

De Gaulle was deeply disappointed by the course of the meeting at Briare because it had never focused on what he saw as the one vital problem – how France should establish herself in Africa in order to continue the war. Churchill's personality and resolve to carry on the fight impressed him, but, as he put it in his Memoirs, the war was entering a new phase and 'the solidarity of Britain and France, the power of France's army, the authority of her government, the loyalty of her military command could no longer be taken for granted. Each participant behaved not like a partner in a joint enterprise but like a man who from now on had his own game to play.'[6]

De Gaulle was right. Churchill came to Briare in order to keep French resistance in France alive as long as possible, because it retarded the German onslaught on Britain as resistance in Africa would not. The Germans did not need to pursue the French into Africa immediately; they could turn their full force against Britain. If they won there, Africa would fall into their hands too. That was why Churchill disappointed de Gaulle by saying so little about Africa. The tactics of Weygand and Pétain on the other hand were to make the British bear as much responsibility as possible for the armistice they had already decided to seek by pressing demands for aid which they knew Churchill would have to refuse. Accordingly Weygand did not admit the battle was lost, as he had told de Gaulle three days earlier, but said that the Germans might still be held if as much British aid as possible, particularly in fighter planes, were forthcoming at once. Pétain backed him up, and so did Reynaud, because it was his policy to avoid a break with the defeatists. But he insisted that France would fight on in any case.

Churchill's generous nature was vulnerable to the reproach that Britain could do so little to aid her ally in her hour of need, and he gave some ground by conceding that the French Army could capitulate if that were considered necessary, without France forfeiting British good will.[7] This was half a point gained for the defeatists. Capitulation was not an armistice, but its acceptance by Churchill meant that he already recognized that France and Britain might have to go their separate ways. De Gaulle had to remain silent during the conference, except on a technical point, but he sat next to Churchill at dinner, presumably on Reynaud's orders, and again impressed him, as he had done in London two days earlier, by his spirit. He alone among the French was full of plans for fighting on.

The meeting ended on the morning of 12 June with a brief session during which Churchill made a formal request which Reynaud accepted: 'that if there was any change in the situation the French government would let the British government know at once so that we might come over and see them . . . before they took any final decisions which would govern their action in the second phase of the war'.[8] Churchill's final words to Admiral Darlan before boarding his plane were another admission that he saw the worst coming as far as the battle of France was concerned. He took him aside and said: 'Darlan, whatever happens, the Germans must never have your fleet.' Darlan swore they would not;[9] and, despite all his subsequent dealings with the Axis, he proved as good as his word.

Back in London Churchill reported his conclusions by telegram to Roosevelt: 'The practical point is what will happen when and if the French front breaks . . . The aged Marshal Pétain is, I fear, ready to lend his name and prestige to a treaty of peace for France. Reynaud, on the other hand, is for fighting on, and he has a young General de Gaulle who believes much can be done.'[10] De Gaulle had made his mark again.

After the conference at Briare, Reynaud convened a Cabinet meeting which de Gaulle did not attend because he was busy planning with the military experts for the move to North Africa. Here the defeatists made the next move in their game. Weygand reported to the Council what he had withheld from Churchill – that the battle was lost and an armistice must be sought. Most of the ministers spoke against the idea. France was still bound, after all, by the Anglo-French agreement of 28 March 1940, concluded at British urging as soon as Reynaud had become Premier, which laid down that neither party would negotiate a peace or armistice without mutual consent. No decision was reached. It was agreed instead, at the suggestion of Chautemps, who had the senior rank of Minister of State along with Pétain, that Churchill should be invited to come over again at once for the meeting between the two governments which he had demanded 'if there was any change in the situation'.

De Gaulle, arriving late in the evening at Reynaud's residence, the Château de Chissay, found that the only subject on the minds of the ministers present was where they should retreat to next, Bordeaux or Brittany. De Gaulle naturally argued for Brittany, which could be defended for a time and from which the government could gain Africa or Britain when necessary, but Weygand angrily opposed him. The choice was made by Reynaud on the morning of the 13th in favour of Bordeaux.

About noon on 13 June Churchill reappeared, accompanied this time by Halifax, the Foreign Secretary, and Beaverbrook, Minister of Aircraft Production, to confer with Reynaud at Tours. De Gaulle only heard of it by a last-minute telephone call from Margerie, Reynaud's *Directeur du Cabinet*: 'You're not invited, but I suggest you come.

Baudouin is at work, and it looks bad to me.'[11] In principle this was an intergovernmental meeting, not one of the Supreme War Council, but Reynaud chose to come to it accompanied only by Baudouin. He intended to speak both for his own views and for those of Pétain, but it seems that he did not explain this curious procedure clearly to the British. As at Briare, each side had its own game to play.

When the meeting finally began at the Prefecture in Tours, Reynaud, after saying he was sending a final appeal to President Roosevelt, announced that Weygand had told the Council of Ministers that the battle was lost and urged that an armistice be sought. The majority of the Council had not approved a demand for an armistice but had asked him to consult Churchill. The British Premier's aim remained the same as in the previous meeting. He said at once that Britain would fight on to victory and hoped France would do so too, 'south of Paris down to the sea and if need be from North Africa. At all costs time must be gained.'[12]

In reply Reynaud asked the vital question foreshadowed at Briare. What would be the British attitude if a French government had to demand an armistice?

According to the British record quoted in Churchill's *The Second World War*, he replied: 'In no case would Britain waste time and energy in reproaches and recriminations. This did not mean that she would consent to action contrary to the recent agreement [that of 28 March] . . . Let them await the answer [to Reynaud's message to Roosevelt] before considering anything else. If England won the war, France would be restored in her dignity and in her greatness.'[13]

Churchill then asked for an interval for reflection. While the British were talking in the garden, de Gaulle made his belated arrival. On the resumption of the meeting Churchill confirmed that his colleagues were of the same mind as himself. Reynaud 'having obtained all that could be obtained' as he puts it in his Memoirs, then announced to Churchill that: 'all I had said so far reflected the opinions of certain of my colleagues and that I myself had not changed and remained confident of Allied victory'.[14]

On this curious note the meeting ended, with an agreement to consult again when Reynaud received the American President's reply to his appeal for help.

Once more de Gaulle was dissatisfied. He felt that Churchill had been too sympathetic to the case stated on behalf of the defeatists. In his Memoirs he says: 'Referring to the eventuality of a Franco-German armistice, which I thought would electrify him, he displayed on the contrary understanding and commiseration.'[15] The British record of Churchill's words to Reynaud shows that there was some justice in de Gaulle's reaction. De Gaulle tried to limit the damage by warning General Spears, Churchill's liaison officer with Reynaud, that Paul Baudouin was already putting it about that Churchill had said Britain would understand if France had to make a separate peace.[16] The defeatists were indeed thinking of a separate peace and not just an armistice, as became apparent when Pétain took over.

De Gaulle was uncertain even of where Reynaud himself now stood. He sought him out in the Prefecture immediately the meeting was over and asked him: 'Is it possible that you seriously think that France might request an armistice?' Reynaud replied: 'Of course not. But we must impress the English in order to make them more cooperative.'[17] De Gaulle realized that the response was frivolous and that Reynaud was giving way. He returned to his quarters to write his letter of resignation. There he found awaiting him his friend Jean Auburtin, now a member of his staff. In the most passionate terms he told him he was determined to reject an armistice and would seek a new command and die at the head of his troops rather than accept it.[18]

Reynaud meanwhile said goodbye to Churchill without telling him that the Council of Ministers was expecting to confer with him. No doubt he felt that equivocation would be easier if he did not allow Pétain and Churchill to confront one another again. In that he was right, as the evening's Council meeting showed. It began in a mood of irritation at the failure of the British Prime Minister to attend, which was manifestly Reynaud's fault. Marshal Pétain then read a prepared statement demanding an armistice, which contained the words: 'The French government cannot quit the country without being guilty of desertion. Whatever happens, it is the duty of the government to remain in the country, on pain of forfeiting its legitimacy if it departs.'[19] The majority dissented from Pétain's view, and Reynaud spoke of fighting on overseas. But no firm decision was reached either way. It was agreed to await President Roosevelt's response. Pétain had made an important advance. He had served warning that he would use his influence to challenge the authority of any government that left the country and purported to exercise French sovereignty from abroad.

Returning home from this meeting, Georges Mandel, the Minister of the Interior, was informed by de Gaulle's anxious *Chef du Cabinet* Jean Laurent that his chief was about to send his resignation to the Prime Minister. Mandel, who was strongly in favour of continuing the war, immediately invited de Gaulle to come and see him and urged him to reconsider. He pointed out that there was still a majority in the Council against an armistice. The worst had not yet happened and, if it did, his position as a minister might be useful to him. There was a long war ahead and de Gaulle would have a great part to play in it. 'Think only of what must be done for France,' was Mandel's advice.[20] De Gaulle accepted it. If he had followed his own inclination, he would have forfeited his chance of going to England when Reynaud fell. Mandel had sensed his political destiny while de Gaulle himself was still thinking of a return to the Army.

On 14 June the government made its retreat to Bordeaux, and de Gaulle returned to the charge with Reynaud. He said that he personally refused an armistice, and argued that Reynaud must order a withdrawal to Algeria if he meant to fight on. Did he? Reynaud said he did. De Gaulle then asked to be sent to London to arrange for the British shipping that would be necessary for the move. Reynaud agreed that he should go, travelling via Brittany to see what could be shipped from there. 'We shall meet next in Algiers' were his parting words.

Before setting out de Gaulle dined at the Hotel Splendide. At another table was Marshal Pétain. 'I went to pay my respects to him without saying a word,' de Gaulle related in his Memoirs. 'Silently he shook my hand. I was not to see him again, ever.'[21]

In fact there was hardly a civil word the two men could have exchanged. De Gaulle was in a towering rage against the great soldier who was preparing to surrender to the enemy. The next day, in conversation with the Admiral commanding at Brest, he launched into a furious diatribe against Pétain, calling him a traitor. On this journey to England he was thinking about the future in a new way, thanks no doubt to Mandel's advice. What would he do if there were an armistice? His train of thought was revealed in a question he put to the captain of the *Milan*, the destroyer taking him to England. 'Would you be ready to fight under the British flag?' The reply was negative.[22]

When de Gaulle reached London on the morning of 16 June, it was high politics, not shipping, that took priority. Corbin, the French Ambassador, and Jean Monnet, head of the French Economic Mission in London, came to see him. They reported that the French government had on the evening of 15 June decided that Roosevelt's reply to Reynaud's appeal for aid, though sympathetic, was inadequate, and had formally asked the British for release from the accord of 28 March. Only a dramatic gesture by Britain, said Corbin and Monnet, would enable Reynaud to withstand the growing pressure for an immediate armistice coming from Pétain and Pierre Laval. They then told de Gaulle of the proposal for an Anglo-French Union, an immediate pooling of resources and citizenship, which they had worked out with the Foreign Office. If the British Cabinet would at once approve the offer of this union to Reynaud it might, they believed, provide him with the ammunition he needed to fight off the advocates of the armistice. Would he, de Gaulle, commend it to Churchill, with whom he was to lunch?

De Gaulle, though fully aware of the practical difficulties of the proposal and unsympathetic to it in principle, bowed to the desperate circumstances of the moment and supported it in discussion with Churchill over lunch. Churchill, who already knew of the proposal and shared de Gaulle's feelings about it, was won over for the reasons which had convinced the General. The party then repaired to 10 Downing Street, where de Gaulle telephoned Reynaud to tell him what was in the offing and waited in an ante-room while Churchill sought the agreement of the British Cabinet.

As soon as British approval had been given, Churchill emerged from the Cabinet room and handed the text of the Union proposal to de Gaulle, who telephoned it to Reynaud in Bordeaux. Reynaud was delighted. He promised to put it before the Council of Ministers at once and urge its acceptance and the continuance of the fight against Germany. Churchill then took up the telephone and confirmed arrangements to meet Reynaud the next day at Concarneau in Brittany, to make plans on the new basis. He also sent de Gaulle off to Bordeaux in a RAF plane with the text of the Union plan. De Gaulle says in his Memoirs: 'We agreed that the plane should remain at my disposal, foreseeing that events would cause me to return.'[23]

De Gaulle had not entirely neglected shipping during his hectic day. In the morning he had ordered the French ship *Pasteur*, carrying arms from America to Bordeaux, to be diverted to a British port. It was the only part of his day's work that was not to be undone before it ended. The artillery, machineguns and munitions of the *Pasteur* went to British troops and replaced some of the losses of Dunkirk.

When Reynaud read the plan for Anglo-French Union to his Cabinet at their 5 pm meeting, he received hardly any of the support he had expected. It was as if the defeatists had been forewarned of the proposal and had armed themselves with arguments against it. (No doubt this is what had happened. Hélène de Portes had been in Reynaud's office when the British proposal was telephoned through, and had read it.)[24] They argued that they were being asked in effect to allow the British to absorb France and her Empire. Pétain said he did not want France to be tied to a corpse.

There was little fight left in Reynaud by this time. The British proposal was swept aside without even a vote being taken, and Chautemps revived the demand that armistice terms should be sought. At that point Reynaud should have tabled the earlier British messages, suspended in favour of the Union proposal, stipulating that the French Fleet must be sailed to British ports before an armistice was requested and that the British government must be consulted about German terms when received. They clearly became relevant again as soon as the proposal for Union was rejected. But he did not do so. He said that the British government had not released France from her obligations and that he would not head a government that sought an armistice. After more confused argument, he announced that he would resign, and sent a message to President Lebrun to that effect. He then went to see Lebrun and told him that if he desired the formation of a government that would request armistice terms, he should give the job to Pétain. Lebrun obeyed.

When de Gaulle's plane landed in Bordeaux, his staff met him at the airport with the news. He knew at once that capitulation to the enemy was certain, and decided at once that he would leave for Britain next morning.

From the moment that de Gaulle ceased to be a Minister, he came under military orders once more, and Weygand, if he had had the slightest inkling of de Gaulle's intentions, would certainly have put him under arrest. It therefore behoved him to move carefully until the morning came and he could depart on the plane which Churchill had fortunately placed at his disposal. His plan also needed clearing with the British, since he would be arriving this time not as a minister but as a refugee totally dependent on their good will.

De Gaulle began by going into Bordeaux to see Reynaud at the Prefecture. If he had entertained any lingering hope that Reynaud might still try to take back the reins of office and order the move to North Africa, it was dashed. The ex-Premier had no illusions about what Pétain would do, yet he was relieved to be free of the burden of leadership himself. De Gaulle said nothing to Reynaud at that stage about his own intentions, but revealed them to the British Ambassador, whom he met outside Reynaud's office. General Spears, who was with the Ambassador, said he would accompany him and telephone Churchill to forewarn him. This he duly did.

Only at this point did de Gaulle send a message to Reynaud announcing his plan. In return Reynaud sent him 100,000 francs (just over £500 at the time) from secret funds still at his disposal. This money was his sole resource when he arrived in England.

He also asked Margerie for his wife, who had now moved to Brittany, to be sent the passports she would need in order to journey to England. But in fact it was not passports Madame de Gaulle needed – she still had the passports the family had used in their years in Syria – but money. Banks and post offices were closed. Early on 17 June, without having received the message from Bordeaux, she went to Brest with her children to borrow money from an aunt and to seek news of her husband from the British Consulate. She knew he had been working with the British on shipping for Africa, but did not know where he was. She found the Consulate in the process of closing down. There were two ships in the harbour loading passengers for Britain. She asked if she and her children might take passage in one of them. The answer was affirmative. So she went to her aunt and borrowed not only the francs for which she had come to Brest, but also a hundred pounds which happened to be available. Then she and her children took ship. They arrived in Falmouth on 18 June, and stayed there for twenty-four hours trying to discover the General's whereabouts.

De Gaulle, who had expected them in London on 18 June, was alarmed when they did not appear, and spoke to General Spears. Churchill, informed by Spears, sent a flying boat and a motor torpedo-boat to search for them along the Breton coast.

On the morning of 19 June the de Gaulle family, still in Falmouth, read in the newspapers that the General had spoken on the BBC the previous evening. Madame de Gaulle succeeded in reaching him by telephone. 'Oh, so you've arrived?' he said. 'Take the train for London.' So the family were reunited; the seaplane that was seeking them was lost without trace.[25]

This drama proceeded in parallel with that of de Gaulle himself. His decision to return to Britain included acceptance of the risk of separation from his family and of their exposure, if they were left behind, to all the hazards at the hands of the Germans that would follow. De Gaulle had to take that risk or abandon his enterprise. It was thanks to his wife's resourcefulness that she and her children were able to catch the last boat from Brest.

De Gaulle himself had flown to Britain early on 17 June with Courcel, his ADC, and General Spears. In order to conceal his intentions until the last moment he made appointments for later in the day with his staff in Bordeaux before driving to the airport and did not climb into the plane until it was ready to move off.

In later years his enemies spread the story that he had been more or less smuggled out of France by General Spears. Irritated by this de Gaulle protested rather too strongly in his Memoirs that he had left 'without romantics or difficulty'.[26] But he acknowledged in a letter to Churchill in 1948 that he had taken 'some precautions' when departing.[27]

In fact the danger of arrest in Bordeaux on 17 June for leading opponents of the armistice was real. Mandel was seized later in the day, though soon released again at Pétain's order. De Gaulle might have been less fortunate. As it was, he arrived in London at high noon. He describes in his Memoirs what then confronted him: 'As I looked for a place to live and Courcel found the Embassy already stand-offish when he telephoned, I felt stripped naked, like a man on a beach planning to swim an ocean.'[28]

But there was a friend awaiting de Gaulle. Spears took him to Downing Street, and there he was welcomed by Churchill. The Premier agreed that as soon as Pétain sought terms for an armistice, he should broadcast an appeal to the French nation not to abandon the fight. Doubtless at that point Churchill expected that bigger French fish would cross the Channel; so did de Gaulle. Neither he nor Churchill could have foreseen on 17 June how big a fish de Gaulle himself was to prove.

# 11   DE GAULLE ASSUMES FRANCE

On 18 June 1940 the name of General de Gaulle meant nothing to the great world, and 18 June was known only for being the date of the battle of Waterloo. The events of the day in London were to change all that, but only as the result of another battle which was fought out in Downing Street between those who wanted to back de Gaulle and those who thought it more important not to offend Pétain. In its way it was almost as near-run a thing as Waterloo itself.

The story begins with the meeting of the War Cabinet at 10 Downing Street on the morning of 18 June. In the absence of Churchill, involved in urgent business elsewhere, Chamberlain took the chair which had been his until five weeks previously. Among the items on the agenda was the proposal that the BBC should be authorized to give facilities that evening to General de Gaulle to broadcast a message to the French people urging them to carry on the struggle and calling on those who could to rally to him in London. The justification for the proposal was that Marshal Pétain had not only announced to the French people on 17 June that he was seeking terms for an armistice but had said: 'We must stop the fight.'

The objections to allowing the broadcast were obvious. De Gaulle was unknown and had no authority to speak. He was simply an ex-minister and a serving officer in the French forces. There were no grounds at that stage for challenging the legitimacy of Pétain's new government. It had made an enquiry about peace and armistice terms but it was still at war with Germany and Italy, and in relations with Britain. It would be more prudent, it might be argued, to wait and see how the Franco-German negotiations went before allowing de Gaulle's appeal to be broadcast. That is what the Cabinet decided to do.

But Churchill learned of the decision from de Gaulle's outraged supporters, led by Spears, who were allowed by John Colville, his private secretary, to interrupt his afternoon siesta and plead their case. He agreed that de Gaulle should speak after all, provided the members of the War Cabinet were prepared to reverse the morning's decision. They were consulted individually by telephone and fell in with Churchill's wishes. The BBC was authorized to let de Gaulle speak and in the early evening he duly launched his appeal to the people of France. It seems that he was unaware of the battle that had been fought on his behalf.

The words of what has gone down in French history as *L'Appel du 18 Juin* were:

The leaders who have been at the head of the French armies for many years have formed a government.

This government, on the pretext that our armies have been defeated, have made contact with the enemy in order to cease the fight.

Certainly we have been, we are, overwhelmed by the enemy's mechanical strength, on land and in the air.

Far more than the numbers of Germans, it is their tanks, their planes, and their tactics which have taken our leaders by surprise and brought them to where they are today.

But has the last word been said? Must hope be abandoned? Is our defeat complete. No!

Believe me when I tell you that nothing is lost for France. I speak in knowledge of the facts. The same means which have defeated us can bring us victory one day.

For France is not alone! She is not alone! She is not alone! She has a great empire behind her. She can unite with the British Empire which rules the seas and is continuing the fight. Like Britain, she can make unlimited use of the immense industrial resources of the United States.

This war is not restricted to the territory of our unhappy country. This war has not been decided by the Battle of France. This war is a world war. All our errors, all our delays, all our sufferings do not alter the fact that the world contains all the resources needed to overwhelm our enemies one day. Struck down today by mechanized might, we can conquer one day in the future by superior mechanized might. The fate of the world turns on that.

I, General de Gaulle, now in London, call on all French officers and soldiers now present on British territory or who may be so in future, with or without their arms; I call on engineers and specialist workers in the arms industry now present on British territory or who may be so in future, to get in touch with me.

Whatever happens, the flame of French resistance must not and will not be extinguished.

Tomorrow, as today, I shall speak on the radio from London.

De Gaulle records in his Memoirs how he felt the past dropping away from him as he spoke, and a new life beginning. 'As the irrevocable words went out over the air, I felt a whole life coming to an end, the life I had led in the framework of a stable France and an indivisible Army. At the age of forty-nine I was entering on an adventure, like a man whom Fate had cast into uncharted waters.'[1]

The language of the appeal of 18 June was itself relatively moderate. It did not irrevocably condemn the Bordeaux government, and blamed the military, not the political, leaders for the predicament of France. Twenty-four hours later, however, de Gaulle spoke again on the BBC and went much further. He talked of 'a dissolving government enslaved by the enemy' and asserted that he was speaking in the name of France. He called on the French people to fight on everywhere they could, and above all in Africa.

There was no possibility of a reconciliation between de Gaulle and Pétain after this declaration on 19 June. But for several days de Gaulle continued his efforts to coordinate his action with that of other French notables. On 20 June, in reply to a telegram ordering him to report for military duty, he wrote to Weygand offering to join him within twenty-four hours if he refused to capitulate to the Germans, or else to be of service to him in London. On 19 June and again on 24 June he sent messages to General Noguès, the Commander-in-Chief in North Africa, offering to serve under his orders if he continued the fight as he had shown signs of wishing to do. He sent telegrams to French leaders in the Middle and Far East as well, urging them to take part in forming a French National Committee to continue the war.

But only from General Catroux in Indo-China, the friend of Ingolstadt days, did de Gaulle receive a positive response. He had hoped to form at once a National Committee of distinguished Frenchmen rallying to him. But they did not rally, and illustrious Frenchmen who happened to be in London also held back.

In Bordeaux the conclusion of an armistice with Germany was announced on 23 June and one with Italy followed the next day. The terms provided for German military occupation of most of France, including the entire Atlantic and Channel coasts. But an unoccupied zone from south of the Loire to the Mediterranean was left to French government. So were French possessions overseas, subject to the presence of German and Italian control commissions. The Fleet, apart from ships assigned to the protection of the Empire, was due to be collected in ports to be specified and disarmed under German or Italian control. Hitler made no response to Pétain's enquiry about peace terms.

A few days later de Gaulle had to shelve the idea of forming a National Committee. Neither he nor Churchill could raise enough prominent candidates. Against all expectations, nobody senior or even equal in rank to de Gaulle came to London to join him. He remained the leading advocate of resistance, and on 28 June the British government issued a communiqué stating that it recognized him as leader of 'all free Frenchmen, wherever they might be, who rallied to him for the defence of the Allied cause'. It was at that moment that de Gaulle may be said to have completed the assumption of France which he began with his Appeal on 18 June. That he was able to do so was due almost entirely to the support of Churchill, who had forced the decision to recognize upon the Cabinet despite the reservations of Lord Halifax.

It was a meteoric rise: on the last day of May de Gaulle still ranked merely as one of the countless colonels in the vast French Army. Just four weeks later France had fallen and he had risen to the status of her leading champion still in arms.

On 31 May, Oliver Harvey, the Minister in the British Embassy in Paris, surveying the *débâcle*, had asked in his diary: 'Will the next few days bring out some Frenchman of destiny?'[2] De Gaulle was to provide the answer. He had been preparing himself for this moment since childhood.

# 12  THE DARKEST HOURS

The French defeatists, wallowing 'in base euphoria' as de Gaulle put it in his Memoirs, were not alone in expecting that Britain would soon follow their example, change governments, and seek terms with Germany and Italy. The image Britain presented to the world was not yet one of single-minded resistance to the enemy. Churchill had been Premier for less than two months and the leading lights among the former appeasers, Chamberlain and Halifax, were still prominent among his Cabinet colleagues. Might they not find new support if they reverted to their earlier ways in this desperate crisis? Questions put down for answer in Parliament at this period show that there was anxiety on this score among at least a few M Ps and suggest that some news had reached them of the proposals for mediation by Mussolini between the Allies and Germany prepared by Lord Halifax and shelved by the Anglo-French Supreme War Council on 26 May.[1] Doubts felt in Britain were echoed abroad, despite Churchill's magnificent affirmations of the nation's will to fight on alone.

It was against this uncertain background that de Gaulle raised the standard of French resistance in London. His intentions were clear in his own mind from the outset. He had no thought of raising a force of French volunteers to serve under the Union Jack. His aim was to form a French force which would keep France in the war. He saw that to do this was essential in order to preserve the prestige of France and the self-respect of Frenchmen after the war. In his first broadcast on 18 June he said: 'Whatever happens, the flame of French resistance must not and will not be extinguished.' On 22 June he was already speaking of '*La France Libre*', a formula which was consecrated in the British government's recognition of him on 28 June as leader of the Free French. Churchill gave him whole-hearted support because he saw in de Gaulle's venture a means of reducing the shock to British and American opinion of the fall of France.

As July began, the volunteers who rallied to Free France were few in number and lacking in distinguished names. Some eminent Frenchmen who arrived in Britain, such as André Maurois and Alexis Leger, formerly Secretary-General at the French Foreign Ministry and equally well known as the poet Saint-John Perse, elected to go on to the United States. Others, like Raymond Aron, the young philosopher, remained in London but did not join de Gaulle. Most of the officers and men of the French Army and Navy, who happened to be in Britain with units in transit from Dunkirk or Norway, opted for repatriation rather than enlistment with the Free French, when given the choice. There were some successes, however. On 29 June de Gaulle recruited most of two battalions of the Foreign Legion and 200 Chasseurs Alpins on a visit to their camp at Trentham Park.

Sometimes de Gaulle and his supporters even had difficulty in gaining access to the camps where French military units were housed, in order to seek volunteers. Neither the Admiralty nor the War Office felt much sympathy for their endeavours. They saw little sense in retaining foreign troops when there was not enough military equipment in the country to rearm the British forces returned from France, and their representatives sometimes encouraged French soldiers to choose repatriation. When the news of these officially created obstacles to de Gaulle's efforts came to Churchill's ears, he had what his private secretary, John Colville, remembers as one of his most spectacular explosions of rage of the whole war.[2] He immediately gave orders which removed Free French problems over access.

But de Gaulle was now about to encounter a far graver problem with Churchill himself. It arose because the British War Cabinet decided on the simultaneous seizure or destruction around the world of as many French warships as possible in order to eliminate the risk that they would come under Axis control. The action, Operation Catapult, was ordered for 3 July. Churchill did not forewarn de Gaulle.

French ships in British ports were seized with only two or three casualties and later manned by Free French sailors. In the Western Mediterranean, however, a 'deadly stroke', as Churchill called it, could not be avoided. A powerful French naval force under Admiral Gensoul was divided between the adjoining ports of Oran and Mers-el-Kebir in French North Africa. At dawn on 3 July a still stronger British force under Vice-Admiral Somerville appeared and offered terms to Admiral Gensoul. His ships and men could come over to the British side completely, or sail their ships to Britain and leave them there, or sail under British escort to the French West Indies, where they would be demilitarized. Hours of fruitless negotiation followed. Then in the late afternoon, the British opened fire. The two French battleships and a battle-cruiser were put out of action. The other battle-cruiser, the *Strasbourg*, though damaged, escaped and gained Toulon, as did most of the smaller ships. Fourteen hundred French sailors were killed.

The attack at Mers-el-Kebir was a ruthless act, and for that very reason its impact at the hour of uncertainty was all the greater. The effect on Britain's foes was summed up by the Italian Foreign Minister, Ciano, in his diary: 'It proves that the fighting spirit of His Britannic Majesty's fleet is quite alive and still has the aggressive ruthlessness of the captains and pirates of the seventeenth century.'[3] Far more important, the action at Mers-el-Kebir exerted 'a particular effect on Roosevelt' according to Robert Sherwood, the biographer of Harry Hopkins, the President's trusted adviser.[4] It did much to convince him that the British truly meant to fight and that it was therefore worth taking the political risks involved in giving them strong support.

If the news of Mers-el-Kebir was a tonic for the British, it was, inevitably, a cruel shock for de Gaulle and his small band of followers. De Gaulle told General Spears, who had been put in charge of a liaison mission to the Free French, that he understood Churchill's decision, which was no doubt inevitable from the British point of view; nevertheless he would have to reflect whether he could continue cooperation with the British war effort or should withdraw to Canada. The next morning he had overcome his crisis and decided to accept what his hosts had been forced to do.[5] On 8 July he broadcast to the French people telling them that what had happened at Oran was 'deplorable and detestable', but that it was better for their proud ships to go to the bottom than to risk being used one day by the Axis against the cause of freedom. He asked the British people not to regard 'the cannonade of Oran' as a naval victory. Duff Cooper, the Minister of Information, had the good sense to agree that de Gaulle should on this occasion speak without his manuscript being seen in advance by any British authority.

If de Gaulle bowed to the inevitable, his feelings remained bitter. He took Mers-el-Kebir as a harsh reminder that the British would always be guided by their own interests in dealing with France. The British were still what they had been at Fashoda and would not hesitate to treat the French Empire with the same brutality as they had shown to the Fleet, if it suited them to do so. If he was to be the guardian of French interests, he must be hard in his dealings with his hosts, all the harder because of the weakness of his position among them.

He showed his feelings during a large party at 10 Downing Street one day in July. Mrs Churchill expressed the hope that some of the French ships would soon rejoin the battle; de Gaulle replied that what would really please them would be to turn their guns on the British. He then launched into a diatribe against Britain bitter enough to shock Mrs Churchill, who spoke better French than her husband and had a better idea of how far he was permitting himself to go. 'You have no right to speak like that,' she said to him. 'You are an ally, and you are a guest.' The next day de Gaulle sent her an immense bouquet of flowers, and the two became firm friends.[6] Churchill himself attached much more importance to what de Gaulle had said on the BBC about Mers-el-Kebir than to his outburst at the lunch-table.

De Gaulle was a welcome visitor at Chequers during July and August. Churchill derived comfort from his serene confidence in the ultimate victory of the Allies. Their favourite topic of conversation was not the varying fortunes of the aerial battle going on literally above their heads, but the nature of the postwar settlement they should impose on conquered Germany.

De Gaulle recorded in his Memoirs that when they discussed the events which had shattered the West they agreed that 'Britain was an island, France the cape of a continent, and America another world'.[7] But the way in which they saw America was different all the same. To de Gaulle she always remained 'marginal', as he put it, whereas she was at the centre of Churchill's thoughts both of war and the peace that would follow. The two men were never to see eye to eye about America's role in Europe, and the difference in their viewpoints was later to be the source of the deepest dissension between them.

After the tragedy of Mers-el-Kebir the thin stream of volunteers rallying to de Gaulle grew even thinner for a time, but the Free French movement began to develop form and substance nonetheless. It acquired a symbol of its own which rapidly became well known, when de Gaulle approved the use of the two-armed Cross of Lorraine as an ensign for fighting units. By the end of July he had a force of 7,000 at his disposal. The Free French were also given regular time by the BBC for broadcasting to France.

No leading politicians had joined the General from France, but he had acquired a number of followers, both military and civil, who had made a mark in their professions and were destined to go further. Among the sailors, Vice-Admiral Muselier, who arrived in June, was his senior adherent, an eccentric but able man and the obvious choice as Commander of Free French forces. Captain Thierry d'Argenlieu, a Carmelite monk when not fighting, was another naval personality. General Magrin-Verneret, later to be known as General Monclar, and Captain Koenig, both of the Foreign Legion, were among officers on their way home from Norway who elected to join Free France. General Legentilhomme and Colonel de Larminat rallied from the Middle East. Colonel de Hauteclocque, who was to become famous under the name of General Leclerc, and Captain Dewavrin, who was given the task of organizing an intelligence service and carried it out with remarkable success under the pseudonym of Passy, also joined.

On the civilian side René Pleven, the economic expert, René Cassin, the jurist, Georges Boris and Jean Marin, journalists, Pierre-Olivier Lapie, the radical politician, and Maurice Schumann, who achieved fame as the radio spokesman of Free France, were among de Gaulle's early adherents. Others who were on the way to London were General Catroux from Indo-China, Jacques Soustelle, already well known as an archaeologist, from Mexico, and Gaston Palewski, Reynaud's former *Chef du Cabinet* and a friend and ally since 1935, from North Africa.

It was necessary to define the financial and juridical relationship of Free France to the British government, and negotiations went on throughout July. The leader of the French delegation, René Cassin, received clear instructions from de Gaulle at the outset as to the position of principle he was to maintain. 'We are France,' said de Gaulle.[8] There were practical reasons why Britain could not accept this contention. While Vichy controlled the French Fleet and Empire and part of Metropolitan France, they had to recognize the authority of its government, but Churchill's personal sympathies were with de Gaulle's claim, and Free France benefited from the fact. Churchill agreed not only to negotiations with the Free French on practical matters but also to an exchange of letters between himself and de Gaulle on the subject of postwar British intentions towards France.

The result was a series of agreements signed at Chequers on 7 August by Churchill and de Gaulle. It was laid down that the British government should meet 'all the costs involved in the formation and upkeep of the French forces' against ultimate repayment, and that these forces, though normally serving under British operational command, should constitute a national entity under the supreme command of General de Gaulle, preserving 'to the greatest extent possible the character of a French force'.

Another provision to which de Gaulle attached importance was that 'this force will never bear arms against France'. 'France' in this context did not of course cover the Vichy forces, as he agreed in an exchange of letters with Churchill which was kept secret. The clause afforded some protection against the inevitable charge that the Free French were no more than British mercenaries. The principle of the unbroken continuation of the French military effort against the Axis powers was preserved by these agreements, and the notion of absorbing it in the British effort by recruiting French volunteers in the British forces, which some in Whitehall still favoured, went by the board once and for all.

The British government also undertook to help the Free French to acquire British nationality if they chose not to return home after the war. This was evidently a precaution against the contingency of a compromise peace, a possibility which neither the British nor de Gaulle could realistically ignore at the time.

If agreements did a great deal for the status of the Free French, they did even more for de Gaulle's. The British government's memorandum named him personally as the leader to whom the French volunteer forces owed obedience.

If de Gaulle had secured no more than this, it would have been a formidable achievement for a penniless Brigadier exiled in a land whose language he did not know. But there was more. The British government also committed itself to the complete restoration after victory of the independence and the greatness of France. The word used for 'greatness' in the French version of the text was *grandeur*. Tradition relates that de Gaulle wrote it into the draft in his own hand.

This was a generous engagement for Churchill to assume to an ally who had made a separate armistice, and it was only made possible by the fact that de Gaulle had kept the standard of French resistance flying. To Churchill, beleaguered as he was in those desperate days, the gift of de Gaulle's support was politically precious, and his own gift in return was no less so. But de Gaulle was not satisfied. He was disquieted by the absence of a British undertaking to restore the full territorial integrity of France and her Empire. In an exchange of confidential letters annexed to the arrangements of 7 August, Churchill sought to propitiate him by stating that, when the course of the war was so uncertain, Britain could not make such a specific commitment, but that it was her intention to do her best for French interests. In reply de Gaulle recorded his hope that at a later stage Britain might be able to take a more positive view. He explains in his Memoirs what he had in mind in seeking this extra assurance. 'On the one hand ... the hazards of war might lead Britain to make a compromise peace; on the other hand she might perhaps be tempted by one or other of our overseas possessions . . .' His suspicions never slept.[9]

By the time that these agreements were signed, the name of de Gaulle was beginning to be known in the world. A handsome house in Carlton Gardens became his headquarters instead of modest offices on the Embankment. Because he had risen so suddenly from relative obscurity, his British hosts took the unusual step of engaging a professional public relations agent, Richmond Temple, to run a publicity campaign on his behalf. He was able to claim some success, although he found de Gaulle himself most uncooperative. *Le Connétable* was at this stage contemptuous of publicity.

One way and another the British had already made a substantial investment in de Gaulle by August 1940. This helped to give many people, among them President Roosevelt, the false impression that he was no more than an instrument of the British. The President never wholly shook off this view, and much harm came of it.

The Pétain government also made its contribution to de Gaulle's growing fame. It had moved headquarters from Bordeaux to Vichy after the armistice, and on 10 July the Chamber of Deputies had voted full powers to the Marshal to prepare a new Constitution. Pétain replaced President Lebrun, and a new French State, of which he was head, replaced the Third Republic. De Gaulle attacked it in his broadcasts from London and denied its authority. In return he was condemned to death as a deserter by court martial on 2 August. Pétain is said to have told friends in private that the sentence was a matter of form and would never be carried out.[10] But the verdict was published and drew both attention to de Gaulle's name and sympathy to his cause. He of course publicly rejected the judgement as null and void.

The governments of the world accepted the legitimacy of Pétain's State without question. The United States, the Soviet Union and the Vatican all remained in diplomatic relations with the new régime, moving their Embassy staffs from Paris to Vichy. Even Britain recognized Pétain's government and, though diplomatic relations remained broken after Mers-el-Kebir, continued to accept Vichy consuls in the United Kingdom until 1943. De Gaulle's verdict on the Marshal's pretensions was harsh but not pitiless: 'The saviour of Verdun has become a traitor . . . It is the shipwreck of old age,' he said.[11]

Apart from governments in exile in London, the first outside organization to establish contact with the Free French was the Zionists. A representative of the Jewish Agency called on 15 July and offered help in spreading news of the Free French movement in the United States and the Middle East, as well as Agency reports on the political situation in the United States. He also stressed the Agency's interest in Syria and proposed financial aid for 'confidential propaganda operations' there. The contact prospered, and a Free French directive of 7/8 August ordered the appointment of liaison officers with Jewish refugee groups and Jews in general in neutral countries. On 9 August General de Gaulle himself expressed his sympathy with Jewish victims of Nazi persecution and promised restitution of equal rights and justice for wrong done under the occupation of France when liberation came.[12] Jews had naturally been numerous from the outset among the French who joined de Gaulle in London.

So de Gaulle began his fight against the men of Vichy for the soul of France, as he put it in his broadcasts. But victory for him depended on victory for Britain, which was under German onslaught. On 10 July, Hitler, seeing that his hopes of a British appeal for peace were vain, launched Operation Sealion, his invasion plan, the first phase of which was an all-out air assault. From then on the RAF fought the Luftwaffe daily for mastery of the skies above the invasion route. The few airmen of Free France played their part, but de Gaulle wanted to do more. The issue of the great battle was still in doubt when, at the end of August, he left Britain to carry the fight to the enemy.

# 13   To Africa and Back

Although he was now a political figure, de Gaulle still conceived of his main task as being to lead French forces back into action against the Axis powers as soon as he had assembled and equipped a sufficient number in Britain. Africa was clearly the target area and he discussed various plans with the British chiefs of staff and Churchill himself. His first preference was for landing a force at Konakry in French Guinea and marching overland on Dakar. But this would have taken a considerable time. Churchill therefore favoured a direct Anglo-French descent upon Dakar, and despite their initial doubts, de Gaulle and the chiefs of staff were won over to his view. The attractions of Dakar were obvious. The capital of French West Africa, it possessed a naval base and seaport which could be of great utility in maintaining control of the South Atlantic sea lanes. If it rallied to Free France, its example could well be followed by all the numerous French colonies in Western and Equatorial Africa. Encouraging messages from supporters in many of them reached de Gaulle in July and August.

Speed was essential, since the Vichy authorities were taking steps to round up dissidents and strengthen their hold on Africa. Preparations were pressed forward by Churchill, but there were some delays before an Anglo-French force finally set sail from Liverpool on 31 August. De Gaulle was in command of the French contingent, numbering 2,000 men. There were about the same number of Royal Marines and a strong British naval squadron, with supporting French units. It was hoped that the sight of this small armada would induce the inhabitants of Dakar to rally to the Free French envoys who would be the first to go ashore, but force would be used if necessary, and a Free French administration would be installed under General de Gaulle.

Good news arrived from Africa in the days immediately preceding the expedition's departure. On 26 August the colonies of Chad and

Cameroon rallied to Free France. On 28 August the Congo and on 29 August Oubangui-Chari (now the Central African Republic) followed their example. At Brazzaville Colonel de Larminat assumed power in the name of Free France. Thus de Gaulle's authority was established in most of French Equatorial Africa. But this situation was still precarious. The forces at work on both sides were tiny, and Vichy might yet turn the tables.

While the expedition was heading for Dakar, a new and major threat was suddenly posed to its chances of success. A Vichy French naval squadron of three cruisers and three destroyers left Toulon and headed for the Atlantic. It should have been stopped off Gibraltar, but, through a chapter of errors and misunderstandings, the British naval forces there did not take action in time. The Vichy ships passed by at full speed on the morning of 11 September and headed south down the African coast. They put in briefly at Casablanca and then went on to Dakar, where they had arrived by 14 September. Efforts to intercept them and order them north again were unsuccessful.

Having weighed this unwelcome news, the War Cabinet tele-graphed its view to the expedition that the hopes of a bloodless success at Dakar had now vanished and that the best plan was for the French contingent to land at Douala in the Cameroons, which had already declared for de Gaulle, while the British forces put in at Freetown. But de Gaulle, although he was at least as anxious as the British to avoid heavy bloodshed at Dakar, protested that it was still worth trying to carry out the original plan. He was supported by the British commanders, and the War Cabinet agreed on 18 September that they could go ahead, despite all the attendant risks.

The Anglo-French expedition arrived off Dakar on the evening of 22 September, and action began the next morning. It was dogged with ill-fortune from the first moment. A heavy fog shrouded the coast and made the approaching armada of thirty-five vessels invisible from the shore. The psychological impact of the attack on Dakar was thus lost. The Free French envoys who landed were rebuffed, and Boisson, the governor, informed the British admiral that he would defend the town by force. An exchange of fire began between ships and shore, much hampered by the persistent fog. A few French marines were landed late in the day but had to be withdrawn again. On the two following days the British fleet tried to shell Dakar into submission but without success. De Gaulle was reluctant to attempt an opposed landing which would have meant inflicting heavy casualties on the defenders. On the 25th, as the bombardment continued, the British battleship *Resolution* was torpedoed by a Vichy submarine and had to be taken in tow. This was the last straw. The expedition withdrew southwards to Freetown. The attempt upon Dakar had ended in failure.

The following few days marked the lowest point in de Gaulle's fortunes, and perhaps in his spirits as well. He once confided in a friend: 'It was a frightful time for me. I even thought of blowing my brains out.'[1] Vichy propaganda was trumpeting from the rooftops that Dakar had chosen Pétain against de Gaulle, and it was true. He knew that his prestige in Britain and America would have sustained a disastrous blow. It was hard to go on alone; but he was equal to the task. Some of his British companions in the troopship *Westernland* were afterwards to say that it was de Gaulle's bearing after the Dakar fiasco that convinced them that he bore the stamp of true greatness. His inner anguish was hidden from the others.

Churchill helped by justifying the Dakar enterprise in Parliament and reaffirming the confidence of the British government in the Free French movement and in de Gaulle personally. It is often alleged that Churchill wished to jettison de Gaulle after Dakar and replace him by General Catroux or Admiral Muselier, but this does not correspond to the facts. What actually happened was that on 17 September, six days before the brief siege of Dakar began, Churchill received Catroux, who had just arrived in London from Indo-China, and said: 'It is in London, I think, that you can be most useful. The Free French movement needs guidance, and I think that you should assume the direction.'[2] At the same time he expressed the greatest admiration for de Gaulle personally. In reply Catroux declined Churchill's suggestion and made it clear that he accepted de Gaulle's leadership, although senior to him in military rank.

Catroux then consulted Lord Lloyd, the Colonial Secretary, who was much involved in dealings with the Free French, as to what precisely Churchill could have meant by his suggestion. Lord Lloyd said that he believed Churchill had indeed been offering him the leadership of Free France. Much as he admired de Gaulle, he had been disappointed by his failure to rally more support.

Lord Lloyd's theory may, however, have been an oversimplification. By direction of the Free French movement in London, Churchill may not have meant the same as overall leadership. On 17 September the Dakar enterprise had been called off by London and Churchill had no way of knowing that it would be reinstated twenty-four hours later. In this situation he may well have felt that the arrangements de Gaulle had made before leaving England, on the assumption that he would soon be installed in Dakar, required revision. De Gaulle had divided his organization in London into a military and civil wing and taken the leadership with him. He would have established his headquarters in Dakar had he captured it. His intention had always been to raise his standard on French territory as soon as possible. On 17 September, however, it seemed that de Gaulle would be heading for a remoter destination in Africa, less suitable as a headquarters, and might be away indefinitely. The question of effective guidance of the Free French movement in London assumed new and increased importance. It may well have been for this reason that Churchill offered Catroux the directing post left vacant there. Perhaps he had thoughts of a duumvirate with Catroux acting as political chief in London while de Gaulle led the forces in the field, and the ultimate leadership was left to depend on results.

But Catroux's refusal and de Gaulle's insistence on attempting the Dakar operation reversed the situation once more. Churchill always loved a man who wanted to get at the enemy, and de Gaulle immediately went up in his estimation, as he told him after his return to London. His support for the General after the failure at Dakar was unwavering. Catroux himself left for Cairo to become the Free French representative in the Middle East. De Gaulle's verdict on the episode was: 'It seems that the Prime Minister did indeed suggest to him that he should take my place. Doubtless he did not intend him actually to make the attempt. His aim was rather to play the classic game of divide and rule.'[3] This Machiavellian judgement probably tells us more about de Gaulle than about Churchill.

Churchill's backing did not prevent de Gaulle's numerous detractors in London and Washington from blaming him and the Free French in general for the Dakar failure. It was said that de Gaulle had prevailed on the British to launch the expedition against their better judgement on the basis of exaggerated reports about his own popularity among the French in West Africa, and that the indiscretion of his followers had prejudiced the security of the expedition and betrayed its destination to Vichy intelligence. The sudden intervention of the naval squadron from Toulon was quoted as proof that the enemy had discovered what was afoot.

President Roosevelt was among those who were influenced against de Gaulle. Shortly after the Dakar affair the American diplomat Robert Murphy was called home from Vichy to be appointed the President's personal representative for affairs in French Africa. He recorded in his Memoirs that:

> Roosevelt – who had never liked the Dakar operation – concluded that de Gaulle had started what amounted to a French civil war, putting his own ambitions above the French and Allied interests. Roosevelt never lost the distrust of de Gaulle's judgement and discretion which he formed then . . . As for security he regarded the French headquarters in London as a leaky sieve, not to be trusted with secret military information.[4]

No Free French indiscretion has ever been proved, however, and it remains possible that the Vichy squadron's appearance upon the scene had a different cause. Its dispatch may have been decided in order to have a steadying effect in the colonies still loyal to Pétain and to recapture those which had gone over to de Gaulle.

The fact that the squadron's first port of call was Casablanca suggests that there may have been doubts about the allegiance of Morocco. These could have been provoked by causes unconnected with the Dakar expedition. The French Ambassador in Madrid, the Vicomte de la Baume, sent a telegram to his Foreign Minister in Vichy, Paul Baudouin, reporting that his British colleague, Sir Samuel Hoare, had told him on 3 September that British officers returning from Morocco spoke of the existence of strong Gaullist sympathies there and of the possibility of Morocco rallying to Free France.[5] Sir Samuel was trying to prevent Spain yielding to the temptation to take the German side at this stage of the war, and any report of a possible growth of Allied strength in the area around Gibraltar was grist to his propaganda mill. It was natural that he should pass it on, but it was also possible that its transmission by the French Ambassador might have been a factor in alarming Vichy into taking naval precautions.

An immediate consequence of Dakar was a crisis in relations between Vichy and London, apparently accompanied by a crisis between 'hawks' and 'doves' in Vichy. The 'hawks' fired the first shot, when on 26 September the French naval attaché in Madrid gave a message to his British colleague, warning that the French Navy would in future protect French shipping between West Africa and Mediterranean ports under Vichy control and would resist by force any British attempt to impose blockade measures. This alarming communication was followed on 27 September by a more reassuring proposal from the French Ambassador in Madrid to Sir Samuel Hoare that they should open discussions on behalf of their two governments with a view to avoiding further clashes such as the one at Dakar and establishing a *modus vivendi*. This offer the British government promptly accepted, while rejecting the message of 26 September.[6] Discussions began on 10 October. The French Ambassador asked that Britain should abandon support for de Gaulle and lift the blockade on imports from Africa into France. If the Germans seized the imports, the French government would move to North Africa and resume the war at Britain's side. Churchill at once telegraphed de Gaulle, who warned him that the offer was a trap. Britain would make a series of concessions under its terms, he said, and, even if the Germans intervened, there would be no possibility of Vichy resuming the fight.[7] Talks continued in Madrid and were one more source of anxiety and suspicion for de Gaulle.

He was soon in action again. By 7 October he was on his way by sea to Douala to join the French contingent from Dakar, who had already arrived there. During the voyage he revealed to a British companion how isolated he felt. 'For me,' he said, 'what is terrible is to feel so alone. Completely alone.'[8] The leader's burden of responsibility never weighed more heavily on him than after Dakar.

Consolation was at hand, however. At Douala on 9 October de Gaulle was for the first time acclaimed on French territory by a French crowd chanting his name. This welcome, coming so soon after the mood of black melancholy that had overcome him at sea, seems to have had the force of a mystical experience for him. He wrote:

From then on, I was always to encounter the same enthusiasm and emotion, whenever the crowds appeared. The result was a permanent sense of obligation. The fact that I embodied for my companions the destiny of our cause, for the French in general the symbol of their hopes, and for foreigners the image of an indomitable France was destined to impose on me an attitude and a character which I was incapable of changing. It was a permanent inner discipline, a heavy yoke.[9]

At Douala de Gaulle received from the Africans the first of those *bains de foule* which were in later years to be such a feature of his career. It was a baptism that made him in a sense a new man, aware that his behaviour must please the public as well as impress the élite.

In the territories that had rallied to him, de Gaulle was able to see that Free France was already in possession of a considerable apanage, stretching, as he put it, 'from the Sahara to the Congo, from the Atlantic to the sources of the Nile'. He took military and political action to strengthen his position. In Chad he gave orders for a column to be formed to advance northwards into the desert of Italian Libya, seize Fezzan, and press on to the Mediterranean. He put Colonel Leclerc, who had played the leading part in the seizure of the Cameroons, in charge of this far-sighted enterprise. But first Leclerc had to command the forces assigned to wrest Gabon from the Vichy grip. He successfully occupied Libreville, the capital, on 9 November, not without a sharp engagement and bloodshed between French and French.

On the political front de Gaulle's activities were determined by the course of events in Europe. As the autumn wore on, it became increasingly evident that there would be no German invasion of England in 1940; that the defenders had won the Battle of Britain; and that the war was likely to spread to new theatres. In this situation Hitler's interest in drawing Vichy France into military collaboration with the Axis began to increase. After a preliminary talk with Laval, he arranged to meet Pétain on 24 October at Montoire in German-occupied France. It was not a satisfactory conversation for Hitler, but at first the public aspect of the encounter mattered more than the private. Hitler and Pétain were photographed shaking hands. This first shock to French opinion was amplified when in a radio address on 30 October the Marshal declared that in order to maintain the unity of France in the framework of the new European order 'I enter today on the course of collaboration . . . I alone, will bear the responsibility for that decision in the judgement of history.' His tactics at and after Montoire did him harm with public opinion in France and even more in Britain and America. One byproduct of his behaviour was to doom to failure the secret mission to London of a Vichy envoy, Professor Rougier, sent to negotiate a *modus vivendi* which would ease the British blockade.

De Gaulle immediately seized the opportunity given him by Montoire and affirmed more categorically than before that legitimacy, the authority of the French Republic, rested with him and not with the puppets of Vichy. This he did in a Manifesto issued in his own name and published in Brazzaville on 27 October. The first part of it explained his view of his mission:

There no longer exists a French government properly so called . . . the organism situated at Vichy is unconstitutional and subject to the invader . . . A new Authority must therefore take over the task of directing the exertions of France in the war. Events impose on me this sacred duty. In it I shall not fail . . . I solemnly promise to account for all my actions to the representatives of the French people as soon as it is possible to designate them freely.[10]

The Manifesto of Brazzaville also proclaimed the creation of a Council for the Defence of the French Empire. Nine of the leading civil and military personalities who had so far rallied to Free France were named by de Gaulle as members. The Council was to exercise the powers of the State in Free French territories, but its functions were advisory only. 'Decisions will be taken by the Chief of the Free French after consultation, when appropriate, with the Council.' This provision, laid down in Article 3 of Ordinance No. 1 constituting the Council, was signed by de Gaulle alone. In effect de Gaulle was proclaiming that he himself, subject to his ultimate accountability to the future elected representatives of the people, was the sole fountainhead of legitimate French authority. On 5 November he sent a note to the British government, which he had not consulted in advance, informing it officially of what he had done and asserting once more the illegitimacy of Vichy. By then, however, the British had realized that their initial fear of the consequences of Montoire was exaggerated. Laval had not triumphed and Vichy had not passed into the enemy camp. In order not to provoke Pétain, they had therefore suppressed publication of de Gaulle's condemnation of Vichy and made no statement of their own; but they tacitly accepted the Manifesto of Brazzaville, although its pretensions disquieted the Foreign Office.

On 17 November de Gaulle flew back to England. His vision of his future had changed in his months in Africa. He had abandoned the idea of making Africa the headquarters of Free France at this stage. Britain was the political and military centre of resistance to Hitler, it was in close touch with America, and it was near to France. It was therefore the only possible centre of operations for the statesman who had assumed the leadership of Free France. The transformation which had begun when de Gaulle broadcast his appeal to the French people on 18 June was now complete. He had made himself a temporary sovereign.

# 14 THE WIDENING WAR

Soon after de Gaulle's return to Britain, there was a sensation in Vichy. On 13 December Pétain suddenly dismissed Laval, making public no reason except that he had lost confidence in him. The real reason was that Laval, who had taken over as Foreign Minister from Baudouin after Montoire, had angered Pétain by trying to extend collaboration with the Germans to the military field. He had attended Franco-German staff meetings at the German Embassy in Paris which had studied plans for Vichy forces to recapture Gaullist colonies in Africa, beginning with Chad. Pétain could not say so openly, but he had no wish for military cooperation with Hitler. He took Roosevelt's victory in the presidential election on 7 November as a sign that America would give increasing support to Britain, and soon afterwards told the US chargé d'affaires in Vichy, Freeman Matthews, that an Anglo-American victory would be more in France's interest than a German one.[1] This was the background to the dramatic move he made on 13 December, which amounted to rejection of the policy of reversal of alliances that he had appeared to be embracing at Montoire. He replaced Laval as Foreign Minister by Pierre-Etienne Flandin, a former appeaser. There was a moment of tension between Vichy and the Germans, but plans for recapturing the dissident colonies were shelved for a time, and Hitler acquiesced in Laval's departure.

This turn of events was less welcome to de Gaulle than to Churchill. It meant that Vichy still seemed worth cultivating both to Roosevelt, who sent his friend Admiral Leahy as Ambassador to Pétain, and to the British, who kept communications open through ambassadors in Madrid and through the Canadian minister in Vichy, Pierre Dupuy. Roosevelt sent Robert Murphy to discuss with Weygand, now installed as Vichy's Delegate General in French Africa, arrangements under which he would resist Axis infiltration in Africa with the help of limited American supplies of oil, food and consumer goods to sustain the local economy. De Gaulle accepted the need for the British and Americans to try to influence Vichy and Weygand in the interests of the Allied war effort but he urged Churchill not to be so conciliatory or to discourage the Free French movement.[2]

As 1940 ended, de Gaulle set to work in London to consolidate his organization and increase its contribution to the war effort. At every turn he had to ask for help from a British administration that was desperately hard-pressed in dealing with its own problems, yet much was achieved during the winter months to regulate the affairs of Free France on the basis of the agreements of 7 August.

Communication and contact with France, occupied and unoccupied, were high on the list of subjects that required negotiation. It was agreed with the BBC that the Free French should have two periods of five minutes at their disposal daily for broadcasting to France and that de Gaulle should speak free of censorship, as he had done *de facto* in July and August. The text of the main BBC transmissions to France was also to be prepared in consultation with the Free French.

It was, inevitably, more difficult to reach agreement over secret intelligence work in France. De Gaulle had created his own services. The *Service d'action* and *Service de Renseignements* under the direction of Dewavrin, *alias* Passy, now a Major and later a Colonel, were responsible for sabotage in France as well as for intelligence work. He also maintained a separate organization for political intelligence work, much to Passy's annoyance. The British Secret Service, usually known as MI6 or SIS, maintained relations not only with the Free French but with Vichy intelligence services, in which many old friends from pre-Pétainist days were employed. The SIS insisted on running its own agents, including Frenchmen, into France without consulting anybody. This liberty of action was unacceptable in principle to de Gaulle, who wanted his team to coordinate Allied efforts, but in practice he had to acquiesce. A *modus vivendi* was established, and Passy began to receive more British help over transport and communications equipment. The Free French also began dealings with the new sabotage organization that the British were building for use in enemy-occupied territory, quite separately from the SIS. It was to become known as SOE (Special Operations Executive). But relations remained generally difficult.[3] Many in the British intelligence community regarded the Free French as dangerously incompetent amateurs.

The intelligence world provided the background to the first major clash of 1941 between de Gaulle and the British government. It began on New Year's Day when Admiral Muselier was arrested on suspicion of espionage and incarcerated in the Tower of London by the Prime Ministers's orders. Anthony Eden, newly installed as Foreign Secretary in place of Lord Halifax, who was sent to Washington as Ambassador, told de Gaulle that there was conclusive evidence that Muselier was in secret contact with Vichy, and had tried to give Darlan advance information of the Dakar expedition. De Gaulle made his own investigations and soon satisfied himself that the British authorities had acted on false information trumped up by two French agents planted with Passy by a British intelligence organization whose aim was to discredit the Free French. On 8 January he summoned General Spears and issued an ultimatum to the British government. If they did not exonerate and release Muselier within twenty-four hours, he said, the Free French movement would sever all relations with them, whatever the consequences.

Spears returned late the same day to announce, without admitting British guilt, that it had been discovered that Muselier was indeed innocent. The guilty parties were punished and amends were made to the insulted Admiral. Regrets were promptly expressed by Churchill and Eden, but they did not efface the impression made upon de Gaulle. 'This lamentable incident,' as he was to put in his Memoirs,[4] 'illustrated the precarious nature of our relations with our allies at all times and did not fail to have its influence on my philosophy as to how to handle dealings with the British authorities.'

This philosophy of de Gaulle's called for intransigence in negotiation and suspicion as to the motives of the other party. He offers justification for this intransigence towards the British early in his Memoirs:

To start with . . . I was nothing. Not the semblance of a force or an organization was behind me . . . But my very poverty showed me the line to take . . . Only if I acted as the inflexible champion of the nation and the state could I win support among the French and respect from foreigners. The critics who persisted in frowning on my intransigence refused to see that I was controlling countless conflicting pressures and that the least yielding would have led to total collapse. Precisely because I was alone and without power I had to climb to the peaks and never afterwards descend from that level.[5]

As to reasons for distrust, he believed that the Muselier affair showed that he had dangerous enemies in Britain, some of them in the ranks of British intelligence services. One way of maintaining his guard was to use Passy's organization to spy on the British as well as on the Germans, and there is reason to believe that de Gaulle did this – perhaps even earlier than the Muselier affair.

With the Muselier drama settled, de Gaulle was able to direct his attention to the Middle East. Syria, Lebanon and French Somalia were under Vichy control but contained Free French sympathizers among the population. De Gaulle had hopes that, with encouragement, they might rally to his cause. He also wanted to increase the contribution made by Free French troops to General Wavell's operation against the Italians. He offered to send a symbolic French force to Greece, which had been attacked by the Italians in October and was fighting back most effectively, but British shipping was not made available. This disappointment increased his feeling that if France was to play a perceptible and honourable part in impending events in the Middle East, he must go there and take personal charge of her interests. He decided, with Churchill's approval, to fly to Cairo early in March.

Before setting out he was invited to Chequers for the weekend. With his usual talent for being in the right place at the right time, he happened to be there at a turning-point in the war. 'At dawn on 9 March,' he records 'Mr Churchill came and woke me up to tell me, literally dancing with joy, that the American Congress had passed the Lend-Lease Bill.'[6]

The event was well worth a dance to Churchill and to de Gaulle as well, although he does not record that he joined in. It meant that Britain was no longer menaced by running out of the dollars needed to pay for the immense and broadening river of American supplies of food, weapons and manufactures that was pouring into the beleaguered island and had become indispensable to the British, and therefore the Free French, war effort. The United States would in future find the dollars itself in return for counterpart funds in Allied currencies. America had become the 'arsenal of democracy' and had taken a stride towards involvement in the war.

American policy was changing the situation in the Far East as well. Economic sanctions were hurting Japan, but in so doing they increased the attractiveness to her of the food and raw materials available in the Western possessions in Southeast Asia. In the early months of 1941 the Japanese occupied key points on the coast of French Indo-China and brought the whole area into their economic sphere, while leaving the French colonial régime, which was loyal to Vichy, nominally in charge. De Gaulle had no power to do more than declare these infringements of French sovereignty as without legal effect, and to prepare as best he could in cooperation with Britain, Australia and New Zealand the defence of the French territories elsewhere in Asia which had rallied to him.

De Gaulle set out by plane for the Middle East on 14 March 1941, accompanied, at Churchill's request, by General Spears as liaison officer. As he says in his Memoirs in a famous phrase: 'I flew to the complicated Orient with straightforward ideas.' He was resolved 'to spare no effort on the one hand to enlarge our field of action and, on the other, to safeguard as much as was possible of France's position'. He was well aware that the latter function might embroil him with his allies rather than the Germans.

De Gaulle wanted to concentrate the Free French forces in the Middle East and use them in an invasion of Syria and Lebanon, but he found from General Wavell that there was no hope of the British cooperating in the near future. Their hands were too full elsewhere. General Rommel's Afrika Korps had just made its first appearance in Cyrenaica and was driving British forces back towards Egypt, and at the same time Wavell was obliged to reduce his strength in the desert by sending troops to Greece. Wavell had a third front in Eritrea and Abyssinia, where Italian resistance was crumbling but not at an end.

De Gaulle had to accept the situation. He departed on a tour of Equatorial Africa, not without many an anxious backward glance at Syria. Events in April rapidly increased his feeling that Allied action there was becoming urgent. First, the German Army came to the rescue of the Italians and swept like a tidal wave through Yugoslavia and Greece. By 24 April the last British troops were being withdrawn by the Navy from their last toehold on the European mainland apart from Gibraltar. Second, Vichy entered on a new phase of collaboration with Hitler. Admiral Darlan had replaced Flandin as Foreign Minister and there were signs both that Vichy-German collaboration was extending to the Middle East and that the project of recapturing the Free French territories in Africa might be revived.

The British reaction to these events seemed to de Gaulle designed not to challenge Vichy but to appease the régime by treating its colonies gently. Negotiations were in progress with the governors of both Syria and Somalia which were apparently aimed at establishing a *modus vivendi*. He suspected, rightly, that the British were following the American lead in their handling of Vichy. The last straw was a telegram of 9 May from General Spears in Cairo advising him that no operations were envisaged in the near future involving Free French forces, that there was no advantage in his returning to Cairo, and that it would be best for him to proceed to London. He reacted the next day with a salvo of protests to Cairo and London attacking the soft line taken with Vichy, and announcing his intention of recalling Catroux from Cairo, while remaining himself in Chad to direct military operations against Libya.

It is easy to imagine how irritating these protests were to Churchill and Eden. There was nothing they could have wanted less at this juncture, with the entire British position in the Middle East imperilled, than to spend time paying attention to complaints – and even threats – from de Gaulle about the use of a few thousand of his troops against Vichyite dependencies which the Free French had neither the power to capture nor the appeal to win over by themselves. But it was precisely for this reason that de Gaulle felt it necessary to raise his voice in complaint. If he kept silent, he risked being categorized then and afterwards as the sort of loyal collaborator of secondary importance who can be trusted to accept with a good grace explanations after the event instead of consultations in advance of it. If de Gaulle accepted that status for himself, he accepted it for France as well. To do the former would have been uncongenial; to do the latter was inconceivable. So *Le Connétable* protested and threatened.

Ironically enough, de Gaulle's broadside to London was unnecessary. Spears's unlucky telegram was out of date as soon as it had been sent. Events in Iraq and Syria had just changed Churchill's view of the right tactics to adopt. Information had come in that Rashid Ali, the pro-Axis Prime Minister of Iraq who had been working to change the established pro-British policy of his country ever since seizing power in March, had asked Hitler for armed help on 2 May. Hitler had immediately decided to fly to Rashid Ali's aid and had decreed that Vichy's consent should be obtained. Darlan had agreed as soon as asked, and the Luftwaffe planes were reported in Syria on 9 May 1941. The same day Churchill telegraphed Wavell telling him what was afoot:

You will no doubt realize the obvious danger of Syria being captured by a few thousand Germans transported by air . . . Admiral Darlan has probably made some bargain to help the Germans . . . we can see no other course open than to furnish General Catroux with the necessary transport and let him and his Free French do their best, the RAF acting against German landings. Any improvement you can make on this would be welcome.'[7]

Churchill had decided at this stage to ignore repercussions on Vichy, and the susceptibilities of the Americans, who were still trying to coax General Weygand to re-enter the fray. So de Gaulle received a message from the Premier telling him that the situation had changed and urging him to keep Catroux in Cairo and go there himself.

De Gaulle now had Churchill on his side for a brief period, although supporting him raised problems for the Premier both with President Roosevelt and with General Wavell. On 21 May Lord Halifax made representations in favour of de Gaulle to the US Secretary of State, Cordell Hull, whose memorandum on their talk reveals all the reserve of the American attitude:

The British Ambassador . . . enquired whether we could recognize General de Gaulle in any more conspicuous way than heretofore. I replied that of course we were seeking to salvage whatever we could from the situation of Weygand in North Africa and from the government at Vichy, and that if Weygand should stand up, de Gaulle would have to become subordinate. To this he agreed.[8]

If de Gaulle had seen this record, neither Cordell Hull's words nor Lord Halifax's agreement with them would have surprised him.

In Cairo the desperately overburdened General Wavell imagined, like de Gaulle, that Free French representations in London rather than the course of events had overborne his advice against intervening in Syria. If this was so, he telegraphed to the Chief of the Imperial General Staff, he would prefer to be relieved of his command. Churchill had to reassure him that his advice counted most, while insisting that for political reasons the Syrian operation must proceed. Wavell, appeased, came back into line, but the Prime Minister had had to face and avert the danger of losing his Commander-in-Chief in the Middle East at the very height of the Battle of Crete, and the whole affair had arisen because of de Gaulle's protest and its repercussions. Churchill cannot have felt grateful for this addition to his burdens.

Planning for the invasion of Syria then went ahead. De Gaulle unrealistically asked for four British divisions and a strong air force to be assigned to the operation alongside the Free French, but Wavell could spare only a single Australian division and some sixty aircraft. General Wilson was to be in command. Meanwhile the Vichy authorities in Syria enlarged the scope of their collaboration with the Axis. Arms were sent to Rashid Ali's men in Iraq and more German and Italian planes made use of Syrian airfields. Admiral Darlan had been received by Hitler at Berchtesgaden on 13 May and had undertaken to cooperate loyally with the new order in Europe. He justified his policy in a radio address after his return to Vichy, describing it as a choice between life and death for France.

Political as well as military preparations were needed for the Syrian operation. The British, as was made clear to de Gaulle, were aiming at a profounder change than the mere replacement of Vichy's authority in Damascus and Beirut by that of the Free French. They wanted the Allied occupation to appear as an important step towards the independence of Syria and the Lebanon, and they privately intended that a generous share of the credit in Arab and American eyes for this work of liberation should accrue to themselves. De Gaulle, on the contrary, wanted all the credit to go to Free France; and while willing to have the independence of Syria and Lebanon proclaimed in principle, he wished to maintain French sovereignty in practice until after the war. Accordingly he rejected the British proposal that a joint Anglo-French proclamation of the forthcoming independence of the two territories should be made at the moment of invasion. France should make the proclamation, he said, and the British role should be military. De Gaulle and Churchill were out of step once more.

While arguing with the British, de Gaulle still had leisure to reflect on the general course of the war. He concluded that the entire British position in the Middle East was in peril. If it was lost, the threat to the Free French possessions in Africa would become acute, and increased American support would be even more precious than British. On 31 May he telegraphed his headquarters in London: 'In general the centre of interest is gradually shifting to Washington. It is absolutely essential that we should begin to exist there.'9 On 4 June, without informing the British, he sent a letter to Roosevelt warning him that the Americans could no longer count on bases in North Africa or Egypt being available if they entered the war, and offering instead facilities in the safety of Equatorial Africa in preparation for the possible entry of the United States into the war. He acknowledged that the United Kingdom might serve as an alternative zone of preparation but advised against choosing it as the base for the main American effort because of differences between American and British 'temperaments, ideas and methods'.[10]

This seems to have been de Gaulle's first personal letter to Roosevelt. It did not show him at his best, but it remains of interest as an example of de Gaulle's method of approach. He addresses the President as partner in a joint enterprise without a hint of the deference that Churchill always used towards him. This, in his eyes, was the only possible way to begin 'existing' (a favourite word of his) in Washington. What he wanted was a direct relationship with the leader who took the supreme decisions in Washington. But Roosevelt sent no reply.

On 8 June the Anglo-French invasion of Syria began. De Gaulle appointed General Catroux as Governor-General of Syria and Lebanon, and in his new capacity Catroux immediately made a proclamation to the inhabitants, the terms of which had been approved by de Gaulle: 'I abolish the mandate and proclaim you free and independent . . . Your independence and sovereignty will be guaranteed by a Treaty negotiated as soon as possible between your representatives and me . . .'[11] The British government followed up, to de Gaulle's displeasure, with its own independence guarantee.

Meanwhile the invasion went ahead. General Wilson had rather fewer men at his disposal than the 35,000 whom General Dentz, the Vichy Commander-in-Chief in Syria, could muster. There was hard fighting for the first ten days, but the Germans had lost interest in Syria when the anti-British movement in Iraq collapsed at the end of May and Rashid Ali, its leader, fled to Berlin. Some of the British forces in Iraq were soon free to cross into Syria and bring pressure to bear on the Vichyites from a new direction. Dentz accepted the inevitable, and on 18 June a message was sent to the British, but not to the Free French, asking for armistice terms.

At a conference in Cairo on 19 June de Gaulle, the British Ambassador, Sir Miles Lampson, and the British commanders-in-chief in the Middle East agreed on the terms to be offered to Dentz and recommended them to the Foreign Office by telegram.[12] The provisions included the representation of France in the Levant by the Free French; no reprisals against Vichy captives, but full opportunity for all those desirous of joining Free France, whether military or civilian, to do so; confiscation of all war material by the Allies; and the participation in armistice negotiations of a representative of General de Gaulle.

As the negotiation for an armistice hung fire for a time, fighting went on, and the Allies occupied Damascus on 21 June. General de Gaulle arrived to a tumultuous welcome two days later and gave General Catroux instructions to negotiate treaties of independence and sovereignty with the qualified representatives of Syria and Lebanon, together with the alliance of the two states to France. The words in the directive linking independence with the conclusion of a new alliance with France had a less generous ring than the original proclamation of 8 June.

On 28 June de Gaulle sent a message to Churchill stressing 'the extreme importance for the future of our alliance which British behaviour towards us in the Levant will have'.[13] But according to his Memoirs he had already concluded from various indications, including the attitude both of Anthony Eden, with whom he had exchanged telegrams, and of British officials in the Middle East, that the terms of the armistice in Syria were bound to fall far short of the wishes he had stated in Cairo on 19 June. In this he was right. The Americans had been pressing London to give more generous terms to Dentz. Without waiting for negotiations to end, de Gaulle withdrew to Brazzaville on the other side of Africa.

Here we see de Gaulle using for the first time in his political career a tactic which was to become a favourite of his when preparing to meet a crisis. It was 'to gain height and distance', as he puts it, by withdrawing from the centre of the scene to a retreat from which he could make a spectacular return at the appropriate moment. He felt that this manoeuvre gave more impact to his ultimate intervention. The results were often to prove satisfactory, and he remained faithful to this technique to the end.

The Syrian armistice was finally signed by Generals Wilson and Verdilhac at Acre on 14 July. Catroux had taken part in the negotiations but had been unable to persuade Wilson to pay attention to Free French requirements. In consequence, when the terms were reported to de Gaulle at Brazzaville, he found them as unacceptable as he had expected. They purported to transfer effective power in Damascus and Beirut from Vichy to the British military command virtually without reference to the Free French, and provided for the early repatriation of all the Vichy forces without allowing time or opportunity for the Free French to seek recruits among them. This was the kind of situation for which he had been preparing himself. He first announced that he rejected the terms of the armistice and then set out for Cairo to see the newly-arrived British Minister of State in the Middle East, Oliver Lyttelton. At their first meeting on 21 July he announced that he would withdraw Free French troops from British command in the Middle East in three days unless the armistice was revised to meet his requirements. His attitude towards Lyttelton was deliberately offensive.

Lyttelton had left the armistice negotiations to General Wilson and had already expressed his unhappiness, before de Gaulle arrived, at some of the concessions Wilson had made to Dentz, over the protests of Catroux. Faced by de Gaulle's cold fury, he backed down all along the line. A new agreement interpreting the armistice was signed by de Gaulle and Lyttelton on 24 July. This made it possible for the Free French to seek recruits among the Vichy forces, to take over all war material left in Syria and to assume charge of the native levies assigned in the armistice to British control. On 25 July Lyttelton wrote to de Gaulle assuring him that Britain recognized the historic interests of France in the Levant and accepted that, when Syria and Lebanon attained the independence promised them, France should continue to enjoy the leading position in that area among the European powers.

The crisis was resolved, and de Gaulle left for Beirut, where he began taking over the administration. Lyttelton followed him on 7 August and agreed that further administrative improvements desired by the General should be made and an Anglo-French defence plan for the territories jointly drawn up. From these events de Gaulle could hardly fail to conclude once again that, in dealing with British ministers, toughness paid.

A period of relative détente followed. Six thousand of the Vichy troops rallied to Free France, which was a useful gain, but the majority, numbering some 25,000, chose to return to France. De Gaulle's suspicions of the British remained alive, but his followers made him aware that they did not wholly share them. A long telegram of 10 August from the delegation in London, signed by Maurice Dejean, one of the first fairly senior French diplomats to join de Gaulle, ended by saying: 'Threats impossible to carry out can only reflect discredit on us. Moreover, we know that, because they come from you, these threats have much pained Mr Churchill.' In reply de Gaulle stuck to his guns: 'During the three weeks since the signing of the Anglo-Vichy armistice the local attitude of the British authorities has been intolerable.' His conclusion was: 'The grandeur and the force of our movement consists exclusively in the intransigence we show in defending the rights of France. We shall have need of that intransigence up to and including the Rhine.'[14]

De Gaulle accepted, nevertheless, the advice of the delegation that he should make an early return to London. He had done what he could in the Levant for the time being, and he realized that the German invasion of Russia had transformed the war. In mid-August he set out for London, resolved to explore and exploit the new situation.

But even before reaching his destination, he had provoked another crisis with Churchill, the consequences of which nearly clipped his wings for good.

# 15  CRISIS WITH CHURCHILL

On his way from the Middle East to London de Gaulle made a brief stop in Brazzaville. While there he gave an interview to an American correspondent which led to the most dangerous to him of many clashes with Churchill. The main purpose of the talk with George Weller, of the *Chicago Daily News*, was to further his campaign to make Free France 'exist' in America, but in response to questions he also revealed much of his accumulated bitterness against British policy. He made no mention of Anglo-French dissensions over Syria but dwelt on British policy towards Vichy.

Weller led into the subject by asking: 'Why, in your opinion, does not London finally close the door upon Vichy by recognizing your government?' 'England is afraid,' replied de Gaulle.

England is afraid of the French fleet. What in effect England is carrying on is a wartime deal with Hitler in which Vichy serves as a go-between. Vichy serves Hitler by keeping the French people in subjection and selling the French Empire piecemeal to Germany. But do not forget that Vichy also serves England by keeping the French fleet from Hitler's hands. What happens in effect is an exchange of advantages between hostile powers . . . if Vichy should lend or lose its fleet to the Germans, Britain would quickly bring the suspense about recognition to an end.[1]

He had not a single friendly word for his British ally. By contrast he praised the United States for its disinterested support of freedom and predicted that it would be the real victor in the war. He said he had already offered to lease naval bases in Africa to US forces for use against Hitler.

De Gaulle did not see a copy of Weller's text until he was in the plane on his way to London. He at once sent a telegram to Brazzaville demanding that publication should be held up while changes were made. In particular he denied saying that the British were 'afraid of' the French Fleet or that he had offered to put French bases 'at the disposal' of the Americans, a formula which would have been incompatible with his notions of French sovereignty. But his telegram arrived too late. Weller had been allowed to cable his report and it appeared prominently in the *Chicago Daily News* on 27 August headlined 'US Offered Africa Ports by de Gaulle'. It was carried generally in the American press and created something of a sensation. Secretary of State Hull was questioned and denied all knowledge of the offer of bases.

De Gaulle learned this while still on the way to Britain and had a general *démenti* issued by his office in Washington, stating that Weller had completely misrepresented him. He also ordered that Weller should be barred from territories under Free French control. Meanwhile the news of the interview was at once flashed to Churchill. It first reached him in the form of an inaccurate précis prepared by an official, which summarized de Gaulle's main charge against Britain as follows: 'Britain is keeping open the Vichy channel with a view to an ultimate deal with Nazi Germany.'² This went infinitely further than was justified by the text of Weller's article, substituting the idea of a compromise Anglo-German peace for a tacit wartime arrangement.

The accusation, as wrongly reported to him, touched Churchill on the raw. Presenting Britain's war aims and effort in a favourable light to American public opinion was one of his dearest concerns at this stage of the war. Only a week previously he had returned from his first wartime meeting with President Roosevelt, their celebrated rendezvous at sea. At this they jointly signed and issued to the world the Atlantic Charter, a declaration of common Anglo-American aims among which was 'the final destruction of Nazi tyranny'. It was a triumph for Churchill that Roosevelt had been willing to commit the United States, still neutral, to this purpose in a document signed jointly with a belligerent. America had taken another stride towards the war, and Roosevelt had run a risk with his own public opinion. Now, at this supremely delicate moment, de Gaulle had apparently told the American public that Britain was meditating a compromise peace with Hitler rather than 'the final destruction of Nazi tyranny'. To make it worse, the accusation first appeared not in an anti-British newspaper but in the friendly *Chicago Daily News*, the property of Colonel Knox, Secretary of the Navy in Roosevelt's Cabinet. Might not many Americans suspect there was something in such a charge from such a source? Might not even the eternally suspicious Stalin, himself perhaps thinking of a compromise peace with Hitler, have his doubts? This was an infinitely more serious matter for Churchill than a dispute over Syria.

His reaction was fierce, although he did not take it for granted that the résumé that had reached him was accurate. 'If the de Gaulle interview with the American press at Brazzaville is authentic,' he telegraphed to Oliver Lyttelton, 'he has clearly gone off his head. This would be a very good riddance and would simplify our further course. De Gaulle has put himself entirely out of court.'[3]

When he saw the full text of the interview on 29 August, the Prime Minister minuted that it was not as bad as the résumé, and ordered that a further check should be made.[4] The result must have diminished his resentment against de Gaulle. He had made a metaphorical reference to 'a wartime deal with Hitler' but he had clearly not been talking of a peace settlement. The original précis had grossly exaggerated his offence.

Was it the error of an overworked official, or a deliberate effort to turn Churchill still further against de Gaulle, mounted perhaps by troublemakers of the same breed as those who had been behind the false charges against Muselier? The evidence does not admit of an answer, but it is fair to say that if de Gaulle himself had studied it as carefully as he did the case against Muselier, his suspicions would have been thoroughly aroused.

Churchill's wrath, however, was far from being extinguished when he saw the full text of what de Gaulle had said. He decided that this time he would show his resentment, which had already been stoked by other reports of the general's behaviour in the Middle East. He sent orders to Anthony Eden that no notice was to be taken of de Gaulle's return to Britain on 1 September, and that the main questions currently under negotiation with the Free French should be blocked until further notice. But he added: 'It is not intended that all contacts . . . shall come to an end.'[5]

De Gaulle wrote on 1 September, the day of his arrival, asking for an interview, but Churchill's reply the next day was cold in the extreme. He demanded an explanation of the reports in the American press of the de Gaulle-Weller interview. 'Until this is received,' he said, 'I am unable to judge whether any interview between us would serve a useful purpose.'[6]

De Gaulle saw danger ahead, and took steps to avoid it. Churchill had never used such language to him before. He replied on 3 September saying that he had been falsely reported and that his one purpose was to fight on to victory alongside the British. In a talk the same day with Major Desmond Morton, the Prime Minister's special assistant for dealings with the Free French, he claimed that the justice of his complaints against British authorities in the Middle East was proved by Oliver Lyttelton's intervention on his side on 7 August.

He blamed General Spears for much of the trouble that had arisen, alleging that Spears had intercepted telegrams addressed to him by Lyttelton.

Churchill now decided to see de Gaulle after a suitable cooling-off period. He sent Morton to him to make an appointment for 12 September. During the intervening days he and other ministers gave some thought to the best way of imposing restraint on de Gaulle's future activities, and concluded that part of the solution might be to revert to the idea of June 1940 that a Committee of National Liberation should be set up to direct Free France. Meanwhile de Gaulle, presumably reassured by Churchill's agreement to see him, sent a telegram to Brazzaville revoking the ban on George Weller. The authenticity of Weller's reporting, apart from details, was evident to anybody who knew de Gaulle's opinions.

On 12 September the interview duly took place at 10 Downing Street. Nobody else was present except an interpreter. Churchill spoke first and did not mince his words. He said he had 'witnessed with very great sorrow the deterioration in General de Gaulle's attitude towards His Majesty's Government'. He now felt that 'he was no longer dealing with a friend'. He accepted de Gaulle's letter explaining the American press interview but there was evidence from many sources that throughout his travels he had 'left a trail of Anglophobia behind him'.

On Syria, Churchill repeated Lyttelton's assurances that the British had no wish to supplant France, whose special position they recognized, but he spoke forcefully about the need to meet the desire of the local populations for independence: 'Clearly the securing of our position in the Arab world involved a transfer of many of the functions previously exercised by France in Syria to the Syrians themselves . . . The Arabs saw no sense in driving out the Vichy French only to be placed under the control of the Free French. They desired their independence and had been promised it.' He rubbed in the vast superiority of British resources over French in the Middle East and made it clear that the French interest in the Levant must be subordinated to the wider requirements of British relations with the Arab world and of winning the war.

De Gaulle's reply was remarkably defensive by his normal standards. He insisted that the record proved that neither he nor the Free French were anti-British, but admitted that the humiliating treatment accorded to the Free French in Syria along with all the other difficulties in his position as the champion of a fallen country might have caused him to say wounding things about the British government. If so, he had no hesitation in expressing his regret. As to Syria, Free France had promised her independence, and he accepted the need to cultivate the good will of the local populations, in the interests of the Allied war effort. Free French forces would cooperate loyally with the British, who must exercise supreme military command in the Middle East. He had always recognized Churchill as the chief of the Allied coalition.

Churchill then produced his main proposal, which was that the Free French should set up a formal Council 'which would have an effective voice in shaping the policy of the movement of which General de Gaulle was the head'. The British government would deal with the Council, and their relations with the Free French movement would improve when it had a broader basis. De Gaulle replied that he had already been thinking of some such move, but not before 1942. He saw difficulties because a Council might introduce political disagreements into the movement, whose unanimity was already producing a revolution in French opinion, but he promised to give the Prime Minister's proposal his earnest consideration.

Churchill then delivered his final thrust. He warned the General how important it was to give no ground for belief that he was anti-British, because 'already some British figures entertained a suspicion that General de Gaulle had become hostile and had moved towards certain Fascist views'. De Gaulle promised to give 'the utmost weight' to this advice.[7]

By the end of this meeting of an hour and a half, relations between the two men had reached the point of détente. The private secretary, John Colville, who entered the room expecting to encounter stormy weather found them sitting side by side on a sofa smoking cigars.[8] But the cigars were not pipes of peace. If there was détente, there was no entente. Churchill still meant to clip de Gaulle's wings; de Gaulle knew it and meant to take avoiding action. The fight was still on. The contestants were resting between rounds.

The next round was soon under way. Churchill's idea was that Free France should be given the decision-making structure of an advanced British colony, with a Governor-General, de Gaulle, presiding as the symbol of a constitutional monarch over a Council which would take decisions automatically binding on him. De Gaulle was to be 'put in commission' as British colonial parlance had it. Thus he would remain of symbolic utility to Allied propaganda but for practical purposes his powers would be very limited.

The British did not leave it to de Gaulle to set up a Council on his own initiative as a result of the Prime Minister's advice. They had already heard complaints from certain of the Free French about the General's autocratic ways, and now various intermediaries tried to stimulate support for the idea of more democracy in the movement. There was no lack of intermediaries – Lord Bessborough, who had a French wife and worked in the French Welfare Section of the Foreign office, Admiral Dickens, Chief Naval Liaison Officer, Desmond Morton, and the Spears Mission were all involved – and they found willing hearers. After taking soundings, they decided that Admiral Muselier, who had not so long ago been incarcerated in the Tower on suspicion of spying, was the right man to exercise effective power in a Council, as a chief minister would do in an advanced colony. André Labarthe, the Socialist editor of *La France Libre*, who had become disenchanted with the General, and Captain Moret, of the Free French Navy, who had been in the *Deuxième Bureau* (French Intelligence) before the war, seemed suitable colleagues. Moret, who was known by British Intelligence, would be welcome as a replacement of the 'dangerously inefficient' Passy at the head of the Free French Secret Service.[9]

Muselier, playing the British game, made the next move. On 18 September he sent de Gaulle a letter proposing himself as effective head of a Committee under the General's titular leadership. The two men met on 21 September and de Gaulle rejected Muselier's proposal. He said he was ready to form a Committee but that he himself would be its head. Muselier replied that he would not serve on such a body and then left.[10]

De Gaulle understood by this time that he was dealing with a conspiracy which he must suppress if he was to maintain his authority. In the course of 22 September Muselier provided him with an opening that made his task easier. He telephoned de Gaulle's office and announced that if the General held by his decision of the previous evening, he, Muselier, would withdraw the Fleet from the Free French forces and carry on the war independently at the side of the Royal Navy.[11] Apparently he shared Darlan's illusion that his ships belonged to him and not to France.

De Gaulle could now counterattack. He summoned Admiral Dickens later the same day and told him he would have to dismiss Muselier because of personal differences that were not serious but made collaboration impossible. Dickens, who knew the truth but could not admit it, urged de Gaulle to hold his hand while he reported to his superiors, which he did immediately. The Prime Minister was alerted that a row was brewing.

On the morning of 23 September de Gaulle asked for an immediate interview with Churchill, who, perhaps expecting that he was going to be asked to arrange a compromise, received him at 10 Downing Street at 1 pm.

De Gaulle took him by surprise by stating that a serious obstacle had arisen to the formation of a French National Committee as desired by Churchill, because Muselier had demanded its leadership and on being refused had threatened to break away and take the Fleet with him. He appealed for assurances of support from the Admiralty if he had to dismiss Muselier and incidents followed. He felt confident that most of the Fleet was loyal to him, de Gaulle, but obviously 'a painful scandal' might be impending.

Churchill was in an awkward position. De Gaulle had unexpectedly asked him for support against a threatened mutiny, to which he was entitled under the accords of 7 August 1940, and not for help in a political row; and he did not want to reveal that he knew more about the matter than de Gaulle had told him. He said that an open quarrel would be a very serious matter, and requested de Gaulle to take no action for twenty-four hours while he considered the situation with his advisers. Then he would see de Gaulle again and hoped to make proposals. He added, no doubt reluctantly, that 'any attempt to divert the allegiances of the Free French sailors as a result of this controversy could clearly not be tolerated'. It was an important concession which de Gaulle would exploit. He agreed to the requested delay and withdrew.[12]

That night at 11 pm Churchill called a crisis meeting at No. 10 with Eden and Alexander, the First Lord of the Admiralty, and decided to leave it to them to settle matters while he himself stayed in the background. He drew up a very firm directive for Eden laying down that he should impose on de Gaulle the formation of a Council headed by a 'Governor-General in Council' and composed of six or seven 'Frenchmen of Right and Left', not office-holders in Free France, to guide the movement. The creation of a Cabinet-style Council, which was what de Gaulle was planning, was not to be permitted; control of the Free French secret service must be vested in someone acceptable to the new Council and to the government; while Muselier must withdraw his statements, written and verbal, to de Gaulle.

The directive ended by confiding the charge of all these matters to Eden, with the mission of imposing British wishes on de Gaulle as to the leadership of the Free French, including the appointment of an acceptable head of their secret service in place of Passy, 'not hesitating to use whatever process may be necessary including the forcible restraint of individuals'.[13] The reference to 'forcible restraint' in this context is unclear. Perhaps it was simply a reminder to Eden that Churchill had already issued orders that de Gaulle was not to be allowed to leave Britain, but it sounds more like a reference to wartime powers of detention. If so, only de Gaulle or Passy, or both, can have been the intended victims.

Churchill's directive sounded very fierce, but in the event its language mattered much less than the fact that he had recoiled from the fray himself. Perhaps he sensed that a confrontation with de Gaulle on what was an internal Free French matter might lead to an irreparable break between them and the disruption of the Free French movement, in which his political credit was engaged. He preferred not to risk it, and de Gaulle must have detected a sign of weakness in the other camp when Morton told him of the change of plan the next morning and asked him to take no action until he and Muselier had seen Eden and Alexander. He flew into a rage, accused the Admiralty of encouraging Muselier to rebellion, and declared his determination to maintain his leadership of Free France.

During the day he made two other moves in preparation for his meeting with Eden. He drew up and signed an ordinance setting up a National Committee of which he himself was President. The eight members were to be commissioners with portfolios, that is it was to be a Cabinet-style Committee such as Churchill had forbidden; and they were all leading members of Free France, not independent 'Frenchmen of Right and Left'. Labarthe and Moret were omitted.

Then he received Muselier and shocked him by stating that the British had already recognized him, de Gaulle, as head of the new Committee and that, as Muselier had been disloyal to him, they could not work together in future.[14] By the time that the midnight meeting began at the Foreign Office the unfortunate Admiral, who had also been told by his British fellow conspirators that he must withdraw all that he had said and written to de Gaulle, was in a state of total confusion.

Eden never had a chance of carrying out any part of the Prime Minister's mandate. He and Alexander led the British team to a complete defeat. Muselier had broken in their hands, and there was no other rival to de Gaulle whom they could produce. They ended by bowing to his *fait accompli*, in return for his accepting Muselier on the new Committee. The news was not announced in the press until 26 September. Before then Lord Bessborough had given the conspirators' verdict in a letter to the Prime Minister which described the new body as 'a Committee of yes-men, which only confirms de Gaulle in his dictatorship'.

In a minute to Eden on 26 September, Churchill sent him Bessborough's comments to read and wrote his gloomy epitaph on the affair:

> This is very unpleasant. Our intention was to compel de Gaulle to accept a suitable Council. All we have done is to compel Muselier and Co. to submit themselves to de Gaulle. I understood you were going to make sure that the resulting Government represented what we want. It is evident that the business will require our closest watching, and that our weight in the immediate future must be thrown more heavily against de Gaulle than I had hoped would be necessary.
>
> I am renewing my directions that he is on no account to leave the country.[15]

There was no practical inconvenience to de Gaulle at the moment in being a kind of prisoner in Britain, although it became a serious grievance later. He had saved his personal position intact, and that was what mattered for immediate purposes. On 1 October he saw Churchill again and assured him, it is to be hoped with a straight face, that the new Committee had made a good start.

A secret minute about the Prime Minister's views after talking to de

Gaulle on 1 October said: 'He continues to regard support for the Free French movement as an integral part of Allied policy. General de Gaulle is at present the only possible leader of that movement. His name stands for a great deal in Metropolitan France. His character and personality may prove him to be a greater man than recent events have caused some to suppose.' Greatness recognized greatness. But the minute repeated: 'The Free French movement should set up a Council to exercise effective control over the General's activities and utterances.'[16]

Churchill was to cling to this vain idea with singular obstinacy. It never had a chance of working, because, as Eden pointed out when defending himself against Churchill's reproaches, there were no 'no-men' in the Free French movement. The only man who might have stood up to de Gaulle effectively was Churchill himself, and he chose not to do so on the question of the Council.

Neither of the great men gives much account of this clash in his Memoirs. Churchill, the loser, understandably omits all reference to it. De Gaulle mentions that he had an interview with Churchill which started badly but ended well, and that he had to brush off certain pretensions of Muselier's. But he does not link the two events. He writes as if he had set up the National Committee on his own initiative rather than as a result of having his hand forced by Churchill's pressure.

De Gaulle, despite his victory, took Churchill's warnings about 'Fascist ideas' to heart. The Soviets were now involved in the war and the Americans were playing a larger and larger part. This had its effect on the political climate in the West. In 1940, after the fall of France, it had been possible to condemn the role of the French system of democracy, the constant quarrelling of the political parties, in causing that tragedy. De Gaulle, himself, in his early days in London, had vowed that he would never make use of the words 'democracy' or 'republic'.[17] But the Russians and the Americans both regarded themselves as democrats. Their sentiments commanded respect. De Gaulle reverted to the language of revolutionary tradition at a great meeting of the Free French held on 15 November at the Albert Hall. 'We say "Liberty, Equality, Fraternity" because it is our will to remain true to democratic principles,' he proclaimed.

De Gaulle understood that the world was changing, but he did not see the National Committee as imposing democratic limitations on his own authority. He had made that point in a letter of 19 September to Morton, so the British were under no illusions about it. In his Memoirs he acknowledges that the Committee eased his task and was always loyal, but it did not share his responsibilities. He sums up the situation in a sentence: 'In the struggle for liberation it was still myself alone [*le pauvre moi*] who was responsible for everything.'[18]

These were proud but not megalomanic words. They accurately expressed the constitutional position set forth in the Brazzaville Manifesto. De Gaulle did not preside over his National Committee like a British colonial governor in council, as Churchill had intended; nor as a British Prime Minister presides, '*primus inter pares*', over his Cabinet; he dominated them as Louis XIV had dominated the *Conseil du Roi*.

Churchill's embargo on dealings with the Free French was now lifted, and they resumed their normal prickly but quite productive course. But relations between Churchill and de Gaulle had been permanently changed by the conflicts in the summer, and the evidence they had produced of what Churchill called the General's 'Anglophobia'. He never again regarded him as a friend, as he had in the early days. On the other hand he had an enhanced respect for de Gaulle's potentialities as a statesman. De Gaulle, who kept personal ties on a different plane from politics, had never felt much friendship for Churchill, but he had admired him and counted on him as his principal support in the British camp. Henceforth he continued to admire him – and might still refer to him as '*mon ami*' when it suited him – but, realizing the change in his attitude, he began to cast about for other British supporters. In particular he started to cultivate Anthony Eden, who had given him his way at the midnight conclave on 24 September.

# 16 Dealings with the Russians and Americans

Once his immediate crisis with Churchill was over, de Gaulle turned much of his attention to the Russians and Americans. As an ally, he had little enough to offer in the material sense: the least advanced parts of the French Empire and some sixty thousand men under arms, wholly dependent on British support. But morally he counted for much more. His voice was heard and his name known increasingly in France, both occupied and unoccupied. He was becoming a symbol of and a synonym for resistance.

Hitler's attack had swiftly produced a reversal of Soviet attitudes towards Pétain and de Gaulle. Vichy, acting on German directions, broke off relations with Moscow a few days after the invasion began. De Gaulle proclaimed support for the Soviets with equal promptitude. Contact was then established with Ivan Maisky, the Soviet Ambassador in London, who passed on an offer to de Gaulle from Moscow to send the chief French Communists in the Soviet Union, Maurice Thorez, André Marty and Raymond Guyet, to join him in London.[1] This proposal went further than de Gaulle wanted, and the Russians cannot have been surprised when he rejected it. But discussions continued and led to an exchange of letters in London on 26 September between de Gaulle and Maisky whereby the Soviet government agreed to enter into relations with the Council for the Defence of the French Empire, to give aid to the Free French, and to work for the full restoration of the independence and the grandeur of France after victory. Soon after this the Soviet government accredited as its diplomatic representative to the National Committee the same General Bogomolov who had previously been its Ambassador in Vichy. It was an effective way of showing that in Soviet eyes de Gaulle had now replaced Pétain as representative of France.

De Gaulle wanted more than this. He hoped to create an entente with Moscow which would strengthen his hand in dealings both with 'the Anglo-Saxons' and with the Resistance in France, in which the Communists had begun to be active. He saw to it that French ships played a modest part in the Arctic supply convoys to Murmansk, and sent a military mission to Russia, which opened discussions about dispatching French troops, pilots and planes to the Eastern front. Gradually this careful cultivation bore fruit, and an air squadron, the Normandie-Nieman, but no troops, went to the Russian front.

Another step in collaboration was to be taken during Molotov's visit to London in May 1942. De Gaulle undertook to back Soviet efforts to make the Western powers open a second front in Europe – which meant in France – in 1942; in return Molotov promised Soviet support with the British and US governments for Free French efforts to regain more of the Empire from Vichy and restore national unity. The Soviet government also agreed that no foreign government had the right to encourage French resistants to reject the authority of General de Gaulle. This promise was honoured, and proved of value to de Gaulle in his dealings with the French Communists.

As far as diplomatic relations were concerned, de Gaulle had more cause to worry about the Americans than the Russians. Whereas Britain and the Soviet Union had both promised to do their best to restore the grandeur as well as the independence of France after victory, the United States had entered into no such commitment, and it was the United States that was most likely to be in the position of arbiter after the war. President Roosevelt had made it clear that he wanted to see the democratic liberties of France restored, but that was all, and he had given little sign of regarding the Free French movement as important. On the contrary Roosevelt and the State Department concentrated on encouraging Pétain and his ministers to stand up to German pressure for more complete collaboration. The Americans had also sent food supplies in limited quantity to French North Africa, with British consent, and schemed to bring the French armies there back into the battle. De Gaulle played a very minor part in their calculations: Weygand was their main hope.

This policy was nourished by the reports of Robert Murphy, American Consul-General in Algiers and the President's special representative for Africa, who found both the Free French and the British very unpopular in North Africa, whereas the French settlers held the United States, so they told him, in high esteem.² So the Americans confined themselves to various practical dealings with the Free French, over the use of air bases in the Pacific for instance, which were kept in a low key. Behind all this lay Roosevelt's belief that the postwar world would be unfriendly to the European colonial empires, that they were all likely to break up by degrees, and that it would be to the benefit of the United States and the rest of the world if they did.

In the hope of improving matters, on 17 October 1941 de Gaulle sent a personal letter to Roosevelt.³ It was an effort to convince him that what had happened to France in 1940 was due to the 'failure of an élite', not the faults of the mass of the people; that the country was still sound at heart and devoted to the Allied cause and to democracy; and that the Free French movement represented what was best in the nation. It was an important letter and another gesture of independence vis-à-vis the British, whom de Gaulle did not tell what he was doing, but it had no effect in Washington. Roosevelt never replied to it.

On practical matters, however, there was some progress. In November 1941 President Roosevelt signed a directive authorizing the supply of Lend-Lease aid to the Free French on the grounds that 'the defence of the territories that have rallied to Free France is vital to the defence of the United States'. At the end of November, General Weygand was deprived of his post in North Africa on German insistence and recalled to France. This was a major disappointment to the Americans, but their hopes of stimulating resistance in France and North Africa still centred on Vichy.

Then on 7 December 1941 came Pearl Harbor and the Japanese declaration of war on the United States and Britain. A few days later Germany and Italy declared war on the United States. The war had become worldwide, as de Gaulle had frequently forecast. Only the Japanese Empire and the Soviet Union maintained an uneasy peace.

But diplomatic relations between Washington and Vichy were undisturbed. The Germans did not require Pétain to sever them, as they had done in the case of Vichy's relations with Moscow at the time of their attack on the Soviet Union, and the United States took no action to alter the situation either.

At this point, just when closer contact between Washington and the Free French might have been expected, their relations were disturbed by one of the most spectacular storms that blew up in any teacup throughout the war. It happened in the tiny islands of St Pierre and

Miquelon off the coast of Newfoundland, French possessions with a population of a few thousand. Like the French West Indies they were under an administration loyal to Vichy and were covered by an agreement reached between Washington and Vichy in the summer of 1940 which provided for the effective neutralization of the islands and the French naval forces in them for the rest of the war. Suspicions had arisen on the Allied side, however, that a radio station on St Pierre was broadcasting weather reports and other information that might be useful to German submarines in the North Atlantic, and consideration had been given in the months before Pearl Harbor to ways and means of putting a stop to this. De Gaulle had written to Eden in October saying that Free French forces were ready to take over the islands, but Eden had asked him to await US and Canadian reactions, and nothing had been done.

Pearl Harbor seemed to de Gaulle to be the signal for action. In a letter of 10 December he told Churchill that Admiral Muselier was on his way to occupy the islands with a force of three corvettes, and asked whether the British government saw any objection to '*ce petit coup de main*'. Churchill saw none but, as de Gaulle had expected, referred the question to the Americans, who said 'No'. A Free French occupation would violate their understanding with Vichy about French colonies in the New World, and they had a visceral dislike of European military activities, even friendly, in their hemisphere. The British and Canadians accepted the American veto, and the Foreign Office so informed de Gaulle on 17 December. In the face of this opposition de Gaulle decided in the course of 17 December, or early the following day, to abandon his project. He instructed Muselier to return to London and had a letter sent to the Foreign Office on 18 December stating that the islands would not be occupied.

If matters had been left there, St Pierre and Miquelon might have been allowed to recede into the Labrador mists, but no sooner was de Gaulle's letter of renunciation received than the Foreign Office wrote to him again, still on 18 December, to tell him that Canadian forces would shortly be proceeding, with American consent, to land on St Pierre and neutralize the offending radio transmitter. Presumably this letter was meant to reassure de Gaulle that the restraint he had shown would not result in extra danger to Allied shipping. If so, it was a miscalculation. The General was enraged at the news that the Americans, after vetoing French operations on French territory, had given their agreement to foreign action.

As de Gaulle saw it, his restraint had been repaid with contempt. If he did not react, the Americans would feel free to ignore France's sovereignty over her possessions whenever it suited them. He sent further instructions to Muselier later on 18 December saying that the Canadians intended to destroy the radio transmitter at St Pierre themselves and that in these circumstances he must proceed to rally St Pierre and Miquelon 'by your own means and saying nothing to foreigners. I take the entire responsibility for this operation, which has become indispensable in order to preserve these French possessions for France.'[4]

To the British de Gaulle protested against Canadian intentions but did not reveal the change in his own.

The new orders reached Muselier at Montreal as he was preparing to return to London by air. After some hesitation he decided to obey them, although he was reluctant to flout American and Canadian wishes. He set sail from Halifax with his small force and landed at St Pierre at 8 am on Christmas Eve. The islanders welcomed him enthusiastically and rallied to de Gaulle at once. There was no bloodshed, and a referendum held on 25 and 26 December ratified the adhesion of St Pierre and Miquelon to Free France. In London, at about the hour of Muselier's landing, de Gaulle informed the British authorities that all previous undertakings about St Pierre and Miquelon were cancelled and that he intended to proceed with Free French occupation on his own responsibility.[5]

The reaction of the State Department to de Gaulle's move was prompt and hostile. A statement was issued on 25 December referring to the 'arbitrary' action at St Pierre and Miquelon by 'so-called Free French forces' and announcing that the US government was consulting the Canadian government to learn what measures it proposed to take to restore the status quo.

It happened that Churchill was in Washington at this time for discussions with Roosevelt. It was his first visit to the United States since the war, and he was the hero of the hour. De Gaulle had the audacious idea of appealing for support to the man who had so little trust in him that he had been keeping him confined to Britain and whose government he had just hoodwinked. He made his approach in terms which showed a profound understanding of Churchill's

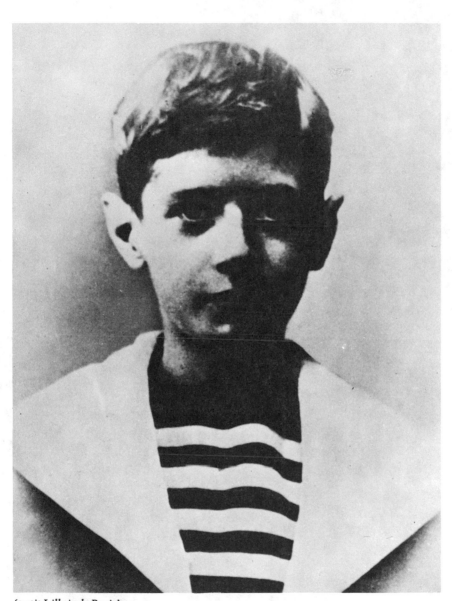

*'petit Lillois de Paris'*

At St Cyr

The young officer

Family wedding, 1922

Prisoner of war

De Gaulle shows his tanks to President Lebrun, October 1939

De Gaulle's début as minister,
6 June 1940

*L'Appel du 18 Juin* (1940): 'As the irrevocable words went out over the air, I felt a whole life coming to an end . . .'

De Gaulle, back from Africa, in his London headquarters, November 1940; 'a temporary sovereign, self-appointed'

Jean Moulin, chief organizer of the Resistance

*Above* First appearance as liberator, Bayeux, 14 June 1944

De Gaulle is welcomed at the White House; Roosevelt smiles but does not change his mind

Churchill and de Gaulle reviewing troops in Marrakesh; the crowd thought
they were friends

The consecration of de Gaulle, 26 August 1944

The American parade in Paris, 29 August 1944

character. His telegram put the question on the high level of honour, and the will to fight the enemy:

I have good reason to fear that the present attitude of the State Department towards the Free French and Vichy respectively may do much harm to the will to fight in France and elsewhere.

I am afraid of the unfortunate impression that the preference which the United States government is openly according to the authors of surrender and the sponsors of collaboration is bound to produce on opinion in the Free French forces and territories, as well as in France, which is not yet liberated.

It does not seem right to me that in time of war, the prize should go to the apostles of dishonour.

I say this to you because I know that you feel the same and that you alone can say it as it should be said.[6]

This was the right note to strike: no talk of political or juridical considerations, or of de Gaulle's obsession with protecting French territory from foreign encroachment; simply an appeal to back the fighter against the quitter.

Churchill could not refuse. He took up the cudgels in Washington for his prisoner, and did it to good effect, both with Roosevelt and in public. He also referred to the St Pierre affairs in a speech in Canada in terms which infuriated Mr Hull.

Fortunately President Roosevelt's feelings were less engaged than those of Secretary Hull, who took Muselier's occupation of the two islands as virtually a breach of the Monroe Doctrine – 'It jeopardizes the whole delicate structure of inter-American relations,' he minuted to the President.[7] But the sympathy shown by American public opinion for the Gaullist coup combined with Churchill's arguments to force Hull to give ground. There was a moment of tension in mid-January when de Gaulle warned Muselier of the possibility of a US naval attack on the islands. Muselier repeated to the US consul what he had already told him at the time of his arrival, that he would, with the greatest reluctance, use force to resist American naval intervention, if he had to. De Gaulle said the same to Eden in London. Happily the question remained academic. Churchill returned to London and worked out a formula which appeased both sides. The administration installed by Muselier was to remain in charge of the islands, but Muselier and his naval forces were to withdraw, and American and Canadian officers were to join the Free French in charge of the radio transmitter. Thus honour was satisfied all round, and de Gaulle had obtained the essence of what he wanted. St Pierre and Miquelon remain in the war and under his control. The price he paid was an increase of the distaste felt for him by Hull and the State Department.

Oddly enough, the hero of the affair of St Pierre and Miquelon, Admiral Muselier, was almost as displeased as Cordell Hull at its outcome. While still in the islands he told the American consul in confidence that de Gaulle had consulted nobody and behaved like a dictator, and that he meant to resign from the Committee when he returned to London.[8]

This he did on 3 March 1942, immediately he was back in England. The affair unfolded rather like another round in the contest of the previous September. De Gaulle accepted Muselier's resignation and treated it as applying both to his membership of the Committee and his command of the Navy. Muselier, however, proclaimed his intention of remaining at the head of the Free French naval forces and obtained the backing of the Admiralty, who thought that they were so loyal to Muselier personally that they would cease to function effectively if he departed. Eden and Alexander called on de Gaulle on 5 and 6 March and urged him to keep Muselier at his post.

For the General of course this amounted to direct British intervention in the internal affairs of Free France. He felt, as he says in his Memoirs, that he was facing another intrigue devised by Muselier with the help of his anti-Gaullist friends, French and British. Naturally he was determined to resist at all costs and said so to Eden. In fact he demanded British support against Muselier, much as he had the previous September, and retired to the country to await events. While there he even prepared a last political testament for the Committee to publish in the event of his resigning and being unable to explain the reasons himself. It seems that he suspected the British might be thinking of putting him under restraint,[9] as Churchill had apparently had in mind during his earlier bout with Muselier.

The British, however, found themselves in an embarrassing position when it turned out that the Free French naval contingent was loyal not to Muselier but to de Gaulle. They had no choice but to back down, with the result that Muselier brought his connection with Free France to an end.

The major military preoccupation of the Americans in 1942 was the opening of a second front in the West. The question was whether to attempt the invasion of Europe for which the Russians were insistently pressing or to make the indirect approach by way of Africa which the British favoured. In either case French territory would be involved and the mobilization of all possible French help was a high priority. At the urging of his chiefs of staff Roosevelt had accepted the primacy of military requirements as a principle of his foreign policy for the duration of the war. In the eyes of the President's military advisers, help from Gaullists or Pétainists was equally acceptable. The over-riding consideration was to further military operations with as little expenditure of American lives as possible.

President Roosevelt, however, set limits on the degree of coopera-tion he was prepared to accept. He was ready to give military aid to the Free French, but politically he was determined to keep to the principle that the French people must be free to choose their future leadership by the democratic process after the liberation of the country. This meant he would allow nothing to be done that might give the impression that the United States government either wanted or expected de Gaulle to be the postwar leader of France. The only gesture Roosevelt permitted towards de Gaulle was, accordingly, almost drained of political content. The US government issued a statement on 9 July recognizing the Free French contribution to the war effort, promising more aid, and affirming community of war aims. Admiral Stark and General Bolte were named as the representatives of the US government accredited to the French National Committee.

This was a modest satisfaction for de Gaulle, but he had no success in his efforts to persuade the Allies to make a direct descent upon France in 1942 rather than to aim at Africa. He had promised Molotov in May that he would use his influence to this end, but only because he considered it the right course in the interests of France. He gives his reasons in his Memoirs:

The best solution was the one which would diminish the trials of the invasion and hasten national union . . . No doubt Vichy would continue to bow to the Germans, but in so doing it would lose whatever credit remained to it. The invader would doubtless occupy the free zone . . . but then the Army in Africa, and perhaps the Fleet, would return to the battle and many more inside France would have joined the Resistance. It would become possible to reunite the various French authorities under a single power to suppress subversion at home and to create an imposing representation of France abroad.[10]

De Gaulle certainly expected that that single power would be his own, but he might have been mistaken, as his position inside France was by no means as strong in 1942 as it had become in 1944.

De Gaulle's views corresponded to the inclinations of the American military planners in favour of a direct descent on France, but they counted for little against the firm opposition of Churchill and the British chiefs of staff, who felt the Allies were not yet strong enough for such an operation. In a series of meetings in late July, their reluctance to take such a grave risk prevailed. Roosevelt accepted Churchill's view that French North Africa offered better chances of success, and issued orders that its invasion, Operation Torch, should be prepared for the autumn. De Gaulle was not informed. His help was not to be sought and the Free French were to know nothing of the invasion planning. They had achieved tactical surprise over St Pierre, and Roosevelt intended to return the compliment many times over.

# 17 FRANCE: RESISTANCE GROWS AND TURNS TO DE GAULLE

The General does not seem to have given much thought to the potential of resistance inside France during his early days in London. He conceived of liberation as being the task of Allied armies and his own Free French movement. Agents were sent to France to seek intelligence rather than stimulate rebellion. The first action he called for in occupied France itself was of a symbolic nature: to remain indoors between 3 and 4 pm on New Year's Day 1941.

By then news had reached London of the first stirrings of resistance inside France. Schoolboys had demonstrated against the invaders on the Champs Elysées on 11 November, and some had been shot. Groups soon sprang up in the unoccupied zone too, which were actively or passively anti-German, and interested in Free France. Learning of their existence, Passy sent an agent, Fourcaud, to make contact early in 1941, but there was no significant result. According to Henri Noguères' *History of the Resistance in France*, the active resistants during the first twelve months after the armistice 'did not constitute in statistical terms even an appreciable minority'.[1]

The German invasion of Russia brought about a radical change in the situation. Resistance strengthened and sharpened when the French Communists took up the struggle. It was they who began the shooting of individual German soldiers which provoked the mass killing of hostages as a reprisal. On 21 October 1941 forty-eight Frenchmen were executed in retaliation for the shooting of Colonel Holz. French opinion was appalled, and hostility to the Germans spread and became more active.

De Gaulle resolved to exploit this situation and asked for British assistance in setting up 'a new organization in France designed to prepare . . . for a nation-wide uprising at the appropriate time'. This proposal confronted the British government with a problem. They were willing to provide technical help with the project, but not to aid de Gaulle in fastening his political leadership on the Resistance or to prejudice the freedom of their own services, SIS and SOE, to operate independently inside France. These points were made clear in a letter which Anthony Eden sent the General on 22 November.[2] De Gaulle accepted collaboration on these terms, although his long-term aims were precisely those which the British had divined and did not wish to aid. He gave a hint of his thinking in a letter about the working of the new project which he sent Eden late in December and which contained a reference to 'the adherence, public or secret', which the French National Committee had now obtained from the great majority of French citizens.

Eden's reply was discouraging. He said he could not promise that the British would operate in France 'entirely through Free French channels' and ended by rejecting de Gaulle's claims on behalf of the National Committee: 'It would not, we fear, be provident to rely for the purposes now in question, on the assumption that the National Committee enjoys the adherence, open or secret, of a very great majority of the French people.'[3]

This was a pointed rebuff of a certainly exaggerated claim. De Gaulle's name now meant a good deal in France, but his Committee did not yet command the allegiance of the great majority, even secretly. All the same, he was working hard to make his claim come true. In January he launched a plan to bring the whole of the Resistance under his wing. In this enterprise his inspiration and his instrument was Jean Moulin, of all the Frenchmen who rallied to de Gaulle in London probably the most remarkable and the most influential. He came to offer not only his services but his ideas, and in so doing he enlarged de Gaulle's vision of the means available to him inside France for carrying out his mission of liberation.

Jean Moulin, who was still in his thirties, had entered the administrative civil service before the war and had been *Chef du Cabinet* to Pierre Cot, Minister of Aviation in the Popular Front governments of 1936–7. To be acceptable in such a post he must have shared Cot's left-wing sentiments to some extent. Jean Moulin's instincts had made him a resistant from the moment of his first meeting with the German Army. This took place in June 1940 at Chartres, where he was serving as *préfet*. The Germans asked him to endorse a report they had drawn up blaming French African soldiers for a killing which villagers had already told him was the work of the Wehrmacht. Moulin refused. The Germans threw him in prison and beat him up. Later he was released, but he could not come to terms with Vichy and was suspended from the civil service. In 1941 he undertook a tour of unoccupied France, made contact with budding resistant groups and then, after the German invasion of Russia, set out for London, where he arrived in October. De Gaulle gave him a cordial welcome. State servants of his calibre were rare in the ranks of Free France in 1941.

Jean Moulin brought with him an impressive report of growing resistance in France and an appeal for aid to both the British and the Free French.[4] He told of a general desire for coordination allied with much sympathy and respect for de Gaulle himself. De Gaulle began to realize that the Resistance in France was acquiring a political consciousness and a voice, or voices. These developments required his attention. Together de Gaulle and Jean Moulin worked out a plan of action. Moulin was to return to France as the representative of the General in the Vichy zone and to win the allegiance to him of the entire Resistance as head and symbol of their movement. He was also to begin building the cells which were to form the nucleus of the secret army for the national uprising at the moment of liberation.[5]

Moulin was parachuted into Vichy France on 1 January 1942, and by March had prevailed on the Resistance groups there to come together in a council under his presidency. Representatives of the most important component organizations went to London to meet the General. Coordination was inevitably much harder to achieve in the occupied zone, but Moulin's message spread there too, and the pilgrimage of leaders to London began. Among the first was Christian Pineau, a trade unionist from the north. Not without difficulty, he was able to persuade the General of the need to allay suspicions that he was an ultra-conservative and to entrust him when he returned to France at the end of April 1942 with a message for Resistance leaders about his policies in which he made it clear that the National Committee aimed at the restoration of the liberties of the Third Republic in a society which would make economic and social security accessible to all.[6] As a result, left-wing groups began to feel more confidence in de Gaulle, and Jean Moulin's task of organization became easier.

De Gaulle's decision to unite the Resistance behind him involved the rejection of the rival course of trying to form a group or party of his own followers inside France who would join the returning Free French to create a specifically Gaullist political organization after the Liberation. This idea was advanced by the ex-Socialist Pierre Brossolette, who arrived in London in March 1942.[7] He argued that the collapse of 1940 had discredited the prewar politicians and parties in France and that new organizations as well as new personalities would be required after the war. Gaullism as such would have to exist. This view certainly had its appeal to the General, but its application there and then would have been incompatible with the mission he had already assigned to Jean Moulin. De Gaulle did not take Brossolette's advice.

This was a fateful choice. Thanks to it and to the success of Jean Moulin's work of unification, de Gaulle was able to appear as a national leader after the Liberation, entitled to appeal for the loyalty of all Frenchmen, including the Communists, as long as the war lasted. But, after victory had been won and democratic diversity was fully restored to political life, the General found himself without an organization of his own to further his views. In 1947 he had to found the *Rassemblement du Peuple Français* – the Rally of the French People – to supply this need. If Pierre Brossolette had had his way, the RPF would have been founded in 1942 or 1943.

While Moulin was pursuing his mission, there were changes in Vichy. Pierre Laval replaced Darlan as Prime Minister in April 1942. From this time onwards Laval, completely committed to the German cause, began to overshadow Pétain, whose grasp of affairs was diminishing. Darlan remained at the head of the armed services and kept his position as heir apparent to the Marshal, but was not in Laval's government. The Admiral was having second thoughts about banking on a German victory and made secret contact with the Americans.

A new figure appeared upon the scene in early May when General Giraud, an army commander who had been captured in 1940, escaped, with outside help, from Germany to Switzerland. De Gaulle tried to invite him to London, but there was no reaction. Instead Giraud went to Vichy and promised Pétain he would do nothing to disturb relations with Germany. The Americans began to cultivate him too.

During the summer Laval committed himself even more completely to the Nazi cause. On the anniversary of Hitler's attack on Russia, he shocked most French opinion by declaring that he hoped for a German victory over Bolshevism. On 23 June the clandestine press replied by publishing the text of the assurances the General had given to Pineau in April about the restoration of French liberties. All these developments helped de Gaulle to grow in stature with the Resistance.

Meanwhile de Gaulle's relations with the British remained a paradox. The British maintained their support, while at the same time confining him to the United Kingdom. Churchill personally continued to harbour dark suspicions about de Gaulle's intentions. This became apparent in April 1942, when the General told Charles Peake, the Foreign Office representative who acted as liaison officer with him, that he wished to begin a tour of inspection of French Equatorial Africa in about three weeks' time. Churchill, seeing Peake's report, minuted to Eden: 'I have for some time forbidden the use by him of any aircraft to leave the country. Please talk to me about this.' Eden urged in reply in a minute of 10 April that de Gaulle be permitted to make his journey 'now that the Muselier affair is patched up'. But Churchill was not satisfied. In a cryptic reply he said de Gaulle's project was 'most dangerous' and directed that the matter should be raised in Cabinet.[8] It was decided that de Gaulle must be asked to postpone his tour.

Perhaps Churchill's reluctance to let him loose in Africa at this point was due to the knowledge that the British were about to carry out an operation in the French island of Madagascar that was bound to enrage the General. Since Japan's entry into the war de Gaulle had repeatedly urged Churchill and Eden to agree to a Free French occupation of Madagascar with British support. The risk of the Japanese implanting themselves there with German approval and Vichyite collaboration became increasingly evident as their forces advanced through Southeast Asia. A Japanese naval base on the island could be a grave menace to Allied shipping in the Indian Ocean. But the British remained reticent until on 6 May, without warning de Gaulle, they occupied the port and naval base of Diego-Suarez on Madagascar by themselves.

The main reason for excluding the Free French from the operation could hardly be imparted to the General. It was that the British and the Americans felt that this would make the move less provocative to Vichy, and with the invasion of France or French North Africa a certainty before the end of the year, Pétain's susceptibilities mattered more to them than de Gaulle's.

Eden, who received de Gaulle a few days after the event, did his best to placate him: he gave assurances that no challenge to French sovereignty was intended and that the administration would be handed over to the Free French in due course. De Gaulle's reaction was restrained. He urged on Eden the need to occupy the whole of Madagascar, since the local representatives of Vichy were not to be trusted, and declared that Free French forces were available to carry out the task and take over the administration. Perhaps his relative moderation averted a crisis. His secret services are said to have had a report at this time that the British government were thinking of the withdrawal of recognition from de Gaulle and his internment in the Isle of Man.[9] Perhaps the policy which Churchill had in mind when he sent his minute of 23 September 1941 to Eden authorizing 'the forcible restraint of individuals' was once again under consideration. If so, wisdom again prevailed, and Churchill continued to bear the Cross of Lorraine.

In the hope of providing further consolation to de Gaulle, Eden revived with Churchill the idea of enabling him to visit Africa. But Churchill remained adamant. 'I cannot agree,' he minuted. 'There is nothing hostile to England that this man may not do when he gets off the chain.'[10] Eden persuaded de Gaulle to wait another six weeks before renewing his request, but his suspicions were thoroughly aroused by these repeated delays. He felt convinced that the Anglo-Saxons must be hatching some other plot like the seizure of Diego-Suarez and that it was for this reason that they were determined to keep him in Britain, where more control could be exercised over his words and deeds than would be possible in Africa. Were they going to seize Dakar without him? He resolved on a complete break with the Anglo-Saxons if that happened, and sent a warning to the British on 6 June, alerting his chief representatives abroad at the same time.[11]

This was not all de Gaulle did on 6 June. He also saw the Soviet Ambassador Bogomolov and asked him to discover if the Free French movement could be based in Russia in the event of a break with the British.[12] He presumably made this move in order to let the news leak out and serve as proof that he was serious about a possible confrontation with the British.

Perhaps as another warning signal, de Gaulle was already blocking French cooperation in the Levant with the British intelligence services. The head of the SIS was then in the Middle East and had complained to Richard Casey, Lyttelton's replacement, that de Gaulle's move was 'a blow to the war effort'.[13] A meeting between Churchill and de Gaulle was arranged for 10 June.

At this moment of tension a new event in the Western Desert, the first considerable feat of arms of the French land forces, providentially improved the climate of Anglo-French relations. Five and a half thousand men of a Free French light division under General Koenig stood firm at Bir Hakim for fourteen days against heavy German attack until ordered to withdraw, which they did successfully on 10 June. Koenig's exploit captured the imagination of the Allied world and obtained much publicity at a time when good news was in short supply. De Gaulle records in his Memoirs that, when the news of the successful withdrawal reached him, he locked himself in his room and wept with joy. For the first time in the war French forces had shown themselves a match for Germans.

The defence of Bir Hakim served to convert what might have been a stormy interview between Churchill and de Gaulle on 10 June into a relatively friendly affair. The Prime Minister warmly congratulated him on the performance of his forces and it was agreed between them that the official title of 'Free France' should henceforth be changed to 'Fighting France'. Churchill also reassured him about British intentions towards Madagascar, Dakar and the rest of the French Empire, and reminded him that he had always been a friend of France. 'That's true,' replied the General, 'you even had the merit of continuing to play the card of France after the Vichy armistice. The name of that card is de Gaulle. Don't lose it now . . .' 'We must see each other again,' said Churchill in farewell. 'I won't let you down. You can count on me.'[14] Relieved of his darkest fears, de Gaulle passed the six weeks of waiting which he had promised to Eden in a calmer mood. During this period he finally yielded to Passy's pleadings and put him in charge of all Free French intelligence services as head of a new directorate entitled *Bureau central de renseignements et d'action*, BCRA.

A valuable new link with the Resistance was formed in July when André Philip, a prewar Socialist and a leader of *Libération-Nord*, one of the stronger groups in occupied France, came by arrangement to join de Gaulle in London. He was immediately appointed Commissioner for the Interior in the National Committee and much publicity was given to his arrival. Philip played de Gaulle's game by telling the press that he was not rallying to a general but joining a minister of the last legitimate government of the French Republic.

It was 25 July before de Gaulle renewed his proposal to go abroad, this time for three weeks in Syria and Africa. On the 28th he saw Eden, who recorded that he was in a 'helpful mood'. The General said he thought no difficulties remained and that he would not have to send back telegrams from the Middle East like those of his 1941 visit. The next day Churchill received him at 10 Downing Street and wished him '*bon voyage*'. *Le Connétable* was no longer confined to England, even though he had paid no attention to Churchill's urgings that he should enlarge his National Committee.

So de Gaulle came to the end of his longest continuous stay in Britain, a matter of eleven months. During the whole of that time he had been in effect confined to the island by Churchill's orders, but this had not prevented him growing in political stature. He had established a satisfactory relationship with the Russians, and if his dealings with the British had been marked by a series of storms, they had not been unproductive. As to the Americans, he could at least feel that he had achieved his aim of making Free France 'exist' in the New World. Public opinion there was distinctly more sympathetic towards him than the sentiments of the White House and the State Department, as had been shown to his profit during the affair of St Pierre and Miquelon.

De Gaulle's chief gain during this period had been the increased support he drew from the Resistance in France. Nothing had done more to enhance his prestige in the West. The thinking of Resistance leaders had its effect on his own. In his speeches in these eleven months in Britain he showed a new awareness of the need to establish a more just social order after the war. He saw the need to identify Free France with a revolutionary spirit, and began to do so in his speeches. 'Let's not mince words,' he said to factory workers in Stafford in October 1941, 'this war is a revolution.' His speeches in 1942 showed the same broader vision, and at his first press conference, which was held on 27 May, he spoke again of the need for a new postwar order and of the unity in working for it of Fighting France and the Resistance.

On 5 August de Gaulle took off for the Middle East once more. On the way, at Gibraltar, he encountered the Socialist Félix Gouin, who had just succeeded in making his way there from France, where he had been active in the Resistance. Gouin asked him how much truth there was in stories reaching France of his difficulties with the British. 'Our British friends are not easy to deal with,' replied de Gaulle. 'That harsh desire for power, which is their dominant national quality' had, he said, been intensified by the struggle to the death with Germany. His duty was to protect the patrimony and the grandeur of France against the designs of the British. 'And the weaker I am,' he added in a determined voice, 'the more intransigent I shall be.'[15]

This was a less encouraging forecast of what his mission to the Middle East might produce than the one he had offered to Eden a week earlier. It proved to be nearer the mark.

During these years of struggling against the odds, the fixed point in de Gaulle's turning world was the presence in England of his wife and children. At first they lived in a rented house in Petts Wood, Croydon, but soon they moved to the country, first to Shropshire and then, in the course of 1941, to Berkhamsted, just north of London. Elisabeth proceeded from school to Oxford, and Philippe joined the Free French Navy in 1940, while the handicapped Anne remained with her mother. De Gaulle spent weekends and holidays with them and lived in the Connaught Hotel in Mayfair, close to his headquarters in Carlton Gardens until, after German air attacks on London had clearly ceased, they moved to a house in Frognal, Hampstead. An eye-witness has described to me how he gradually relaxed in the course of an evening with them.[16] He played simple games with Anne, who was always cheered by his company, and took her hand in family card games. It is easy to imagine how much would have been added to the burden of his anxieties if his wife had not succeeded in catching the last boat from Brest.

# 18 'THE MUTES OF THE BRITISH SERAGLIO'

The Japanese attack on Pearl Harbor had wrought an immediate change in the General's attitude to the war. On the evening that the news reached him, he said to his ADC Captain Billotte: 'The war is over. Of course there are years of fighting ahead, but the Germans are beaten. Unfortunately we'll make so many mistakes on the Western side that by the time this war is finished, we shall have created all the conditions for another one with Russia.'[1] From this time on de Gaulle's aims became more predominantly political than before. He could take military victory for granted and knew that the force of circumstances would prevent France from playing more than a minor part in the battle. But he wanted his forces to participate at least symbolically at the vital places and the vital moments in order to strengthen France's claim to the status of a great power after the war and ensure the regaining of the whole of her Empire.

As he revealed in his conversation with Félix Gouin at Gibraltar, it was France's patrimony, as he liked to call the Empire, that was in the forefront of his mind as he flew to Cairo. He was disturbed by reports from Syria that local British representatives, military and civil, were constantly encroaching on the authority of the Free French and pressing for the grant of more powers to the Arab governments in Damascus and Beirut. During the summer Catroux had been strongly urged by Casey to organize elections in Syria and Lebanon before the end of the year and had undertaken to do so. De Gaulle meant to have none of this. 1943 would be soon enough for elections, and he meant to force the local British to respect the paramount position of Free France as laid down in his agreements of the previous summer with Oliver Lyttelton.

When he reached Cairo, de Gaulle found Churchill there on his way to Moscow, and they agreed to review the difficulties in Syria with their respective local authorities and discuss the results later. Then Churchill turned to other matters, far weightier for him. He had to replace the chief British commanders in the Western Desert after the summer's failures on the battlefield, and break the unpalatable news to Stalin that there was to be no second front in Europe in 1942.

But to de Gaulle Syria remained the vital matter. He told Casey bluntly at their first meeting in Cairo on 8 August that the National Committee had decided there would be no elections in the Levant in 1942 any more than in the British sphere of influence in the Middle East. The military situation was too grave, he said, with Rommel so close to the heartland of Egypt. Then he flew on to Damascus and Beirut.

There he found matters even more unsatisfactory than he had expected. The British, on the grounds of war necessity, were interfering in the distribution of wheat and oil, whose import they controlled, and in many other administrative matters that de Gaulle considered to be the exclusive responsibility of the mandatory power under his agreement with Oliver Lyttelton. The activities of General Spears, who had been at the head of the British Mission since the beginning of the year, he found particularly offensive. It seemed to him that Spears was positively trying to stir up difficulties for the French with the local populations.

De Gaulle complained to Churchill, by then back in London, but the Premier rejected his charges and suggested that he should come back to London and discuss matters personally. The General agreed in principle but waited in Beirut until 10 September in order to receive Wendell Willkie, who was on a mission as President Roosevelt's personal envoy, and try to involve him personally in the Syrian affair. He sent a vivid and typical message to the Committee on 10 September while Wendell Willkie was in Beirut with him:[2]

British irritation and alarm is due not so much to our reactions themselves against their policy in the Orient as to two other considerations which make themselves constantly felt:

The first is that we have made the Oriental question a matter of inter-Allied diplomacy. But we literally had to do this or let ourselves be strangled by the mutes of the British seraglio . . . Given British usurpation here for more than a year, we have no choice if we are to save the situation.

The second factor to trouble the British is my presence here at a time when they would prefer to have my movements and statements under control. This shows . . . that important events concerning France or the French Colonial Empire are imminent.

As to the nature of these events he had already drawn some remarkably accurate deductions. As early as 27 August he had sent a telegram to Pleven and Dejean saying:

I am convinced by many indications that the United States have taken a decision to land troops in French North Africa . . . The operation will be launched in conjunction with an impending British offensive in Egypt . . . The Americans think they will obtain at least the partial passivity of the Vichy authorities . . . They have secured the good will of our supporters, particularly in Morocco, by pretending they are acting in accord with us, while intercepting all communications between them and us . . . Marshal Pétain will undoubtedly give the order to resist the Allies in Africa as aggressors. The army, navy and air force will not fail to obey. The Germans will be able . . . to intervene . . .[3]

If the Americans had consulted de Gaulle, they might have benefited from such warnings. But Roosevelt's veto stood firmly in the way. De Gaulle might guess, but he was not to know and not to help.

In the matter of Madagascar, de Gaulle was rather better treated. On 10 September Pleven and Dejean telegraphed that Eden had told them under the seal of strict secrecy that the British had decided to extend their military control from Diego-Suarez to the entire island and to invite the Fighting French to take over its administration. But, Eden said, this invitation would have to be held up until the argument over Syria was settled. So would the General please return soon and talk to Churchill, as the Premier had suggested.[4] The bait was sufficiently tempting, and the General had already done as much as was possible locally to consolidate his position in the Levant against 'the mutes of the British seraglio', as he now called British officialdom in the Middle East. He left for London on 22 September, just the day before British troops occupied Tananarive, the capital of Madagascar.

On 30 September Churchill, along with Eden, received de Gaulle at 10 Downing Street and they discussed Syria and Madagascar. It was one of their angriest interviews and ended in deadlock on both questions. When de Gaulle made his now ritual threat to cease cooperation with the British, Churchill challenged his right to speak in the name of France. 'You say you are France. You are not France! I do not recognize you as France!' Still angry, he went on: 'I admit that General de Gaulle and his followers are an important and worthy part of the French people. But no doubt we could find some other authority which would be of value.' De Gaulle rejoined by asking why Churchill discussed French interests with him if he did not regard him as representing France. Later in the meeting Churchill flared up again and accused de Gaulle of Anglophobia and personal ambition. Then Eden intervened and arranged for the contentious issues to be discussed by officials. Contact between the two leaders was severed for a while.

While negotiations with the British were under way between officials, de Gaulle busied himself with other matters. He received several important leaders from the Resistance in France and warned them to be ready for an American invasion of North Africa. They told of increasing support for him in France. The same message came in letters from Georges Mandel and Léon Blum, both in German custody, from the President of the Senate, Jules Jeanneney, and others. De Gaulle did his best to impress all this on the Americans. In the course of October he sent André Philip to Washington to deliver another long personal letter to Roosevelt. In essence it was an appeal for trust and cooperation. This time Roosevelt did at least read the letter, but he was not impressed. He minuted that it was too long and two years too late, and that de Gaulle had no understanding of the advantages the Allies had gained through American policy towards Vichy.[5] De Gaulle received no reply.

The usual détente soon developed after the row of 30 September between Churchill and de Gaulle. War pressures required it to do so. On 23 October, as the battle of El Alamein opened, Churchill sent de Gaulle a message saluting the presence of Fighting French forces with Montgomery's army. A week later Field-Marshal Smuts, who had arrived from South Africa, called on de Gaulle and assured him that the British would soon hand Madagascar over to his charge; and so they did. A joint Anglo-French announcement that the island was to be placed under Free French administration was issued on 6 November. In his discussion with de Gaulle, Smuts had added to his words about Madagascar the prophecy that sooner or later de Gaulle would take over French North Africa as well. This more daring forecast was to take a good deal longer to come true.

De Gaulle did not know it, but Churchill had timed the transfer of Madagascar to the Free French exactly as he wished. It was the curtain-raiser for Operation Torch, the American and British descent upon French North Africa with forces under the command of General Eisenhower.

# 19 OPERATION TORCH LIGHTS A POLITICAL BLAZE

In the first week of November 1942 the character of the war changed. The Allies seized the initiative from Germany and, save for a few fleeting episodes, held it for the rest of the war. In the Pacific the Americans had already begun to dictate events in August with the capture of Guadalcanal by the United States Marines. There too the change proved irreversible.

Three events marked the reversal of roles in the European theatre. On 4 November the Eighth Army broke the German-Italian front in Egypt and began a general advance; on 7 November the Russian armies closed a ring around German forces at Stalingrad; and on 8 November Anglo-American forces, borne to the area by armadas from Britain and the United States, commenced the invasion of French North Africa just as de Gaulle had predicted to Pleven and Dejean three months earlier.

On American insistence, de Gaulle had been kept in the dark even at the eleventh hour as to the nature and timing of the North African operation. Churchill had wanted to put him in the picture on 7 November, but Roosevelt vetoed even that.[1] Some of the exiles in London were better informed, however. At a reception on the evening of 7 November, Masaryk, the Czech Foreign Minister, had whispered to one of the National Committee: 'It's for tonight.' So when General Ismay telephoned de Gaulle's military secretary, Colonel Billotte, at 1 am on the 8th to tell him the landings had begun, it was unnecessary to awaken the General. He had gone to bed with the news.

Billotte passed on Ismay's message at 7 am. De Gaulle emerged in his dressing gown, looking furious, and said to those awaiting him in the next room: 'Well, I hope the Vichy people drive them into the sea. They can't break into France like burglars.'[2] His wrath was genuine, but his words were calculated and contained a warning he meant to be repeated to the Allies, that if they tried to behave like masters in the house they were entering, he would oppose them. Their duty was to hand it over to France, that is, in the circumstances of the time, to *Le Connétable de France*.

In fact de Gaulle had had ample time to consider his reactions, since he had predicted these events as long ago as late August. He soon had a chance to pass his views on to Churchill, who later the same day invited him to Downing Street and gave him an account of the Allied plan and how it was going thus far. Churchill emphasized that this was an American affair in which he was acting as Roosevelt's lieutenant, and that de Gaulle's exclusion from all part in it was an American decision. He indicated that he hoped Britain would have more of a voice at a later stage and that she would be true to her commitments to support Fighting France. In reply de Gaulle criticized Churchill's acceptance of a subordinate role, arguing that the British had been fighting the Axis in Africa for years, along with the Free French, whereas the Americans were newcomers, and that the British contribution would at least equal the American. He also criticized the Allied invasion plan itself for failing to include a landing at Bizerta in Tunisia, the port by which German and Italian forces were most likely to enter. On Churchill's news that resistance by the Vichy troops was stiffer than expected, de Gaulle observed that the Americans were paying the price of banking on Vichy rather than on him. But he forecast that given the basic feelings of the French soldiers, the fighting would not last long.

Churchill had two surprises for de Gaulle. The first was the news that the Americans had offered the command of the French forces in North Africa to General Giraud, and that he had accepted. The second was that Admiral Darlan had been caught in the invasion. De Gaulle replied that he could cooperate with Giraud and would get in touch with him, but Darlan's record since June 1940 made any sort of association with him impossible. The men of Vichy in North Africa and their régime must be swept from the scene.[3]

In public de Gaulle allowed none of his reservations to appear at this stage. Speaking on the radio the same evening, he called on the French in North Africa to take the side of the invading forces and so to prepare the liberation of France herself.

Pétain's public attitude was as clear as de Gaulle's. He issued a statement condemning the invasion as an aggressive act and called on his forces in Africa to resist to the utmost. But when the US chargé d'affaires, Mr Tuck, called with the official copy of a message from Roosevelt appealing to him not to oppose an invasion aimed at the liberation of France, Pétain showed no sign of personal displeasure. Finally he said an affable goodbye to Tuck, as if wishing to leave him under the impression that, despite his protest, events in North Africa were not too unwelcome to him.[4]

But if Pétain was playing a double game, he was doing so with only half a mind. He was now too old to concentrate and to act. He continued to vacillate during the next few days, while Laval went to Berchtesgaden to confer with Hitler. He was seriously considering, it has been alleged, ordering resistance to cease in North Africa and the fleet to put to sea from Toulon.[5] At the same time, however, he refused suggestions from both American agents and Vichyite supporters that he should leave France for North Africa himself. Laval, returning from Germany on 11 November, swiftly put an end to these waverings. He warned that, if the government did not remain true to the policy of collaboration with the Axis, he would resign and the Germans would treat France as they had Poland. Pétain and the rest submitted. Their last chance had gone. In the following days the German Army moved into the unoccupied zone and the men of Vichy were from then on physically at Hitler's mercy.

Across the Mediterranean, the Americans continued to play the hand. They found it difficult. The groups of friendly Frenchmen, some of them Gaullists, whom Robert Murphy had mobilized before the landings did their best to seize power in Algiers and Casablanca, but they failed. Many were placed under arrest, and a few officers were threatened with court martial. Giraud, when he arrived belatedly, had no impact on the situation at all. His appeal to the Army and administration to rally to him was universally ignored. Algiers surrendered to the Americans on the night of 8/9 November, but elsewhere fighting continued. There were naval engagements off Casablanca between American and Vichy warships. Pétain's order to resist was being obeyed.

The joker in the North African pack was Admiral Darlan. Nobody had foreseen his presence and he had not foreseen the landings. He angrily told Robert Murphy that the Americans should have coordinated their invasion with him.[6] During 8 November in Algiers he parleyed with the Americans and communicated with

Pétain, trying to make up his mind what to do. When Algiers surrendered, he was in the power of the Americans. With Giraud a failure, they decided that they must make use of him if they could, in order to bring resistance to an end. German and Italian troops and planes were already arriving in Tunisia, far sooner than expected.

Darlan was hesitant at first, but agreed on 10 November with General Mark Clark, who was negotiating with him on General Eisenhower's behalf, to order a ceasefire 'in the name of the Marshal', and to assume authority throughout French North Africa. But he wavered again when a message arrived from Pétain denouncing Darlan's proclamation. Clark put him under arrest, fearing he would disavow his action. Soon afterwards Darlan announced to the Americans that he had received another message from Pétain in a secret naval code stating that he had issued his denunciation under duress. The Americans released him, and from then on he was their willing and valuable, though controversial, servant until his murder on Christmas Eve.

Thanks to Darlan's orders the Vichy forces abandoned their resistance to the Allies on 11 November – by which time each side had lost some 3,000 men – and prepared to join the impending battle with the Germans. British forces hurrying eastwards made contact with the Germans inside Tunisia on 16 and 17 November. A ragged front formed, with General Juin's French troops alongside British and Americans. The initial Allied hopes of a swift and triumphant end to the campaign were thus disappointed. The end of January became the new target date for completing operations.

But well before the end of November military events had been overshadowed by the political consequences of the Clark–Darlan agreement. Darlan's usefulness was proved by the obedience given to his orders by all subordinate French authorities. General Eisenhower confirmed Allied acceptance of him on 13 November, by which time Darlan was able to justify his actions to loyal Pétainists by arguing that the Marshal was no longer a free agent. He proceeded to create an Imperial Council, to which he named the chief Vichy proconsuls, and appointed Giraud as military Commander-in-Chief, while assuming for himself the title of High Commissioner. The American generals acquiesced in all this as a matter of military utility, with the endorsement of President Roosevelt. Their action looked like the legitimization of Vichy's policies by the greatest power in the world, and a precedent for what would be done when the Allied armies landed in Metropolitan France.

There was an immediate sense of shock and revulsion in Britain, and Churchill sounded an anxious note in private to both Roosevelt and Eisenhower. 'Anything for the battle,' he cabled Eisenhower, 'but the politics will have to be sorted out later on.'[7] Nevertheless, his commitment to the military enterprise under American leadership kept him silent in public.

De Gaulle had no such inhibitions. He warned Churchill of the consequences of putting military considerations first:

It is a strategic error to flout the moral character of this war. We are not in the eighteenth century . . . We make war today with the spirit, the blood and the suffering of peoples. If the people of France discover that the Anglo-Saxon liberation means Darlan for them, there will be only one victor in this war: Stalin.[8]

Churchill allowed him to use the BBC on 17 November and succeeding days to broadcast a statement emphasizing that Free France had no hand in the political manoeuvring under way in Algiers, and would not accept the continuation of the Vichy régime there. But when de Gaulle tried to speak on the same theme himself on 21 November, he was told that it was impossible because the Unites States government, which had a right to clear statements relating to the North African campaign, had not given its approval to his text. Eden tried to have the ban lifted, but Churchill insisted on maintaining it.

Censorship did not, however, prevent the political storm from gathering. Messages of support, orchestrated by Jean Moulin, reached de Gaulle from Resistance leaders in France. American public opinion, as over St Pierre and Miquelon, showed a distinct tendency to sympathize with him too, and to query Roosevelt's policy. The President tried to reassure his critics by stating at a press conference on 18 November that General Eisenhower's arrangements with Darlan were 'only a temporary expedient'. This immediately aroused apprehension among Darlan's supporters. Field-Marshal Smuts, who was in Algiers, cabled a warning to Churchill: 'It would be a great mistake to create impression that he is to be discarded at an early date. Military situation may call for his retention for fairly long period.'[9] Further evidence of Darlan's usefulness was provided on 23 November when Governor-General Boisson rallied to him and brought over Dakar and all French West Africa to the Allied side.

President Roosevelt was under the full weight of these rival pressures of expediency and principle when he finally received the envoy de Gaulle had sent him in early October, André Philip, who was accompanied by the Free French representative in Washington, Adrien Tixier. The Frenchmen made the mistake of trying to be as tough as their master without the benefit of his moral stature. They lacked the grace to say a single word of gratitude for the sacrifice of life which the Americans were accepting in their effort to liberate French territory, but confined themselves to complaining, in accordance with their instructions, about the use being made of Darlan. Their attitude irritated the President profoundly, as Winant, the American Ambassador in London, later told members of the National Committee. Consequently the exchanges were sharp. According to the French record[10] the President justified his tactics in terms of *Realpolitik*:

I will use Darlan as long as I need him. I use him on a day to day basis. He has to obey or he will be broken. The time has not come to set up even a provisional French government, or to make a choice between French leaders who are prepared to take part in the war against the Axis . . .

Roosevelt ended by saying that he hoped de Gaulle would visit him in Washington to discuss the situation. That semi-invitation was the only gain the French envoys made from the meeting, but it was important. De Gaulle began discussing possible dates with the State Department. He had tried and failed to enlist Roosevelt's sympathy by letters and through envoys. A personal meeting seemed to offer the last chance. It was clear from the President's words that 'temporary expedients' in North Africa might last a long time and might set the pattern to be followed when France was invaded. There was an evident danger that the truth of the French proverb 'Nothing lasts like the provisional' might be illustrated at the expense of Free France.

But at this point Darlan suffered an important rebuff. It was administered, ironically enough, by the French Fleet at Toulon, which he had so long regarded as his faithful servant. He had sent them instructions as early as 11 November to put to sea and make for North Africa if in danger of capture by the Germans. But Admiral Laborde, who was in command, decided that his allegiance was to Pétain. The Fleet stayed in Toulon, and when the German Army finally approached on 27 November it scuttled itself at its moorings. Three battleships and eight cruisers went to the bottom, along with many smaller ships. If they had obeyed Darlan's orders, they could have made a great contribution to the Allied fight against the German submarine menace, which was now approaching its peak, and done much to raise French prestige. De Gaulle felt this catastrophe keenly. He records in his Memoirs how he received on the telephone Churchill's condolences 'nobly phrased, but with a note of underlying satisfaction'. All de Gaulle's historical vision of ruthless England instinctively hostile to French sea power is compact in these words. He could never bring himself to believe that Churchill truly desired the restoration of France as a great power capable of pursuing the foreign policy of its choice.

After the sabotage of the Fleet, Darlan's prestige began to wane and sympathy for the Free French showed signs of growing. In Algiers and other cities, painted slogans of '*De Gaulle au pouvoir*' and '*Mort à Darlan*' appeared. The rumour grew that Darlan's enemies were plotting to assasinate him. It was no more than the truth, as events were soon to show.

A new element was introduced when a representative of de Gaulle, General François d'Astier de la Vigerie, arrived from London on 19 December, with General Eisenhower's authorization, in order to discuss with Giraud and others how to coordinate the war effort of all French tendencies. De Gaulle had been trying to send a mission to Algiers ever since the landings, but his earlier requests to Churchill and Roosevelt for facilities had been unsuccessful. François d'Astier was a senior member of de Gaulle's intelligence team. His brother Emmanuel was head of *Libération*, a Resistance group in the formerly unoccupied zone of France, and an ally of Jean Moulin; another brother, Henri, lived in Algiers and had been one of Robert Murphy's principal collaborators before the invasion. After it he had been made chief of police in Algiers. He was a monarchist but in close touch with local Gaullists too.

François d'Astier's activities soon produced shock waves. He brought encouragement and dollars to the local Gaullists and named three of them – René Capitant, Louis Joxe and Henri d'Astier[11] – as the General's principal representatives in North Africa. He found and stimulated anti-Darlan sentiments among many local French personalities. Even Giraud agreed to discuss military coordination with de Gaulle. Finally he was received by Darlan himself, surrounded by the principal figures in his new régime, including Giraud. Darlan tried to browbeat d'Astier, asserting that he alone had the authority to unite the French against the Axis, and that he must therefore stay in office until the end of the war, when he would retire.

D'Astier replied bluntly that de Gaulle was the symbol of French resistance and its only possible leader and that the sole contribution Darlan could make was to retire from office without delay. The meeting broke up in disorder, and d'Astier was ordered to leave North Africa at once. On 24 December he was back in Britain and reporting to de Gaulle that he did not think Darlan would keep his place much longer.[12]

D'Astier's prophecy was fulfilled the same day. On the afternoon of 24 December, Admiral Darlan was shot dead when entering his offices at the Palais d'Eté in Algiers. His assassin, a young man of twenty named Bonnier de la Chapelle, was arrested on the spot. After a summary court martial ordered by General Giraud, Bonnier was put to death on the morning of 26 December, only thirty-six hours after his deed.

Mystery still surrounds the killing of Darlan. The assassin was known to be a royalist militant, and the official American theory, relayed by Cordell Hull from Robert Murphy to Roosevelt, was that the killing was the fruit of a royalist plot with or without the knowledge of the pretender to the throne, the Comte de Paris, who was in Algiers at the time and ought, in Murphy's view, to be forbidden to remain there.[13] It was widely believed at the time that the Comte was hoping to form a coalition of all anti-German French leaders, including de Gaulle and Giraud, of which he would be the head. Such ideas added to the acute tension in Algiers. Early in January the Comte was obliged to leave Algiers for his residence in Morocco[14] at the request of General Giraud, prompted by both British and Americans, who wished to calm the situation and concentrate on the battle in Tunisia.

De Gaulle, on the other hand, in his Memoirs points the finger of suspicion at the Americans without actually naming them. He suggests that the exponents of the 'temporary expedient' had come to feel that Darlan was now counterproductive and had therefore arranged for his elimination. As evidence in support of his theory he advances the indecent haste and the secrecy with which the assassin was put to death. Not even his name was revealed to the press before his execution, and there had been no time to interrogate him adequately.

It was as if those in authority were anxious to conceal what might lie behind his deed – and those in authority were Giraud and the Americans. De Gaulle does not conceal his sympathies with Bonnier de la Chapelle, whose motives he thought were patriotic.[15]

There was another suspect too. Many people in Algiers, including General Giraud and the military judge, Albert Jean Voituriez, who investigated the crime,[16] believed that the Gaullists might have become involved in what was originally a monarchist plot and that General d'Astier might have brought approval from London to his brother Henri for the liquidation of Darlan. Obviously those who suspected the Gaullists must also have suspected de Gaulle himself.

The judicial investigation which was carried out at the time cast no conclusive light on the affair. It resulted in the arrest on suspicion of complicity in Darlan's assassination of Henri d'Astier, the Abbé Cordier – a royalist priest and Bonnier's confessor – and a commissioner of police, Garidacci. But no charges were brought, and in September 1943 the report of the investigating judge, Albert Jean Voituriez, was shelved and the suspects liberated by order of another judge. Finally on 21 December 1945 a review tribunal of the Court of Appeal of Algiers, set up by an ordinance of General de Gaulle, annulled the verdict against Bonnier de la Chapelle himself on the grounds that documents discovered after the Liberation proved that Darlan had been a traitor, and that therefore 'the act for which Bonnier was condemned was accomplished in the interests of the liberation of France'.[17] Since then it has been the practice of Gaullist commentators on these events to speak of 'the execution of Darlan'.

The 'execution' of Darlan had the immediate effect of postponing de Gaulle's visit to Washington. He was due to leave England on 27 December, but Churchill intervened when the news arrived from Algiers to suggest that priority should be given to dealing with the new crisis in North Africa, which was preventing the Allies from concentrating on the military campaign. Roosevelt agreed, which left de Gaulle, who was privately convinced that Roosevelt had prompted Churchill's intervention, with no choice but to acquiesce. At this point Churchill dispatched Harold Macmillan to be senior British representative in North Africa with ministerial rank, a move which much increased British influence on the course of events there.

On 26 December Giraud was appointed by the Americans as 'civil and military commander-in-chief in North Africa', in succession to

Admiral Darlan. De Gaulle immediately telegraphed to him that Darlan's death made it more necessary than ever to set up a national authority and proposed a meeting on French territory in Algeria or Chad. Giraud sent an evasive reply, playing for time to settle himself in the saddle, but de Gaulle went on pressing. Then, suddenly, the Anglo-Saxons intervened. It was announced that Roosevelt and Churchill were conferring in Morocco, and Churchill sent de Gaulle a message on 17 January inviting him to come and meet Giraud.

This was a highly disagreeable invitation to de Gaulle, as he told Anthony Eden. He had no wish to meet Giraud under foreign patronage, and there was no indication that the President associated himself with Churchill's message. He replied with a refusal: 'Your invitation is unexpected. The overheated [*surexcité*] atmosphere of an Allied meeting and this sudden proposal of yours do not seem to me to promise an agreement. Direct and simple conversations between French leaders are the only good formula.' Roosevelt telegraphed to Cordell Hull in Washington: 'We have produced the future bridegroom, General Giraud . . . but our friends can't deliver the bride . . .'[18] Thereafter 'The Bride' became a favourite description of de Gaulle with the President.

Churchill, stung by having to admit to Roosevelt that he had so little influence with de Gaulle, reacted more brutally than usual when he sent a message threatening to withdraw financial support from Free France as long as de Gaulle was its chief, if he refused to come to Casablanca. He softened the blow by adding that Roosevelt joined in the invitation and that they would be happy to discuss North African questions with him. De Gaulle had the good sense to give way, and arrived in Morocco on 22 January.

The delegations were gathered at Anfa, the most opulent suburb of Casablanca, under close American security guard, for which de Gaulle repeatedly expressed his distaste. He had a series of separate meetings with Giraud, Churchill, Roosevelt and their followers, at which the main subject of discussion was how to bring de Gaulle and Giraud together and create a single French authority in North Africa. The Allied proposal was that a Committee should be formed under the triple presidency of Giraud, de Gaulle and General Georges, an old friend of Churchill's, who had commanded the French northern armies in 1939–40. The Vichy proconsuls, Noguès, Boisson, Peyrouton and others, were to be among the Committee members. Giraud was to have primacy among the triumvirs and to be Commander-in-Chief of the French forces in North Africa. Indeed Roosevelt had already signed an agreement with Giraud in that capacity, without consulting de Gaulle, making supply arrangements for North Africa, and recognizing his right to represent France's military, economic and financial interests in French North and West Africa.

De Gaulle could not accept such a proposal, which asked him in effect to surrender his leadership and merge Free France in an authority under Giraud which would derive its status from an agreement with the United States and Britain. In a series of difficult meetings he maintained his refusal, advancing for his part the plan which François d'Astier had already put to Giraud on his behalf, whereby under a strictly French agreement he would be the political chief and Giraud the military commander.

The most important meeting was the first between Roosevelt and de Gaulle, which took place one evening in the President's villa. They were alone together, except for a host of American armed guards half-hidden behind curtains. Describing the scene, de Gaulle says: 'We vied with one another in the exchange of courtesies.' But de Gaulle, characteristically, judged that Roosevelt was possessed by that 'tendency to dominate' which he attributed to all Anglo-Saxons, and aspired himself to play the role of the saviour of France.[19] He thought him 'troubled at the core of his being by the painful infirmity against which he fought so bravely' (Roosevelt had been confined to a wheelchair since being stricken with polio in 1920). He had, however, been accessible to Roosevelt's charm – 'He is a patrician,' he told Gaston Palewski after the meeting[20] – and was correspondingly wounded when he learned later that the President was making jokes about his attitude and accusing him of imagining he was Joan of Arc. The meeting did nothing to bring the two men, or their views, closer together.

At the final session deadlock developed. De Gaulle refused to accept the draft communiqué on the French talks approved by the President and the Premier. Then Roosevelt devised a way of saving at least appearances. He asked if de Gaulle would agree to be photographed by journalists shaking hands with Giraud. 'I will do that for you, Mr President,' replied de Gaulle in English. They went outside into the sunshine, and, with Roosevelt and Churchill sitting in the background looking benevolent, the two rivals clasped hands before the press cameras. Then they went away to prepare and issue their own communiqué on the talks, uncleared with the Anglo-Saxons. In the circumstances it sounded remarkably positive – and entirely Gaullian:

We have seen each other and talked. We have confirmed our complete agreement on the goal to be attained, which is the liberation of France and the triumph of human freedom through the total defeat of the enemy.

This goal will be attained by the union in the war of all Frenchmen, fighting side by side with all their allies.

The conference at Anfa was a searching test of de Gaulle's qualities as a statesman. He had to withstand the combined pressure of the two most powerful and eminent leaders in the Western world, on whom in the material sense the liberation of France, and his own political future, must depend. His will and his skill proved equal to the test. He refused Anglo-American patronage of a French united front, maintained his independent leadership of Free France, captured an immense amount of publicity, and established the bridgehead in North Africa which he had been striving to create ever since the Allied landings. This he did by securing Giraud's agreement in their bilateral talks to an exchange of liaison officers. Thus Giraud committed himself to receiving in Algiers a representative of the London Committee for further discussions on ways and means of achieving French unity. Giraud was to send a liaison officer to de Gaulle as well, but this was of much less real significance.

Robert Murphy's verdict on the conference is worth quoting: 'This professional soldier, who never had participated even in national politics before the war, now put on such a sparkling performance in international power politics that he took the star role away from the two greatest English-speaking politicians.' In Murphy's judgement, Casablanca was an 'unproclaimed victory' for de Gaulle.[21]

Immediately after Anfa, Giraud seemed to be in a strong position. Under the Americans he appeared to be the undisputed master of North Africa. But the truth was very different, as became apparent in the following months. The active minority in North Africa who had favoured the Allied cause and sought to help the invasion could no longer be suppressed and imprisoned as they had been in Darlan's time. Roosevelt and Churchill's visit brought a wind of freedom which continued to blow after their departure. When Giraud tried to take repressive measures against his critics in early March, the public outcry and the embarrassed reactions of the Allied representatives were such that he soon had to cancel them and, in a speech on 13 March, proclaim his devotion to democratic liberties.

On 14 March Giraud wrote to Catroux declaring his readiness to welcome de Gaulle to Algiers to discuss the achievement of national unity. De Gaulle had now achieved the position he enjoyed, in which he was being pressed to accept a proposal and could refuse it. He instructed Catroux to state that the National Committee wanted evidence that Giraud had abandoned his negotiating position of Anfa, i.e. the Roosevelt-Churchill proposal giving primacy to Giraud, before de Gaulle came to Algiers. Many messages and visits to London from Resistance leaders brought de Gaulle assurances of their full support. The great Jean Moulin came in February, his work of unification nearly completed. He returned with de Gaulle's instructions to set up without more delay the National Council of the Resistance under his own presidency. The plan the two men had made in December 1941 was about to bear its full fruit.

At this point de Gaulle received for the first time a message of support from an eminent American. It came in the shape of a telegram dated 3 April from the High Commissioner in Noumea, reporting what General MacArthur had said to his Free French liaison officer, Commandant Laporte. He had spoken in his most elevated style:

As an American and a soldier, I am ashamed of the way my country has treated your chief, General de Gaulle. The shame with which my government has covered itself in the sorry business of North Africa will take a long time to efface. I am a long way away from all that, but I cannot restrain myself from expressing to you all my disgust at the attitude of Roosevelt, and even of Churchill, towards General de Gaulle. Send him all my affection and admiration . . . He must not retreat before Giraud . . . He has the backing of the majority of the American and British peoples . . . He is supported by public opinion, just as I am . . . it is impossible to destroy an ideal as pure as his . . . with all my heart I pray to God for his success.[22]

De Gaulle sent a warm reply and stood as firm as his new friend wished. He remained an admirer of MacArthur's from then on. He always got on better with Republicans than with Democrats.

Eisenhower also veered towards acceptance of de Gaulle during April. Early in the month he had wanted to keep the General away from North Africa while the battle of Tunisia was approaching its climax, but on 21 April he told Macmillan that he no longer opposed de Gaulle's arrival.[23] Under pressure from Jean Monnet, who had come from America in February, and from Macmillan, Giraud sent de Gaulle a memorandum on 27 April in which he made a vital concession by renouncing his claim to primacy in any authority that was set up. It only remained to agree where the two men should meet. Giraud suggested a venue out of the limelight, such as Marrakesh, but de Gaulle insisted on Algiers. On 12 May, with the Tunisian campaign ending at last in triumph for the Allies, Giraud agreed.

The way was now clear for de Gaulle to come to North Africa on his own terms. On 13 May Axis resistance in Tunisia came to an end. The French forces in North Africa now numbered 450,000, including 150,000 European Frenchmen. They had played a worthy part in the battle, and some units were now demanding to be placed under the orders of General de Gaulle, whose Free French contingents, smaller in number but richer in glory, had come into Tunisia with the victorious Montgomery. In Metropolitan France too de Gaulle's star was in the ascendant. On 15 May came news from Jean Moulin that the National Council of the Resistance had been set up and had declared its complete support for the principles represented by General de Gaulle, whom they wished to see as head of a provisional government in Algiers and who, whatever the result of his negotiations with General Giraud, would remain the sole chief of the Resistance movement. The first formal session of the Council was held under Jean Moulin's presidency on 27 May and confirmed the message of 15 May. The convening of the Council in German-occupied territory was a hazardous enterprise and its success spoke volumes for the courage and diplomacy of Moulin. The news was published and brought priceless support to de Gaulle at a critical moment.

Triumphant on all fronts, except that of Washington, de Gaulle prepared his departure from England, which was no longer to be the headquarters of Free France. He wrote to King George VI to thank him, his government and his people for their welcome in 1940 and their hospitality since then. In the absence of Churchill in Washington, he sent him a letter on 27 May 1943:

As I leave London for Algeria, where I am called by my difficult mission in the service of France, I look back over the long stage of nearly three years of war which Fighting France has accomplished side by side with Great Britain and based on British territory.

I am more confident than ever in the victory of our two countries along with all their allies; and I am more convinced than ever that you personally will be the man of the days of glory, just as you were the man of the darkest hours.

Yours very sincerely,
Charles de Gaulle

It is an honest letter, expressing admiration but not gratitude. It does not acknowledge the truth that Churchill had made de Gaulle. This was a letter that would remain on record, and it was essential to de Gaulle's independent standing that he should not appear to be under any obligation to the British government. So his thanks went to the constitutional monarch and not to his First Minister.

De Gaulle had taken refuge in England in June 1940 as a professional soldier with twelve days' experience as a junior minister. He left three years later as a seasoned statesman known throughout the world. It had been his singular destiny to become a statesman while he was stateless, living in exile under sentence of death. It would have been a hard task and a severe moral strain in any part of the world. But for a Frenchman to learn the statesman's trade in exile in England – a Frenchman moreover with such a finely developed sense of history – was particularly testing and difficult. He had come among the adherents of a rival faith as strong as his own, hereditary foes and only recent friends of France. And he was among them without resources, as poor as they were rich.

De Gaulle among the British was like the Prince of the Babylonian Captivity who in Milton's words 'knew no state but the pipes and shawms of his own proud spirit'. He represented a prostrate nation with such inflexible resolution that he compelled respect for her and opened a path to her out of the abyss into which she had fallen.

The hardest part of his task had been done when he was able to establish himself on French soil in Algiers. There were difficulties and dangers immediately ahead, but he was not thinking exclusively of those during his final days in Britain. His mind was ranging far ahead to the days when France would have been restored to the rank of a great power. In a conversation with one of the Resistance leaders who visited him during May, General Cochet, he revealed his thoughts: 'I have no more confidence in the Anglo-Saxons. From now on my policy will be based on the Russians, and perhaps on the Germans.'[24] In terms of immediate action his words did not mean much, but one day they were to count for a great deal.

# 20 DE GAULLE IN NORTH AFRICA: CONFLICT WITH ROOSEVELT

While de Gaulle was making his farewells in Britain, his position was once more in danger. The President of the United States was pressing Churchill very hard to remove him from the leadership of Fighting France and Churchill was inclined in response at least to make another effort to bring him under the control of a strong Council.

Roosevelt had opened his campaign as soon as the capture of Tunis and Bizerta had brought military operations in North Africa to an end, apart from mopping up. On 8 May he sent a message announcing his intentions to Churchill, who was then on his way to America by sea to settle plans for the new phase of the war:

I am sorry, but it seems to me that the Bride's behaviour is getting worse and worse. His attitude and actions are intolerable.

The war in North Africa has almost reached its objective without any material contribution from de Gaulle, and the internal situation, despite the dangers it contains, is developing satisfactorily ... There is no doubt, however, that de Gaulle is making use of all the tricks of the most shameless propaganda to stir up agitation among the people, including Jews and Arabs ... Unfortunately there are already too many who are beginning to believe these disorders are being financed partly or wholly by the British government ...

... I tend to think that when we go into France we will have to think of a military occupation with British and American generals in charge ... I think we should talk about a new Committee of Liberation whose members would be approved by you and me ... not a provisional government but a consultative council.

I don't know what to do with de Gaulle. Perhaps you would like to make him Governor of Madagascar.[1]

The injustice of these charges is evident. Even if the accusation were true, it would have ill become the man who had insisted on excluding the Fighting French from all part in the invasion to complain that de Gaulle had given no material help to the campaign. In fact he had helped. He had from the outset called on the French forces in Africa to join the Allies against the Germans, and the Fighting French with the Eighth Army had played a part in the final battles.

What really irked Roosevelt was that since Casablanca, de Gaulle had won majority support in North Africa, as well as widespread sympathy in Britain and the United States, for a Fighting French takeover of the administration. The High Commission under Darlan and Giraud had been a failure and American prestige had declined as a result. Roosevelt, painfully conscious of these facts and of the profit his Republican adversaries might draw from them in order to attack his policies in the election campaign of 1944, naturally wanted to strike back. It was equally natural that he should aim at de Gaulle through his British paymasters, themselves funded by the Americans via Lend-Lease.

Roosevelt's ire was understandable enough. Only American power could rescue France from the consequences of her military defeat by Germany. Roosevelt could do the job without de Gaulle; de Gaulle could not do it without Roosevelt. Why should Roosevelt allow the credit for the liberation of France to go to de Gaulle?

The President took the question up as soon as Churchill arrived in Washington. Churchill was now permanently torn between irritation and admiration as far as de Gaulle was concerned, but he had gone through his own crisis of deciding whether or not to jettison the General in 1941–2, and had come down on the side of keeping him on board and trying to bring him under better control. When he had received de Gaulle on the morning of the invasion of North Africa, he had renewed his promise that Britain would not let him down. He was not now disposed to depart entirely from that undertaking. After all, his own reputation was by now bound up to some extent with that of the leader of Fighting France.

So Churchill adopted the expedient of telling the President that he would have to refer the question to the Cabinet in London. They argued that it would be disastrous to discard the General at this juncture, which enabled Churchill to defer a final decision without using up much of his own credit with Roosevelt by defending de Gaulle. Late in May he left Washington for Algiers, where he was to review the situation before the impending Allied invasion of Sicily, still under pressure from the President to rid him of the turbulent Frenchman and accept the idea of setting up an Anglo-American military government in France when it was liberated. Perhaps de Gaulle already had an inkling of Roosevelt's intentions when he spoke so bitterly to General Cochet.

On 30 May de Gaulle arrived in a French plane at Boufarik, a French-controlled airfield near Algiers, and was greeted by a French guard of honour and a military band which played the Marseillaise. French dignitaries, including Giraud, were in the front rank of the reception committee; Allied representatives were behind them. De Gaulle describes the occasion in his Memoirs with an attention to these details of protocol worthy of Saint-Simon. The precedence assumed by the French in his welcome made an agreeable contrast with the circumstances of his arrival for the Anfa conference in Morocco, in a British plane at an American-guarded airfield. At Boufarik the Prince could feel that he had returned home from his captivity.

Giraud hurried de Gaulle off to an immense festive luncheon in the French fashion. The chief supporters of the two men were among the forty-odd guests. It was an animated scene. As de Gaulle observed: 'Looking around, you might have thought nothing tragic had happened in the last three years . . . All the same, two rival teams were around the table.'²

During the next few days, the rivalry was acute. Discussions began on setting up a new National Committee to take over from the one in London, and immediately they ran into difficulties. De Gaulle wanted the new Committee to have the character of a provisional government with authority in all fields, including that of control over the armed forces. Giraud, however, was determined to remain military Commander-in-Chief in his own right and saw the new Committee not as a government but as an instrument for exercising his authority as 'civil Commander-in-Chief'. In fact he regarded the Clark–Darlan agreement and his own nomination by Eisenhower after Darlan's death as remaining in force even after the establishment of the new Committee.

The deadlock aroused intense excitement in Algiers. The city was full of rumours. Each side suspected the other of planning to launch a putsch to seize power and imprison its rivals. Giraud and de Gaulle both imparted their fears to Eisenhower's political advisers, Murphy and Macmillan. Then on 3 June agreement was suddenly reached on the formation of a Committee of seven members. Giraud and de Gaulle were the co-presidents. The other five were General Georges, General Catroux, René Massigli, André Philip and Jean Monnet. De Gaulle was fairly well placed for support in this body. Catroux, Massigli and Philip had all joined him in London and, without being unconditional adherents, would always tend to share his point of view; Monnet had recently arrived from Washington, where he had been since refusing to join de Gaulle in 1940; and Georges had been spirited out of France by order of Churchill in the hope that he would provide a brake on the General. They were not de Gaulle's men but neither were they Giraud's.

The Committee proclaimed that it was the central French authority, absorbing both the London Committee and the Algiers organization of the civil and military Commander-in-Chief; that it would exercise French sovereignty over all territories situated outside the power of the enemy; and that it would direct the national war effort. It undertook to restore the Republican régime and all French liberties, and to hand over its powers to the provisional government that would be created as soon as the territory of France was liberated. An ordinance in the names of General de Gaulle and General Giraud set up the new body under the title of *Comité Français de la Libération Nationale*. It became known by its initials as CFLN.

This looked like a victory for de Gaulle. The Committee was assuming the authority of a government, as he had wished, and the Vichy proconsuls, his enemies, had been excluded from it at his insistence. One of them, Peyrouton, had resigned, and Catroux took over from him as Governor-General of Algeria, while remaining a Committee member. The other two, General Noguès, Resident in Morocco, and Governor Boisson at Dakar, remained at their posts, but they were now subject to the authority of the Committee.

Churchill, who was still in Algiers conferring with Eisenhower and other commanders, invited the French Committee members to lunch on 4 June to celebrate their union. Then he flew back to London, where he immediately received a telegram of 5 June from Roosevelt reminding him that he was still expecting action against de Gaulle. The President expressed the view that basically there was British-American military rule in North Africa and that the two of them could use General Eisenhower to do what they wanted. This was a wholly different concept of sovereignty in North Africa from de Gaulle's, and was bound to lead to a clash with him if openly asserted. It was a prospect which did not deter Roosevelt. His message went on to call for a vigorous Anglo-American propaganda effort against de Gaulle and ended with the words: 'Best of luck in getting rid of our mutual headache.'

On 6 June Churchill replied:

We had the whole French Committee to luncheon on Friday (4 June) and everybody seemed most friendly . . . If de Gaulle is violent or unreasonable, he will be in a minority of five to two, and possibly completely isolated. The Committee is therefore a body with collective authority with which in my opinion we can safely work.

I consider that the formation of the Committee brings to an end my official connection with de Gaulle as leader of the Fighting French, which was set out in the letters exchanged with him in 1940 and certain other documents of later date, and I propose, in so far as is necessary, to transfer these relationships to the Committee as a whole.[3]

He added that they could wait for a time before deciding what measure of recognition to give the new Committee. On 8 June he announced his intentions to the House of Commons.

Thus the stage was set for the British subsidies, on which de Gaulle's whole capacity for effective action had hitherto been based, to be transferred to a body in which he was believed to be in a minority. Churchill evidently hoped that this move, combined with press attacks, would bring the General under control and meet American requirements without obliging the Allies to break with him completely. But he was deceiving himself if he seriously believed that the General would fail to dominate the Committee. This was the terminal form of an illusion which Churchill had nourished ever since the idea of converting de Gaulle into a Governor-General in Council had first occurred to him.

Meanwhile in Algiers the lull of 4 June had been followed by new storms. De Gaulle pressed for the establishment of a Commissioner for National Defence to exercise the Committee's military powers, and asked for the post himself in addition to his co-presidency. A meeting on 8 June ended in deadlock, and the next day the exasperated de Gaulle wrote to his colleagues saying that he 'could no longer associate himself with the activities of the Committee' as it was functioning at present and that he was no longer to be considered either as President or member of it. He returned to his villa and put it about that he meant to withdraw to Brazzaville – familiar tactics.

If Giraud had been a resolute man with a political sense, and if he had been given firm Anglo-American backing, this was the moment at which he might after all have ousted de Gaulle from the leadership. De Gaulle had announced his resignation without taking into account the implications of Churchill's announcement of 8 June in London that British subsidies would in future be paid to the Algiers Committee. Perhaps he did not even know it when he resigned. Withdrawal to Brazzaville in the new conditions could have led to penniless isolation, and he had given Giraud the chance to thrust it upon him.

But the possibility was theoretical only. Giraud wavered. De Gaulle made it clear that his resignation was not an abdication. He remained chief of Fighting France, and he was evidently the favourite of the crowd in Algiers and the French local councils in the big coastal cities. Moreover, firm Anglo-American backing for a hard line was not forthcoming. Macmillan advised Giraud and Georges against accepting de Gaulle's resignation: 'I see in this the danger of very grave events and a complete break-up of the French Empire,' he told them.[4] His advice prevailed, and the deadlock dragged on.

At this point the President's demand for a propaganda campaign against de Gaulle began to bear fruit.

Official briefing to the press in London about events in Algiers became much more critical of him, and it was put about that Churchill had drawn up a Cabinet memorandum of de Gaulle's sins against the Allied cause and given copies to American correspondents. On 13 June the *Observer* ended a hostile article by saying: 'If General de Gaulle continues his displays of intransigence . . . he will soon find himself without friends . . . We can do our duty to the people of France in other ways.' It was believed that Churchill himself had written it.[5]

Pierre Viénot, the Fighting French delegate in London since de Gaulle's departure, reported anxiously to Algiers both the more menacing tone of the press and the administrative difficulties following on Churchill's decision to transfer subsidies to the Algiers Committee. A crisis rapidly developed over aid to the Resistance in France. It was vital to de Gaulle to remain the channel through which help flowed from Britain to the Resistance if he was to preserve his leadership of it in any sense, and a menace to his position now developed. The BCRA were told on 14 June that help would no longer be channelled through them. The British withheld eighty million francs (about £450,000), the monthly subsidy which was due to be sent to France for the support of the *réfractaires*, as they were called, the young refugees who had taken to the hills to avoid being sent to Germany as forced labour. But General d'Astier appealed to the SIS from the verdict of the SOE, and was successful. The BCRA received their funds after all, though uncertainty still hung over the future.[6]

While the crisis simmered on, King George VI arrived at Algiers on a tour of the Mediterranean war theatre. On 14 June he gave a luncheon for the French leaders who were still at loggerheads. Afterwards de Gaulle asked Macmillan how he proposed to spend the afternoon. Macmillan replied that he was going to Tipasa, where there were Roman ruins and a beach. De Gaulle asked if he could accompany him, and alone. Macmillan relates the sequel in a letter to his wife: 'So I had three and a half hours of driving, walking in the ruins and continuous talking with this strange – attractive and yet impossible – character. We talked on every conceivable subject . . . All was more or less related to the things which fill his mind.'[7]

Later the Englishman bathed naked in the sea while the Frenchman in uniform 'sat in a dignified manner on a rock'. They dined together and went home. Macmillan concluded: 'I think I have persuaded him to remain in the Committee for the present and give the thing a chance.'

De Gaulle did not record his conclusions, but the reason why he sought Macmillan's company at this critical moment is apparent from a telegram on the crisis which he sent to Cassin and Soustelle in London on 12 June: 'Macmillan, whom I often see, now seems to have understood the realities. Murphy is still vague and difficult to communicate with.'[8] He had detected in Macmillan someone who was more of a friend than his chiefs in London. This was a correct judgement and was to be of importance in the fresh political storm that de Gaulle was about to provoke.

The fact was that in urging de Gaulle to stay in the Committee Macmillan had been preaching to the converted. De Gaulle was thinking not of leaving the Committee but of bending it to his will. His withdrawal to Tipasa was a modified version of that disappearance from the scene of the crisis which he so often practised before the moment of action. Tipasa was a substitute for the too distant Brazzaville, and, while in Macmillan's company there, de Gaulle was planning a dramatic move.

The next morning he went into action. Members of the London Committee had by now arrived in Algiers and de Gaulle took the view that they were entitled to compose half the membership of the new Committee. He wrote to Giraud explaining that his own withdrawal applied only to the group of seven and suggesting that a plenary session of the Committee should be called by the two of them jointly for the same afternoon to seek a solution of the problems of military organization. Provision for an enlargement of the Committee had been made in the ordinance of 3 June setting it up, so de Gaulle's proposal was not necessarily objectionable as a way out of the continuing deadlock. But the ordinance did not specify the number or identity of the extra members, and de Gaulle was taking advantage of this to propose an enlargement that would strengthen his own hand.

Unwisely, Giraud accepted de Gaulle's proposal and the plenary session duly took place with fourteen members of the Committee. In this body support for de Gaulle was much stronger. Giraud turned to the Americans, complaining that he had been duped by the advice of Jean Monnet into accepting the enlargement of the Committee.[9] Murphy sought instructions from Washington.

Roosevelt's reaction to the news of the packing of the Algiers Committee was explosive. In a furious message of 17 June to Churchill he called for a renewed effort to cast de Gaulle off completely:

> I am fed up with de Gaulle, and the secret and personal machinations of that committee in the last few days indicate that there is no possibility of our working with de Gaulle . . . I agree with you. We must get rid of him.[10]

At the same time the President sought Churchill's agreement to instructions he had sent to Eisenhower to summon de Gaulle and Giraud and lay down Allied requirements to them. These were that Giraud should remain sole Commander-in-Chief of French Forces in North and West Africa, and that the Allies should deal with him alone on all questions relating to their use of French military facilities in North Africa and their re-equipment of French forces. Roosevelt no doubt hoped that de Gaulle would reject this ultimatum and so give the Allies a good reason for putting him out of political circulation. He telegraphed Eisenhower: 'It is important that you should know for your very secret information that we may possibly break with de Gaulle in the next few days.'[11]

Churchill hastened to send a reply on 18 June which ostensibly agreed with the President but actually left de Gaulle a loophole:[12]

> If de Gaulle resigns, he will put himself in the wrong with public opinion, and the necessary measures must be taken to prevent him creating a disturbance. If he submits, this will be better than sweeping away a Committee on which many hopes are founded ... We should prescribe the conditions essential for the safety of our forces and place the onus on de Gaulle. At any rate it would be wise to try this first.

Roosevelt did not dissent. The loophole was left.

The Fighting French delegates in London and Washington, Pierre Viénot and Philippe Baudet, kept de Gaulle well informed of the mounting danger. Viénot telegraphed him a résumé of the off-the-record briefing given to diplomatic correspondents on 17 June by Brendan Bracken, the Minister of Information and Churchill's close friend. Bracken had castigated de Gaulle for pursuing personal ambitions, systematically stirring up trouble for the Allies in North Africa, and showing 'unpardonable ingratitude' to Britain. 'Britain is tough and won't allow an ambitious General to upset the plans of Eisenhower and the United Nations.' A correspondent asked if this meant that Britain would go as far as placing de Gaulle under restraint. 'Yes,' replied Bracken.[13] Viénot's telegrams attribute some of his information to secret sources and provide evidence that the BCRA employed agents to collect intelligence in Britain about the British government's intention.

Thanks to his men in London and Washington, de Gaulle had a good idea of what was at stake when he went with Giraud to see Eisenhower on 19 June. Eisenhower's tone was more moderate than that of Roosevelt's instructions to him. He did not emphasize the President's view of where ultimate sovereignty in North Africa lay, but asked for assurances that as long as important Allied operations were being conducted from bases in North Africa, there would be no change in the supreme command of French forces in North and West Africa or in the arrangements for Allied use of French facilities. De Gaulle asked Eisenhower to put his demands in writing and said that they would be presented to the Committee, although he described them as intervention in French affairs.[14]

An allied memorandum which ended with assurances of respect for French sovereignty was delivered the following day, and on 21 June the Committee met to consider it. This was the critical moment for de

Gaulle. If the Committee tamely accepted the Allied documents, it would be a success for Giraud and a heavy blow to his own prestige. On the other hand if he caused the Committee to refuse, he was running the risk of consequences which might go as far as his arrest and the end of his political career.

The Committee's deliberations were lengthy and a compromise was not found until the following day, after informal consultation with the Allies. It amounted to giving Eisenhower what he wanted in practice without taking up any position about who held the ultimate authority in North Africa or entering into any commitment about duration. The decision was reached to set up not a Ministry of Defence but a Military Committee composed of de Gaulle, Giraud, and a few senior generals. Under the Military Committee there were to be two High Commands, one for North and West Africa under Giraud and one for the rest of the Empire and the Resistance in France under de Gaulle. These decisions were announced and, at de Gaulle's suggestion, no direct reply was sent to the Allied memorandum.

Eisenhower, with the encouragement of Macmillan, chose to regard this as a satisfactory outcome. By this time, according to the account in Macmillan's Memoirs,[15] Eisenhower had become disillusioned with Giraud and unenthusiastic about the President's policy of working exclusively through him for the rearmament of the French forces. If Eisenhower was satisfied, the President had no valid reason to demand action against de Gaulle, and Churchill took no action in the absence of pressure from Washington.

So the gathering storm which had seemed so dangerous on 17 June did not burst upon de Gaulle's head after all. It gradually dispersed, and the flow of anxious telegrams from Viénot and Baudet dried up. When René Massigli, who was in charge of foreign affairs in the Algiers Committee, visited London in early July, he took the chance to emphasize to Churchill the dangers that would follow the removal of de Gaulle from his position of leadership. But the plea was no longer necessary. As they sat in the garden of 10 Downing Street, Churchill 'talked at length about General de Gaulle. He paid tribute to his remarkable gifts but expressed the fear that he pursued personal ambitions . . . de Gaulle had said to him one day that precisely because of his situation he had to show his independence of Britain in everything. But that had led him to go too far . . . He must take his place in a team.' There was no more talk of eliminating de Gaulle. On the contrary Churchill spoke as if he had been trying to save de Gaulle from Roosevelt all along. He told Massigli that the enlargement of the Committee had caused him a lot of trouble with Washington, but that the latest news was better.[16]

Meanwhile the President had invited *his* French General, the good non-political Giraud, to tour the United States and discuss the equipping of the French armies, and Giraud left Algiers on 2 July full of naive pleasure at an invitation which he thought would raise his prestige. But the field of his battle with de Gaulle was Algiers, not Washington. The French maxim that '*Les absents ont toujours tort*' proved true in this case. Giraud's visit to the United States was treated by his hosts, in accordance with their policy, as a purely military affair without political overtones. In consequence it had little public impact either in America or North Africa, except when Giraud made an astonishingly foolish speech in Detroit praising the magnificent achievements of the Nazis in reconstructing German society.[17] In Giraud's absence de Gaulle passed the month of July touring the country and attending victory parades amid scenes of great popular enthusiasm; and his wife and daughters joined him from London.

The Allies invaded Sicily on 10 July and discovered that all the logistical support they could wish from French North Africa was forthcoming, although de Gaulle was in charge and Giraud away in the United States. In early July the French islands in the West Indies rallied to Fighting France and thereby completed the union of the French Empire in the war against the Axis under the Cross of Lorraine. The result was that by the time Giraud returned to Algiers on 29 July de Gaulle had a solid majority in the Committee. On 31 July the Committee, including Giraud, approved a new set of proposals. They were that the co-presidency should continue nominally, but that de Gaulle should be sole chairman of the Committee; that a Committee of National Defence should be set up, with de Gaulle in the chair; and that Giraud should be Commander-in-Chief of all French forces.

Thus Giraud conserved the title the Allies had insisted he must have, but everything was settled in principle as de Gaulle wished. He was now the unchallenged and unchallengeable leader of all the French who were fighting against the Axis, and only Roosevelt and Hull refused to see that he was the predestined chief of the first government of France after its liberation.

# 21 TOWARDS LIBERATION

By August the Algiers Committee had clearly come to stay, and both Churchill and Eisenhower urged Roosevelt to agree to its recognition by the Allies. He held out until the end of the Anglo-American conference at Quebec and then gave way grudgingly. On 26 August the United States, British and Soviet governments made separate declarations of recognition. The American statement was the most restrictive of the three, making it clear that the decision only applied to French territories under the Committee's control and not to the future administration of liberated France.

Allied victories on all fronts made it evident that the ring was tightening around the Axis powers and that 1944 would be the year of the great landing in France. Inside the country Hitler's exactions grew as the strain on his war machine increased. French rations became the lowest in Western Europe and more and more French labour was conscripted and shipped off to German factories and farms. Under this pressure the nature of the Resistance movement changed. The groups of relatively disciplined men who had been its backbone in the earlier years were now joined by masses of youngsters who had no training and whose inspiration was the wish to avoid being sent to Germany. The active Resistance became much larger but less organized. Some of the results were tragic. On 10 June the newly formed Council of the Resistance was surprised at a meeting, and nearly all its members, including its leader, Jean Moulin, fell into the hands of the Gestapo. Moulin was tortured to death. General Delestraint, leader of the military side of the Resistance, the secret army that was being formed with British help to launch a general rising when the word was given, was also captured in June. In the next few months the same fate overtook Moulin's successor and other leading Gaullists working in senior posts in the Resistance. It became more and more difficult for de Gaulle to give direction to the movement inside France. The influence of the Communists grew at his expense. But his titular leadership was unchallenged. The cornerstone of Jean Moulin's great work remained in place.

De Gaulle was resolved that the French forces should play the maximum possible part in the liberation campaigns in France. A memorandum of 18 September signed by him and Giraud put this view to the Big Three, as the United States, Britain and Russia were called by the press. The salient point was that the main effort of the French forces should be devoted to a landing on the Mediterranean coast, but that certain elements should be included in the cross-Channel invasion, among them an armoured division assigned to the liberation of Paris. A second memorandum made proposals for organizing cooperation between the Allied armies and the civil administration in France. It was based on the assumption that the Algiers Committee would direct the civil administration.

With recognition granted to the Algiers Committee it would have been logical for the Allies to adopt a generally more positive attitude towards Fighting France. Vichy's susceptibilities could now be ignored. All the assets it had possessed a year earlier, the best part of the Empire, the Fleet and the unoccupied zone itself had disappeared. There were strong arguments for treating Fighting France as a nominal equal and taking de Gaulle into Anglo-American confidence with regard to all future military planning, and in particular that of the invasion of Normandy. This was what he wanted, and to grant it at this stage might have made him an easier ally in war and peace.

The British government, which had severed its link with Vichy through ambassadors in Madrid as long ago as 18 March, might have adopted this policy. But American opposition to recognizing that the Algiers Committee had any authority in France was adamant, and it was the basic principle of Churchill's war policy to keep in close, friendly, and indeed deferential relations with President Roosevelt. So he aligned the British position upon the American.

In consequence de Gaulle, despite his much increased strength, was still kept in a subordinate position in Allied councils. He was given no information about operational planning, nor was he officially told, although he knew, about the preparations beginning at the President's behest for the Anglo-American military administration of civil affairs in France. A training school was set up at Charlotteville near Washington to give two-month training courses to candidates for the task!

De Gaulle was told as little about Allied negotiations with Italy as about operational planning. Marshal Badoglio had replaced Mussolini as Premier on 26 July, and had immediately made a secret request for an armistice. This was signed on 3 September and, after a delay designed to enable Allied troops to land in Southern Italy, was made public on 8 September. Only tardy and confused information was given to the French, and they were unable to send a representative to take part in signing the armistice. There were also difficulties about representation for France on the Commission set up to deal with the political side of the occupation of Italy. Only at the end of November did Fighting France become a member of the newly-created Advisory Council for Italy, but even then she was not given a place on the more exalted European Commission which was set up at the same time.

To de Gaulle this whole process of grudging and limited acceptance was a sign that the Anglo-Saxons wished to keep France in a state of tutelage even after the liberation. He saw to it that his feelings were reflected in the French North African press, and a campaign was mounted accusing the Americans of still favouring the men of Vichy and intending to make them their instrument of government when the Allies occupied France. To the Americans it was a traumatic experience to be attacked in this way by people they had just liberated. De Gaulle was blamed, and resentment in official Washington was bitter.

With the approach of winter the Allied leaders began to consider a meeting to discuss high strategy for 1944. From this of course de Gaulle was to be excluded. He was left free to concentrate on shaping the course of events and opinions in the French Empire and occupied France. An ordinance of 17 September decreed the formation of a Consultative Assembly to support the Algiers Committee in its work. It had over a hundred members, some fifty of them from the Resistance in France, and its first meeting on 3 November was a moving occasion. De Gaulle opened it with an important political declaration claiming legitimacy from the outset for his own movement and denying it to Vichy.

By this time Giraud had prepared his own downfall on the Committee. In July and August he had sent arms to Resistance groups in Corsica without consulting or informing his colleagues. In September, at the moment of the announcement of the Italian armistice, which had the effect of neutralizing the Italian garrison of eighty thousand on the island, he gave the order for an armed uprising. Only at that point did he tell de Gaulle of the coup he had been preparing and suggest that troops should be sent from North Africa at once to back the insurgents against the German forces. When the battle in Corsica had been won, de Gaulle had no difficulty in settling accounts with his Commander-in-Chief. After the Consultative Assembly had held its inaugural meeting in Algiers on 3 November, de Gaulle proceeded to reorganize the Committee. Representatives of the Resistance were brought in, and Generals Giraud and Georges were among those who departed.

The new arrivals who came to Algiers for the Assembly by the now well organized, if hazardous, route from France saw matters very differently from those who had been abroad for most of the time since 1940. Their chief concern was to secure a rapid increase in aid to the Resistance. The grandeur of France, as de Gaulle observed to his regret, meant relatively little to them, nor did they all fall under the spell of his own personality.

One with whom de Gaulle had immediate difficulties was a young man called François Mitterrand, who had made his way from France via England. When the General received him, his first observation, in a reproachful tone, was: 'You came in a British plane.' This criticism seemed hardly justified to Mitterrand, since he had come from the west of England, where no other planes were available. He declined to fall in with de Gaulle's plans for his Resistance group, and the interview ended as badly as it had begun. The antipathy was apparently mutual, because Mitterrand found it impossible to obtain transport back from Algiers to France. He finally managed to hitch-hike to England in General Montgomery's plane, and made his way to France from there.[1] Thus began a relationship of great importance to the Fifth Republic.

There immediately followed the unnecessary distraction of another Anglo-French crisis over the Levant. The elections which de Gaulle had refused to hold in 1942 took place in July 1943 and resulted in the victory in both Syria and Lebanon of nationalist parties eager to affirm complete and immediate independence without the prior conclusion of a treaty with France. In November the government in the Lebanon passed a new constitutional law purporting to do away with the French mandate. The High Commissioner, Jean Helleu, had been authorized to make concessions, but instead he was unwise enough to dissolve the Assembly and imprison the President and ministers. Arab leaders throughout the Middle East raised an immediate outcry and, inevitably, complained to the British. The CFLN tried to escape from this predicament by calling Helleu to Algiers and ordering Catroux to go to Beirut and patch matters up by making concessions.

A solution might have followed, but unluckily the British government faced a special problem which made it urgent to dissociate itself from Helleu's action and resolve the crisis. Churchill was on his way to Tehran to meet Roosevelt and Stalin and knew that he would be held responsible in that gathering for the situation in the Levant. Casey was therefore sent to Beirut to present Catroux with an ultimatum demanding the release and reinstatement of the Lebanese leaders by 22 November, failing which British forces would assume responsibility for law and order. When the Committee met in Algiers, de Gaulle was for refusing to carry through the reinstatement under a British threat. On 20 November, however, he was outvoted in the Committee, which favoured seeking a compromise. They ended, on Catroux's advice, by accepting the British demands in full after outvoting de Gaulle a second time.

Thus a military confrontation was narrowly averted. But, if a new Fashoda was prevented, a new grievance on de Gaulle's part was not. He felt that the British had intervened in order to gain the credit for a setttlement which the French were in fact achieving on their own initiative.[2]

An instructive aspect of this affair was de Gaulle's acquiescence in being outvoted in the Committee although the ultimate power of decision was his. In the circumstances this was only common sense, but it is worthy of note that the General allowed common sense to be his guide. It should be remarked that he never lost the capacity to bow to the majority in a Council of Ministers. His willingness to do so was to reappear at the end of his career during the crisis of May 1968 and to have its influence on the course of events. De Gaulle was always pragmatic even about displaying intransigence. Inflexibility was a tactic which appealed to his temperament, but it remained a means to an end, not a principle.

At the end of November the first summit meeting between Roosevelt, Churchill and Stalin took place at Tehran. In de Gaulle's absence both he and France were discussed. Stalin's views were clear-cut and brutal. De Gaulle, he said, was unrealistic. He represented an imaginary France, but the real France had backed Pétain and aided the Axis. France should be punished for that; her colonies should not be returned to her. 'De Gaulle continues to behave as if he were at the head of a great power . . . I attach no importance to him.' Roosevelt was hardly more charitable. He asserted that France should not have Indo-China back, and that some kind of international control should be established at strategic points like Dakar and New Caledonia. He did not agree, he said, with his friend Churchill that France could soon become a Great Power again after the war. Only Churchill spoke up in defence of France. She had been overwhelmed by superior force in 1940, he argued, and the free world would need a flourishing France after the war.[3] But his plea made no impression at Tehran. At Yalta, happily, he was to be more successful.

Evidently Stalin attached no importance to the Soviet commitment of 1942 to work for the restoration of the grandeur of France as well as her independence after the war. Perhaps both he and Roosevelt were working off some of their sense of grievance at the fall of France in 1940. If she had stood upright against the German onslaught, Hitler would not have been strong enough to make war on either Russia or America.

Of more immediate importance to de Gaulle than the hard words of Stalin and Roosevelt was the decision taken at Tehran that there should be an invasion of Southern France in 1944 as well as the cross-Channel assault, and that it should be given priority in assignment of resources over other Mediterranean operations. This confirmed that the Western Allies could give full acceptance to the military aspect of his proposals of 18 September. He was given the good news at a meeting in Algiers on 27 December with General Eisenhower, who had been chosen as commander of the operation to be launched from England. On the other hand, Eisenhower had no reply to offer to the other aspect of the proposals of 18 September, liaison between the Allied armies and the civil power in France.

On one point de Gaulle would have agreed with Stalin at least in principle: collaborators with Hitler deserved punishment. The members of the Consultative Assembly who had come from occupied France were also insistent that major culprits should be brought to trial. As a result a number of leading Vichyites living in North Africa were arrested just before Christmas, including two ex-ministers, Pucheu and Flandin; two proconsuls, Boisson and Peyrouton; and two military men, General Bergeret and Admiral Derrien.

The principle thereby asserted was of capital importance. It was that the administration headed by de Gaulle had the power to put

Frenchmen on trial for acts performed by orders of the Vichy régime at any period of its existence. This was a slap in the face for all the foreign governments which, like the United States and Russia, had sent ambassadors to Vichy. Roosevelt and Churchill felt it necessary to intervene. The President was furious at the arrest of Boisson and Peyrouton, who had both been helpful to the American forces, and Churchill sympathized with Flandin, a prewar friend. De Gaulle was not prepared to agree to the release of any of the three, but promised that their cases would be held back until after the war.

Churchill fell gravely ill in North Africa on his way back from the Tehran Conference, and had to pass a period of recovery there over Christmas and the New Year. His convalescence provided a chance for the first serious tête-à-tête conversation between the two men since de Gaulle's departure from England in May 1943. De Gaulle came to lunch at Marrakesh on 12 January.

It proved to be one of their more amiable encounters. Mrs Churchill helped by taking de Gaulle for a preliminary walk in the garden which the convalescent Prime Minister did not join, and reminding him that it was important 'to hate one's enemies more than one's friends'.[4] It was a repetition of the lesson she had read him after the tragedy of Mers-el-Kebir, and the General again took it in good part. In his conversation with Churchill he argued once more against the plan to set up an Anglo-American military government in liberated France and pleaded for more aid to the Resistance. Churchill promised to do what he could for the Resistance and asked de Gaulle to discuss the administration of liberated France with the newly arrived British representative, Duff Cooper, who was to replace Macmillan.

In fact Churchill did not agree with Roosevelt's plans for military government, but it would have been against his principles to tell de Gaulle that he sided with him against the President on such an issue. He contrived none the less to say a few things that must have been music to de Gaulle's ears. He said that he had triumphed in French North Africa, as Churchill had predicted; and that he would triumph in Metropolitan France too. As a reward de Gaulle invited him to review a parade of French troops in Marrakesh the next day, and the two men stood side by side in apparent amity before a large and enthusiastic crowd.

Attitudes in official Washington remained, however, firmly hostile. In January 1944 the State Department prepared a letter of guidance for President Roosevelt to send to Murphy's replacement, Edward Wilson, which read like an indictment. It condemned every aspect of de Gaulle's 'political activities which retard and are a constant threat to the Allied military effort' and ended:

> I am only bringing these facts to your attention in order that you may lose no opportunity to point out to General de Gaulle and the members of the Committee the harmfulness of their present course not only to the cause of the United Nations but to France herself.[5]

An envoy saddled with such instructions faces an uphill task. When Wilson said at one of their early meetings that he hoped no misunderstandings would cause trouble in future, de Gaulle replied that it was not misunderstandings but American policy that caused the trouble.[6] After a few months Wilson gave up his post.

By this stage of the war the demand for decolonization was beginning to make itself felt in the empires of the Western Allies. The language of the Atlantic Charter was doing its work. De Gaulle was aware of the strength of this current of feeling in the French possessions and sought, while there was still time, to direct it into channels of cooperation. He still believed that the French presence in the Empire must continue, but he was willing to consider concessions of both form and substance if they would satisfy the rising expectations of the colonial peoples.

In pursuit of this policy the CFLN first liberalized voting rights in Algeria and then convened a conference on the African territories at Brazzaville in January 1944 to recommend measures of economic, social and political improvement that might be applied within the French Community, as the Gaullists now began to call the Empire. In his opening address de Gaulle emphasized that the process of change would be lengthy and would be carried out by France alone in exercise of her sovereignty. The culmination would be not independence but new forms of administration that would enable the people to take part in the direction of their affairs under French authority.

On returning from Brazzaville, de Gaulle fell seriously ill with malaria and kidney trouble. Like Churchill's malady after Teheran, it was well timed. He was fit again by the time he had to be. His attention was absorbed by the twin problems of preparing for the invasion and managing relations with the Resistance. The trials of the Vichyites detained in Algiers were adjourned until after the Liberation with the exception of the case against Pucheu, which was especially grave because he had been Minister of the Interior in 1941–2. It was said in particular that in one case where the Germans had decided to shoot hostages he had indicated to them whom to shoot and had chosen Communists. In March he was tried and condemned to death, desite the fact that General Giraud, in his capacity as civil and military Commander-in-Chief, had given Pucheu a guarantee of safe conduct before he came to North Africa of his own free will after the Allied landings. Pucheu had violated its terms by drawing attention to his presence in the country instead of living quietly, but Giraud still felt obliged to ask de Gaulle for a reprieve. De Gaulle refused an act of clemency which would have been most unpopular with the Resistance, above all with the Communists, and Pucheu was put to death. Giraud was bitterly resentful, but the Resistance rejoiced, and the Communists announced their willingness to nominate representatives to the CFLN, which they duly did after a brief negotiation.

At this point de Gaulle decided to wait no longer for an Allied response to his proposals for administering liberated territory. On 21 March an ordinance was proclaimed laying down that the CFLN would move to France and assume its responsibilities there as soon as enough territory had been freed. Lists of commissioners to take charge in the various regions had already been published in January, and policy decisions were announced on a few matters of the highest administrative priority. Credit and the various sources of energy were to be nationalized; welfare services were to be improved; and women were to be given the vote for the first time in the history of France. Speaking on 27 March in the Consultative Assembly de Gaulle described the Committee for the first time as the provisional government and proclaimed that it would take no lessons from foreigners in its work of restoring democracy in France. His words were a direct challenge to Roosevelt's plans, by now well known, for installing a military government and were prominently reported in the American and British press. The CFLN was now the instrument with which he meant to rule France. His hold on the Resistance had slackened with the loss in France of Pierre Brossolette and other Gaullists.

Preparations for military command were also completed. De Gaulle assumed the title of head of the French armed forces on 8 April. Giraud refused the consolation post of Inspector-General and preferred to retire to his house at Mostaganem in Algiers stripped of all his offices. Roosevelt was angry but powerless to help him.

Later in April with the approach of the invasion season, Britain put all communications with the outside world, including diplomatic, under tight security control. Communications between the French delegation in London and Algiers were cut. De Gaulle considered that special arrangements should have been made for the Fighting French as they had been for the Americans and protested vigorously. For a time he refused to receive Macmillan's successor Duff Cooper, the British Ambassador in Algiers. But when Duff Cooper asked on 23 May to deliver a special message from Churchill, the interdict was lifted. The message was an invitation to visit Britain to discuss questions of recognition and of administration in liberated France. Churchill was still hoping to find a compromise between Roosevelt and de Gaulle. Assistant Secretary of State Stettinius reported to Mr Hull from London that 'the British fear the United States will repeat its Darlan policy, and they are resolved to back the CFLN and nobody else'.[7] This over-statement had some truth behind it.

Duff Cooper explained in delivering his message that Churchill hoped the visit would coincide with the Allied invasion. De Gaulle accepted and arrived on 4 June in the Premier's personal plane which had been sent to Algiers for his journey. On the same day Allied forces were entering Rome after an advance in which the initial break-through had been made by French troops under General Juin.

Churchill received de Gaulle at his invasion headquarters, a specially equipped train near Portsmouth not far from the coast where British, Canadian and American armies were poised to launch their attack, and at long last revealed to him what Operation Overlord was to be.

# 22 TRIUMPH

De Gaulle's intentions, as usual, were firm. He did not come to Britain to discuss governmental arrangements in liberated areas of France, and therefore he brought no colleagues with him. He had pressed for such discussions for many months in vain; now it was too late. He had settled the matter. As he told the CFLN representative in London, Pierre Viénot, in a message of 25 May about his impending visit: 'We are the administration.' Thus there was a painful disappointment in store for Churchill and his hopes of finding a Franco-American compromise.

On the other hand military discussions held much interest for him. He wanted to know how the Allies were going to invade; he wanted to make sure that General Leclerc's armoured division, which was still short of transport, would be fully equipped in time to play its part in the occupation of Paris; he wanted to make the symbolical act of presence at the scene of the invasion which befitted the chief of Fighting France. To be in England at the moment when the liberating forces set out was important, and far more important still would be the opportunity, if he could achieve it, of landing in France in the early days and making his first appearance to his fellow citizens in the guise of their leader.

Churchill's exposition of the Overlord plan was a moment of deep emotion to de Gaulle, and he expressed it frankly. He congratulated Churchill on his achievement 'after Britain had valiantly overcome so many trials and had thereby saved Europe'.[1] But when Churchill turned to political questions, the tone changed. The Premier, who was flanked by Eden and Bevin, proposed that they should negotiate a draft tripartite agreement on the administration of France which de Gaulle would then take to Washington to submit to Roosevelt. This would lead, he predicted, to some form of American recognition of the CFLN as the provisional authority in France. De Gaulle promptly rejected this approach. A provisional government already existed under his leadership, he said, and there was no question of his seeking American, or British, authorization. On the other hand a tripartite agreement covering relations between his government and the invading Allied forces was extremely urgent, though it could not be concluded in the absence of an American representative. He implied that the British were acquiescing in American policies with which they did not really agree, and this charge provoked a memorable outburst from Churchill:

How can you expect us to differ with the United States? We are able to liberate Europe only because the Americans are with us. Any time we have to choose between Europe and the open seas [*le grand large*], we shall always be for the open seas. Every time I have to choose between you and Roosevelt, I shall choose Roosevelt![2]

De Gaulle never forgot Churchill's words and frequently quoted them in later years as proof that the British were not at heart Europeans.

On this disagreeable note the meeting ended and de Gaulle repaired to General Eisenhower's nearby headquarters for a military briefing. Trouble arose when he was shown the text of the declaration Eisenhower intended to broadcast to the French people at the moment of the landings. Its language, obviously approved by Roosevelt, implied that Eisenhower was assuming supreme authority in France. De Gaulle showed his displeasure and departed.

The next day de Gaulle made an effort to prevail on Eisenhower to modify his proposed radio address, but was told it was too late to change the text. As a protest, he withheld the larger part of the contingent of French liaison officers assigned to Overlord, and refused to join the exiled rulers in London when they spoke in support of Eisenhower on the morning of 6 June as the descent on the beaches of Normandy began. De Gaulle insisted on making his own separate statement on the BBC that same evening. In this he called on the French people to give all possible help to the liberating forces, but asked them to obey lawful French authorities, by which he meant his own representatives, and made no mention of Allied authorities. He also called on the Resistance for an immediate and general rising against the Germans, whereas Eisenhower had urged the civil population to remain quiet until the Allies approached.

De Gaulle summed up his impression of the first three days in

England in a vitriolic telegram of 6 June to his colleagues in Algiers:[3]

1. The British, when inviting me, knew that the Americans would not be present at the talks.
2. . . . I refused to appear to approve Eisenhower's declaration . . .
3. I ordered our liaison mission not to leave because it would have seemed to condone Allied military government . . .
4. Churchill is in accord with Roosevelt. My journey here was engineered to give cover to their deal.
5. Eden wants general talks . . . but Churchill has become blind and deaf.
6. If I can set foot in a town in Metropolitan France, I will . . .
7. Why is Massigli delaying proclamation of the provisional government to foreign powers?

Other telegrams followed in the same wrathful vein. He accused the Allies of issuing an occupation currency without French agreement, and of confirming the Vichy administrators in office in the first towns liberated. But it soon became clear that de Gaulle's anxieties were exaggerated. This was in large measure due to the way in which General Eisenhower applied his directive from President Roosevelt, which left him discretion as to whether or not to consult local representatives of the CFLN. Eisenhower chose to have them consulted. The Allies were not in fact hesitating to deal with Gaullist representatives and did not challenge the Algiers Committee when it informed foreign powers that it was assuming the functions of a provisional government in liberated areas. Nevertheless de Gaulle tried through his Ambassador in Moscow to persuade the Soviet government to urge the Allies to be more cooperative. On 10 June, Molotov replied politely that the Russians could not intervene directly but were sure he would surmount his difficulties, as he had others.[4] In this they were right, as soon began to appear. Much of the press, American as well as British, espoused de Gaulle's cause, as soon as dissatisfaction was made public.

Anthony Eden tried to pour oil on the troubled waters. He suggested tripartite talks at official level on civil affairs in France and urged Churchill to agree to de Gaulle visiting the beach-head in Normandy. Churchill assented 'provided de Gaulle was more reasonable', and arrangements were made. Then on the evening of 13 June, as de Gaulle was dining with Eden, Attlee and other ministers before embarking for Normandy, Churchill sent a message to Eden in a last-minute effort to withdraw his tentative agreement to the venture. But Eden and Attlee persuaded him to let it proceed.[5] Early the next morning de Gaulle, with a few companions, landed on a Normandy beach at the same time as a contingent of Canadian troops. His exile from France had lasted three days less than four years.

In the circumstances it was an astonishing achievement on de Gaulle's part even to have arrived in France. There were no French units yet in Normandy and Roosevelt and Churchill considered that he was positively hindering the Anglo-American military effort. But they knew that he had the power to be even more troublesome if they kept him away from his own land, and that he would use it. To public opinion in the West, de Gaulle had come to represent France, and the President and the Prime Minister had to accept the fact.

Now began a day as charged with destiny as any in the General's life so far, the day of his first confrontation with the people of France, to whom he had been unknown four years before, since when he had become known as a voice and a symbol but not in the flesh nor in photographs. First he called on General Montgomery, commander of the forces in the beach-head, and then he went on to Bayeux, the principal township liberated so far. He had sent emissaries there direct from his landing-point to assume civil and military authority.

This is how he described his welcome:

We walked through the streets. When the inhabitants realized that this was General de Gaulle, they gazed in silence at first – in a sort of stupor – then burst into cheers and tears. They came out of their houses and joined me, full of emotion. Children surrounded me, women smiled and sobbed, men shook my hand. We walked on like one family, overwhelmed with joy and pride, feeling the hope of our nation rise with us from the depths.[6]

He received local dignitaries at the Sous-Préfecture and made a brief address to the assembled population. Then he went on to the villages of Isigny and Grandcamp. Everywhere he was greeted with enthusiasm and his authority was accepted without question. His tour was a triumph. Liberated France had recognized him for what he was, the man who could give her a place of honour among the victorious powers and abolish the heritage of Vichy. American and British reporters in the beach-head sent the news around the world.

General Marshall, chairman of the US chiefs of staff, made his own report to Washington as well. He had hurried over to London and the invasion beaches as soon as Overlord had been fairly launched. On 15 June he telephoned Henry Stimson, the Secretary for War, and told him: 'De Gaulle's trip to the beach-head has made him feel stronger than ever.' Marshall found the political situation in Britain 'appalling'. Churchill and Eden were quarrelling over de Gaulle. He had witnessed one of their violent disputes and 'was quite convinced that it was genuine'. That Marshall thought it necessary to give Stimson this assurance speaks volumes for American distrust of the British. It shows that he believed – and knew his Washington audience did too – that the Prime Minister and Foreign Secretary of Great Britain were capable of mounting a charade of disagreement over a vital matter of foreign policy in order to pull the wool over the eyes of their American allies.

'Eden is out to do everything de Gaulle wants and the Prime Minister is sticking to his guns,' reported the anxious Marshall. He had tried in vain to shake Eden by telling him that if the American public knew that de Gaulle's attitude had 'impaired military operations' and obstructed the progress of the invasion 'they would tear him limb from limb'.

Yet there were elements in the report that were favourable to de Gaulle. Marshall acknowledged that he was encouraging his followers to fight the Germans and that the reaction of resistance groups in France had been magnificent. Roosevelt, he reported back to Stimson, who would not necessarily be aware of the fact, had sent a personal telegram directing him to make full use of the de Gaulle organization, 'provided that he does not impose it by force of arms on the French people'. The President had added that 'he had no objection to the beach-head visit arranged by the British'.[7]

Since there was no need to impose de Gaulle on the French people, who were welcoming him with open arms, Roosevelt's new instructions cleared the way for full practical collaboration between Eisenhower's forces and the Gaullists. General Koenig, who was on Eisenhower's staff as commander of the French Forces of the Interior (FFI) provided the necessary contacts. An improvement in political relations was bound to follow.

De Gaulle returned to England on 15 June a different man. His beach-head welcome had removed any remaining doubts as to what the French people felt for him. Their attitude had the value of a consecration, ratifying the claim he had so long maintained to be the legitimate spokesman of France. On 16 June before leaving for Algiers he had a final talk with Eden, who hastened to send a hopeful telegram to the Embassy in Washington for transmission to the State Department. 'The General,' he said, 'was in a more reasonable mood than I have ever known him and emphasized that, despite the difficulties there had been, his desire was above all to work closely with us and the Americans.' De Gaulle had said he would not be able 'to calm apprehension in Algiers' about the state of relations with the Allies and 'to improve matters' as far as the critical tone of the French press was concerned.[8]

After Bayeux, de Gaulle felt strong enough to undertake his much delayed visit to Washington. It was in his interest to make it before the landings in the south of France took place, in which the bulk of the re-equipped French forces, some seven divisions, were to take part along with American troops under General Devers. But he was resolved to be suitably received by Roosevelt, who did not intend to invite him formally as a head of government, and to make it clear that he was not coming as a suppliant for favours, *'un demandeur'*. While arrangements were being made between Algiers and Washington, he went to Italy to visit his victorious troops and to see the Pope.

Pius XII received him in the Vatican on 30 June. It was another kind of consecration, following on that which the French had given him at Bayeux. Describing the occasion in his Memoirs, de Gaulle observes, without a hint of resentment, that: 'The Holy See, true to its eternal caution, had maintained until this moment a complete reserve with regard to Fighting France and our government in Algiers.'[9] In fact the Holy See had remained in relations with Vichy, and the bulk of the French episcopacy and clergy had always accepted Marshal Pétain's authority and instructed the faithful to do the same. De Gaulle, a good pupil of the Jesuits, never repined. He understood that it was the duty of the Church, while always regarding human affairs *sub specie aeternitatis*, never to confound tomorrow with today. He had been content to wait for her recognition.

On 30 June the moment arrived. With the Sovereign Pontiff de Gaulle talked of the future of Christian Europe under the shadow of victorious communism. Pius XII wanted the nations with a strong Catholic tradition, including Germany, to cooperate in defending Western Europe and building up a new society true to the values of Christian democracy. This was a vision that could be reconciled with de Gaulle's, a vision of a Europe in which there would be a place for French leadership, and which would exercise a powerful influence in the rest of the world.

From the Eternal City de Gaulle hastened to the New World, where preparations for his visit were now complete. On 6 July he arrived in Washington and was received by the President on the front porch of the White House, in accordance with the protocol laid down for visiting heads of government. In the course of the three crowded days that followed he met the grandees of the US government, both civil and military, but the essential part of the visit was contained in three long talks which chiefly concerned Roosevelt's vision of the postwar world and de Gaulle's reactions to it. The result was a lessening of the distance between the two men but no such meeting of minds as there had been between the Pope and the General.

De Gaulle found, without surprise, that Roosevelt's vision assigned too modest a role to the nations of Western Europe. The President saw four Great Powers as the corner-stones of the world order to be established by the United Nations. They were the United States, Britain, China and the Soviet Union. While promising that the United States would aid France generously, he did not hide his feeling that the collapse of 1940 had permanently diminished her stature, and that it would be unrealistic to set her on the same level as the Big Four. De Gaulle knew that this was also the view of the Soviet government, while the British, he believed, wanted a France strong enough to play second fiddle in Europe, but no more. He concluded that France could in the last analysis count only on her own efforts if she was to regain her place in the first rank among the nations, and said as much to the President. Roosevelt smiled and replied, 'We'll do what we can. But when it comes to helping France, nobody can take the place of the French people.'[10]

As de Gaulle left to return to Algiers, the State Department issued a statement on 12 July to the effect that the US government recognized that the CFLN 'was qualified to exercise civil administration in liberated France'. It was not full recognition but it was a step towards it.

This statement, and promises of American aid, added up to a reasonable dividend from the visit, but Roosevelt did not change his mind about de Gaulle. In a letter to a friend a few days later he said he still regarded him as an egoist. The letter found its way to de Gaulle, who observed in his Memoirs that he would never know whether the President had thought him an egoist on France's behalf or his own.[11] The General had in mind no doubt the dictum of Maurras that a man may be disinterested for himself but nobody has the right to be disinterested for France. Roosevelt might have thought himself a Maurrassian egoist – if he had read Maurras – in the interests of the United States; but it can hardly be doubted that he saw de Gaulle as an egoist without the benefit of any qualifying adjective.

The General returned to Algiers to await the moment for the move to France. In obedience to his orders the Resistance was making a maximum effort and engaging in July as many as eight German divisions in the mountainous areas of southern France which might otherwise have been used in the battle of Normandy.[12] Eisenhower's original guidance to the underground forces to remain quiet until the Allied armies were close at hand was widely ignored, and the consequences were sometimes tragic. Uprisings to which the Allies could not give effective aid were crushed by German counterattacks with much bloodshed. Eisenhower was unhappy about this, but it was a price which de Gaulle was resolved to pay. He saw it as an absolute moral necessity that France should contribute as much as possible to her salvation.

At the end of July the battle of France entered a new phase. The Allies broke out of the Normandy peninsula and the Germans began to fall away to the north and east with increasing rapidity. The road to Paris opened before General Patton's tanks and almost simultaneously, on 15 August, Operation Anvil, the joint Franco-American invasion of Provence, commenced. The landings were successful, and penetration inland proved, with the help of important Resistance forces, to be more rapid than foreseen. Lyons was liberated on 2 September.

But during those days the world's attention, and de Gaulle's, had been focused on Paris, not on the battle in the south. He had two preoccupations: that French troops should be in the vanguard of the forces liberating the city; and that he himself should be welcomed by the Parisians as the chief of the provisional government of France.

The military part of his plans was well enough in hand. General Leclerc's Second Armoured Division landed on the Normandy beaches early in August and moved ahead with Patton's forces. Eisenhower recognized that its function was to take part in the liberation of the capital. But on the political side there were two threats which worried de Gaulle. One was the expiring manoeuvres of Vichy; the other, and more serious, was the intentions of the Communists, who enjoyed such a powerful position in the leadership of the Resistance. He had feared that they might make a bid for power in Normandy and Brittany as soon as the Germans were driven out. This did not happen, but de Gaulle's anxieties were not set at rest. Paris was the main bastion of Communist strength, and that was where their effort might be made.

The first move by Vichy was a message delivered on 14 August to Henry Ingrand, the Gaullist representative in Clermont-Ferrand, suggesting that Pétain should take refuge with the Resistance and negotiate the transfer of power to de Gaulle. Ingrand promised Pétain security if he came over but made no political commitment. There was no reaction from Vichy. Either the Marshal could not make up his mind to move, or he was too closely watched by the Germans.

Then Laval took up the running with an intrigue which he had been elaborating for some time and which had already come to de Gaulle's knowledge. With the consent of Ribbentrop, the German Foreign Minister, he fetched Edouard Herriot, President of the prewar Chamber of Deputies, to Paris from his residence under German surveillance near Nancy, and tried to persuade him to reconvene the Assembly, which had not met since July 1940. Laval's idea was that he and the Marshal should resign and that Herriot should obtain the approval of the Assembly for a new government of 'National Union' which should welcome the Allies and de Gaulle to Paris. The way would thus be cleared for an apparent reconciliation of Pétainists and Gaullists, a new government under de Gaulle which would derive its authority from the same source as Pétain had done, and a discreet withdrawal into private life for Laval and Pétain.

The scheme required the support of too many conflicting interests to have any serious hope of success, but it worried de Gaulle, not least because he thought it had American support. He was determined not to accept power from the Assembly which had given it to Pétain or to allow it to speak in the name of France. As to the Resistance, all sections of it were hostile to compromise with Vichy.

De Gaulle instructed Alexander Parodi, whom he had made his delegate to the Resistance in March 1944, to oppose Laval's plan uncompromisingly,[13] and made him a Commissioner of the provisional government to strengthen his hand. A Resistance plot against Herriot's life was prepared. Parodi vetoed it, but warned Herriot of the dangers of lending himself to Laval's intrigues. This, and the growing restlessness in Paris, where anti-German activity was increasing daily, led Herriot to refuse to collaborate. He was taken back to Nancy and by 20 August Laval's plan had miscarried. Pétain was haled off to Sigmaringen in Bavaria by the Germans, and Laval and his government were soon on the same road.

An odd incident occurred in Algeria during these days which may well have been caused by the anxiety of Gaullist supporters over Laval's intrigues. An attempt was made to shoot General Giraud, who was still at home at Mostaganem. He escaped with his life but was wounded in the jaw. The Americans, who still kept an eye on their former protégé, believed that the attack had been made on the instructions of Diethelm, the Gaullist Commissioner for War.[14]

Judging that the time was ripe for the liberation of Paris, de Gaulle set out for France from Algiers on 18 August. The Americans sent a plane which developed mechanical difficulties and delayed the arrival of the party in France for some twenty-four hours. De Gaulle was convinced that the Americans wanted his arrival and the final Allied move on Paris to be retarded in order to leave more time for Laval's plan to come to fruition.[15] In fact it had foundered by the time de Gaulle arrived at Eisenhower's headquarters near St Lo on 20 August and urged an early assault on Paris. Eisenhower was hesitant because the German garrison was still strong enough to provoke a destructive battle in the city if it chose to defend its positions. He proposed to force withdrawal by outflanking them on both sides of Paris. But a destructive battle in Paris was a risk that de Gaulle was ready to run, as he had been in 1940. He argued that a popular uprising had already begun and might soon be crushed with ferocious reprisals if the Germans were not engaged at once.

After some hesitation Eisenhower gave the orders desired by de Gaulle on 23 August, assigning the leading place in the advance on Paris to Leclerc's French division. By then a ceasefire had actually been concluded inside the city between the Germans and the Resistance, who had been alarmed by the failure of Allied forces to come to their rescue, but it was not universally respected and soon broke down.

By the evening of 24 August Leclerc's advance guard was in the heart of Paris, and the next day the Second Armoured Division entered the city in strength, completing a journey for which the first preparations had been ordered by de Gaulle in Chad in October 1940. Part of the US Fourth Division moved in on the right of the French troops, and the Germans began to pull back. General von Choltitz, the garrison commander, came to meet Leclerc at the Prefecture of Police and signed a new ceasefire agreement, ordering the German troops still in the city to surrender their strongholds. Thus Paris was spared the destruction which Hitler had ordered von Choltitz to carry out and the battle which de Gaulle had been willing to risk.

De Gaulle had entered the city from Rambouillet on the afternoon of 25 August while fighting was still going on. At Montparnasse station, just south of the central areas, he met Leclerc, who was accompanied by the Communist Rol-Tanguy, representing the Resistance forces. De Gaulle weighed with nicety the political significance of every move. He expressed disapproval of the form of the German act of surrender because it was made out both to Leclerc and to Rol-Tanguy. It should have been countersigned by Leclerc alone, he said, as the senior officer. He was determined to assert the primacy of the Army over the FFI, and of the provisional government over the Council of the Resistance, which had earlier in the day issued its own proclamation in the name of the French nation without reference to him or his government. In this he saw the burgeoning of an effort by the Communists to seize power in the name of the Resistance. It was the move for which he had been waiting and which he meant to nip in the bud.

The crowds expected him to proceed from Montparnasse to the Hôtel de Ville, where the Resistance leaders headed by Parodi were gathered to receive him. But he took another road. He went first by way of the rue de Bourgogne to the Ministry of War in the rue Saint Dominique. It was from there that he had set out with Paul Reynaud on the night of 10 June 1940, when the government had evacuated Paris. There he returned, in order to symbolize that the government had come back from exile. He installed himself in the Minister's office, which he found unaltered since his departure. The same telephone was in the same place on the same table. Nothing had changed while all was changing.[16]

In his office he received Parodi, who had hurried over from the Hôtel de Ville, and Luizet, the Prefect of Police, and told them of his plan for a triumphal parade the following afternoon from the Arc de

Triomphe to Notre Dame. Then he went to the Prefecture of Police to congratulate the police force on their contribution to liberating Paris. The importance of ensuring their support in the event of a clash with the Communists was evident, and many of them were in need of reassurance. They had taken orders from the Germans during the occupation and had much to hide. De Gaulle's words to them showed that he would have understanding for conduct that their function had made inevitable.

Only then did he proceed to the Hôtel de Ville to meet the chiefs of the Resistance, who were by this time irritated and impatient. The tone of the speeches on both sides at his ceremonial reception was impeccable, but he remained alert to the possible political significance of every gesture. When Georges Bidault, president of the National Council of the Resistance, called on him to proclaim the Republic from the windows of the City Hall he replied: 'The Republic has never ceased to exist. Free France, Fighting France, the French Committee of National Liberation have all in turn embodied it. Vichy always was and remains null and void. I am the President of the government of the Republic. Why should I proclaim the Republic now?' The reply epitomized the political philosophy on which his tactics throughout the day had been based. De Gaulle went to the window and waved a greeting to the enthusiastic crowd, but made no speech.

During the night it became apparent that German forces stronger than Leclerc's division were still immediately north and east of the city, but de Gaulle decided that the risk of a counterattack or a heavy air raid was not a reason for cancelling the celebration which he had planned. Immense crowds, on foot in a city without public transport, were moving from all quarters to line the route of the parade. They were not to be disappointed.

At 3 pm on 26 August de Gaulle appeared at the Arc de Triomphe. This was the supreme moment of glory in all his long career. The population of Paris had been recognized for centuries as the arbiter and chief spokesman of the French people. Now it was to give its response to the appeal of 18 June by hailing him as the saviour of his country.

Followed by old companions, the generals of his armies and Resistance leaders, he walked down the Champs Elysées to the Place de la Concorde wildly applauded by the multitude. It was a moment of triumph such as few men have savoured, a triumph which placed him among the immortals. The dream of his childhood, of winning acclaim for his services to France, was more than fulfilled. He recorded his thoughts and feelings in his Memoirs:

I emerge from the shadow of the Arc de Triomphe . . . Before me is the Champs Elysées.

'Ah! C'est la mer!' Huge crowds are massed on each side of the avenue. Perhaps two million people . . . As far as I can see waves of humanity surge before me in the sun, beneath the Tricolour.

I advance on foot . . . staff officers worry about an air raid, casualties and panic. But I believe in the fortune of France . . . It is true that I haven't the build or the taste for crowd-pleasing gestures, but I am sure they are not expected from me.

I go on, full of emotion yet undisturbed . . . through the storm of voices echoing my name . . . It is one of those miracles of the national feeling which mark our history down the centuries . . . We are one thought, one feeling, one voice together . . . And I in the midst of it all, I feel not a person but an instrument of Destiny.[17]

As *Le Connétable* arrived at the portals of Notre Dame where the Te Deum of liberation was to be chanted, firing broke out, apparently from the rooftops. Solon the Athenian would have judged this the perfect moment for a happy death, but Destiny was far from having finished with her instrument. De Gaulle entered the cathedral, and there was an immediate reply to the firing from the forces on the ground. Similar incidents took place elsewhere in the city at the same moment, and there was more random firing later inside Notre Dame during the singing of the Magnificat. It was thought at first that Germans or Vichyites were at work, but a search produced no culprits. Perhaps the firing of an accidental shot in the supercharged atmosphere had triggered off the whole affair. De Gaulle always suspected that a Communist manoeuvre was behind it, an effort to justify the maintenance of Resistance groups under arms even after the establishment of French authority on the grounds that subversive gangs were threatening public order, but no proof has ever been produced.[18] The fusillade of Notre Dame remains a mystery.

The allegiance of Paris confirmed de Gaulle's position and that of the Algiers Committee of which he was the head. But accounts had still to be settled with the Allies, who had not yet recognized the provisional government, and with the Communists, who might still come to life as a rival power.

Nor was Vichy quite dead. An envoy from Pétain, Admiral Auphan, had appeared in Paris with authority to enter into negotiations with de Gaulle, provided the legitimacy of the Marshal was respected. The proviso ruled out any possibility there might have been of a discussion. It posed the one condition de Gaulle could not accept. 'A call issuing from the depths of our History, and the instinct of the country, had led me to take up the abandoned treasure, the sovereignty of France. It was I that possessed legitimacy. Monsieur le Maréchal, . . . once my chief and model, what have you come to?'[19] Thus de Gaulle described his reaction in his Memoirs. Auphan was dismissed unheard.

On 27 August, the day after the triumphal parade, General Eisenhower came to Paris to congratulate de Gaulle and tell him he meant to establish his headquarters at Versailles. De Gaulle was glad to have him near, but not in, Paris. It was agreed between them that the Americans too should have their parade through the city. There are conflicting versions of how this came about. Eisenhower says in *Crusade in Europe* that de Gaulle asked for American troops in Paris to strengthen his hold against subversion. He could spare none for the task but agreed that two divisions should march through the city to the front.[20] De Gaulle in his Memoirs refers to no such request. At all events the Americans made their march past de Gaulle and General Bradley on 29 August. The Champs Elysées was filled from side to side by columns of good-humoured young men whose ancestors had left Europe with more relief than regret, singing 'Don't fence me in', a sentiment most acceptable to the liberated Parisians, who were present in force once again. The appearance of the Americans served as a warning to the Communists, if it were needed, of where the real power lay.

In dealing with the Communists de Gaulle struck while the iron was hot. On 28 August he summoned the Council of the Resistance for his second and last meeting with them. He told them that the members would be absorbed in the Consultative Assembly which he had summoned from Algiers and that some of the leaders would become ministers in his government. The forces of the interior were to be taken into the Army, and their directing body was to disappear. The National Council of the Resistance, Jean Moulin's legacy, had performed its glorious task in helping to drive out the enemy. Its duty now was not to become a permanently separate political organization but to merge into the national life. There were objections, and it was clear that not all would obey willingly, but de Gaulle had moved very fast, and the message of the American parade reinforced his action.

The General was scarcely generous with the Resistance during these days. In speeches he paid tribute to its achievement, but not lavishly. Men whose enemy had been the Gestapo, for whom capture had meant not the status of prisoner of war but torture followed by death or the concentration camp, might have expected warmer praise and more trust. But de Gaulle behaved as if he felt he could not afford to admire them too much for fear that he and all France might fall under their spell. That he was determined to avoid. There must be no rival centre of authority to the State itself in the France he meant to build, no return in another form to the prewar divisions which had paralysed the country. General Eisenhower's headquarters helped him by announcing that control of civil administration had been handed over to the French authorities. This declaration did not accord with de Gaulle's doctrine that the provisional government of Algiers had been the sole legitimate authority from the day of the Allied landings onwards, but it had practical advantages at the moment. It left him installed in Paris as the unchallenged head of the government of France. It remained to show that he could govern.

# 23  ON TO VICTORY

It was a wasted land that de Gaulle inherited. France depended on America for everything – food, oil and supplies for the civil population; material to rebuild her industries and communications; equipment for the armies she must raise if she was to play a worthy part in the victory over Germany. The eight divisions which had taken part in Overlord and Anvil, seven of them in the lesser of the two operations, would not be enough for that. There had to be constant dealings with the Americans on all these matters.

De Gaulle also had to direct the reconstruction of French society. The machinery of government had to be set up in Paris with all speed and its authority established throughout the country; the French Forces of the Interior had to be assimilated by the regular Army and hastened to the battle front; and restraint had to be imposed on those Resistance groups, Communist and other, in various areas of the country, particularly in the hills of the southeast and southwest, who might, if unchecked, try to act as if they had governmental authority. The Resistance was not to be allowed to govern, but by way of compensation de Gaulle intended that swift satisfaction should be given to its desire for justice upon collaborators. Provision for special courts was made under legislation already promulgated in Algiers.

De Gaulle, established in his offices in the Ministry of War in the rue St Dominique, went to work on this programme as soon as his triumph of 26 August was over. The first meeting of ministers in Paris took place on 2 September. A few days later three Resistance leaders were brought into the government, among them Georges Bidault, the non-Communist chief, who was given the portfolio of foreign affairs. After some hesitation the Communists accepted two posts, although de Gaulle refused their demand for one of the three key ministries, Foreign Affairs, Defence and the Interior. They settled for Air and Public Health. It was a success for him that they chose not to stand aloof when offered so little.

The government formed and functioning, de Gaulle made his first great tour to meet the people. Between 14 and 18 September he visited Lyons, Marseilles, Toulouse and Bordeaux and was everywhere received with enthusiasm by huge crowds. Sometimes, however, his exchanges with the local chiefs of the FFI were difficult. His message was that the days of guerrilla warfare were over, and that the Resistance as such had no political role to play in the new France, and his manner reinforced his theme. He behaved as a superior towards the FFI officers, sometimes kept them standing at attention when talking to them' – which was not at all a normal habit of his – and was even sarcastic on occasion about the exalted ranks they had awarded themselves. Reaching a private soldier at the end of a rank of youthful colonels, he stopped, looked him up and down, and asked: 'What's wrong with you? Can't you sew?' In one area in the southwest, where the Resistance leader admitted conducting trials and executions on his own authority, de Gaulle ordered an investigating officer to be sent from Paris.

Not all the guerrilla chiefs took kindly to de Gaulle's manner, or his message. A Toulouse leader, Colonel Ravanel, remembered his disappointment at de Gaulle's attitude vividly enough to speak of it on a television programme many years afterwards.[2] By and large, however, the General's mission was a success. Nobody openly disobeyed, and the news spread that France had a leader who knew his mind and was immensely popular.

At this period de Gaulle made the acquaintance of many personalities who had not rallied to him in London or Algiers but were destined to play an important part in his future. Outstanding among them was the writer André Malraux, who had been cured by the Nazi-Soviet pact of his prewar attraction to Communism, and had been in the military wing of the Resistance at the end of the occupation. He now became an active Gaullist and a firm friend. The General found in him a kindred spirit who viewed the world from the heights, as he did himself. Even in the days of his final withdrawal to Colombey he enjoyed receiving Malraux and exchanging ideas with him. Another great writer who rallied to him was François Mauriac. This eminent Catholic, already a member of the Academy, became an ardent though often critical admirer. Eminent businessmen were less cordially received. 'We didn't see many of your kind in London,' he said to one of them.

Two others who first met the General in France were his future Prime Ministers, Michel Debré, who had been a Resistance leader in Normandy, and Georges Pompidou. Pompidou, a teacher, had held aloof from all contact with the Germans without being active in the Resistance. The General, hearing of his abilities, decided to employ Pompidou in his private office, precisely because he knew none of the other members of his entourage. Until this time de Gaulle's personal acquaintance with those whose names would have figured in a French *Who's Who* had been limited. Now it rapidly expanded.

De Gaulle was as distrustful as ever of American intentions. He was convinced that Roosevelt did not want any great power in continental Europe except Russia and was delaying both recognition and the equipment of more French divisions for that reason. 'The Allies are betraying us,' he said to his new secretary Claude Mauriac. 'They're betraying Europe, the dirty dogs. But I'll make them pay for it.'[3] He meant what he said.

But Roosevelt was now alone in his thinking. The State Department and the Foreign Office, like General Eisenhower and Jefferson Caffery, the new US Ambassador in Paris, had rallied to the view that de Gaulle was right in telling them that the only alternative to his rule in France was that of a Communist-dominated régime. At the end of September de Gaulle adopted a change of tactics that was calculated to suggest a growing danger. He began to withhold some French troops from the front for duties inside the country. On 29 September, on the eve of a visit to Lille, he told the Commissioners of the Republic, whom he had convened in Paris:

A certain nation [he obviously meant the United States] seems to be afraid of the revival of France and is doing all it can to make it impossible . . . some regions are in outright insurrection, notably Limoges, where the Communists are systematically refusing to recognize the representatives of the central authority . . . So there is a chance that we may crack in the days ahead . . . But I think we'll hold.[4]

The shock waves from such declarations reached the American and British embassies.

In mid-October de Gaulle went further and complained in a speech of the reticence of the Allies towards his government:

Certainly many Frenchmen may feel astonished and saddened at the sort of relegation in which the other powers are at present keeping France in all that concerns the conduct of the war and the preparation of the peace . . . but for the moment, we must accept things as they are.

The British and American press commented anxiously on the lack of solidarity between France and her allies which de Gaulle's remarks revealed.

Then, suddenly, as the date of the American presidential election drew near, Roosevelt changed his mind. On 23 October he sent messages to Stalin and Churchill announcing that the United States intended to recognize the French provisional government immediately. Washington, Moscow and London issued statements of recognition the same day. De Gaulle's reaction was characteristic and caustic. There was no particular reason for France to rejoice, he said at a press conference, because her allies had decided to adjust to reality. He took care not to suggest gratitude. None the less he knew that a card of great value had been added to his hand, and he played it at once. On 28 October a government decree announced that the militias would be dissolved and the French Forces of the Interior absorbed in the regular Army. In the Council of Ministers he singled out the two Communist members and said to them: 'Billoux . . . Tillon . . . This is what the government must do and what it is going to do. Now, if you disagree . . .'⁵ It was the moment for the Communists to withdraw if they did not wish to be implicated in the decision. But they remained at the table. It would have been hard for them to do otherwise five days after Moscow had recognized the French government.

On 11 November Churchill came to Paris at de Gaulle's invitation, and they proceeded down the Champs Elysées together after laying wreaths at the Arc de Triomphe. They received a rapturous welcome from the crowd, but de Gaulle was far less happy than on 26 August. 'Listen to how they applaud him', he muttered to a companion. 'That brigand, that scum [*cette canaille*]!'⁶ The word '*canaille*' was a familiar part of de Gaulle's well-stocked armoury of terms of abuse, and meant less in his mouth than it might have done in many others; perhaps his irritation was due to a feeling that the Parisians had made his own consecration less than unique by greeting Churchill so warmly.

When it came to their conversations on policy, however, de Gaulle did not allow himself to be influenced by personal sentiments. He was now the ruler of France and could speak with a new authority. From this position of increased strength he made a serious effort to achieve a meeting of British and French minds, but his success was limited. Churchill promised to supply more military equipment and to support with Roosevelt and Stalin de Gaulle's demand for a French zone of occupation in conquered Germany, but when de Gaulle urged that Britain and France should join forces to protect continental Europe from being divided between American and Russian power blocs, he met, as ever, with Churchill's refusal to detach British policy from that of the United States. He decided, so he relates in his Memoirs,[7] that a close Anglo-French alliance, such as he would still have welcomed, was not a practical possibility. Britain was still turned towards 'le grand large'. De Gaulle never renewed the proposal he had made to Churchill in these talks.

After Churchill departed, de Gaulle turned to preparing his first encounter with Stalin. It was Stalin who kept Roosevelt and Churchill informed of what was afoot, not de Gaulle. In late November he flew to Moscow, just as France was celebrating the liberation of Strasbourg, the last great city to remain in German hands. Before departing he had made an important gesture. On 6 November he gave a pardon to Maurice Thorez, the leader of the French Communist party, who had deserted from the French Army at the beginning of the war and taken refuge in the Soviet Union. It was a vote of confidence in the readiness of Thorez to cooperate with the provisional government if allowed to return to France, and he knew it would be welcome to his host in the Kremlin.

Thorez played the game. On 30 November at a political meeting at the Velodrome d'Hiver in Paris he made a call for national unity in the interests of victory over Nazi Germany. 'On to Berlin' was the slogan for the Communists, he said. Thus he set the scene for de Gaulle's first meeting with Stalin, which took place in Moscow on 2 December.

De Gaulle has left in his Memoirs a fascinating and fascinated account of his dealings with Stalin.[8] He saw in him a great Russian, a ruler bent on national aggrandizement, rather than a great Communist dedicated to world revolution. He noted that Stalin tended to speak of Russia rather than of the Soviet Union. This was a man with whom he felt he could cooperate as far as national interests coincided. It was necessary to convince him that de Gaulle was not subservient to the Anglo-Americans but was an independent force. This venture was de Gaulle's first experiment in 'basing his foreign policy on the Russians', as he had told General Cochet in May 1943 that he would do. He did not find it easy going.

Stalin wrote no Memoirs, but the American record of the Yalta Conference gives an account of how he described de Gaulle to Roosevelt. He said he had found him 'unrealistic', a visionary seeking to erase from history the fall of France in 1940 and to secure for her in the postwar world a position to which her contribution to Allied victory and her contemporary strength did not entitle her.[9] This was very much what Stalin had said of de Gaulle at Tehran before meeting him, but the results of the Moscow meeting suggest that he was rather more impressed than he admitted to Roosevelt. At least Stalin thought it worth making a last-minute concession in order to establish a basis for a Franco-Russian treaty.

The first subject raised in the talks in the Kremlin was of course Germany. It was agreed that she would soon be defeated and that she must be rendered permanently harmless. As to postwar territorial arrangements, de Gaulle emphasized his independence of British and American views. He even made the extraordinary proposal that the French and Soviet governments should work out bilaterally a plan for the dismemberment of the German Reich which they could then jointly recommend to the other powers.

Stalin, who for the past twelve months had been discussing with the British and Americans how Germany was to be divided between the three of them, cannot have taken this invitation literally, nor can de Gaulle have had any expectation that it would be accepted. Nevertheless it reflected an idea that was central to his thinking about Europe. France, Russia and Germany were continental powers: any European settlement involved their territory and their security. Britain was marginal, America was remote: their involvement depended on their own choice. The security of France had suffered between 1919 and 1939 from the relative detachment of Britain and America. They might again choose a measure of detachment in the future – conceivably they might even have it thrust upon them. But the continental powers would always be present.

But Stalin was interested in the immediate future. He told de Gaulle that the German settlement could only be made in consultation with Britain and America. He was willing to exchange ideas on how to prevent a revival of German power, but not to make bilateral agreements.

While Stalin stood firm on the need to consult Roosevelt and Churchill about German questions, he offered de Gaulle a bilateral Franco-Soviet treaty of friendship on the same lines as the Anglo-Soviet Treaty of 1942. This would put France on the same level as Britain as far as her relations with Moscow were concerned. In return he asked for recognition by France of the Lublin Committee as the government of Poland. Washington and London were resisting such recognition and were, like the French, still in relations with the Polish government in exile housed in London, with which the Russians had broken in 1943. If France recognized Lublin, the Anglo-Saxons would find their negative attitude harder to maintain.

De Gaulle had no illusions about the dangers ahead of Poland, but the Red Army had not yet fully occupied it, and he thought the West could exercise some influence. He was also mindful of the ancient tradition of Franco-Polish friendship, and wanted to be the last not the first to make concessions. He therefore suggested the signature of a Franco-Soviet treaty without preconditions. In reply the Russians told him that the British were opposing the treaty. To sign it would therefore be a concession on their part which merited a counter-concession.

De Gaulle, furious, instructed Bidault to summon the British Chargé d'Affaires and protest at this act of interference. London's reply was that the British government had not opposed a Franco-Soviet treaty but suggested that a tripartite agreement might be worth considering as an alternative.[10] Behind this British proposal was no doubt a certain distaste for a situation in which Moscow had friendship treaties with both London and Paris while the two democracies still had no comparable link between themselves.

De Gaulle promptly told the Russians he rejected the British proposal and wanted a bilateral treaty, but the Russians continued to press for the treaty and recognition of Lublin together. Deadlock ensued and persisted through a series of official discussions and lavish entertainments. Stalin even tried the effect of hinting at his influence over French internal affairs. He praised Thorez to de Gaulle and urged him not to have him arrested – 'at least not yet'. This amounted to saying that Stalin knew the French Communists would collaborate with de Gaulle for the present, unless he gave his faithful servant Thorez orders to the contrary. De Gaulle was displeased, but did not show his feelings as he had so often done on lesser grounds with the

British and Americans. He confined himself to replying coldly that France would treat Thorez according to what she expected of him. If Stalin could speak for Thorez and the French Communists, de Gaulle could speak for France herself.

The deadlock was still unbroken on the last night of the visit, 9 December, when Stalin gave a ceremonial dinner of farewell in the Kremlin. The evening developed into a contest for psychological ascendancy between the two men. Stalin paid little attention to de Gaulle during dinner and spent most of his time proposing a series of flesh-creeping toasts to ministers of his government who were present. 'Here's to the Minister of Railroads. His trains run on time and help our armies. If they didn't, he knows he would pay for it with his head.' His manner conveyed that the fate of the Franco-Soviet negotiation was of no great concern to him.

After dinner Stalin and de Gaulle sat on a sofa with a Russian interpreter. Stalin beckoned to the British Chargé d'Affaires, John Balfour, who spoke both Russian and French, to join them. Around a table close by were seated several members of the Politburo, including Malenkov, to whom de Gaulle had been talking before dinner.

After some desultory conversation with Stalin, de Gaulle turned to his British neighbour and asked him, loud enough for the interpreter to hear: 'Do you think we shall be able to get on with these people after the war?' The diplomat made the diplomatic response. 'Well,' said de Gaulle looking hard at Malenkov and his companions, 'when I see the looks of these future leaders of Russia whom I invited here to meet me tonight, I doubt it very much.' De Gaulle had shown that he could be as offhand and as brutal as Stalin and was equally prepared to face the future without a Franco-Soviet treaty and was already preparing to deal with Russia after Stalin's death.

Later in the evening he emphasized this by declining to stay for a film show Stalin had ordered and making it clear that he regarded this as their last meeting before his departure for France the next morning. At Molotov's request he left some officials behind to make a final attempt to break the deadlock, but he took Bidault away with him. He had put up a performance which Sir John Balfour still remembers with professional admiration.[11]

In the early morning hours agreement was reached. The Russians dropped their demand for recognition of the Lublin Committee as a government and accepted the offer already made by the French of the appointment of an unofficial representative who would deal with the Committee on non-political matters, such as arrangements for the return of French prisoners of war released from German camps overrun by the Red Army. De Gaulle came back to the Kremlin to be welcomed by Stalin and to sign with him the Treaty of Friendship he had wanted, without paying the Russian price.

De Gaulle had done well in Moscow and his achievement was favourably received in Paris. He had established his own line to the Russians and ensured that they would not incite the French Communists against him, at least in the near future. At a Central Committee meeting in Paris on 21 January, Jacques Duclos, the Secretary-General, confirmed what Thorez had said while de Gaulle was on his way to Moscow. He opposed the maintenance of armed groups and emphasized the 'national mission' of the party. Communists should join the Army, he said.

This was a considerable strengthening of de Gaulle's position. He remained anxious lest the Communists should increase their hold on public opinion but there was no further fear of their bidding for immediate power. In retrospect, indeed, it is possible to see that de Gaulle's suspicions about Communist intentions in 1944 were exaggerated. Some groups of enthusiasts among the Resistance, not all of them necessarily Communists, may have had visions of converting liberation into revolution, but no evidence has ever come to light that the French Communists had prepared a plan with Moscow's backing for the seizure of power. Stalin was their master, as events after the outbreak of war in 1939 had shown, and his philosophy in these matters was simple. He believed that it was the occupying power which decided the political colour of governments in liberated countries. He would have expected the Anglo-Americans to intervene and frustrate a Communist takeover in France even if de Gaulle had failed to dominate it. He would never have encouraged the French Communists to mount a coup d'état, and they would never have attempted it without his approval.

Just after de Gaulle's return from Moscow to Paris there suddenly began, on 16 December, Hitler's last offensive in the West. Like his blow in 1940 it was struck through the Ardennes. A group of German armoured divisions achieved tactical surprise and punched a hole of some fifty kilometres in the American front. There was no reason to expect a repetition of 1940 – the material superiority of the Allies was too great – but fear of the Panzers was still a reality, and there was a moment of anxiety in the Western camp. Under its influence Eisenhower ordered the American and French divisions around Strasbourg to pull back to the northwest to help stem the German advance. Overnight the possibility that the Germans would reoccupy Strasbourg emerged. The fear of reprisals and of fresh devastation was immediately aroused.

De Gaulle intervened at once, and made his action public. He wrote to Eisenhower protesting at his orders and stating that he would, if they were maintained, direct French forces under General de Lattre to leave his command and protect Strasbourg alone. In a sense this threat was spurious, because the French were dependent on the American supply system and could not have continued to fight if it had been withdrawn when they ceased to be under Eisenhower's orders.

But de Gaulle's protest (and the attendant publicity, rather than his threat) caused the Americans to think again, and Churchill flew over from London to help resolve the crisis. He sat, in mute but weighty witness, at a conference between Eisenhower and de Gaulle at Versailles. By the time it was held, the Allied forces were rallying and it was already evident that 1940 was not to be re-enacted. Eisenhower agreed to countermand his earlier orders to the American forces in Alsace, and the danger to Strasbourg was dispelled as swiftly as it had arisen. De Gaulle's prompt reaction had corresponded to French national instinct and was immensely popular. From then until 1969 there was a solid pro-Gaullist majority in Alsace in all elections.

The usual winter summit conference took place early in February when Stalin, Roosevelt and Churchill met at Yalta in the Crimea to discuss their plans for the final phase of the war. De Gaulle was not invited. The British and Russians both told him informally that his exclusion was Roosevelt's doing and not theirs, and the Americans did not seek to deny it.[12]

At the Tehran conference Roosevelt still had much to offer to the Russians. At Yalta, Stalin was in the ascendant. His armies had advanced half the distance from Warsaw to Berlin since mid-January, and he was still neutral in the war with Japan, which the Americans expected to last for another eighteen months. He had indicated at Tehran that he would be willing to declare war on Japan once Germany was defeated, but it remained to translate that undertaking into the effective help which the Americans, still unsure that the atomic bomb would work, believed that they would need in the Far East. He would have been the best placed of the three in the negotiations even if Roosevelt had been in possession of all his capacities. But he was not: he was mortally ill, and there was no concealing the fact.

Poland was the most contentious issue and dominated the discussions. Stalin was determined that authority in Warsaw should pass to an administration controlled by the Lublin Committee, whose chiefs were members of the Polish Communist party. Roosevelt and Churchill fought hard, but they had to face the fact that the Red Army was now in occupation of the whole of Poland. The identity of the occupying army was the trump card in the game, as it had been in Italy, France and Greece, where the British had recently driven the Communists from Athens by armed force and replaced them by a régime more to their liking. In the end Roosevelt and Churchill had to agree that a new provisional government in which the Lublin Poles would predominate should be set up in Warsaw and given recognition. Thereafter there would be 'free democratic elections'. It was a face-saving formula for the West, but nobody could doubt who would decide what 'free' and 'democratic' meant in a land controlled by the Red Army. In return Stalin promised to make war on the Japanese as soon after the fall of Germany as he could move the necessary forces to the Far East.

As far as France was concerned, the Three repeated the views they had expressed at Tehran. Stalin argued that she could not be regarded as an equal partner in Germany. Only Churchill spoke up for France and urged the importance of the contribution she could make in containing Germany and stabilizing Europe when the American forces withdrew, as Roosevelt said they would have to do in two years' time at the most. He was remarkably successful. At the first meeting Roosevelt had inclined to Stalin's view of France, but in the end he came round to Churchill's side and prevailed on Stalin to agree that France should be invited to join the Allied Control Commission on Germany. Juridically she was to be on the same footing as the Big Three, but territorially there was to be a difference. Her zones of occupation in Germany and Berlin were to be carved out of the two thirds assigned to the US and Britain. The Soviet Union was to keep its third untouched. Nevertheless much was secured for France. The left bank of the Rhine and the resources of the Saar were to be under her control for an indefinite period; and de Gaulle would be able to say that the Anglo-Americans had sold the pass over Poland without the consent of France.

De Gaulle ought to have been grateful to Churchill, but he never gave any sign of being so. He deeply resented his exclusion from the conference, and was determined that France should accept no responsibility for its decisions, which French propaganda soon began to describe as a division of Europe into American and Russian spheres of domination.

On 12 February, as the conference was drawing to an end, Roosevelt sent a message to de Gaulle asking him to a meeting at Algiers on his way home to the United States. De Gaulle found the invitation unacceptable for more than one reason. For a foreign ruler to choose the time and place of a meeting with the head of the French Republic on French soil was hurtful to the national prestige. But far more important was the consideration that by conferring with Roosevelt immediately after Yalta he might seem to be setting the seal of French approval on its decisions. So de Gaulle chose refusal, not without causing anxiety among his own ministers, notably Bidault, and criticism in the Western press. But he accepted the invitation of Stalin, Roosevelt and Churchill for France to join the Allied Control Commission for Germany.

De Gaulle always maintained that if he had been at Yalta he would have enabled the West to defend the cause of Poland more effectively. The question is academic but not without interest. The argument against his thesis is that his presence would not have relieved the West of its greatest negotiating handicap: the Red Army occupied Poland, and possession is more than nine points of the law in power politics. On the other hand de Gaulle had shown in Moscow that he knew how to be obstinate with Stalin. His example might have stiffened the Americans into using their vast reserves of strength more resolutely than the dying Roosevelt was able to do by himself. This was the role that de Gaulle played to good effect many years later in the Berlin crisis. As it was, he could only criticize 'le partage de Yalta', and Poland was left to live with the results.

In the early spring de Gaulle faced his first economic crisis and was forced to chose between a leftward and a central course. The national economy was reviving but running at a huge deficit. Measures to protect the franc were urgently needed. The leftist Finance Minister, Mendès-France, produced a very austere plan for currency reform, compulsory savings and a freeze on prices and profits. Pleven, the more moderate Minister for Foreign Trade, opposed him and advanced milder proposals which left more scope for profit-making in private enterprise and for borrowing to meet the deficit. After some hesitation de Gaulle, though personally attracted by the rigour of Mendès-France, whom he admired, decided that France was too weak to take the strain of his plan and came down on the side of Pleven. This was an important decision which set the French economy on a liberal rather than a Socialist track and broadened the gap between de Gaulle and the Left. In April Mendès-France left the government.

On 12 April President Roosevelt died on the threshold of the new age which he had done so much to bring to birth. It was Harry Truman, a man of a very different stamp, who was to wield the enormous powers of the Presidency in the promised land of the *Pax Americana*.

Politically the event seemed to offer de Gaulle more cause for hope than anxiety. It removed a man who had a rooted antipathy to his character and aims and replaced him by one who had few preconceived notions about Europe and might be expected to have a more open mind. Senator Truman had only taken over as Vice-President in January 1945. He had not been at Yalta and was a newcomer to the game of international politics at the highest level when he suddenly became President. Probably de Gaulle did not know that Roosevelt had told Truman that he was more worried by what the French and British empires might do after the war than by what the Soviets might do.

At the moment of Roosevelt's death Western and Soviet forces were converging on the heartland of Germany for the kill. On 25 April American and Russians met at Torgau in Saxony and split Hitler's thousand-year Reich in two. It was the junction that de Gaulle had foreseen and demanded in 1914, but he had expected that the French would be there. Now he was eager that the French First Army should play as prominent a part and advance as far east as possible. He authorized General de Lattre to press on and ignore American orders that the French should not advance east of the Black Forest. While an argument between de Gaulle and Eisenhower dragged on, the First Army took Stuttgart and drove on into Bavaria. On 6 May they entered Berchtesgaden, Hitler's mountain stronghold near the Austrian border, and hoisted the Tricolour over his residence, 'The Eagle's Nest'.

By then Hitler himself was dead in Berlin and his successor, Admiral Doenitz, was presiding over the dissolution of the Third Reich. For a few days Doenitz played for time and attempted, as Goering was doing, to drive a wedge between the Western Allies and the Russians. Himmler went a stage further and tried to separate the French from both the Anglo-Americans and the Russians. He sent a message to de Gaulle:

You have won ... When one remembers where you began, one must take one's hat off to you ... But what are you going to do now? Trust the Anglo-Saxons? They will treat you as a satellite and make you lose your national honour. Join the Russians? They will take France over and liquidate you ... The only road that can lead your people to greatness and independence is that of an entente with conquered Germany. Proclaim it at once. Get in touch without delay with the men in the Reich who still have power *de facto* and want to lead it in a new direction.[13]

De Gaulle made no reply, but he was sufficiently impressed by Himmler's argument to quote it at length in his Memoirs and to observe: 'Setting aside the personal flattery addressed to me in this message from the graveside, there is no doubt some truth in the vision which it outlines.'[14] In fact Himmler's assessment of the hopes and risks ahead of France was not very different from his own.

On 7 May at 2.41 am the representatives of the German High Command signed the act of unconditional surrender at General Eisenhower's headquarters at Reims. A French general put his signature to the document along with American, British and Russian commanders. On the following day the act of surrender was repeated at Soviet military headquarters in Berlin. General de Lattre represented France. 'What, the French as well?' exclaimed Field-Marshal Keitel, as he led the German delegation into the chamber where the ceremony took place. It was Keitel who had received the French capitulation in the railway carriage at Rethondes on 22 June 1940. None was better qualified than he to appreciate the reversal of fortune involved in the presence of the French at the surrender of the German armed forces in their own capital. In Paris, at the same hour as Churchill in London and Truman in Washington, *Le Connétable* broadcast to his people the news of total victory over Nazi Germany and Fascist Italy.

Thus the seal was set on the greatest of de Gaulle's services to his country. Despite all her misfortunes and all her frailties France had been present in the first rank of the victorious powers in the hour of their triumph. It was a good fortune which she owed above all to the devotion and the genius of Charles de Gaulle.

The judgement that de Gaulle passes in his Memoirs on the two fallen dictators merits examination at this point because it tells much about the man.[15] The note of moral condemnation generally struck in both the Western and Communist worlds is muted.

Mussolini he dismisses in a few temperate sentences. His aim – the restoration of a Roman Empire – was not ignoble but exaggerated. His fatal error was to join Germany against the natural allies of Italy in the West.

Hitler he treats at much greater length. He might be writing of the protagonist of an Aeschylean tragedy, brought to ruin by *hubris*. Indeed he compares Hitler to Prometheus, of whom Aeschylus made a hero. Perhaps it is to restore the balance that he also compares him to Moloch. Hitler, he says, started from nothing and offered himself to Germany just as she was seeking a new lover. They made an adventurous couple. Fascism, racism, totalitarianism, oppression and crime marked their course to the abyss. Germany remained faithful to him to the last. 'She did more for him than any people ever did for any leader.'

The epitaph is a verdict on human nature, not just German nature. So is de Gaulle's explanation of Hitler's fall from the heights he scaled. The dictator's error, he says, was to count always on the triumph of the baser instincts in his opponents. Because Hitler was at first resisted by weak and timid men who gave way in the hour of decision, he thought it would always be so. Paris and London proved his downfall, because, contrary to his expectations, they refused to acquiesce in the murder of Poland.

From his youth de Gaulle had been fascinated by the appetite of Germany's leaders for undertakings beyond their strength. It is evident in his epitaph on Hitler that the charm still held. His judgement is delivered in the vein of Goethe, recognizing that evil is as much a part of life as good.

In a single graphic phrase de Gaulle shows that he is also a man of sensibility, and an artist. After relating the story of Hitler's death, he asks whether at last 'the Titan' (another invocation of Greek mythology) became a man again 'for long enough to shed a tear at the moment when all was at an end'.

De Gaulle is, as far as I know, alone among Hitler's enemies in having tried to enter into his feelings when he knew beyond a doubt that no hope and no time were left to him.

# 24 DISCORD AND DEPARTURE

With victory achieved in Europe, de Gaulle had nearly completed the task he had set himself in June 1940 of restoring France to independence and to honour. She had recovered the status, if not all the attributes, of a great power, and for the first time since the collapse of Napoleon's Empire in 1814, she was relieved from the presence on her frontiers of a dangerous adversary. Germany had lost her sovereignty and was totally occupied. With the exception of Indo-China, France's overseas possessions had all been gathered in. At home, democratic liberties had been restored and the danger of anarchy or civil war averted.

But problems abounded. The French Empire, like all the European empires, was full of discontents, while on the home front wartime unity began to crumble as soon as Germany surrendered. It was clear that soon there would be elections and that the Consultative Assembly would give way to a legislative body. All the old political parties for which de Gaulle felt such a profound distaste began to sharpen their weapons in preparation for battle. Soon *Le Connétable* would have to carry out the promise he had made in Brazzaville in November 1940, return his powers to the people and render an account of his stewardship. The political parties were by no means persuaded that thereafter he would be indispensable to the government of France. Léon Blum set the new scene as soon as he returned from Germany. He refused an invitation from de Gaulle to join the government, and on 20 May, after only ten days in France, he issued to the nation a stirring call to ingratitude. 'No man has a right to power. But we have the right to ingratitude,' he said. He spoke for many. The guilty returned too, most of them under arrest. Pétain came back at his own insistence, ignoring a message from de Gaulle which urged him to stay in Switzerland, where the Germans had sent him in the final days of the war. Laval was forced to return a few weeks later after a vain attempt to seek asylum in Spain. Both were arrested and indicted. Their fate would in the last resort be a political rather than a legal question, and the General knew that he would be called upon to answer it.

Yet it was North Africa and the Middle East that first required de Gaulle's attention. They began to erupt on the very day of the celebrations of victory in Europe. In Sétif in Eastern Algeria on 8 May a parade turned into a nationalist demonstration, which swiftly developed into an anti-European riot and spread to the neighbouring countryside. In the next five days 103 white settlers, women and children as well as men, were killed, many of them mutilated. Fierce reprisals followed against the native population: an official investigation set the number of killed at between 1,010 and 1,300, but much higher estimates were also made, ranging from 6,000 to 15,000.[1]

De Gaulle dismissed this Algerian drama in a single sentence of his Memoirs, saying that General Chauvigneau nipped incipient troubles in the bud, and omitting any reference to the killings. On the disturbances in Syria, however, he wrote at much greater length. There the British were involved, and the result was a heavy blow to the French position in the Levant, whereas in Algeria French authority survived apparently undamaged.

As at Sétif, the victory celebrations of 8 May were the signal for anti-French demonstrations in Beirut and all the major cities of Syria. Disturbances continued throughout the month, and the French took counter-measures. On 30 May matters came to a head. The Syrians had appealed to the Big Three against French repression, and a mood of strong disapproval of it had developed at the UN conference in San Francisco. Britain had forces in Syria large enough to control the situation; in the eyes of the Arab world she was a passive accomplice of France because of her inaction. When fighting broke out in Damascus, Churchill felt he must intervene. Having first assured himself of the approval of President Truman, he summoned the French Ambassador on the evening of 30 May and told him that, if the French government did not proclaim a ceasefire in Syria, British troops would have to act to put an end to the bloodshed and ensure the security of Allied communications through the Middle East for the war against Japan. De Gaulle was informed at once, and saw the need to prevent any clash between French and British forces. He had the necessary orders sent to the French commander in Syria the same evening.

Once more, as in November 1943, a crisis in the Levant had ended with a French retreat before a British threat of force. De Gaulle expressed his resentment in memorable terms to the British Ambassador in France, Duff Cooper, whom he summoned on 4 June. 'I recognize we are not at present capable of making war on you,' he protested. 'But you have outraged France and betrayed the West. That cannot be forgotten.'²

Churchill was shocked and wounded. He poured out his resentment in a message of 6 June to President Truman on the subject of yet another dispute which was embittering relations with de Gaulle at that time, his refusal to withdraw French troops from the Val d'Aosta on the Italian side of their common frontier in the Alps when requested to do so by General Eisenhower. It was known that de Gaulle wanted minor territorial adjustments to be made in this area to incorporate French-speaking populations in France, but the Americans regarded that as a matter for the peace settlement. Truman sent de Gaulle a message on 7 June stating that he had cut off supplies of munitions and equipment to the French army until it withdrew its forces from Val d'Aosta and expressing his sense of shock that the French commander in the area, General Doyen, had threatened to use force against American troops if they tried to move in.³ The President prepared a public statement but held it back to await de Gaulle's reply, realizing that any reference to the possibility of an armed clash between French and American troops would provoke an immense sensation.

Before dispatching his message to de Gaulle Truman had sent it to Churchill for concurrence. Churchill agreed and, commenting on Truman's decision to withhold publication, said: 'The publication of your message would have led to the overthrow of de Gaulle, who after five long years of experience I am convinced is the worst enemy of France in her troubles.' The General was, he said 'one of the greatest dangers to European peace. No one has more need than Britain of French friendship, but I am sure that in the long run no understanding will be reached with General de Gaulle.'⁴

De Gaulle acted promptly to prevent an open crisis with Truman. He had a soothing reply sent by Bidault to the President denying that it had been the French intention to use force against American troops. The French soon withdrew from the Val d'Aosta but remained in the small French-speaking areas of Tende and Brigue which the Italians duly agreed to transfer to them when the peace treaty was signed.

The ceasefire of 31 May led to the end of the Syrian affair, which had been the greatest single cause of friction between de Gaulle and the British ever since 1941. Soon both French and British forces were on their way out of Syria and Lebanon for good. There was no question of Britain taking the place of France in the Levant. For de Gaulle what had happened there was a failure not only for France but for Britain and Western Europe. If the European Powers could not retain their presence and influence in Africa and Asia, modified of course to conform with the spirit of the times, he did not see how they could contrive to remain great. They all lost by the departure from Syria, and that departure was due, he thought, to British policy. The consequence would be other Western retreats elsewhere. That was what he meant by accusing Britain to Duff Cooper of having betrayed the West.

Churchill's harsh words to Truman about de Gaulle were the product of the heat of the moment and do not represent his balanced judgement. He omits the message from his Memoirs. It is, however, to be found in Truman's *Year of Decisions, 1945* and must therefore have impressed its recipient, whose own assessment of de Gaulle in his Memoirs is none too favourable: 'De Gaulle was a man of dedicated courage who had rendered important services to France in 1940 . . . however . . . his tendency to use force in pressing national claims made for difficult situations.'[5]

De Gaulle won only qualified support in France for his policy in the Levant and the harshness of his criticism of Britain. Had his clash with Truman developed into an open dispute, public opinion would surely have been even more disturbed at so bitter a quarrel over so small a matter with a power to whom France owed so much. But the General knew when to draw back. As Gaston Palewski, one of his closest collaborators, has observed, he sometimes talked impulsively, but he never acted without reflection.[6] Events soon proved that France's standing in the world had not been lastingly affected by what had happened in the Levant. When the UN conference came to a successful end on 26 June, its Charter provided that France should be one of the five powers with a special responsibility for world peace, a permanent seat on the Security Council and a veto. Thus she acquired equal status in the world body with the four powers whom Roosevelt had foreseen as the guardians of peace, the United States, Britain, Russia and China.

The United Nations, however, were to have no voice in the immediate future of Germany. That was reserved for decision by the

Big Three who met in Potsdam on 16 July for what was destined to be the last of their conferences. It was also to be the last international meeting of major importance to which France was not invited. While it dragged along its contentious but decisive way, de Gaulle observed its progress and continued to concern himself with internal affairs, in particular the preparation of elections.

An important question which arose in July was whether the General should approve his own list of candidates for the elections. If he did so, he was certain to have a powerful group of supporters in the Constituent Assembly to represent his views. But the idea was repugnant to him, because it came too close to the formation of a political party. How could he be both a national leader and a party leader? He made the same choice as he had between the views of Jean Moulin and Pierre Brossolette in London. When René Mayer, the Minister of Public Works, raised the question, de Gaulle replied: 'When will you understand that I have never wanted to be the leader of a majority?'[7] This decision proved to be one of the gravest political errors he ever made. Effective representation in the Assembly would have given de Gaulle a good chance of securing the kind of government and the kind of Constitution he favoured. Nobody seems to have realized that he would need such support after the elections because they would mark the end of his own reign as temporary sovereign.

De Gaulle had the trials of the Vichy leaders to deal with at the same time as the debate on electoral preparations. That of Marshal Pétain began in Paris on 23 July. His judges unanimously found him guilty of high treason but were divided as to the penalty. They sentenced him to death by fourteen votes to thirteen, while expressing the desire that the sentence should not be carried out. It is said that the majority in favour of the death penalty was due to de Gaulle having privately indicated that he thought the verdict necessary for *raison d'état*. He immediately commuted the sentence to life imprisonment and Pétain was incarcerated on the Île d'Yeu. De Gaulle states in his Memoirs that it had been his intention to allow Pétain to end his days in his home near Antibes after two years in custody,[8] but when the time came he was not in power and could not exercise clemency. The rulers of the Fourth Republic kept the Marshal in his island prison until his death in 1951.

In October Laval and Darnand, chief of the detested Vichy Militia, were sentenced to death. In their cases there was no question of commutation of sentence. They died on the scaffold.

These trials were the last of their kind. Judgement had already been delivered on lesser offenders. De Gaulle had always recognized that in the first flush of liberation rough justice would be meted out to some by self-constituted judges, but he had striven, not without success, to impose the due process of law as soon as possible. He states in his Memoirs that 10,842 Frenchmen were put to death as collaborators without a regular trial, while a further 779 were executed after condemnation in court.[9] The former figure is a minimum estimate. Some historians of 'L'Epuration' (the purge) have made much higher calculations, none lower.

One of the General's most painful tasks was that of deciding whether to confirm death sentences. He always exercised his clemency in favour of women and nearly always where minors were concerned. He intervened in some other cases as well, such as that of Charles Maurras, whom he had once so much admired. He asked the Minister of Justice (by telephone) to have the trial of Maurras moved from Lyons to Paris, in order to increase his chances of escaping the death penalty for the support he had given the Germans, but later accepted advice that it should take place in Lyons after all.[10] Maurras, sentenced to life imprisonment, became a Catholic and died. An overwhelming majority of the mail received by the General favoured more clemency towards collaborators than it was the policy of his government to accord.[11]

The execution of Laval and Darnand brought this melancholy chapter to a close. So France passed its verdict on a régime that had failed. But the theory that France had needed Pétain and his followers as a shield in 1940 while de Gaulle re-forged her sword did not die so easily. An opinion poll in Le Figaro in June 1980, on the fortieth anniversary of the fall of France, found more than 60 per cent of the public believed that Pétain had been right to ask for an armistice in 1940.

On 2 August the Potsdam Conference broke up. It failed to coordinate policy between East and West, apart from Stalin's reaffirmation that Russia would join the war against Japan. The Big Three settled some procedural questions relating to reparations and trials for war crimes, but they could not agree on how Germany and Eastern Europe were to be governed. They set up an Allied Control Council for Germany without defining its powers, and a Council of Foreign Ministers which was to meet periodically and try to solve the outstanding problems. France was invited to join both these bodies. By the end of the conference it was clear enough what was going to happen. Each occupying power would govern its zone of Germany as it chose, and the Russians would shape as they pleased, without regard to Western wishes, the countries of Eastern Europe occupied by the Red Army, including Poland.

As at Yalta, absence from the conference table at Potsdam brought with it the consolation that France bore no direct responsibility for the fate of Poland and the rest of Eastern Europe. The *modus vivendi* established in Germany was rather acceptable to de Gaulle, because it meant that France was able to occupy her zones on the Rhine and in the Austrian Tyrol and her sectors in Berlin and Vienna and administer them with a minimum of outside interference. The invitations to join the Council of Foreign Ministers and the Allied Control Council were accepted, and, perforce, the Polish government in Warsaw was recognized. Thus France achieved formal parity with the Big Three in Germany and Austria.

In the middle of the Potsdam conference came the sweeping and unexpected defeat of the Conservatives under Churchill by the Labour party under Attlee in the British elections of 26 July. De Gaulle regretted Churchill's departure from power despite all their quarrels. He had always made allowance for the fact that they were defending different interests and that French aspirations to grandeur sometimes reawakened 'the spirit of Pitt', as he put it, in Churchill's breast. Perhaps he took their clashes less personally than the Prime Minister, and he never forgot that it was Churchill who had given the indispensable support to Free France and to himself in June 1940.[12]

Attlee had his eyes as firmly turned towards America as Churchill, and his accession to power held out no hope of a closer Franco-British understanding. De Gaulle took it as a sign that the British people were tired. 'When I learned that Britain had dismissed the captain she had chosen in the hour of the storm, I foresaw the moment when I would abandon the helm of France – but of my own accord, as I had taken hold of it.'[13]

Four days after the end of the Potsdam conference, the world entered a new age, when the first atomic bomb was dropped on Hiroshima. De Gaulle had known about the American project since July 1944, when three French scientists who had been involved told him about it at a secret meeting while he was in Montreal, after his

American visit. He understood that it meant a qualitative and not just a quantitative change in the nature of warfare, and that the American monopoly represented enormous power. This was illustrated at once when Japan surrendered after a second atomic bomb had fallen on Nagasaki on 9 August. The act of surrender was signed aboard the US battleship *Missouri* on 2 September in Tokyo Bay, with General Leclerc acting for France.

Learning from Roosevelt's error after Yalta, Truman made no attempt to arrange a meeting with de Gaulle while in Europe for the Potsdam conference. Instead it was arranged between them that de Gaulle should visit Washington as an entirely separate exercise some weeks after Truman's return there. The General duly visited the United States and Canada from 21 to 30 August. In Washington he established with Truman that there would be no American opposition, if no direct help, to French reoccupation of Indo-China. Truman had not inherited Roosevelt's strong disapproval of the French return which de Gaulle was determined to bring about. It was also agreed that the United States should make a loan of $1,650 million to France. De Gaulle returned to Paris better satisfied than he had been after visiting Roosevelt the year before.

There were, however, practical difficulties about the reoccupation of Indo-China. The Japanese forces there surrendered to the Chinese in the north and to British troops dispatched from Malaya in the south, but some of their weapons fell into the hands of Indo-Chinese resistance forces, under the leadership of the Communist Ho Chi Minh, who aspired to set up a State independent of France. On 2 September the political movement he led, known as the Viet Minh, proclaimed an independent republic in Tonking, Annam and Cochin China. This was the situation when the main French expeditionary force of 80,000 under General Leclerc arrived in Saigon in early October. De Gaulle's directive to Leclerc instructed him not to send forces into Tonking or Northern Annam until he received further orders, but to concentrate on establishing control in the south of the country. In the north, as well as in the protectorates of Cambodia and Laos, only political contacts were to be sought.[14] This task was sufficient to absorb the energies of the expeditionary force for many months. De Gaulle was able to issue no further directive to Leclerc before his retirement from office in January 1946.

In France the events that were to lead to de Gaulle's withdrawal from power now gathered pace. On 21 October a referendum on the future Constitution and the election of a new Assembly took place simultaneously. In the referendum the electors followed de Gaulle's advice. Ninety-six per cent were in favour of the Assembly producing a new Constitution to replace that of the Third Republic, and 66 per cent voted that its lifetime and its powers were to be limited. It was to have seven months to perform its task. In the Assembly the Communists won the most seats but were closely followed by the Socialists and the centrist *Mouvement Républicain Populaire* (MRP). It was evident that the new government would have to be a coalition of these three parties.

On 13 November the Assembly unanimously elected de Gaulle as President of the government. This act might be regarded as setting the seal of the nation's approval on the account he had rendered of his stewardship since 18 June 1840. But he no longer enjoyed the ultimate power of decision that he had in Algiers and in the provisional government formed in September 1944 in Paris, the power he had assumed in the Brazzaville Manifesto of October 1940. The Assembly was now legislative and constituent, not consultative. It could no longer be overriden as in the past. The government needed the support of a majority of its votes in order to pass laws and raise money. Moreover de Gaulle was President of the government, but the Socialist Félix Gouin was President of the Assembly, of which de Gaulle was not even a member. His new status, or lack of it, was borne in on him when he made an enquiry about the Assembly's work on the Constitution. He was told that he had no right to the information because he was not a member. In fact he had no power over the process of constitution-making, which interested him more than any of the day-to-day problems the government was handling. He could exercise influence only by expressing his personal opinion. He had no political party at his command to work for his views in the Assembly. The MRP under Bidault was far from being completely loyal to him.

De Gaulle had forgotten what such a situation was like, and the rediscovery was no pleasure. Very soon he began to think of resigning. The inclination increased as it became apparent in the course of December that there was a majority in the Assembly in favour of a Constitution which would place effective power in the hands of a unicameral legislature which the President of the Republic would not be entitled to dissolve. This was not at all what de Gaulle favoured, and he saw that if he remained in office he would inevitably give the impression of approving a project to which he was profoundly hostile. In fact the political parties, despite all de Gaulle's warnings, intended to return to the system of the sovereign Assembly which had prevailed under the Third Republic and, de Gaulle thought, played such a part in its disastrous end. He, on the contrary, wanted a system not too different from that which prevailed in Algiers and Paris from 1943 to 1945.

Withdrawal from power appeared to de Gaulle the only way of conveying his dissatisfaction with the Assembly's attitude to public opinion. Before the end of the year his mind was virtually made up, but he felt the need, as always before one of his great decisions, for a period of seclusion and reflection. This left time for his government to obtain approval for a few measures of capital importance for the renewal of France. On 1 January 1946 the nationalization of the sources of credit and of energy, that is to say of existing banks and of gas and electricity, was passed into law. The coalmines had already been nationalized the summer before. Thus the shape of the postwar economy of France was defined. Industry, except in cases where its proprietors had collaborated too blatantly with the Nazis, was to remain in private hands. But on the same day he had to fight off in the Assembly a Socialist attack on the defence budget. He had no taste for government by dispute. In his speech he said: 'This is no doubt the last time I shall speak in this chamber.'

Then de Gaulle withdrew to Antibes for a few days of undisturbed reflection on the future. On 14 January he was back in Paris, his mind fully made up. Having made the necessary preparations and allowed the news of his decision to percolate to the embassies most concerned, he summoned his ministers to his office in the Ministry of Defence in the rue St Dominique on the day most inconvenient to them, a Sunday, 20 January. Without inviting them to be seated he read a brief statement:

The exclusive régime of the political parties has returned. I condemn it. But, unless I use force to set up a dictatorship, which I do not desire, and which would doubtless come to a bad end, I have no means of preventing this experiment. So I must retire.

That was all. In a few minutes it was over, and his ministers filed out to face a new France.

# 25 In Opposition

In fact his ministers welcomed his withdrawal, and that was where de Gaulle made his miscalculation. He believed that the parties could not govern for long without him and that either as a result of their internal disputes or of mass demonstrations in his favour he would be brought back to power more or less on his own terms. Friends like Maurice Schumann and Rémy Roure wrote in the newspapers that his departure might be short-lived.[1] This was what had happened when he had withdrawn during wartime crises to brood like Achilles in his tent.

But de Gaulle was mistaken if he expected French politicians to react as the British and American governments had done. Roosevelt and Churchill had a war to win and were always in a hurry. When it came to the point, they were never simultaneously willing to face the effort involved in breaking with a man who was popular and could not easily be replaced. The political parties in France were under no such pressure. They held lawful power and there was no real threat to their enjoyment of it except de Gaulle, who had chosen to go out into the wilderness. They made no effort to prevail on him to change his mind, and the MRP did not come out in support of the position he had taken. On 24 January the Assembly elected Félix Gouin as President in his place. No indignant crowds arrived from Paris to hale him back to power from the house that he had rented at Marly near the capital. He sent to enquire whether the police had blocked the roads. They had not. The people had stayed at home.

There was no demand in Allied countries for his return. The press in the US and Britain expressed surprise at his sudden departure, and there were some forecasts that it would not be of long duration, but that was all. A memorandum of 4 February from Cordell Hull gave the Ambassador in Paris instructions as to the attitude of the US government: 'The Department's view of French credit needs is not adversely affected by the change in the French government. On the contrary . . .'² The tone of relief is perceptible. As to the British, the Foreign Office had advised Churchill the previous June to 'carry on as things are at present and make the best of de Gaulle in the hope that after the elections . . . he may then perhaps disappear altogether'.³ Their hopes were now fulfilled.

In the months after his retirement de Gaulle remained strangely inactive, as if he believed that the prize of a return would fall into his hands without further effort on his part. He waited and began to write the War Memoirs that were destined to bring him a new kind of fame. Meanwhile the Constituent Assembly completed its labours and submitted the result to a referendum on 5 May. As de Gaulle had hoped, the people rejected it, by a margin of a million votes. It then became necessary to elect a new Assembly and to give it another seven months in which to prepare a revised Constitution and put it to the voters. De Gaulle decided that the time had come to break his silence and try to impose his views on the constitutional question. While awaiting a suitable occasion he moved with his family back from Marly to their prewar home at La Boisserie, by then sufficiently restored from the damage done by the Germans to be habitable.

In the new elections the MRP won most seats, but another tripartite coalition was inevitable. While negotiations between the parties were under way, de Gaulle made his political return at Bayeux, at ceremonies held to mark the second anniversary of his appearance there during the Normandy landings. In his speech he called for a presidential system, one in which the head of State would direct the government, choose his ministers and have the power when necessary to dissolve the Assembly and call an election. This was a direct challenge to the ideas of the political parties, which remained bent on creating a sovereign assembly, and to the traditions of French democracy. De Gaulle had publicly committed himself to a plan as controversial as the 'Armée de métier' had been in 1934. He was in effect proposing a 'Constitution de métier', a modernized system of government, and he remained faithful to the Bayeux plan for the rest of his career.

Immediately afterwards a new administration was formed with Georges Bidault as Premier. It was the moment of truth for the MRP. They had presented themselves to the country as supporters of the

General, and had done their best to suggest that he supported them. Would they try to win approval for a Gaullist Constitution? The answer was no. The Assembly opted for a draft which gave rather more standing than previously to the President, but none of the powers which de Gaulle had described as indispensable. The fact was that Bidault disliked the way in which de Gaulle had treated his ministers from September 1944 until October 1945, and had no wish to revert to it. At this time the last possibility that the MRP might rally to de Gaulle and become his political instrument went by the board.

In October it was time for the referendum on the revised Constitution, which the General had denounced repeatedly in a vigorous campaign. Just over nine million voted in favour and nearly eight million against, while eight million more abstained. It could not have been a more tepid endorsement, but it meant that the Constitution became the law of the land, and it only remained to elect the two houses of the new parliament and establish the government. In November this was done, with results not very different from those of June. After some manoeuvring between the parties Paul Ramadier, a Socialist, became Prime Minister on 16 January 1947, and Vincent Auriol, another Socialist, was elected first President of the Fourth Republic. De Gaulle naturally refused to stand for the office, which would, in his eyes, have condemned him to impotence and deprived him of the right to criticize a new régime which was doomed to repeat all the gravest errors of the old.

Thus in January 1947 the Fourth Republic was in precarious existence and de Gaulle was in the wilderness. His prestige was still immense, but his countrymen saluted him in thanks for services rendered rather than in hope of those to come. And yet he remained passionately convinced that a great task still lay before him. The mission on which he had embarked on 18 June 1940 was unfinished. France had regained her independence and the status of a great power, but not her grandeur: only he could restore that grandeur. How was he to find the means to complete his work?

After consultation with his most loyal supporters, he came to his decision just as the Fourth Republic was settling to its manifold problems. He would have to descend into the arena and at least to some extent play the political game, while preserving his unique prestige as a national rather than a party personality. He must create an organization which would use the system to destroy the system and bring him back to power. On 2 February he revealed his intentions in a talk at Colombey with his private secretary Claude Mauriac: 'I'm going to try to rally the people . . . it's the only hope.'[4] 'Rally of the French People' – *Rassemblement du Peuple Français* (RPF) – was the name he had chosen for the group. It was not to be a political party, but it would contest elections and appeal to the people for their votes as the rules of the Republic ordained. De Gaulle decided to launch the new organization in a major speech.

The news soon leaked to Paris in garbled form and caused acute anxiety among the new rulers. Suspicions were aroused that the General might be meditating a coup d'état rather than a lawful political initiative. When he realized that the launching of the new party was imminent, Ramadier paid a secret visit to de Gaulle at Colombey and had two hours' conversation with him during the night of 1/2 April. De Gaulle assured the Prime Minister that there was no question of himself or his followers acting outside the law, but he rejected Ramadier's appeal for support of the Fourth Republic. 'The present constitution will not achieve the greatness of France, the sole object of my preoccupations and supreme goal of my life,' he replied.[5] He must, he said, take political action as he had done in the Resistance. Ramadier warned him that the government would have to distinguish between its treatment of the national hero and the political opponent. The General did not object. At the end of their talk, he accompanied Ramadier to his car and gave him a parting assurance that he would not become another General Boulanger.[6] So the lines were drawn and the government knew what to expect.

De Gaulle took his next step at Strasbourg on 7 April. He received a hero's welcome from a vast crowd that remembered his intervention with Eisenhower and Roosevelt to prevent the withdrawal of American forces protecting Strasbourg. He was speaking to the 'Alsatian Committee for Gratitude to America'. He told them that France and America would always stand together against any new threat to freedom, spoke of current problems and the inability of the present system to solve them, and proclaimed: 'The time has come to form and organize the rally of the French people . . . the great effort of common salvation and the profound reform of the State.' On 14 April came another speech making his plans more precise.

A few days later a call for recruits to the RPF went out, and the headquarters of the movement began full-time activity in Paris. This set de Gaulle on a new course. Like it or not, he was a politician out of power and seeking to return to it by the same means as other politicians – by trying to win elections. It was an enterprise of which he had no previous experience.

# 26 The Rally of the French People, 1947–53

The six years de Gaulle devoted to the RPF are generally regarded as the least distinguished of his career, and he seems to have shared this view himself, for he dismisses them in a few lines of his Memoirs. Nevertheless the RPF may be said to have justified itself in the long run and to have had its positive aspects even in the short term. While it flourished in its early years it kept public attention focused on the gravest weakness of the Fourth Republic, its inability, like that of its three predecessors, to provide France with stable government, and it offered the nucleus of an alternative and more centralized system to which the nation could have recourse if necessary. In carrying out this function it probably helped to prevent the régime from yielding too far to its vice of inter-party quarrelling. The Fourth Republic worked better on the whole when the RPF was strong enough to be a dangerous critic than when it disintegrated.

For de Gaulle, the chief advantage of the RPF was that it formed for the first time a political organization within which his supporters could combine and function effectively. The framework of the RPF survived the organization itself. It was of value to the Gaullists in the crisis of 1958 that brought their chief back to power, and later. The successive organizations they formed as the political climate varied during his Presidency, the UNR of 1958, the UNR and UDT of 1962, and the UDR of 1967, can be regarded as so many reincarnations of the RPF. The operation which de Gaulle launched in the spring of 1947 never really ceased thereafter.

The nature of the RPF was determined in large measure by two political events which immediately preceded its birth. One was the launching of the Fourth Republic in January 1947; the other was the intensification of the cold war which was signalled by the proclamation of the Truman Doctrine in March of that year. In consequence the

RPF was bound to be anti-Communist as well as anti-Fourth Republic, and his years as leader of the RPF were the period of de Gaulle's career during which he was at his most friendly to the United States and his most hostile to the Soviet Union.

These characteristics were accidental, not essential to de Gaulle's political philosophy, but they deeply marked the RPF and were responsible between them for giving the movement a right-wing, semi-totalitarian image which it was never able to discard. The Socialists among de Gaulle's wartime companions were almost all absent from the RPF, and some moderates remained loyal to the MRP, while the Communists, who had so often been in *de facto* alliance with him during the war, were now his most determined enemies. On the other hand many rallied to the RPF who had sympathized with Pétain during the war and done little or nothing to aid the Resistance.

The programme the RPF put forward was on the lines of the General's Bayeux plan, which was compatible with the democratic process. If the party's methods of dealing with hecklers were rough, this was because it often had to protect meetings from physical disruption by the Communists. There were some ugly incidents, but nothing to compare with the systematic brutality of pre-war Fascist organizations; and the RPF never made a practice of attacking Communist or Socialist gatherings. Important RPF meetings certainly tended to appear demagogic, because they had to build up to the appearance and the oratory of the General. André Malraux was responsible for much of the stage-managing of these affairs, and he was at the same time inventing the technique of *son et lumière* for cultural presentations. There was a kind of overlap in his methods of handling the two kinds of occasion. His use of floodlighting and fanfares to create an atmosphere of excitement might seem to Europeans disagreeably reminiscent of Fascist practices, but to Americans this was already familiar as part of democratic electoral campaigns and in no way shocking. In general the RPF can justly claim to have been better than its reputation.

It got off to a remarkable start, and nearly a million applied for membership in the first month. The tension of the summer months, with the expulsion of the Communists from Ramadier's government in May and the hostile reaction of Moscow to the Marshall Plan, maintained a sense of crisis which made many people think of turning to de Gaulle for leadership once more. The first electoral test of the new organization came in October, when municipal elections were held throughout France: they resulted in a triumph. De Gaulle's candidates far outdistanced the other parties and secured about 40 per cent of the popular vote. This brought them control of the municipal councils of most of the major cities in France, including Paris.

If the leaders of the Fourth Republic had faltered at this stage and decided to call a premature general election, the RPF would almost certainly have won enough seats to be able to form a government at some time in the life of the legislature, and perhaps immediately. Public opinion polls suggested that French voters were already divided along much the same lines as during the years of the future Fifth Republic under de Gaulle, with 40–43 per cent pro-Gaullist, 33–4 per cent anti-Gaullist, and the rest undecided.[1] The General issued a declaration on 27 October calling for the dissolution of the Assembly and new elections, and when Ramadier's Ministry fell on 12 November, it seemed that his demand might be met. Communist-organized strikes were putting a heavy strain on the administration. But he would enter into no deals with the parties. When Henri Queuille, who had been in the provisional government in Algiers, made an approach on behalf of the Radicals to Jacques Foccart of the RPF, offering to support fresh elections if they were given certain assurances about policy and places, it was rebuffed because the leadership believed that events would bring the RPF to power on their own very soon without entangling alliances.

Matters did not go that way. The Fourth Republic took on a new lease of life, and the elections which might have put the RPF in a position to force through a new Constitution were averted. It was Robert Schuman who formed a government on 16 November, and its component parties, MRP, Radicals and Socialists, soon became known collectively as the Third Force, both anti-Communist and anti-Gaullist. Jules Moch, a Socialist at the Ministry of the Interior, was its strong man. He acted vigorously against the Communists, and the strike wave subsided in December.

Doubtless it was in November 1947 that the RPF missed its best chance of coming to power. From that time its hold on the popular imagination gradually weakened. Life began to grow more comfortable and an American-Russian equilibrium established itself in Europe. The Fourth Republic held on, and the economy improved as Marshall Aid began to flow into France and the rest of Western

Europe. US policy had the effect of bolstering up the Third Force.

Support for the RPF grew again briefly in November 1950 when China intervened in the Korean War and there seemed to be a risk of escalation that might even lead to a Soviet move against Western Europe. In this crisis people's thoughts turned once more to General de Gaulle, but tension subsided when President Truman dismissed General MacArthur, the advocate of bombing China. By the time that general elections were held in France in June 1951 the RPF was losing ground again.

De Gaulle made an immense personal effort in the final weeks of the campaign, touring and speaking without respite. During this time he received a message that he can hardly have expected. It came from Mrs Churchill and wished him success in the elections. Churchill was then leader of the Tories and hoping to force a tired Labour government with a slender majority into premature elections. When he heard of his wife's gesture, he was anxious lest it should be criticized as intervention in French affairs in favour of what was widely regarded as an anti-democratic movement. But Mrs Churchill firmly defended her right to make her own political choices.[3] In the event her message remained secret, and her husband returned to power in October.

De Gaulle was less fortunate. The results of 17 June fell far short of his expectation of winning some 200 of the 626 seats in the new house. The RPF, with 21.5 per cent of the vote, won only 120 seats. De Gaulle found himself faced with a new situation; the RPF were now a parliamentary party. They were not strong enough to form a government immediately but, if they manoeuvred with skill and showed a willingness to compromise, there was still a good chance that they would be able to lead a coalition of some kind to power in the course of the five years the new Assembly was due to last. But the General had no taste for such tactics. When they were recommended to him by a loyal supporter, his answer was categorical. 'Never,' he said. 'It will be opposition until the régime collapses.'[4]

If the choice was easy for the General, it was less so for the parliamentarians of the RPF. Inevitably, and quite quickly, the influence of Assembly politics began to operate on them. They were no longer simply supporters of the General, they had responsibilities to their constituents, and reputations and careers to protect. Signs of independent thinking manifested themselves early in 1952 when a financial crisis led to the fall of the Third Force administration formed by René Pleven after the elections. Nobody could find a majority in the Assembly independent of RPF or Communist votes, and there was a run on the franc. In this situation the President asked Jacques Soustelle, as the leader of the largest group in the Assembly, if he could form a government. Soustelle hastened to Colombey and suggested to the General that, although there was no question of the RPF taking office, they might go through the motions of accepting Auriol's invitation and try to turn the situation to tactical advantage. De Gaulle told Soustelle to inform the President that he himself was willing to see him, if he thought it would be useful. Soustelle returned to Paris to be received by Auriol at the Elysée for a further discussion. Apparently it did not take the course de Gaulle had wished. Soustelle emerged and talked to the press as if he himself might form an administration.

De Gaulle, who had also hurried to Paris, was furious: at a meeting of his principal companions he criticized Soustelle bitterly for playing the game of the Fourth Republic. 'Could he be jealous?' whispered André Malraux to his neighbour.[5] The RPF did not enter a government, but twenty-seven of its members voted a few weeks later for the investiture of Antoine Pinay as Premier. They felt it their patriotic duty to do so, as they explained to the General, in order to save the franc from the threat of collapse. With the help of their voices Pinay took office and introduced reforms which bolstered up the franc and the Fourth Republic. De Gaulle never forgot Soustelle's *faux pas*.

These incidents marked the point at which de Gaulle abandoned the hope that the RPF might bring him back to power by action in the Assembly. To prolong the life of the system by patching it up, as the parliamentary group were beginning to do, was the opposite of the purpose for which he had created the RPF; in his view, it was fundamentally harmful to France because it postponed the date when the necessary cure could begin. But the pro-Pinay deputies continued in their course, and in July 1952 a quarter of them withdrew from the RPF group in the Assembly.

East-West tension eased in 1952, and the process went further when Stalin died in March 1953 and his successors began to make placatory gestures towards the West. The world wore a different aspect from that of 1947 when de Gaulle had launched the RPF, and the assumptions he then made were proved to have been mistaken.

War was not inevitable. The conflict between America and Russia was taking subtler forms. He had to think again.

He revealed his first conclusions in May, after the RPF had done badly in the municipal elections in April. On 6 May 1953 de Gaulle declared that the parliamentary group should continue to exist and to act according to its principles, but not in the name of the RPF. At his request it took a new title, '*L'Union des Républicains d'Action Sociale*', the URAS. He called them his 'friends in parliament', but emphasized that their activities did not commit him personally. A kind of theological concept of states of grace and sin was developed for members of the RPF. The true RPF was now a popular extra-parliamentary movement the purpose of which was to bring General de Gaulle to power with a mandate to reform the régime; there was also a parliamentary group whose members were in a state of sin because they worked within the system of the Fourth Republic instead of outside it, but who were adherents of the movement; and then there were those who accepted ministerial posts and were thereby excommunicated from the RPF. The first of these were the five who joined the government of Joseph Laniel in June 1953. Many later governments of the Fourth Republic contained Gaullist ministers.

This was a complicated arrangement and de Gaulle did not always describe it or apply it in the same way. But its institution was a sign that he was no longer thinking of a return to power by parliamentary means. It would have to be some great event, some crisis, that would bring him back to the centre of the scene. The RPF could not create the event, but it might help to exploit it once it occurred. He did not therefore dissolve either the RPF or the URAS, although he detached himself from both. It was useful to have friends on guard, organized and available when wanted. He had not understood that in 1946, but now he did. Having made his dispositions, he settled down to wait for the great event that would cause France to turn to him once again.

At this point in 1953, a glance must be spared for aspects of de Gaulle's life during the years after his withdrawal from office which did not fit into the framework of his labours with the RPF. Life in opposition allowed leisure and imposed austerity, for the General was not rich. From June 1946 he lived simply at La Boisserie with Madame de Gaulle and their handicapped daughter Anne. The other children soon married. Philippe pursued his career in the Navy and Elisabeth became the wife of a young Army officer, Captain de Boissieu. De

Gaulle spent some days in Paris every week for his political work and had regular quarters at the Hotel La Pérouse on the Left Bank, not far from the RPF offices in the rue de Solférino.

On 6 February 1948 Anne died of pneumonia at the age of twenty. It was a release from a heavy burden for her parents, but they were grieved. They had always kept her at home despite the gravity of her handicaps. Anne was deeply attached to her father, who had a talent for entertaining and soothing her. When living with the family he tried to devote some time to her every day, however busy he might be.[6] In 1946, with Pompidou's help, he and his wife had already set up the Anne de Gaulle Foundation for handicapped children, which would have cared for their daughter if she had survived them. De Gaulle did not neglect it after her death. He devoted a considerable part of the income from his writings to its upkeep. As they left the graveside on the day of Anne's burial, de Gaulle took his wife's hand. 'Come,' he said 'now she is like the others.' He could not shake off a mood of depression after Anne's death. 'People say it's a merciful release', he said. 'Perhaps they are right. But I feel as sad as if one of the other children had died.'[7]

De Gaulle was a heavy smoker of both cigarettes and cigars until 1948, when he gave the habit up completely because his doctors thought it might be contributing to the deterioration in his eyesight. A strong effort of will was needed, and he forced himself to it by announcing his decision to those around him. His eyesight was not helped and in 1952 he had to undergo an operation for cataract, which was followed by another in 1956. He commented that the only effect of giving up smoking had been to deprive himself of a pleasure; but he never began again.

A subject in which de Gaulle always took the greatest interest, whether or not he was involved in RPF activities, was the defence of France. In the years 1947–51 he sometimes had apocalyptic visions of a third world war in which France would first be occupied by the Russians and then liberated by the Americans, starting from deep in Africa. His aim was to avert the catastrophe of another occupation by strengthening the French forces and prevailing on the Americans and British to station more troops in Europe. Thus he welcomed the conclusion of the North Atlantic Treaty in April 1949 because it made the American commitment to Europe more definite, though still not categorical enough in his view. He repeatedly warned, however, that the existence of NATO did not make strong French forces any less necessary. When the European Defence Community was proposed in 1952 as a framework for a German contribution to the defence of the West, he roundly condemned it because it would absorb most of the French Army. He was insistent that France must be defended by French forces, and that another solution to the problem of German rearmament must be found.

De Gaulle's confidence in American power to defend the West diminished from 1951 onwards because he came to feel that Truman's dismissal of MacArthur had been a turning-point in the wrong direction for the West. In an interview he gave to Jean-Raymond Tournoux in March 1954, when it had become clear that France was losing the war in Indo-China, he said: 'If America had listened to MacArthur in 1951, she would have won the war in Asia. She alone possessed the atomic bomb . . .'[8] In a press conference a month later he proposed for the first time that France should become a nuclear power. Until then he had been content for France to shelter under the American nuclear shield. But now the Russians had the bomb, and he was developing new ideas which were to be central to the defence policy of the Fifth Republic. They were not affected by the fact that his friend General Eisenhower had been elected President of the United States in November 1952.

# 27 WITHDRAWAL

De Gaulle's withdrawal from affairs was interrupted by brief returns to the scene. One came in the spring of 1954, as public opinion in France suddenly began to show resentment at the plight of the country, which was being asked by its allies both to fight harder in a losing war in Indo-China and to dissolve its Army in an international pooling of forces in Europe. At a ceremony at the Arc de Triomphe on 4 April war veterans booed and hustled the Minister of Defence, René Pleven, the man who had originally devised the idea of the EDC. The government had still not dared, despite American urgings, to submit the EDC treaty to the Assembly.

The General, who had made no speeches since the previous November, when he had again condemned the EDC, perceived a sudden gleam of hope. Was the scene at the Arc evidence that the national spirit was turning against the Fourth Republic and might be ready for de Gaulle once more? He decided to test the climate with a new appeal. On 7 April at a press conference in Paris he attacked the EDC once more and proclaimed, for the first time, that France must have her own atomic weapons. But it was the conclusion of his remarks that attracted most of the publicity. He announced that he would appear at the Arc de Triomphe on Sunday 9 May, the feast of St Joan of Arc, and the day following the anniversary of the victory over Nazi Germany, to salute the Unknown Soldier. He asked the people to be present with him to show that they remembered what had been done to save the independence of France and that they meant to protect it. He invited war veterans to surround the Arc and gave directions to the Army and police as to the part they were to play, without referring to the ministers concerned. The occasion was to be an expression of national unity, he said, and complete silence was to be observed by the participants. In giving orders direct to the armed forces, de Gaulle was exercising what he regarded as his fundamental legitimacy, conferred on him by events in June 1940 and still valid whether he was in or out of office.

This was an effort to revive memories of the great demonstration of 26 August 1944 when the people of Paris had welcomed de Gaulle at the Arc de Triomphe as the saviour of France. Some of his more hopeful followers had visions of an upsurge of popular feeling that would sweep him back to power. De Gaulle himself was more sceptical of the results but willing to make the experiment, as he confirmed on 8 May to Louis Terrenoire, who had been Secretary-General of the RPF since the elections of 1951.[1]

In the event, the French war in Indo-China intervened: the fortress of Dien Bien Phu fell on 6 May, after two months of siege by the Viet Minh. The national mood three days later was one of mourning rather than exaltation. The crowd at the ceremony was considerable but in no way to be compared with that of 1944. De Gaulle, standing erect in an open vehicle, drove up the Champs Elysées to the Arc de Triomphe, laid a wreath in silence and departed in silence. As he climbed back into his car, he murmured to his private secretary, Olivier Guichard: 'Le peuple n'est pas tellement là.'[2] The crowd dispersed without demonstrations.

De Gaulle had more than half expected this disappointment, but it was a disappointment none the less. He abandoned the idea he had been nourishing of denouncing the government for the loss of Dien Bien Phu and trying to provoke a ministerial crisis in which he could intervene.[3] Now began the period of his life which Gaullists call 'The Crossing of the Desert'. When his wartime ally, Pierre Mendès-France, succeeded Laniel as Prime Minister in June, he issued a declaration stating that the existing régime could solve none of France's problems and that he would hold aloof from events.

Mendès-France was not a member of any of the major parties but a left-wing critic whose intelligence and integrity had won him much prestige. The Establishment of the Fourth Republic turned to him at this juncture to face up to problems that had become too pressing to postpone but were still too difficult for them to confront. He carried out this ungrateful task with courage and dispatch. He began by undertaking to make peace in Indo-China in thirty days or resign. He virtually met his time limit. In July an agreement was reached by the Great Powers at the Geneva Conference giving independence outside the French Union to Cambodia, Laos and Vietnam, which was divided into northern and southern zones while preparations were made for an election under international supervision. The Communists took power in the north, but there was a non-Communist administration in the south, where French troops were to remain until the election. For France this was a tolerable exit from a situation that had become untenable.

With this achievement to his credit, Mendès-France went on to open negotiations for the grant of autonomy to Tunisia, and to submit the EDC treaty to the Assembly. On 30 August they finally rejected it by a majority of eight votes, with the RPF members among the hostile majority. Thus the French armed forces were saved from integration, thanks in no small measure to de Gaulle's categorical opposition, which he stated for the last time on 28 August, in time for the decisive debate.

The General and Mendès-France had retained much regard for each other from their association during the war, and Mendès-France went to call on him at Colombey in the autumn, perhaps hoping for some sign of approval or encouragement that would strengthen his position. It was not forthcoming, although their talk was friendly. De Gaulle forecast that Mendès-France would be allowed to liquidate a series of problems that the régime had not had the courage to tackle but would be thrown out if he tried to introduce reforms.[4] Events proved de Gaulle right. Mendès-France fell in February 1955 when he tried to introduce reforms in Algeria for the benefit of the Muslims.

Detached at Colombey, de Gaulle observed the passage of events without public comment. The first volume of his War Memoirs, entitled L'Appel, was published in October 1954 and had an immense success. He had the satisfaction of being recognized as a great writer to console him for his exile from power.

Only once did he emerge from the desert, and when he did it was to make his retreat more formal. On 30 June 1955 he gave his first press conference for fifteen months. He began by announcing that he did not know when he would give another conference, since he was not going to intervene any further in 'public affairs'. It was not possible under the existing régime to solve the problems assailing France. 'The change of the régime and, as a consequence, salvation can only come from a re-awakening of the spirit of the nation [l'esprit public]. It is my hope that I shall be able to contribute once again to this re-awakening, whether it comes soon or late.'

De Gaulle went on to state his views on the main international questions facing France. On East–West détente, he said that France was qualified by historical experience to play a leading role in establishing whether better relations with Russia were possible but that she would only be equipped for the task when she became a nuclear power. Finally he called for a revision of the Atlantic Pact in order to give more effective voice to France and greater ability to protect her overseas interests.

On French North Africa, where armed rebellion had been in progress in Algeria since the previous November, he declared that association must replace domination and that France must develop the strength to be an attractive partner. His words implied but did not state that in the last analysis the peoples of North Africa must be free to choose their own political destiny.

Altogether this was an important press conference. The General's policy on three of the subjects which preoccupied him most during his years as President of the Fifth Republic, East–West relations, NATO and Algeria, is already here in embryo. He did not make another major declaration in public until May 1958, when the process of his return to power began. De Gaulle was already prepared to go further in private and spell out the implications of 'association' for Algeria. He did so at this time to his wartime assistant Geoffroy de Courcel, who was dealing with Moroccan and Tunisian affairs at the Quai d'Orsay.[5]

His main preoccupation during these 'desert' years passed at Colombey was the continuation of his Memoirs. The second volume, entitled *L'Unité* and covering the years 1942–4, appeared in June 1956 and was as successful as the first. Then there was an interval during which he underwent an operation for cataract. He spoke of it to Jean-Raymond Tournoux, who visited him on 30 November and found him wearing dark glasses. 'I don't want to appear in public any more,' he said. In fact he did not do so between 2 August 1956, when he addressed the cadets of St Cyr, and May 1958 – except during a brief tour in March 1957 of the Sahara, where dark glasses excited no comment. Sensitivity about his appearance seems to have contributed to his desire to keep out of the public gaze.

De Gaulle had not quite finished the third volume of his Memoirs when he returned to power in May 1958. It came out in September 1959 under the title *Le Salut*, and ended with his resignation in January 1946. When he resumed writing after his final withdrawal from power in April 1969 it was from May 1958 that he began. He did not consider his years out of office worth relating at any length. But he must have had them in mind when writing the last paragraphs of his War Memoirs. There he describes the view from his study in the tower at Colombey over an unbroken vista of forest, and the small park around which he walked 12,000 times during his years of exile. Solitude and monotony are vividly evoked. Finally he presents his vision of France and of himself:

Old land, consumed by the course of time, bearing the scars of storm and flood, exhausted by its fruitfulness, yet always ready to nourish the living generation.

Old France, bowed under the weight of history, bruised by war and revolution, coming and going between grandeur and decline, yet always raised up by the genius of renewal.

Old man, worn by effort, detached from scheming, feeling the eternal cold draw near, yet never weary of seeking in the shadows for the gleam of hope.[6]

De Gaulle had to wait a long time before the gleam of hope for which he was watching finally appeared. When it did, the cause was the increasingly desperate situation in the Algerian war. This soon gripped the Fourth Republic with even more cruelty than had the Indo-Chinese affair from which Mendès-France released it. In law Algeria was part of France, and all parties save the Communists were committed to keeping it so, as were the European settlers, who numbered over a million and were fiercely opposed to any concessions, even negotiations, with the rebels. The great majority of Army officers was also determined to keep Algeria French and prevent a repetition of what had happened in Indo-China. On the other hand the Muslim insurgents demanded nothing less than full independence and had the support of much of the Third World, particularly the Arab nations, who pressed the case for Algerian freedom in the UN General Assembly, where it soon acquired majority support. To add to the complications, the Algerian war was a matter of far greater concern to French public opinion than Indo-China had ever been, because it was much closer to home and national serviceman were a large component in the forces fighting there, whereas the regular army had borne the whole burden in Indo-China. The combination of these circumstances made the Algerian problem almost as embarrassing and intractable for the Fourth Republic as it could be. By 1956 there were 500,000 troops in Algeria and France was rent by the war.

It was in these conditions that she sought relief by mounting the ill-starred Suez expedition along with Britain and Israel in the hope of toppling President Nasser and deflating Arab nationalism. In November 1956 the Suez enterprise ended in disaster and humiliation with heavy consequences for the prestige of the Fourth Republic. Almost at once some Army officers in North Africa began to think of insurrection and the imposition of a strong authoritarian government which would make victory in Algeria its highest priority. Feelings of hostility also began to grow against the Americans, who had opposed France over Suez, and the British, the ally who had failed her in the moment of crisis. France decided to go her own way in the development of atomic weapons, as de Gaulle had urged in 1954, and in April 1958 the Prime Minister, Félix Gaillard, signed the order for the independent production of a French atomic bomb. Almost simultaneously the French Defence Minister, Jacques Chaban-Delmas, and his Federal German colleague, Franz-Josef Strauss, signed an agreement for joint weapon research. It was rumoured, correctly, that a secret supplementary accord extended collaboration to the atomic field.[7]

As matters turned out, however, the humiliation of Suez and its consequences in Algeria gradually produced conditions in France which were more favourable to de Gaulle's return to power. By the autumn of 1957 he had perceived a gleam of hope. While on holiday in Brittany with his brother-in-law Jacques Vendroux he raised the subject of his own accord, as they were walking around the rocks of Trevenelin Finistère on 22 October, and prophesied that events in Algeria would bring him back to office.[8]

# 28 RETURN TO POWER

After Suez there were three separate groups of Frenchmen who began working against the régime. The first consisted of the European settlers in Algeria and their allies in Paris: the second was composed of certain Army officers in Algeria: the third was a handful of Gaullists, centred on RPF headquarters in the rue de Solférino. There was liaison between the first two, but the Gaullists were rather detached from both. The leaders of both the Army and the settlers in Algeria considered de Gaulle's attitude as expressed in his press conference of June 1955 to be dangerously liberal. On the other hand they lacked a leader with de Gaulle's prestige. A convergence of these groups did not seem impossible to de Gaulle's supporters, and they worked to arrange it.

When Félix Gaillard's government was formed in November 1957, its Minister of Defence was Jacques Chaban-Delmas. He chose Léon Delbecque, a former member of the Resistance, as his special envoy to Algiers.[1] Delbecque, an ardent Gaullist like his chief, established close contact with the various discontented elements in Algeria, and commended to them the return to power of de Gaulle as the best solution of their problem. He returned frequently to Paris to report not only to Chaban-Delmas but to Olivier Guichard, de Gaulle's private secretary. On one occasion at least he was also received by the General himself in Paris, and told him that opinion in Algeria, both civil and military, desired his return to power.[2] The General affected scepticism but imposed no veto on Delbecque's activities.

Chaban-Dalmas was not the only supporter who was trying to turn the situation to de Gaulle's advantage. Jacques Soustelle, who had been Governor-General of Algeria from 1955 to early 1957 and had made himself immensely popular with the white population by his uncompromising advocacy of *l'Algérie française*, was also at work, rallying support in Paris for the formation of an emergency government of Public Safety which would appeal to de Gaulle to assume the leadership of the nation once more.

De Gaulle realized that he might soon be confronted with a last chance to return to power. He was sixty-seven years old, and if he failed to exploit this occasion France would inevitably conclude that he was a hero who belonged to the past. Naturally he adopted his usual tactics of weaving 'a close veil of deception' about his intentions. To those who saw him in the early months of the year he abounded in expressions of pessimism about his future. He told Maurice Schumann: 'I shall never come back to power. Never. It's finished now.' When Schumann passed this on, Michel Debré explained: 'If he's told you that he will never come back to power, it means he's hoping to hear you say the opposite. He thinks of nothing else.'[3] Debré was surely right.

At this stage the government of Félix Gaillard suddenly had to contend with an international crisis arising out of the Algerian war. In February 1958 French planes from Algeria bombed a rebel camp at Sakiet, over the border in Tunisia, killing women and children as well as men. There was an outcry, and the Tunisian government appealed to the United Nations. An Anglo-American commission of good offices was set up, but could achieve nothing. French opinion was angered by this international interference, and Prime Minister Gaillard's government fell in mid-April.

A crisis followed, and President Coty had difficulty in finding a successor. On 5 May he sent the head of his military cabinet, General Ganeval, to a secret meeting with Colonel de Bonneval, de Gaulle's ADC, and Jacques Foccart of the RPF to enquire whether de Gaulle would consider forming a government. This was not an invitation to prepare a new Constitution, and was quite unacceptable, but the approach meant that a dialogue had begun between the General and the President. De Gaulle kept it open by having Coty told that it was 'too soon' to state his terms in detail, but indicating that he would want special powers and did not intend to govern with Parliament, which would have to be suspended for a long emergency period.

Coty then turned elsewhere in his search, and on 9 May he persuaded Pierre Pflimlin of the MRP to try and form a Ministry. But Pflimlin was not acceptable to the French in Algeria, who suspected him of being ready to open negotiations with the rebels of the FLN (*Front de Libération Nationale*). The Army commanders shared this view and decided to take an initiative to block Pflimlin's path. A demand had already been made by settler organizations, stimulated by Léon Delbecque, for the creation in Paris of a *'gouvernement de salut public'*, the formula invented during the Revolution for an emergency government with special powers. The military leaders sent a telegram to General Ely, their superior in Paris, asking him to call the President's attention 'to our anguish, which only a government firmly determined to maintain our flag in Algeria can efface'. But President Coty did not change his mind. The Assembly was summoned to vote on the investiture of Pflimlin on 13 May.

Algiers was now united in its resolve to reject Pflimlin, but the division between the partisans of Delbecque and those, more numerous, who distrusted de Gaulle and aimed at a military government now came to a head. While Delbecque dashed to Paris hoping to bring back Chaban or Soustelle to lead a Gaullist coup on the 13th, the rightists decided to forestall him by occupying government headquarters in Algeria on their own account on 13 May and force the Army to assume direct responsibility for law and order.

On 12 May the Gaullists met in conclave in Paris, Michel Debré, Jacques Foccart and Olivier Guichard among them. It was agreed that the hour had come for Soustelle to fly to Algiers and take charge. But Soustelle demanded the authorization of the General before he would accept the responsibility. De Gaulle, at Colombey, was reticent. 'Let Soustelle do what he thinks he ought to do. I don't want to hear anything about it,' was his message.[4] Soustelle hesitated, and sent Delbecque back to Algiers to say that he would intervene after the military had assumed power, but not until then.

On 13 May events came to a head in Paris, where the Assembly met to vote on the investiture of Pflimlin, and in Algiers, where rightist demonstrators attacked and occupied the offices of the Government-General. At this point the strongest personality among the military leaders came to the fore. He was General Massu, who had won immense popularity among the settlers when the tough parachute division which he commanded had broken the power of the rebels in Algiers in 1957. Massu, although a Gaullist of long standing, had no interest in politics and had not been involved in any way in the plotting for a coup. He now entered the government offices and parleyed with the occupiers, who were led by Pierre Lagaillarde, chief of the student movement. As the price of restoring order they demanded the proclamation of a committee of public safety. Massu consulted General Salan, the Commander-in-Chief, who gave him no clear instructions, and then decided to accept the demonstrators' demand.[5] In consultation with Lagaillarde, he scribbled down the names of Committee members. All were colleagues of Lagaillarde; there were no Gaullists save Massu, the Chairman.

At 8.45 in the evening, Massu emerged on the balcony and read to the vast crowd below a hastily drafted proclamation which was received with applause. Salan continued to hesitate. Imagining the day's work was over, Massu invited Lagaillarde to withdraw his men. Lagaillarde, who wanted to force General Salan to commit himself to an Army takeover by maintaining the tension, naturally refused.

The news was flashed to Paris and throughout Algeria. There followed a period of feverish consultations in the Government-General, during which Massu added some officers and some pro-French Muslims to the list of his Committee. Léon Delbecque, returning from Paris without Soustelle or Chaban, then made his belated appearance and persuaded Massu to appoint him Vice-Chairman. At this point, with General Salan still refusing to play Lagaillarde's game, the Committee began to steer a more Gaullist course and sent a telegram to de Gaulle appealing to him 'to take in hand the destiny of the nation'. The hesitant Salan approved this move, but it was Massu who signed the message. At 11.45 pm he read the text to the crowd in the Forum.

During the night the National Assembly in Paris voted for the investiture of Pierre Pflimlin. Massu gave the news to the crowd in the Forum in terms which made it clear that his Committee would not accept the authority of Pflimlin's 'government of abandon' and counted on de Gaulle to save the nation. It seemed that the French in Algeria, civil and military, were in rebellion. But the legal situation was clouded by two other events which occurred in the small hours of the morning. Before transferring power to Pflimlin, Félix Gaillard gave General Salan civil, as well as military, authority in Algeria, because of the absence in Paris of the Governor-General, Robert Lacoste; and Pflimlin confirmed this decision after he had taken over.

On the strength of his new position, Salan issued a proclamation on 14 May calling for a return to order and stating that the Committee of Public Safety represented the 'Franco-Muslim community' and was to maintain liaison between it and the High Command, which was its superior. This was an effort to bridge with words the gap that had opened up between the rival authorities in Paris and Algiers. In fact, however, the gap widened as public safety committees were set up in the main cities of Algeria, where Pflimlin made no effort to impose his authority.

Everybody was waiting for a sign from de Gaulle, but he made no response to Massu's appeal. It had been manifestly unconstitutional, and he wanted to take power legally. He visited Paris briefly and was urged by his supporters to act before the movement in Algeria lost its momentum. But he accepted the risk of continued silence. Then, on the morning of 15 May, General Salan, whose position was just within the law, gave him the opening he needed. He finished a brief address to the crowd permanently gathered outside his office by shouting 'Vive de Gaulle'. The words may have been due to the prompting of the resourceful Delbecque, who was at Salan's side, but they received an ovation and were immediately flashed around the world.

De Gaulle now decided to go into action, as he might well have done on this day even without Salan's appeal. At 5 pm on 15 May, while he remained at Colombey, a short statement was read on his behalf to journalists assembled at his office in Paris. It spoke of the collapse of the State and declared de Gaulle's readiness to assume once more, as in June 1940, 'the powers of the Republic'.

In his Memoirs the General says that from the moment of his declaration nobody doubted that the crisis would end with his return to power.[6] In fact there was no inevitability about the process. The Fourth Republic still had many defenders who had to be dominated or won over. He had announced that he was ready to take power, but he had not said how. Uncertainty was heightened. He followed up his Delphic pronouncement by stating on 16 May that he would hold a press conference in Paris three days later.

During this waiting period the public safety régime in Algeria established its authority and came out in unequivocal support of de Gaulle. Lagaillarde's rightist conspiracy faded away. Great numbers of pro-French Arabs, more than 20,000 it was claimed, joined in a demonstration in Algiers on 16 May calling for the creation of a government under de Gaulle. On 17 May, Jacques Soustelle finally arrived in Algiers after escaping from surveillance in France and began a personal campaign for a new régime dedicated to the integration of France and Algeria. Potentially most important of all, the generals began planning for an airborne invasion of France, to be called *'Operation Résurrection'*. It was a curious semi-political operation, the aim of which was defined as being to arouse a popular movement in favour of General de Gaulle so strong that the Assembly would be obliged to vote his investiture,[7] but it would have had to turn into a coup d'état in the last resort. The ground had been discreetly prepared for this operation months in advance, and several generals and police chiefs in the Metropolis had already indicated their willingness to collaborate.

Pflimlin struggled to cope with the situation in France, and many potential sympathizers with the movement in Algeria were arrested. Meanwhile a debate raged within the political parties. How should they react to de Gaulle's declaration? The Socialists held the key to the parliamentary situation. If they declared for de Gaulle, there would be enough additional support to ensure a majority in the Assembly for his taking office. But if they joined the Communists in opposing him, they would put his supporters in a minority. At this stage the Socialist leaders, Guy Mollet and Vincent Auriol, were already sympathetic to de Gaulle, but the rank and file were hostile and demanded that he should condemn the generals in Algeria before they would even consider him as a Prime Minister. De Gaulle's continuing negotiation with the Socialists was a most important thread in the tangled web of intrigues and manoeuvres that stretched over the next two weeks.

The General's tactics became clearer at the press conference which he gave to a great throng of journalists at the Palais d'Orsay beside the Seine in the heart of Paris on 19 May. The circumstances were dramatic, for an imposing force of police and soldiers, stationed on both banks of the river, sealed off the meeting-place. But there were no disturbances.

It was three years or more since most of those present had seen de Gaulle. He had aged and put on weight, and there was less power in his voice. But he had lost none of his ability to dominate the scene. He praised the Army for having quelled the disorders of 13 May in Algiers and asked why he should be expected to condemn it when the government had not done so. This was his reply to the challenge of the Socialists, but he linked it with an expression of his esteem for Guy Mollet. He went on to say that he was now prepared to restore the authority of the State and national confidence in it. That was what he meant by 'assuming the powers of the Republic'. Obviously this could not be a routine takeover, and he would have to have special powers. But he was no threat to liberty or to the Republic which he had restored. He ended by saying: 'Now I shall return to my village and shall remain there at the disposal of my country.' With that he departed for Colombey.

De Gaulle was treading a delicate and precarious course on the very frontier of legality. He was trying to use the Army's threat of action against the lawful government in the name of *'le salut public'* in order to persuade that government to transfer power by legal process to him. If that were done, he would prevent the Army taking action. If it were not done, he would leave the régime to its fate. He was not willing to sustain it from outside against those in Algeria who asserted that the Republic was in danger, and that emergency means must be used to save it.

As de Gaulle's press conference had no immediate effect on the authorities in Paris, he exerted further pressure on the situation on 23 May by dispatching a message to General Salan, through the proper channels in the Ministry of Defence, asking him to send a representative to Colombey to report on the situation.

The threat from Algeria became more acute on 24 May when Corsica went over to the dissidents and committees of public safety took control. Gendarmes sent from the mainland to restore order allowed themselves to be disarmed. This was proof of the sympathy of the police in France for the Algiers Committee. *Opération Résurrection* was then provisionally set for the night of 27/28 May, with the understanding among the generals in Algiers that it would only be launched if de Gaulle gave his approval. The Ministry of the Interior in Paris was informed of the timing and reported it to de Gaulle. He knew of it through other channels too, for a parachute officer from Algiers had been in touch with his staff at the rue de Solférino. 'The General is opposed to any military movement,' Jacques Foccart had told him.[8]

On 26 May, de Gaulle judged the time ripe for the next move. He invited Pflimlin to a midnight meeting in the house of a friend of his at St Cloud. Pflimlin, knowing that invasion could be imminent, had no choice but to accept. He admitted that the situation in Algeria was out of his control and asked de Gaulle to impose restraint on the generals. De Gaulle agreed to do this, and made it clear that he expected Pflimlin to resign after his admission of inability to maintain order. The next morning Pflimlin was still hesitating when the General issued a statement that he had begun 'the regular process necessary for the establishment of a republican government capable of ensuring the unity and independence of the country'. He added: 'In these conditions I could not approve action from any source which threatened public order.' The signal to the generals was clear. *Opération Résurrection*, which had in the meantime been put back to 30 May, was suspended but not abandoned.

General Salan's representative, General Dulac, appeared at Colombey on 28 May and presented to de Gaulle the report on the situation in Algeria which he had requested. According to the account in de Gaulle's Memoirs, Dulac told him on Salan's authority that if he did not soon take power 'the High Command would be unable to prevent a military descent upon Metropolitan France'. This curious formulation left unstated, for obvious reasons, the authority who would actually order this military descent of the French Army on France. In response to Dulac the General apparently questioned whether enough troops had been assigned to *Opération Résurrection*. The discussion completed, Dulac hastened back to Algiers to report to Salan on the situation at Colombey. Salan promptly radioed his allies in France: 'We have made direct contact with *le grand Charles*. He makes pressing demand that we should avoid any intervention for the moment. Action foreseen for 30 May is cancelled. It will be resumed this week in the event of difficulties for *le grand Charles*.'[9] So the sword of Damocles was still poised over the government if needed; and the man who could release it was de Gaulle.

Meanwhile Pflimlin's hesitations had come to an end. Despite urgings from extreme Left and Right to stand firm he called on President Coty on 28 May and tendered his resignation. Coty now wished to clear the way to power for de Gaulle, but there was still no sure majority for his investiture. He asked de Gaulle to meet the presidents of the two legislative chambers that evening, 28 May. Their discussion was difficult and inconclusive. Le Trocquer, President of the Assembly, was frankly hostile, but Monnerville, the President of the second chamber, showed some sympathy for the demand for special powers, provided its scope were reduced. De Gaulle acted on Monnerville's advice, as subsequent events proved. To Le Troquer he said: 'If the Assembly follows your line, there will be nothing left for me to do except to leave you to sort matters out with the paratroopers and go home to nurse my regrets.'[10]

The next day, 29 May, Coty sent a message to the two Chambers telling them that civil war threatened and that he was calling on 'the most illustrious of Frenchmen' to save the Republic. That evening he received de Gaulle at the Elysée and they made their plans for the final phase of the operation.

It was still necessary for de Gaulle to overcome the suspicions of the Socialists. He was finally successful on 30 May, when he received Auriol and Mollet at Colombey and spoke to them movingly of his devotion to the Republic and its democratic liberties, and his contempt for dictatorship. They returned to Paris converted, and by a great effort prevailed on the rest of their group in the two chambers to reverse their previous decision and agree to support de Gaulle for the premiership. But the majority in favour of the volte-face among those in the Chamber of Deputies was only 77 against 74!

This slender majority removed the last major obstacle from de Gaulle's path. On 31 May he returned to Paris to reveal his intentions to the leaders of the parliamentary groups. The Communists did not attend the meeting at his hotel. The rest were present, and only François Mitterrand expressed disapproval. Then de Gaulle proceeded to form his government. The Vice-Premier was to be Guy Mollet, and Pierre Pflimlin and the financial expert, Antoine Pinay were among the ministers. On 1 June he went before the Assembly and presented his programme. He asked for special powers to deal with the situation in Algeria and in France; for authority to draw up a new Constitution and present it to the nation for approval or rejection by referendum; and for the two houses to go into recess until their next normal session began in October. After a debate, from which he absented himself, he was voted into power by 329 to 224, with 32 abstentions. Opposition had been substantial to the last, and included personalities such as François Mitterrand and Pierre Mendès-France. In his speech Mitterrand said: 'His two companions in 1940 were honour and the nation. Today they are violence and reaction.' But he ended with a tribute to the unique prestige of the man who 'more than anyone else represents a hope for the peoples of our territories overseas'.[11] When the oratory was over, de Gaulle had won. On 2 and 3 June the two chambers voted him special powers and went into recess until October.

It had been a near-run thing, but de Gaulle had seized his last chance. Moreover he had come to power not on the bayonets of the Army but on the votes of the Assembly. His hopes of leaving a durable political legacy to France were much increased by that fact.

# 29 The Birth of the Fifth Republic

De Gaulle was back in power, but he was only Prime Minister. The National Assembly which had voted him special powers might, at least in theory, take away what it had given and even vote him out of office when it convened once more in October. He had originally proposed to President Coty that it should go into recess for two years, but had been persuaded by Monnerville to retreat on that important point. René Coty was still President and the régime of the Fourth Republic still prevailed. Thus the supreme priority for de Gaulle as he set to work was to secure his own position by bringing the new Constitution into effect swiftly, and he gave the task of drafting it with all possible speed to Michel Debré, aided by a team of talented young officials. But there were other matters that would not wait until he became President. New trends had to be set in defence and foreign affairs, and these will be considered in a later chapter. Algeria and finance came first.

On 4 June he flew to Algiers and an extraordinary welcome. He told the crowds 'I have understood you', and on one occasion during his three-day tour he cried '*Vive l'Algérie française*'. Yet he aroused the suspicion of extremists among the settlers because he did not go far enough. He never proclaimed the integration of the three Algerian departments with Metropolitan France, which was what they most wanted to hear.

Their doubts were justified. In de Gaulle's mouth '*Vive l'Algérie française*' expressed a hope, not a resolve. He hoped that, when the time for self-determination came, as he knew it must, the Arab majority in Algeria would choose of their own volition a close association with France. But he knew he had to move cautiously. The Army had opened the road to power for him expecting that he would in return clear the way to victory in their Algerian war. He could not afford to forfeit their support before he was firmly in the saddle in France. This meant that, unless he could soon negotiate an armistice with the FLN, he would have to give the Army a chance to achieve victory in the field. He delayed a decision while his agents established secret contact with the FLN through Switzerland, but their response, when it came, was cold. The FLN insisted on negotiations for independence, not a ceasefire.

De Gaulle returned to Paris on 7 June and spent the following weeks in France – except for a forty-eight-hour tour of inspection of the Army in Algeria in early July – dealing with the most pressing problems in a prodigious burst of activity. With the help of his Finance Minister, Antoine Pinay, he managed to halt a run on the national reserves of gold and foreign currency. A loan which he launched personally in a radio address on 13 June was an immediate success. In July cuts in budgetary expenditure were decided, together with a twelve-month wage and salary freeze in the public sector. The consequent fall in living standards was taken calmly. Confidence returned, and reserves of gold and currency increased.

On Arab and African matters other than Algerian, the General also took a number of swift decisions over problems that had been dragging on inconclusively under previous governments. He announced in his radio address of 13 June that a new relationship was to be created between France and her overseas territories, and in the next few days agreements were signed in Morocco and Tunisia regulating the stationing of French troops in those countries and providing for withdrawal from many points.

Having thus impressed on the great powers the fact that France was speaking with a different voice, he turned to other matters. The draft of the new Constitution was under study by a Committee headed by Paul Reynaud, and he took part in its deliberations. On 14 August a project was published envisaging a régime very much on the lines of the proposals he had first advanced in his speech at Bayeux on 16 June 1946 and repeated from time to time thereafter, which would give effective power to the President of the Republic to direct the nation's affairs. It was to be submitted to a referendum on 28 September, a week before the end of the parliamentary recess. If it were approved by a majority the dissolution of the Assembly and new elections would follow automatically. The politicians would have no further chance to use the rules of the Fourth Republic against him.

There was to be a referendum in the overseas territories too, in which the inhabitants were to decide whether, and if so how, they were to be associated with France in future. A range of choices was open, from the status of a French department through membership of the new French Community to total independence. In the last ten days of August de Gaulle made a rapid tour of Madagascar and Africa explaining to huge crowds everywhere the significance of the decision that lay before them and encouraging them to opt for association with the Community. This involved joint arrangements in the realms of foreign affairs, defence and finance, and qualified the new nations for economic and technical aid from France.

By the end of the month he was back in Paris, his mission largely accomplished. He had succeeded in doing what had always been beyond the ability of the leaders of the Fourth Republic. He had perceived and anticipated the inevitable, which was freedom for the black African territories to choose their own political future. He had offered it to them instead of temporizing while the danger of armed rebellion grew. A different and more friendly future relationship was made possible. It was almost an advantage that one country, Guinea, had chosen to sever all links with France. Her fate could serve as an object lesson to the rest. De Gaulle intended that the severance should be total. He was not interested in Prime Minister Sékou Touré's professed willingness to go on accepting French aid without links.

On 28 September the constitutional referendum was held and resulted in a triumph for de Gaulle. Eighty-five per cent of the electorate voted in France, and 79 per cent of them were in favour of the new system, the purpose of which was to bring about a major shift in the balance of power within the State away from Parliament towards the Executive. The President, little more than a figure-head under the previous régime, would now become an elective monarch entitled to determine the main lines of national policy and to enforce them through the instrumentality of a strong government under the Prime Minister of his choice. He could also dissolve Parliament and call fresh elections after consulting the Prime Minister and the Presidents of the two chambers; but this he could only do once in twelve months. In addition the President had powers under Article 16 to take 'the measures required by the circumstances' in the event of a national emergency. The large discretion thus accorded to the President aroused some disquiet, but de Gaulle let it be known that it was designed for use only in a crisis such as that of June 1940.

The National Assembly and the Senate, though weakened, were not reduced to impotence by the changes. The Assembly voted the laws and the budget and could pass a vote of censure on the Government. It would clearly be difficult, if not impossible, to rule indefinitely against a hostile majority in the Assembly. But Parliament lost the power it had enjoyed under the Constitution of 1946 of electing the President. That was confided to a large electoral college of some 80,000 in which representatives of local assemblies and mayors predominated. Elections were to be held for the new and no longer sovereign parliament, and for the office of President, where the real power would in future reside and for which the General was the predestined candidate. De Gaulle's supporters immediately took the important step of launching a political organization, the UNR (*Union pour la Nouvelle République*) to contest the elections. They made use of the administrative machinery of the RPF in order to rally recruits.

The election results overseas were as satisfactory as those of the constitutional referendum. All the black African territories except Guinea voted by huge majorities for membership of the Community. Guinea chose independence and had isolation thrust upon her. De Gaulle ordered the cessation of aid and the recall of French officials. Equipment owned by France was removed. Even telephones were ripped out. De Gaulle made a definite effort to deter others from following the course chosen by Guinea, and complained to Dulles when the Western allies began to send her aid, and supported her application for admission to the United Nations.

In Algeria too the results were encouraging. The rebels had ordered the Arab population not to vote, but 3.5 million out of an electorate of 4.5 million ignored their directions. Ninety-six per cent of them voted for '*l'Algérie Française*'.

Strengthened by this success, de Gaulle felt the time had come to make a fresh approach to the Algerian rebels who had responded so coldly to his overtures in June. First he acted to reassure the settlers about their future and to take the army in Algeria out of politics. He went to Algeria immediately after the referendum and announced in a speech at Constantine a plan for expanding the country's economy with the help of increased aid from France. He also ordered all military officers to resign from the still existing committees of public safety.[1] Then, back in Paris, he made his appeal to the rebels. In a press conference on 23 October he called for an armistice, a *paix des braves*. It was a striking phrase, which put the two sides on a basis of moral equality, and he made it clear that he was ready to negotiate a ceasefire with envoys from the rebel leadership based in Cairo. But he did not speak of negotiating independence. His offer assumed a continuing French association with Algeria; and the insurgents were invited to approach the French lines with a white flag if they wished to accept it. This smacked too much of surrender. The response of the FLN was a swift and blunt refusal. Their leader, Ferhat Abbas, speaking in Tunis on 25 October, declared that the problem of Algeria was not military but political. There must be negotiatons not on a ceasefire but on the whole question of Algeria's future. He called on the rebels to continue to fight.[2]

This was a painful setback. De Gaulle had provoked the distrust of the French in Algeria without conciliating the rebels. Talk of 'another 13 May' began to spread among the settlers who had been shocked by the appeal for 'a peace of the brave'. The obduracy of the FLN left de Gaulle with no choice but to turn to the Army for help. He replaced General Salan by General Challe, who was to direct the great offensive.

The parliamentary elections brought consolation. They were held in two rounds in November under the new system of the single transferable vote. The result was an impressive success for the UNR, which won 206 of the 536 seats in the new Assembly and could be sure of finding enough allies to provide a Gaullist government with a working majority. It was now abundantly clear that the presidential election on 21 December would be no more than a formality. So it proved. De Gaulle received 78 per cent of the votes cast in the special college of 'notables' and so surmounted the last obstacle on his path to the power he sought.

Before assuming office as President, de Gaulle spoke to the nation on radio and television on 28 December. Most of his speech dealt with the measures which he had decided to take in order to put the national economy on a firm basis before it was exposed to the challenge of the Common Market, which was to come into operation on 1 January 1959. These had been prepared by a committee headed by the conservative economist Jacques Rueff, and had remained secret until

The RPF (*Rassemblement du Peuple Français*) meets, 1952

Disappointment at the Arc de Triomphe, May 1954; the masses were not there

'You have been the flood and the dam'; de Gaulle to Massu, Algiers, June 1958

French government poster celebrating peace in Algeria, 1962

Family wedding, summer 1962; the plot to assassinate him there miscarried

De Gaulle with his new Prime Minister, Pompidou

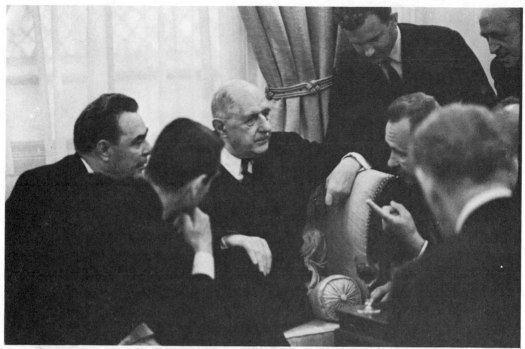

With Brezhnev and Kosygin in Moscow, June 1966

German mediator President Luebke between Johnson and de Gaulle at Adenauer's funeral, April 1967.

De Gaulle with Prime Minister Johnson, Quebec, 1967

The Latin Quarter, May 1968

Gaullists demonstrate in the Champs Elysées, 30 May 1968; the turn of the tide

Ireland, June 1969; the final chapter

this post-electoral moment. As de Gaulle says in his Memoirs, if they were good for the State, they were hard on the citizens. The essence of them was that taxes were to be increased and social services cut. Finally, and most important of all, the franc was to be devalued (by 17.5 per cent, but de Gaulle left it to Pinay to announce the figure) and, thus protected, to become convertible for foreign transactions. Ninety per cent of trade with Europe and 50 per cent of trade with the dollar area was also freed of controls.

De Gaulle was announcing the second general lowering of living standards since his return to office, and at the same time the first steps in the dismantling of the protective commercial barriers behind which France had lived since the nineteenth century. She was preparing to compete on equal terms with Germany, Italy and the Low Countries in the Common Market. It was a major exercise in modernization, a change such as the Fourth Republic had often discussed but never been equal to introducing, and it was accepted calmly by the citizens.

At the year's end de Gaulle was entitled to feel satisfied at the results of his advance on a broad front since June. Above all, the new Constitution had been accepted by an overwhelming majority of votes, and had endowed France with a system of strong government such as he had desired all his life. In one sector only had he encountered real disappointment, and that was Algeria. He had not yet found the key to that problem.

On 8 January 1959 de Gaulle drove to the Elysée, to take over from René Coty. He records how, as he returned alone from the ceremony of laying a wreath at the Arc de Triomphe, he heard the gates of the palace close behind him. 'From now on,' he says, 'I was the prisoner of my mission.'[3] He was also the master of the Fifth Republic, vested with powers not much less than those he had exercised during the war; and this time they had been conferred on him by the votes of the French people.

# 30 ALGERIA, 1959—62

Now for the first time de Gaulle had the power systematically to pursue what had always been his aim, the aggrandizement of France. He made his loyal follower Michel Debré Prime Minister of the new government, from which Guy Mollet resigned in disapproval of the economic measures announced on 28 December. De Gaulle hoped, as he said in his Memoirs, to endow the country with an administration which would restore the stability it had lacked 'for the past hundred and sixty-nine years', ever since the great revolution of 1789. As was so often the case, de Gaulle's idea of change involved in part a reversion to an earlier state of affairs.

If there was no impediment to the exercise of de Gaulle's will at home, other than criticism from minorities of Left and Right, there was still an obstacle overseas: Algeria. He must surmount it before the road to the building of the new France lay straight before him. The problem was so preoccupying for the next three and a half years, until peace had come, and had so little direct connection with France's other concerns, that it is best treated on its own.

De Gaulle's first overtures had already been rejected by the rebels, and it was necessary to strike another note. Manifestly there was no question of his turning back to the idea of integration. He had avoided using the word on his visit to Algeria in June 1958, when the *pieds noirs* – as European settlers born in Algeria were called – and the generals had been hoping to hear it. He understood that, even if the Muslims had been willing to accept integration, its implementation in any real sense would have imposed an intolerable financial burden on France. It would also have meant war to the bitter end with the FLN, who had made their commitment to independence even clearer by forming a provisional government in Cairo (*Gouvernement provisoire de la République algérienne*, GPRA) in September 1958, which Peking, but not Moscow, had already recognized.

How then could he give an acceptable sense to the formula of 'association instead of domination' to which he had been committed since 1955? He produced no immediate answer but introduced two new factors into the situation. One was the formation of the new Community of Madagascar and the French African States which he hoped might have some appeal for the Algerian rebels; the other was the opening in March of the biggest offensive yet launched by the French Army in Algeria.

In Algeria General Challe's forces struck hard. After June the rebel forces (*Armée de la libération nationale*, ALN) were unable to operate in units larger than companies. Challe achieved dispersion of the enemy but not annihilation.[1] From 27 to 30 August de Gaulle went on a tour of inspection, his first visit to Algeria for nine months, and saw that the Army had achieved the objective he had set. It was master of the terrain even in the wild hill country. From then on the rebels had no hope of inflicting another Dien Bien Phu on the French. But de Gaulle drew from this success the opposite conclusion to that of his generals. They thought that *Algérie française* could and should continue to exist indefinitely under the protection of the Army. De Gaulle, on the other hand, had to take into consideration the fact that the mass of the Algerians wanted to decide their own fate, that the majority of world opinion increasingly supported the rebellion and condemned French action against it, and that the Army's effort was ruinously expensive. He regarded the military success as the occasion for a new peace offer from a position of relative strength, and he tried during his tour to explain his thinking to Challe and the officers of the élite regiments which constituted the spearhead of the French forces. He made few, if any, converts, but he judged that the Army would obey his orders even if he made a radical departure from the Algerian policy of the European settlers.

On 16 September de Gaulle took his fresh initiative in an address to the nation. He announced that France would give the people of Algeria the right to determine their own future by a free vote: they could opt for independence without France, as Guinea had done; or '*francisation*', a new word for integration; or independence in association with France and aided by her, which was of course the choice he commended to them. After the war had ended, there would have to be an interim period of up to four years before self-determination took place. De Gaulle would decide the timing. The political organization behind the rebellion would be entitled to take part in the elections on the same terms as other movements in Algeria.

The use of the word 'self-determination' radically changed the situation. It sounded the death-knell of *Algérie française*, unless the Algerians themselves opted for it, which was inconceivable. It therefore enraged the French in Algeria, for whom de Gaulle was now exposed as a traitor, and it shocked the Army. An armed civilian organization, the *Front National Français*, was formed in November by right-wingers. To the rebels, however, de Gaulle had once again offered too little. Shaken though they were by their losses in the field, they could hardly be expected to accept a ceasefire and an interregnum of political activity under French control which might last as long as four years. Once they abandoned the fight, it would be immensely difficult for them to resume it if de Gaulle disappeared from the scene and his successors changed policy, and there was no assurance that they would win an election after years of peace. The GPRA spokesman in Cairo welcomed the use of the word 'self-determination', and did not rule out the possibility of negotiations on certain conditions, but in fact the rebels did not shift from the position which they had publicly adopted as long ago as 1956: no ceasefire before independence, no negotiations except for independence. De Gaulle was disappointed once more.

In December 1959 there was disappointment for him in Africa too. The newly-formed Community already showed signs of losing its cohesiveness. The governments of Madagascar and Mali informed him of their wish to leave it and adopt a looser form of association with France. De Gaulle had hoped that the Community would last much longer as an institution, and that a liberated Algeria might even elect to assume in it that 'place of choice' of which he had spoken in the past, but it was evident that this possibility was now disappearing. He put the best face he could on the matter and promptly accepted in a speech at Dakar the principle that any member of the Community might make the same choice as Mali and Madagascar and still remain on friendly terms with France. In the course of 1960 all members of the Community were duly to make this choice.

In January 1960 an unforeseeable incident produced the threatened explosion among the white population. General Massu, the most popular soldier in Algeria with the settlers, gave an indiscreet interview to a German journalist in which he said that the Army no longer understood de Gaulle's policies and that its chiefs would not give him unconditional obedience. He went so far as to concede that perhaps it had been a mistake to bring him back to power in 1958. Massu thought the interview was off the record, but on 18 January it was published in the *Süddeutsche Zeitung*. De Gaulle recalled Massu from Algeria at once, and administered a thunderous rebuke, but he recognized that he had been misled into his indiscretions. There was no court martial. Massu remained a General, temporarily unemployed. Challe pleaded in vain for him to be sent back to Algeria, warning that his dismissal might have dire consequences.

The news that their hero had been so summarily removed was, however, more than the *pieds noirs* could bear. The extremists, already organized, saw their chance to appeal both to the civilian population and the Army. They called a general strike for 24 January, and armed groups occupied and barricaded key points in Algiers the day before. Their leaders, Ortiz, Susini and Lagaillarde, asked their military allies, of whom the most important were a number of colonels, Argoud, Massu's chief of staff, Gardes, an expert in psychological warfare, and others, to bring the Army over to their side. Their aim was stated by Susini to members of the FNF: 'The hour to overthrow the régime has struck. The revolution will start in Algiers and move to Paris.'

But there was no serious planning behind Susini's wild words. He and his followers had no party or political leader to turn to in France. Their only chance of achieving results lay in the Army's response to their appeal. It turned out that the influence of the friendly colonels was limited. There was plenty of sympathy for the FNF among territorials, paratroopers and Foreign Legionnaires, but senior officers hesitated. Suddenly everything depended on General Challe, who had just returned from an interview with de Gaulle in Paris.

Challe had been preoccupied by his campaign against the ALN, and did not realize how far some officers had gone towards conspiring against the State. He was for *Algérie française*, but still loyal to de Gaulle. Deciding reluctantly to do his duty and clear the FNF out of the city, but with minimum use of force, he ordered gendarmes and paratroopers to carry out the task on the evening of 24 January. The FNF opened fire on the gendarmes, killing 14 and wounding 123. The paratroopers, no doubt deliberately, arrived too late to go into action. The operation was a failure. 'Barricades Week' had begun, and for the first time Frenchman had killed Frenchman in Algeria.

On the night of 24/25 January de Gaulle broadcast to the nation calling on the rioters to lay down their arms, ordering the Army to obey him, and vowing that he would make no concessions. It was an uncompromising statement, and public opinion in France endorsed it. The FNF stood fast behind their barricades and fraternized with the paratroopers who were supposed to be confronting them. But the generals did not go over to them, and on 28 January Challe and Delouvrier, the Governor-General, withdrew to a secure airbase outside Algiers to avoid any risk of being kidnapped. The hopelessness of the extremist cause began to appear, and de Gaulle administered the final blow in another televised appeal to the nation on 29 January. Dressed in uniform in order to recall what he had meant to France during the war, he reaffirmed the right of the Algerians to choose their own future, but denied that he wanted a break between France and Algeria. 'On the contrary I think everything can be settled, and settled in France's favour, when the Algerians have had an opportunity to make known their will.' He appealed for the trust and support of all, so that France might not become 'a broken plaything'.[2]

The impact of the speech was tremendous. Declarations of loyalty flooded in from all quarters, including Army units in Algeria. The insurgents behind the barricades melted away. On 1 February Ortiz and Lagaillarde surrendered. De Gaulle had won. Debré, who was out of sympathy with this policy of self-determination for the Algerians, offered to resign as Premier, but de Gaulle insisted that he should remain in office. Only Soustelle and Cornut Gentille, who were committed to the cause of integration, left the government.

The victory, however, was not conclusive. The Army had resisted the temptation to join forces with the *pieds noirs*, but some elements had wavered and had to be disbanded. Captured ringleaders were sent for trial. De Gaulle had to face the fact that the Army was deeply unhappy about his intentions. There was danger too in the state of French opinion. Polls taken in February showed that 72 per cent supported de Gaulle's Algerian policy, but 75 per cent still hoped for a free Algeria closely linked with France. De Gaulle took this into account when touring Army units in Algeria during March 1960. He repeatedly expressed confidence that the Algerians would choose close association with France. 'Independence is a monstrosity. France must remain in Algeria.' These were Delphic pronouncements that misled many of his hearers as much as had his cry of '*Vive l'Algérie française*' in June 1958.

In fact the prospects of the FLN accepting any form of association with France were growing more remote. In January just before 'Barricades Week' a National Council of the rebels held in Tunis had given more power to the extremists, among whom Boumedienne, the Chief of Staff of the Army, was increasingly prominent. These hardliners interpreted the drama in Algiers as proof that French unity was cracking and that they had only to fight on in order to gain complete independence. On the battlefield, however, Boumedienne was prudent. He withdrew part of his hard-pressed forces to Tunisia to regroup and wait for better days.[3]

Just when there seemed no hope of rapprochement from either side, an event as unforeseeable as Massu's outburst to the press changed the atmosphere. Again it was an expression of the fighting man's impatience with political manipulation, but this time it came from the Algerian side. The chiefs of the Fourth Wilaya (Military District), the most important of the six into which the FLN had divided Algeria, decided that de Gaulle's peace proposals gave the rebels the essence of what they wanted and that negotiations should be opened for a ceasefire which would put an end to the sufferings of the men in the field. In a series of radio messages, which were intercepted by the French, they told the leadership in Tunis that unless the GPRA approached the French, they would do so themselves. When the GPRA replied evasively, Wilaya Four made good its threat and sent envoys to the nearest French official to request secret contact with a high authority from Paris.

This looked like the fruit of the Challe offensive, which had hit Wilaya Four, adjoining Algiers, very hard. The commander of a single district was not in himself an adequate negotiating partner for de Gaulle, because he could not commit the FLN and deliver peace. But there was the hope that the leadership outside Algeria, who knew what was happening, might themselves show more flexibility in order to prevent the break in their front becoming public and perhaps infecting other Wilayas. De Gaulle therefore sent his chief adviser on Algeria, Bernard Tricot, to parley in secret with Wilaya Four and play on the fears of the men in Cairo and Tunis. At the same time he had General Challe posted to Germany and put a damper on military activity.

Discussions went forward with Wilaya Four until in June de Gaulle decided to see its commander, Si Salah, in person. With a couple of companions Si Salah was flown to France and received in secret at the

249

Elysée on the night of 10/11 June. To the simple Algerian it was an adventure out of the Arabian Nights. He was wafted through the air from his native desert to a palace where he was courteously received by its ruler. But, again like the Arabian Nights, the welcome concealed a trap. De Gaulle, though courteous, proposed no agreement. He told his guest that he was first going to make a new offer of negotiations to the GPRA and that, if they did not accept, he would deal with him instead. Evidently there was no need to bring the Algerian to Paris in order to give him such an inconclusive message. De Gaulle must have wanted the meeting to become known to the GPRA leaders in order to sharpen their fears of being outflanked if they were too rigid and so to induce a positive response.

In the event the rebels did send an unprecedentedly swift and forthcoming reply to de Gaulle's speech of 14 June in which he appealed to them to come 'and find an honourable end to the fighting, after which the way to self-determination would be open'. Their delegates arrived at Orly on 25 June and were housed at the prefecture at Melun. Discussions broke down after only a few days, because de Gaulle refused the Algerians' demand that he should take part personally. No doubt they felt entitled to be received at the same level as Si Salah. That unfortunate went on a mission to a neighbouring Wilaya on 21 June and never returned. De Gaulle did not have the option of turning back to him after the breakdown at Melun, even had he wished to do so. He had sacrificed a minor piece for a questionable result.

In his Memoirs, de Gaulle professes satisfaction with what was achieved at Melun, in that the two sides had sat around a table for the first time. But the failure to make progress looked like a setback for him. The rebel leaders, no longer threatened by Si Salah's initiative, made no further move. In the autumn the GPRA had the encouragement of being recognized by the Soviet government. Then, in November, Senator Kennedy, long an outspoken advocate of the right of the Algerians to self-determination, was elected President of the United States. De Gaulle would have preferred the defeated Nixon, who as Vice-President under Eisenhower had learned the importance of showing consideration for the susceptibilities of France and her leader. Clearly the international climate was growing less sympathetic to the French position in Algeria.

Pressure for change was mounting in France too. On 5 September 1960 'The Manifesto of the 121' was issued. Signed mainly by left-wing, but non-Communist, intellectuals, it called on conscripts to refuse military service in Algeria. The subversive appeal to the Army was not without danger, but, since the manifesto showed increasing readiness in France to accept the further concessions over Algeria that de Gaulle now knew were inevitable, it cannot have been wholly unwelcome to him. Speaking on 4 November he declared he had chosen the road to 'an Algerian Algeria' which would decide its own destiny. Later in the month he appointed for the first time a Minister for Algeria, Louis Joxe. Then, in early December, he made a tour of Algeria. He was better received by the Muslims than by the *pieds noirs*. This was one of the few occasions on which de Gaulle, so used to enthusiastic welcomes all over the world, faced hostile crowds. He cut short his tour and returned to Paris, having changed his itinerary but not his intentions.

Speaking to the nation on radio and television on 20 December, de Gaulle announced a referendum on the Algerian question. On 8 January 1961 the French people, including of course the population of Algeria, were to be asked if they approved the grant of self-determination to the Algerians when peace had been restored. The Algerians could break with France if they wished, but, said de Gaulle, every practical consideration favoured a close association. Over a million Europeans lived in Algeria, who were essential to the country's life 'and whom, come what may, France, whose children they are, is determined to protect'. He ended by saying that France was ready to receive at any moment the delegates of those who were fighting her. As soon as the bloodshed stopped, the French government could settle 'with the various tendencies in Algeria, and, in particular, with the leaders of the rebellion' the procedure for exercising free self-determination. He appealed for a massive vote in favour of his proposals.

The call for a referendum improved the atmosphere and eased international pressure on France, to which de Gaulle was sensitive. The UN General Assembly, always sympathetic to the FLN, contented itself with a vote passed on the day of de Gaulle's speech which affirmed the right of the Algerian people to self-determination. Some Third World governments even urged more flexibility on the FLN.

On 8 January 1961 the French people gave de Gaulle the massive vote for which he had asked. Of those going to the polls in Metropolitan France, 75 per cent approved his proposals, as did 71 per cent in Algeria. The boycott of the elections proclaimed by the FLN had only a limited effect; there was a 59 per cent turnout. The one discordant note was struck by the *pieds noirs*. The negative vote of 786,536 in Algeria corresponded closely to the numbers of the adult settler community.

Among them, the sobering effect of the failure of 'Barricades Week' had worn off. The mood now was one of desperation, and those leaders who had made good their escape to Spain began actively plotting another coup, in consultation with General Salan, retired from the Army and settled in Madrid. General Challe also retired from the Army, prematurely, in January 1961, embittered by the use de Gaulle had made of his successful offensive in Algeria. However, he did not immediately join the plotters, who in February formed a new movement which they called '*Organisation Armée Secrète*', to fight for *Algérie française* by terrorist methods. A wave of bomb outrages perpetrated by the OAS soon began in Paris. They could not have chosen a method better calculated to alienate French and world opinion if they had tried.

On 30 March the French government and the GPRA published simultaneous announcements that peace talks would begin at Evian on 7 April. De Gaulle had cleared the way by abandoning his insistence on a prior ceasefire. Delay was immediately caused when the suspicions of the rebels were aroused by a statement by Louis Joxe that he would be negotiating with more moderate Algerians as well as the FLN. The talks did not begin on 7 April, but the announcement of them hastened the final preparations of the conspirators in Spain for a new putsch in Algiers. Challe agreed late in the day to lead a rising headed by four retired generals, himself, Salan, Jouhaud and Zeller. They knew they could count on the support of the French in Algeria, and believed – on inadequate grounds – that the armed forces would this time desert de Gaulle. Some of them even harboured the illusion that they could count on the support of the CIA because of American dislike of de Gaulle's disruptive influence on NATO. Challe had no plans for invading France. He believed he could hold Algeria for long enough, about three months, to win the war against the rebels and present France with the *fait accompli* of an *Algérie française* completely pacified. Reconciliation would inevitably follow, he thought. Some of his fellow conspirators had different ideas. Nothing was firmly organized, as events were soon to show.

The plotters were smuggled into Algeria by various routes. Their secret was ill kept, but, despite the warnings that reached them, the French authorities took no effective precautions. Challe launched his putsch on the night of 21/22 April and General Gouraud, commanding at Constantine, declared for him. His supporters seized Oran, and most of Algiers, but only part of the Army came over, while the Navy and much of the Air Force stayed aloof. De Gaulle made a passionate speech on the night of 23 April, condemning the 'quartet of generals' who had attempted the putsch and appealing to their soldiers not to follow them. Opinion in France at once rallied to him as strongly as it had in January 1960. The Ministry of the Interior was besieged by Gaullists demanding arms, and the Communists echoed the demand on behalf of their own militants. President Kennedy gave assurances of firm American support. De Gaulle did not respond to any of these offers, but he took emergency powers under Article 16 of the Constitution, and some 1,800 suspected sympathizers with the putsch were arrested.

In Algeria events took the same course as in Barricades Week. Support drained away from the wavering generals. Gouraud returned to his allegiance, and on 27 April Challe gave himself up. Zeller did the same some days later, but Salan and Jouhaud went underground to work with the OAS.

The infection of the Army had proved only partial, but it had gone deeper than the year before. A purge had to be carried out. Five generals and some two hundred officers were placed under arrest. All officers had to account for their movements during the days of the putsch, and disloyal regiments were disbanded. Generals Challe, Zeller and Gouraud were sentenced to long terms of imprisonment. The morale of the rest of the Army was profoundly affected, and yet it stood firm upon the terrain in Algeria. The ALN contented itself with bombings and small-scale activities. Boumedienne kept his main army in reserve in Tunisia and made no effort to exploit the situation.

When the peace talks at Evian finally opened on 20 May, the negotiating hand of the French had been gravely weakened by the Generals' Putsch. The European settlers in Algeria had sided with the conspirators and were still supporting the OAS. In these circumstances it was not easy to secure from the FLN guarantees of their rights in an independent Algeria. The other principal aim of the French team, led by Louis Joxe, was to obtain assurances that their stake in the oil of the

Sahara would be respected, but the FLN were unhelpful on this too. By the end of July, the talks had reached an impasse. The Algerian delegation, which had yielded nothing, returned to Tunis to meet a barrage of criticism from FLN extremists for their excessive flexibility. The war did not flare up again, but there was no peace and countless terrorist incidents between OAS and FLN. In France too the OAS continued with their bombings. One of their most mindless atrocities was to murder the unfortunate mayor of Evian, merely because his town had been chosen as the venue for the peace talks.

In the FLN camp, negotiations with the French had once again been followed by internal disputes. The fourth National Council took place in Tunis in August and Boumedienne and the army chiefs, supported by Ben Bella from confinement in France, criticized the political leadership for its weakness. Leftist influences gained ground at the expense of the more liberal approach of the original organizers of Algerian revolt. The veteran Ferhat Abbas was replaced as President by the more youthful Ben Khedda, an ally of Boumedienne. Krim Belkacem, the leader of the Evian delegation, lost his post as Foreign Minister to one of his subordinates, Saad Dahlab.[4] The outcome of the meeting was another shift towards extremism, which augured ill for the future of negotiations. In September the extremists on the other side, the OAS, came near to killing de Gaulle when they set a trap for his car at Pont-sur-Seine near Paris. Only the skill and courage of his chauffeur, who kept the car under control through a barrier of flaming oil, enabled the General and his wife to escape.

Faced with an apparent impasse, de Gaulle was more eager than ever to find a way of liberating France from the burden of the Algerian war. He even considered, if agreement with the FLN proved impossible, creating a coastal zone under French sovereignty in which European settlers and loyal Muslims would form the majority, and letting the rest of the country go its own way, except for the oil-rich part of the Sahara. But this course would never have been accepted by the FLN or endorsed by the Third World or the United Nations. He therefore decided to signal increased flexibility, while making the FLN aware through private channels that the danger of an imposed solution existed, if they were intransigent. In his New Year address to the nation he stated that France meant to free herself 'one way or another' of the ties which bound her to Algeria. Whatever happened, he went on, 1962 would be the year of the regroupment in Europe and modernization of the greater part of the French Army. Withdrawal from Algeria would begin in January.

This was a clear message to the FLN that France meant to disengage from Algeria soon on almost any terms. Negotiations resumed by mutual consent in late January, and the lines of an agreement finally emerged on 17/18 February, after de Gaulle had authorized Joxe by telephone to make concessions on all points still in dispute.[5] It was announced that the two sides would meet for a final session at Evian on 7 March. They did so, despite the doubts of Boumedienne. On 18 March at Evian the accords for the transfer of power were signed and at midday on 19 March the ceasefire came into effect.

The accords were conditional on approval by referendum in France and Algeria. The result was a foregone conclusion, but the procedure conformed with de Gaulle's insistence that independence should be granted by France and not wrested from her. As Algeria was not yet sovereign, the Evian agreements did not constitute a treaty. They were promulgated in a declaration by the French government, and a High Commissioner, Christian Fouchet, was appointed to preside over the transfer of power.

The terms agreed were:

1. Citizens of each country had the right to live and work in the other.
2. Property rights were guaranteed for French remaining in Algeria.
3. Algeria was to be sovereign in the Sahara. France would cooperate in exploitation of oil and keep her nuclear research installations.
4. Algeria would receive economic and technical aid, and remain in the franc zone.
5. Cultural cooperation.
6. Mers-el-Kebir and some air bases would remain in French hands for fifteen years.

The referendum in France was held on 8 April, and 91 per cent of those voting endorsed the accords.

De Gaulle asserted that the agreements contained all that he wanted. On paper indeed they provided for a form of association between France and Algeria, and although the French had had to give way over sovereignty in the Sahara, they had preserved valuable oil rights and their nuclear testing grounds. Certain guarantees had also been secured for the settlers, even if they were less generous than had been hoped. But the behaviour of the OAS and the settlers deprived the accords of much of their potential value for France even before they went into effect. Jouhaud and Salan were captured in March and April respectively, and the direction of the OAS fell into more extremist hands. A 'scorched earth' policy was proclaimed: the European population were ordered by the OAS to leave the country after destroying all that they had created in Algeria since the arrival of the French in 1830. The majority of them obeyed, and 300,000 left for Europe in May alone. The French government had reckoned with having to resettle 100,000 in six months! Meanwhile a special military tribunal condemned Jouhaud to death. De Gaulle had not intended to commute the sentence, but when the equally guilty Salan only received life imprisonment, he reluctantly agreed that the same penalty would suffice for Jouhaud.

Then on 17 June the OAS suddenly abandoned the fight in Algeria. They signed a truce with the FLN, 'in order to reconcile the two communities'. It was too late. The exodus continued. When it was over, only 100,000 of the million whites remained. In a way this unforeseen development simplified the future for France. De Gaulle had observed gloomily the year before that France was negotiating to secure the creation of a million hostages. Now the hostages were gone.

On 1 July the referendum was held in Algeria in peaceful conditions. An overwhelming majority gave an affirmative answer to the question 'Do you want Algeria to become an independent state cooperating with France in the conditions laid down by the Declaration of 19 March 1962?' On 3 July France recognized the independence of Algeria.

In September Ahmed Ben Bella, the former leader who had been a prisoner of the French for the past six years, became the first President of Algeria. Before long he was demanding the renegotiation of the Evian accords. It mattered little. France had turned her back on the Algerian problem, and de Gaulle was directing her attention elsewhere, to modernization, to a leading role in European affairs, and to a part that he believed no other nation was equipped to play in the great game between the superpowers.

In his Memoirs de Gaulle describes his management of the Algerian problem in Olympian style, as if he had been in control of the situation all the way and had finally succeeded, through tact and timing, in imposing the solution he had in mind from the beginning. This treatment was no doubt an artistic necessity for a writer whose model was Julius Caesar's account of his exploits in Gaul. But it does less than justice to the qualities he displayed in surmounting difficulties that were greater than he admitted. Not only had he to steer French public opinion in the right direction, but also it was essential to maintain his ascendancy over the Army in Algeria. After May 1958 that Army was conscious of its political power. De Gaulle had to manage it carefully until he had strengthened his position at home. A successful mutiny in Algeria in 1960 or 1961 could have had incalculable consequences for France, and would certainly have put an end to his hopes of being of service to her. Future rulers of France might have been dependent on the support of a political military establishment, a kind of Praetorian Guard. He avoided these perils and finally devised a solution of the Algerian war on terms laid down by France herself instead of being obliged to appeal to the Great Powers as Mendès-France had done over Indo-China in 1954.

De Gaulle's failure was with the European settlers. He never succeeded in persuading any significant number of them that the only course which might give them a future in Algeria was to acquiesce in a transfer of power in exchange for guarantees of future status. Their ferocious intransigence sealed their fate after independence. The Algerian rebels too were inflexible. They had less respect and more distrust for de Gaulle than he suggests. They might, if he had shown less imagination, have postponed a solution and distracted him indefinitely from his work of renewal in France. Algeria was not Vietnam. France could have held it for a long time without military defeat, but only at the cost of bitter political dispute at home and increasing international disapproval.

That was the trap which he avoided by making the necessary concessions. It was a remarkable achievement, the more so for being repugnant to the instinct of his youth to defend to the last gasp the patrimony of France. Mao Tse-tung paid a just tribute to it, when discussing the General with a French visitor in 1970. He told him that he considered de Gaulle the greatest statesman of his day because he had known when to say No and when to say Yes. He had resisted the Nazis in 1940, and he had yielded to the Algerians in 1962. No other political figure of the time, said Mao, would have been capable of doing both, and he had won great prestige thereby. That was why the structure he had built in France had stood the test of crisis and could be passed on as his legacy to future generations.[6] Mao's tribute can serve as the last word on the qualities de Gaulle displayed in extricating France from the colonial era.

He nearly paid with his life. The OAS did not abandon the quest for revenge in France at the same time as the fight in Algeria. On 22 August the General had a miraculous escape, along with his wife and son-in-law, when their car was riddled with bullets in an ambush at Petit Clamart outside Paris. Nobody was hurt. Those responsible were later captured and their leader, Colonel Bastien-Thiry, was executed. The OAS did not get so close again.

# 31 THE TIME OF TRIPARTISM

Despite the urgency of what he had to do at home and in Algeria, de Gaulle lost no time when he came to power in 1958 in launching France on a new foreign policy. He wished to bring about a profound change in the nature of her relations with the Anglo-Americans, as he persisted in calling them, the Germans and the Russians. In his *Memoirs of Hope*, begun after his final withdrawal from power but unfinished at his death, he described his purpose as follows:

To detach France not from the Atlantic Alliance which I intended to maintain as an ultimate precaution, but from the integration under American command which NATO had brought about; to establish with the States of the Eastern bloc, and first of all with Russia, relations directed towards détente, and then towards entente and cooperation; to do the same, when the time came, with China; and finally, to acquire a nuclear capacity such that nobody could attack us without risking frightful wounds. But I wanted to travel the road step by step, in accordance with general developments and without upsetting the traditional friendships of France.[1]

In addition his plans envisaged the gradual formation of a concert of European States, East and West, which might ultimately become a confederation. But this was evidently a vision of what might lie far in the future when the cold war had been replaced by cooperation. The first step would be to launch the EEC, which was due to begin functioning on 1 January 1959, and even this first step depended on France reaching a prior understanding with Federal Germany. At the root of these projects was of course de Gaulle's eternal dream of restoring to France the greatness and the capacity for independent action which she had once enjoyed. Now at last he had the power to make the attempt. Looking at the world around him he saw that two essential elements of greatness were the possession of nuclear weapons and a stock of gold. Accordingly he set himself to obtain these for France.

He attended first to Germany. On 13 June his Foreign Minister, Couve de Murville, informed Bonn that the new government would not carry out the Franco-German accord of 1958 which could have led to the Federal Republic acquiring nuclear weapons.[2] While Chancellor Adenauer and his Defence Minister, Franz-Josef Strauss, were meditating on the implications of this news, de Gaulle turned to the Anglo-Saxons. They had reacted to his return to power with the same mixture of hope and apprehension as Adenauer. There would be less cause to worry in future about the instability of France, but how, they wondered, would de Gaulle use the strength that he imparted to her?

The first of the Anglo-Saxons to arrive was Premier Macmillan, who came for talks at the end of June. De Gaulle made it clear that he wanted France to be given more weight in the Atlantic Alliance, and they announced agreement 'on the overriding importance of organizing the defence of the free world'. For his part Macmillan pressed de Gaulle strongly not to agree to the launching of the Common Market but rather to fall in with the British proposals then under negotiation for the formation of an industrial free trade area in Europe. Macmillan compared the Common Market of the six with the economic blockade of Britain which Napoleon had tried to mount. On this de Gaulle made no commitment. It was a subject he wished to discuss with Adenauer before making up his mind.

John Foster Dulles, President Eisenhower's Secretary of State, was the next visitor. He prepared for his visit to Paris on 4–5 July with meticulous care,[3] but it was inevitably a failure. It was Dulles's mission to urge that France should accept a pledge of close consultation in place of the formal creation of a tripartite American–British–French directorate of the Alliance such as the General was already known to favour. He also wanted France to acquire American nuclear weapons under the 'double key' arrangement, rather than go to the expense of making her own. De Gaulle left the matter of procedure on consultation open, but made it clear to his visitor that he had no hope of persuading him on nuclear policy. According to the State Department record, he told Dulles:[4]

He could be certain that France would have atomic bombs. Of course, he said, the French program could in no sense be comparable to that of the United States or the Soviet Union and it might take 25 years before France would have a significant nuclear potential . . . If France were given nuclear weapons or produced them thanks to the United States' assistance, this would be an economy and thus a reinforcement of the alliance. France would use such weapons as it had used other US military equipment, and as the United States had in the past used French military equipment.

The American report summarized the General's position thus:

(1) France must really be associated with the defense of the free world. While no treaties were necessary, France must play a role at the summit and feel that it was really participating in strategic plans and armament; (2) any nuclear arms made available under NATO planning on French soil must be under the direct responsibility of France, with the United States participating in this control . . . (3) NATO must be extended towards Africa and the Middle East, and the command structure must be reformed.

No agreement was possible on de Gaulle's three demands, but there was no deadlock either. Clearly the General had issued a declaration of nuclear independence, but would he be able to make it good? Dulles departed with his thoughts on the next round, bearing a cordial message from de Gaulle to Eisenhower and 'his hopes that the United States would maintain its strength and its liberal spirit'.

Next, de Gaulle turned again to the Germans. On 14 September he received Chancellor Adenauer at his home at Colombey for conversations which were destined to have historic consequences. The General had chosen the setting of his own house, in order to give a special air of intimacy to the occasion. Madame de Gaulle was not best pleased at this introduction of politics to La Boisserie, whose domestic atmosphere she resolutely defended at all times. She insisted that, if the German Chancellor were to come to her home, he should be treated no differently from family guests. All would be done by the scanty staff of Colombey. This she augmented by borrowing from her brother Jacques Vendroux, the Mayor of Calais, but there were no servants, no catering, no silver or china from Prime Ministerial resources in Paris. The General bowed to her wishes, which he had not foreseen, and the result was highly successful.[5] Adenauer was flattered to be received in such intimate surroundings for a meeting he had approached with the trepidation which de Gaulle's tactics had nourished.

All the Chancellor knew for sure of the General's intentions toward the Federal Republic when he arrived at Colombey was that he did not mean to give effect to the Franco-German nuclear accord of March 1958. He did not know how de Gaulle meant to manoeuvre between the Americans and the Russians, nor whether he was ready to accept the measures necessary to bring the Common Market into operation in January 1959, which included a first step towards lowering the tariff barriers behind which France had so long protected herself. Realization of the Common Market meant a great deal to Adenauer, and de Gaulle had often spoken critically of it.

Thus the proposals which the General now advanced had a double impact on his guest. They were welcome in themselves and they came as a happy surprise. De Gaulle told Adenauer that he believed the time was at last ripe for an historic Franco-German reconciliation. Of course the Federal Republic would have to renounce nuclear weapons; would have to realize that the Eastern frontiers set in 1945 were permanent; and could only hope for reunification within Germany's existing frontiers in a remote future. If the Chancellor could proceed on this basis, France and Germany could establish a special relationship – *'des liens préférentiels'*. There were no comparable conditions that France needed to accept, because the war had left her in a better situation than Germany. Her relationship with the Federal Republic would not, realistically speaking, be one between equals. (This was de Gaulle's invariable theme with the Germans.) But, in the interests of a historic reconciliation, she was willing to allow the organization of the EEC to proceed, once there was a Franco-German agreement on terms. The two essential conditions were that agriculture, as well as industry, should be included in its scope, and that Britain, 'as long as she is what she is', should be excluded. France would not always remain a member of NATO, which was dominated by the United States, but she would make her own contribution to the security of the Federal Republic. That was his offer.

Adenauer accepted these proposals with enthusiasm, while insisting that the Federal Republic had an absolute need of the American guarantee of her security and must therefore remain in NATO. He also pointed out that opinion in Germany favoured British entry into the EEC and that this fact must determine the official position of Bonn, but he promised that he would not allow this consideration to prejudice the process of Franco-German entente.

De Gaulle found all this acceptable, given the position of the Federal Republic. The two men agreed to remain in close personal contact, and Adenauer promised to support de Gaulle's idea of instituting regular political consultation between the foreign ministers of the six EEC countries. So the compact between the leaders of France and Germany was sealed.[6]

The understanding reached at Colombey was a major diplomatic success for de Gaulle. It promised to provide him with exactly the kind of ally France needed to restore to her some of the strength and status that was disappearing with her loss of Empire, a partner powerful but subordinated. If Adenauer was as good as his word, de Gaulle might hope to create an association of France and West Germany which would have many of the advantages of Charlemagne's imperial system, among them the primacy of the French and the absence of the English.

The predestined victim of the Colombey entente was Britain. Western Europe, economically and politically, was to be organized without her. This was not, however, immediately apparent. The intentions that de Gaulle had revealed were kept secret. In diplomatic exchanges Adenauer tried to play down the importance of what had happened at Colombey. De Gaulle gave him an opportunity to do this convincingly when, forty-eight hours after the Chancellor's visit, he sent a memorandum to Eisenhower and Macmillan proposing 'that an organization comprising the United States, Great Britain and France should be created and function on a world-wide political and strategic level. This organization would make joint decisions in all political questions affecting global security and would also draw up and, if necessary, implement strategic action plans, especially as regards the use of nuclear weapons.'[7] He had not told Adenauer of his intentions and the Chancellor complained of the fact to the Anglo-Saxons as well as the French. Obviously the proposal was unattractive to the Germans who would have been left out of the directorate, but Adenauer's disquiet cannot have been very serious, since he must have been morally certain that there was no chance of the Americans accepting the idea. So must de Gaulle, because Dulles had already told him that 'formalization of groupings for directing the free world would be resented' by the smaller allies.

When the answers arrived they were negative on the essential point as he must have expected. Eisenhower's letter of 20 October turned down his proposal for the reason already given by Dulles. 'Evasive' is the word he rather unfairly uses for these replies in his Memoirs. He felt his hands were free. When he received Dulles again in December, it was recognized on both sides that there could be no organic tripartite directorate, with veto power for each member, such as his memorandum had demanded.[8] As a substitute, the Americans tried to promote a form of three-power consultation in Washington between the State Department and the French and British ambassadors, but it never worked effectively and faded out in the course of 1959. De Gaulle's concern shifted to carrying out the threat in his memorandum that, if no tripartite directorate was set up, France would not take part in any further development of NATO and reserved the right to demand reform of the organization or to leave it.

When de Gaulle sent his memorandum to Eisenhower and Macmillan, he was repeating for the last time the demand he had so often made to Roosevelt and Churchill during the war that France should be treated as an equal in status, although she was not one in power. On this last occasion the demand was pitched extraordinarily high. He was asking for nothing less than a worldwide veto on the use of the American deterrent, and he could offer in return only a veto on a nuclear force that he had told Dulles might take twenty-five years to become significant. This was not a bargain to interest a Great Power. He would have hesitated between delight and suspicion if it had been accepted, but 'not for an instant', in the view of one of his highest officials did he expect it to be. He made his proposal for other reasons. In the first place, its rejection would rally popular support in France for disengagement from NATO; but, secondly, there was a problem in the functioning of the Alliance which was of real concern to him. If France had American nuclear weapons on her soil, her security was at risk as soon as an American nuclear weapon was fired anywhere in the world, thereby inviting reprisals. The fate of France was out of French hands, therefore, unless she had a universal veto on the use of such weapons. France had to put her position on record.

Ironically enough, however, as de Gaulle remarked to Dulles at their second meeting, which took place in Paris in December 1958, just as he had freed his hands for action, the Russians launched a crisis over Berlin, which was the only part of the world where Allied tripartism was a reality. The Berlin crisis lasted on and off until the summer of 1962, and did a great deal to retard both disengagement from NATO and overtures towards Russia as far as de Gaulle was concerned.

The drama began, after one or two curtain-raising speeches by Khrushchev, when a Soviet note was delivered to the Western powers on 27 November demanding the withdrawal of their forces from West Berlin and its conversion into a Free City. It threatened that, if the situation were not changed by then, the Soviet government would in six months' time sign a separate peace treaty with the German Democratic Republic and thereby extinguish Allied occupation rights in Berlin. Allied access would then be possible only through or over territory controlled by the GDR. The note did not spell out all the implications, but a blockade of Berlin which the Allies could only break by using force was clearly one of them. De Gaulle promptly assured Adenauer of firm support against this Soviet pressure on Berlin. His view was that the West should refuse to negotiate as long as the Russians made threats. He expressed himself forcefully to Dulles on 15 December: 'we should most certainly not retreat in the face of a menace . . . He believed that if the Soviets threatened war, we should accept that challenge, even if it meant war.'[9]

This was robust language considering that nearly all the trained French forces were engaged in the Algerian war. To be uncompromising when weak was a rule that de Gaulle had made for himself during the war, but he had never pushed inflexibility to the lengths of folly. He had not gone to the lengths of defying Churchill's threats when he thought they were seriously meant, as they were over his initial refusal to attend the Casablanca conference and even the Syrian crises of 1943 and 1949. No doubt he judged from the outset that Khrushchev's purpose was not to seize anything the Allies held in Germany but to consolidate the Russian hold on what they and their allies had occupied in 1945 by forcing on the West recognition of East Germany's frontiers. In any case his American allies were not weak, and he would earn Adenauer's gratitude by encouraging them to stand firm.

He was even firmer when Dulles came to Europe again in February 1959 to discuss plans against the contingency that the Russians might hand over control of Allied access from West Germany to West Berlin to the East Germans. Dulles telegraphed back to President Eisenhower:

The French, unlike the UK, seemed quite specific that we could not accept a substitution of the German Democratic Republic for the Soviet Union . . . The French would, I think, be willing immediately on May 27th or as soon as Soviet turnover is an accomplished fact to attempt to use force to go through. I doubt whether they have thought this out and realize all the implications. In any event they accepted my view that though we should at that time begin military preparations, we should not actually move until we had made a final effort to mobilize world opinion against the Soviets . . .

By this time the Americans were in the position of having to hold the General back, at least on paper! They realized that force could escalate to a choice – for them, not France – between using nuclear weapons and accepting defeat. Towards the end of the meeting Dulles raised another matter about which de Gaulle had expressed discontent, the fact that the French Mediterranean Fleet was assigned to NATO, whereas the US Sixth Fleet in the Mediterranean was not. He said he thought this was a matter that could be negotiated with NATO with a view to achieving parity. According to the American record 'De Gaulle said that this was a "very important" statement, and it obviously gratified him.'[10]

De Gaulle interpreted this rather involved statement in the way that suited him best, and withdrew his Mediterranean Fleet from NATO a few weeks later. There was much publicity about what the press saw as a disobliging gesture to NATO. Neither the French nor the Americans chose to reveal that it had been more or less cleared by Dulles in advance. In April, de Gaulle took a step of more practical consequence when he forbade the presence of American nuclear weapons, whether on planes or launching-ramps, in France. US planes that carried such weapons had in consequence to move to Britain or Germany. Before the Soviet ultimatum expired, France was no longer a target for the Russians, if they should wish to strike at the American deterrent.

De Gaulle had already sent another signal to the Russians before this to indicate that the French position on Germany was not the same as that of the Americans. Without consulting his Allies or the Germans he declared in a speech that France regarded the Oder–Neisse frontier between Poland and Germany as permanent. Adenauer was so grateful for French firmness over Berlin that he refrained from open criticism. But, for the sake of German opinion, he urged the Anglo-Americans not to imitate the General, and they agreed. He also asked the General not to repeat what he said. It was a request to which de

Gaulle could easily accede, since he knew that Khrushchev had heard the first time and understood that French influence in Bonn, unlike American, was now openly committed to opposing West German irredentism.

In May a four-power conference on Berlin began in Geneva. The East Germans were permitted to attend on an equal footing with the West Germans, as the Russians had demanded. A few weeks later Khrushchev allowed his six-month ultimatum to expire without action against the Allied position in Berlin. He was willing to wait longer now that talks had begun. The conference adjourned in August. No decisions had been reached, but the atmosphere was more friendly. Khrushchev went on a much publicized visit to the United States as Eisenhower's guest. Tension eased, but the respite could end whenever the Russians chose.

After the Khrushchev visit, President Eisenhower, who had begun to play more of a personal part in foreign affairs since the death of John Foster Dulles in May, embarked on an effort to woo de Gaulle back into the NATO fold. In Paris from 2 to 4 September Eisenhower repeated the offer of American missiles under the 'double key' procedure which Adenauer had accepted for the Bundeswehr. When de Gaulle replied that France would only buy American arms if she could use them without seeking consent, Eisenhower reproached him with a lack of confidence in American intentions towards Europe. De Gaulle's answer was that the Americans and Russians possessed nuclear deterrents which protected their own national territories, but not the territory in between them, Western and Eastern Europe. If the Russians bombed France and not America, how could the French be sure, he asked, that America would riposte with bombs on Russia, when the inevitable consequence would be Russian bombs on America?

For Russia and America deterrence exists. But it does not exist for the respective allies of the two. What would prevent Russia and America from wiping out what lies between their frontiers, that is to say essentially the European battlefield? Isn't that what NATO is preparing to do?[11]

These were hard questions. In fact the Americans are still trying to find a satisfactory answer to them today. The two presidents parted on good terms, and on 16 September de Gaulle announced in a widely publicized address at the National Defence College in Paris that

France was to have her independent nuclear force, to which he gave the name 'strike force' (*force de frappe*). In January 1960 she duly joined the atomic club when her first bomb was exploded at her Algerian testing grounds.

Eisenhower was soon back in Paris on a different mission. Khrushchev indicated that he was not prepared to allow the German question to lie dormant indefinitely. He wanted a meeting with the three Western leaders. De Gaulle received Eisenhower and Macmillan in Paris from 19 to 21 December to discuss the situation. They were willing to meet Khrushchev, but the problem was how to manage a summit so that it would not provoke a new Berlin crisis. Chancellor Adenauer was in attendance to plead against the offer of concessions on Berlin. As usual, it was de Gaulle who rallied to his support. He was agreeable to a summit meeting but not to treaty negotiations as long as Khrushchev backed up his demands by threats against the Allied position in Berlin. He also insisted on the delay of the four-power summit until Khrushchev had time to pay an official visit to France like those he had already made to Britain and America. Eisenhower and Macmillan, who would have been ready to negotiate, accepted the French position in the interests of Western unity. De Gaulle thus increased the Chancellor's debt of gratitude to him.

Agreement was reached with Khrushchev that the four should meet in Paris. But the Russian leader's State visit to France had to come first. It was a long affair, involving, at de Gaulle's insistence, a tour of the country comparable to his programme in the United States. It lasted from 23 March to 3 April, and there was ample time for talks between the two leaders. These ranged wide, for de Gaulle was trying to create an atmosphere of confidence. He was firm on Berlin, but agreed with his guest that Germany should accept as permanent its frontiers of 1945 and should renounce the possession of atomic weapons. Nevertheless Khrushchev did not hide his distrust of the special relationship between Paris and Bonn. The visit ended amicably, with agreements being made for technical and cultural cooperation. De Gaulle records that he was inclined to believe that something of importance had happened in 'the centuries-old relations between Russia and France'.

After Khrushchev's departure de Gaulle made official visits of his own to Britain, Canada and the United States in rapid succession, and everywhere received not only ceremonial honours of exceptional splendour but also an enthusiastic public welcome. It was a striking tribute to him and to his France from the Anglo-Saxon world with whose leaders he was so often at odds. The long-awaited and much delayed East–West summit conference finally met in Paris on 15 May. It proved to be a fiasco and broke up without serious discussion because of the consequences of the shooting down of an American U-2 'spy plane' over Soviet territory on 1 May. Khrushchev demanded by way of apology and amends more than Eisenhower could yield. De Gaulle emerged with credit from the acrimonious exchanges which took place. He firmly supported Eisenhower against Khrushchev's excessive demands, and thereby won American gratitude and respect, whereas Macmillan tried to find a compromise. The damage to détente was limited by Khrushchev's announcement that he would make no fresh move over Berlin until he had a chance to discuss the German problem with the new American President who would take over from Eisenhower in January 1961.

On the whole de Gaulle was reassured by what he had seen of the tempestuous Khrushchev at his worst. In the hearing of some of his ministers he summed him up thus: 'Khrushchev makes a lot of noise, but he doesn't do anything. If you want to be a Hitler, you must make war. Khrushchev won't make war, and everybody knows it, beginning with Khrushchev.'[12] If de Gaulle was right, there would be no war over Berlin even if the Allies stood their ground. He proceeded on this assumption, and on 6 July wrote to President Eisenhower recommending absolute firmness on Berlin.

In another letter to Eisenhower, de Gaulle took the initiative of suggesting 'a tripartite meeting at heads of government level to work out a joint plan for organizing united action on world problems and for reorganizing the Atlantic Alliance'.[13] But Eisenhower fobbed him off with a request for a memorandum regarding his views on NATO, and nothing came of the matter.

In January 1961 a new era opened, with the arrival of John Kennedy at the White House. On 31 May de Gaulle, fresh from victory over the rebellious generals in Algeria, welcomed to Paris the new President, fresh from catastrophe in the Bay of Pigs.

Kennedy was on his way to meet Khrushchev in Vienna, but Germany and Berlin – on which, as ever, de Gaulle counselled absolute firmness – were by no means the only subjects discussed in Paris. Kennedy asked for French support in the ex-Belgian Congo, where he was trying to restore stability with the help of political and military intervention by the United Nations, and in Southeast Asia, where he planned to sustain anti-Communist forces with American power. De Gaulle never liked such American intervention in former French or French-speaking territories. He advised against both courses of action and recommended economic aid instead. Kennedy also renewed the arguments of Eisenhower against an independent French deterrent. It was not a fruitful meeting.

De Gaulle was also disappointed by Kennedy's behaviour after his encounter with Khrushchev. Kennedy was firm enough in Vienna, but was shaken all the same by the vehemence and confidence of Khrushchev, and sensed that a new crisis was not far away. After returning to Washington, he ordered the strengthening of American forces in Europe. At the same time, however, he began to press his Western colleagues to agree to the opening of negotiations with the Russians on the German problem, and hinted in an address to the nation on 25 July at concessions, 'the removal of actual irritants' in Berlin. A flood of refugees had been pouring into West Berlin from East Germany ever since that Vienna meeting; now it increased dramatically. Macmillan was as eager for negotiations as Kennedy, so it was once more left to de Gaulle to defend the cause of firmness.

The argument continued in a four-power meeting held from 5 to 7 August in Paris, and French inflexibility prevailed. When Gromyko, the Russian foreign minister, asked the Western ambassadors in Moscow if he might expect a proposal on negotiations – he knew in advance that the Americans and the British favoured them – he was told that no decision had been taken in Paris. The following weekend, in the early hours of Sunday 13 August, the East Germans severed all communications between East and West Berlin, except for controlled movement through a few heavily guarded checkpoints. A few days later they began to build a wall along the sector borders. It became clear that unless the Allies intervened by force to remove the barriers inside the Russian sector of Berlin, free movement within the quadripartite city was at an end, and with it the flow of refugees from East to West Germany.

On the other hand Allied access, both official and military, to East Berlin through the checkpoints was uninterrupted; and the conditions of movement between the Federal Republic and West Berlin were unchanged. The Soviet Army continued to supervise Allied traffic. The threatened handover to the East Germans did not take place.

There could be no question of the Allies knocking down the wall in the Russian sector. They contented themselves with reaffirming their access rights from West Germany by running a large American military convoy into the city on 20 August. There it was met by Vice-President Johnson, who had come on a twenty-four-hour visit.

De Gaulle's inflexibility was certainly one of the chief causes of the Berlin Wall being built when it was. An agreement to negotiations with the Russians would at least have postponed it. But the negotiations could only have been successful if concessions had been made by the West, and if negotiations had been held and failed, West Berlin might have suffered more than it did from the Wall. This was the line of argument de Gaulle used in justifying his refusal of negotiations to the French public. At all events the Allied position in the city was preserved intact, which was what Adenauer wanted most; and war did not result.

The building of the Berlin Wall was a blow to West German morale, for it deepened the division between the two Germanies. It was seen as a failure for Adenauer's policy, and in the general elections of the following month his Christian Democratic party (CDU) lost its overall majority. In order to remain Chancellor, Adenauer had to form a coalition with the small Free Democratic party and to promise to retire in two years' time, halfway through the normal four-year span. He did not blame de Gaulle for his political misfortunes, and remained as loyal as ever to their understanding, but now its days were numbered.

The Russian action of 13 August was not at first correctly understood in the West. It was regarded as intensifying the crisis rather than easing it. In fact it was essentially a defensive move aimed at stabilizing East Germany by damming the flow of refugees rather than the more aggressive course of forcing the recognition of the Communist State on the West. The Anglo-Americans still urged negotiations with Russia, and de Gaulle still said No. Early in 1962 the Americans became so exasperated with French rigidity that they began informal bilateral conversations about Berlin with the Russians, keeping their French and British colleagues informed – at least up to a point. The Americans brought up again all the ideas the Western Allies had thought up at various times for easing the Berlin situation. In effect the talks could have become a bilateral negotiation if the Russians had wished, but they showed no sign of interest in any of the options tabled by the Americans.[14] They led to nothing. Before long the French also launched on informal conversations with the Russians without mentioning the fact to the Anglo-Americans.[15]

As Berlin became less of a preoccupation, both the Americans and the British began to weigh once more the question of giving some nuclear aid to France. Their motives were different. Washington still hoped to link France more firmly to NATO, while London's aim was to make de Gaulle look more favourably on the application Britain had made late in 1961 for membership of the EEC.

In the event, President Kennedy's decision taken in April was against giving nuclear aid to France,[16] but despite this fact the Defence Secretary, Robert McNamara, agreed in May to sell a squadron of Boeing jet tankers to France which would enable the aircraft of the *force de frappe* to refuel in the air, and so greatly increase their range.[17] Harold Macmillan, on the other hand, told General de Gaulle, when they met at the Château de Champs on 2–3 June, that Anglo-French nuclear collaboration was possible[18] – on the implied condition that Britain was admitted to the Common Market on acceptable terms. Negotiations in Brussels on the British application went slowly, however, even after Champs. The subject will be treated in more detail in the next chapter.

Then came the Cuban missile crisis. The Americans discovered that the Russians were secretly installing a nuclear weapons system in Cuba. Khrushchev's plan, so he later alleged in private, was to activate the system and then offer to dismantle it in return for the withdrawal of the Allies from West Berlin.[19] In an address to the American people on 22 October, Kennedy told them what was happening and made it clear that he was ready to use force to frustrate Khrushchev's plan. His will prevailed. On 27 October Khrushchev ordered the withdrawal of his missiles.

De Gaulle played a part in every act of the Cuban drama. To begin with, it was French Intelligence which in August passed the Americans their first information about the arrival of nuclear missiles in Cuba. Secondly, when the crisis broke, de Gaulle immediately told Dean Acheson, the special envoy whom Kennedy sent to Paris to brief him, that, if there was war, France would back the United States; and he initiated a prompt declaration of support from the six member governments of the EEC. The gesture was the easier to make because no American missiles were based in France, and so she would not be an early target, even if it came to a nuclear exchange. Nevertheless the Americans were grateful and compared his firmness favourably with the irresolute attitude of the British government. Macmillan, however, had to take into account that Britain housed American Thor missiles and was therefore in a more dangerous position than France.

Kennedy emerged as the winner in the Cuban conflict, but de Gaulle, although he sent him a letter of congratulations, privately criticized his failure to exploit his success. In the General's opinion Kennedy should have insisted on the departure of Castro and should not have withdrawn American missiles from Turkey as he did a little later.[20] Still, the public image of the young President had certainly much improved, and the General's standing benefited from having been his firmest supporter in Europe.

Cuba marked the end of the period of threats in international affairs which Khrushchev had inaugurated in 1958. The superpowers had drawn back once more from the brink of war, as they had done in Korea in 1950–1. As de Gaulle had said, since they would not make war, they would have to make peace, but the change, and the new chance it offered to the General's ideas of East–West détente, only became apparent gradually. The point which the French at once began to make in the wake of the Cuban affair was that the Americans had taken action without consulting their allies and had only informed them on the eve of a confrontation which might have spread to Europe at very short notice. This was a strong argument, the French contended, in favour of Europe having its own nuclear deterrent.

The Americans of course took the opposite view. The Kennedy administration regarded small nuclear forces as dangerously vulnerable and, in the phrase of Robert McNamara, 'prone to obsolescence'. It was an important aim of Kennedy's policy that America alone in the Western alliance should wield the nuclear deterrent. Dean Rusk, Kennedy's Secretary of State, had been brutally frank on the subject in talks with the French Defence Minister, Pierre Messmer, early in 1962. 'If you target your nuclear force independently, we shall target it with ours,' he said.[21] A more tactful American formula was: 'We shall never allow 5 per cent of the deterrent to trigger off the other 95 per cent.' Dean Rusk's warning did not of course pose an immediate problem, since France was still years away from possessing an operational nuclear force, but de Gaulle took careful note of his words.

Immediately after Cuba a nuclear problem arose which brought all these considerations into play. In 1960 the US and British governments had signed an agreement under which Britain would purchase for their nuclear air force the Skybolt missile which the Americans were developing. The British then abandoned the more costly programme for producing their own Blue Streak ballistic missile and accepted dependence on American technology. Now, in December 1962, McNamara told them that Skybolt had proved unsatisfactory and was not to be produced. The Americans had plenty of other systems available, but the British were left without the weapons on which they had been counting for extending the life of the V-bombers, their only nuclear force, into the 1970s. Prime Minister Macmillan hurriedly made arrangements to see President Kennedy, but first visited de Gaulle. They met at Rambouillet on 15 and 16 December for their first exchange since their talks at Champs in early June.

De Gaulle told his guest plainly that he felt the negotiations at Brussels had proved that Britain could not yet assume the obligations of a member of the Common Market. Macmillan, however, argued strongly that success was still possible. As to Skybolt, the two men agreed that Europe needed independent nuclear forces and that Macmillan should be guided by this view in his talks with Kennedy. De Gaulle seems to have had the impression that, under the impact of being let down over Skybolt, the British might decide to abandon nuclear collaboration with the Americans and work with France instead, perhaps on a revival of Blue Streak.

French hopes on this score may have been encouraged by the conclusion on 29 November of an Anglo-French agreement for the joint production of a supersonic airliner, Concorde. This accord was of more benefit to the French than to the British, whose aeronautics industry was larger and more advanced. Only the British were capable of building the engines that would power Concorde, and the knowledge that the French would acquire by their collaboration would be of service to them in designing engines for their nuclear air force. The Concorde project therefore involved a measure of indirect British aid to the construction of the French *force de frappe*. It was a firm commitment, since the agreement contained no provisions for unilateral termination, and it might naturally stimulate French hopes of more collaboration with Britain.

But Macmillan dashed hopes of any further collaboration at Nassau. He decided that the future British deterrent force should be submarine instead of airborne, and that it should be equipped with the Polaris missiles which Kennedy offered to sell to Britain, provided she built the nuclear warheads and submarines herself. Macmillan also accepted the American stipulation that British nuclear forces should be assigned to NATO and become part of a multilateral force to which the US would also contribute; but it was provided that in a national emergency Britain could withdraw her submarines and operate them herself. In theory therefore her independent nuclear capability would be preserved: in practice, since the NATO Commander-in-Chief was always American, Kennedy had achieved one half of his aim of assimilating European deterrents to the American deterrent. Only the *force de frappe* remained to be brought into line.

Kennedy immediately offered de Gaulle Polaris missiles on the terms accepted by Macmillan, but rejection was a foregone conclusion. De Gaulle's idea of nuclear independence was very different from that of the British Prime Minister. He took his time in replying, and asked some questions through his Ambassador in Washington which revealed that there would have to be lengthy negotiations even if he said Yes to Kennedy,[22] but he can never have contemplated putting the *force de frappe* under an American commander.

De Gaulle felt that a turning-point in his foreign policy had now been reached, and he resolved to give the fact dramatic expression. In order to put matters in perspective, however, it is necessary to return in time and to examine how de Gaulle's effort to organize the EEC in the way he wished had been progressing. For the European and the Anglo-American streams of his policy, which he had kept separate since 1958, were about to converge.

# 32  EUROPE FOR THE EUROPEANS

In returning to power in 1958 de Gaulle saw Europe, as he puts it in his *Mémoires d'Espoir* divided between Soviet domination of the Centre and the Balkans and 'the organization imposed on the Atlantic Alliance, which amounted to the military and political subordination of Western Europe to the United States'.[1] He intended France to take a lead in changing this situation and working towards the creation of what he liked to call a 'European Europe'.

'My policy', he stated, 'aimed therefore at the creation of a concert of European states whose solidarity would increase as they developed links of all kinds ... that purpose led us to put into effect the Economic Community of the Six and organize political concertation between them, and to ensure that certain others, above all Great Britain, should not lead the West towards an Atlantic system which would be incompatible with any possibility of a European Europe, but should on the contrary decide to change orientation and become part of the Continent themselves'.[2] He goes on to talk of the need to develop détente, entente and cooperation with the countries of Eastern Europe.

The formula 'European Europe' caused a certain amount of confusion when de Gaulle began to use it, because he applied it to both phases of his European policy, the immediate building of a system of exclusive relationships between the six members of the EEC and the much remoter development of a loose association of all the nations of Europe that might one day grow out of entente and cooperation between East and West. Another phrase which he sometimes used for this latter concept was 'Europe from the Atlantic to the Urals'.

Development of policy in Western Europe took priority over that in the East, to a greater degree probably than de Gaulle wished, because the Berlin crisis provoked by Khrushchev was a major obstacle to any significant move towards détente. In the West, on the other hand,

France could move ahead once de Gaulle had concluded his agreement with Adenauer, which was an essential preliminary.

Not until mid-December 1958 did de Gaulle reveal his intentions towards the EEC. His hands were free because Pflimlin's government during its brief tenure of office had sent its Minister of European Affairs, Maurice Faure, on a rapid tour of the capitals of the Five to inform them in strict secrecy that because of her precarious finances France would not be able to assume her obligations under the Treaty of Rome on 1 January 1959 and must ask for an indefinite postponement.[3]

De Gaulle's return to power had soon led to a spectacular improvement in the economy, and by December money was flowing into France instead of out, but uncertainty persisted as to what would happen in the EEC at the New Year. Then on 15 December de Gaulle began to unmask his batteries. The French government announced its withdrawal from the British-sponsored negotiations for an industrial free trade area, and, to the surprise of the British, Erhard followed suit for Federal Germany, as instructed by Adenauer. Five days later it was confirmed that France would make the tariff adjustments required to launch the Common Market on 1 January 1959. So the EEC came to birth on the due date after all.

De Gaulle allowed some months to elapse before he raised the question of political coordination between the members of the new organization. In June 1959 he revealed his ideas to the Italian government in the course of a state visit, the first of his Presidency. He advocated regular consultation between the Six at all important levels, presidential, ministerial and parliamentary, on politics, economics, defence and culture. This was a far-reaching programme and the reaction of the Italians was cautious. Defence consultation without the United States and any sort of regular consultation without Britain seemed to them undesirable, but they promised to reflect. De Gaulle had made a start. The rest of the Six were briefed, and in November it was agreed that foreign ministers should meet every three months. But there was no accord on the more delicate question of defence talks between the Six, which were what de Gaulle wanted above all else.

In 1960 quarterly meetings between foreign ministers became part of the calendar of the Six, and de Gaulle began to prepare the next stage with Adenauer. In talks with the Chancellor at Rambouillet at the end of July he repeated the proposals for general and regular consultation between the six governments which he had first put to the Italians, this time with the additional suggestion that a permanent secretariat should be set up in Paris to prepare meetings and pursue their results. This new proposal would make Paris the decision-making centre of the six governments, the political capital of the members of the EEC, and relegate to lesser status Brussels, where the EEC Commission – the servant of the six governments and no more than that in de Gaulle's eyes – was based. Adenauer promised to support de Gaulle's plan at a summit conference of the Six. De Gaulle proceeded to put his ideas to the rest of the Six and then to air them at a press conference on 5 September.

At this point the British intervened, as de Gaulle had doubtless anticipated, and informed all concerned of their dislike for a system of regular European political consultations from which they would be excluded. They found a particularly sympathetic hearing in the Hague, and when the summit of the Six took place in Paris in February 1961, no decision was reached on de Gaulle's proposals, largely because of the opposition of the Dutch. As a compromise, a commission was set up under the chairmanship of Christian Fouchet, French Ambassador in Denmark, to report back to the next meeting of heads of government. A contest between French and British influence had been engaged.

The next round took place in Bad Godesberg on 18 and 19 July under the shadow of a new Berlin crisis. The Six agreed that Fouchet's Commission should draft a treaty of political union, as it was called, providing for regular meetings designed to work out a common foreign policy having due regard for the need to cooperate with other nations of the free world in matters of defence. This last proviso was inserted by the friends of NATO, but was vague enough to be acceptable to de Gaulle. The idea of a political treaty between the Six seemed promising for the French cause. No supranational implications were involved. 'Political union' meant no more than an institutional attempt at coordination of policy between the six sovereign states of the EEC.

Britain chose this moment, however, to inform the Six on 21 July of her desire to open negotiations to establish whether the conditions existed for her to join the EEC. De Gaulle had no doubt of the motives behind this move. '. . . the English attack again', he says in his Memoirs. 'Having failed to prevent the birth of the Community, they now plan to paralyse it from within.' In the autumn the British Government proceeded to make a formal request for negotiations with the Six, which was accepted. De Gaulle asserts that he saw from the beginning that there were so many conditions attached to the application which required account to be taken of Britain's special relations with the Commonwealth and EFTA, as well as her agricultural interests, that there was no hope of a successful outcome and that since his five partners would not have the courage to say No to the British, the day would come 'when I should have to accept the challenge and either put a stop to the time-wasting or pull France out of a venture which had lost its way as soon as it set out'.[4]

January 1962 was an important month for the Common Market, because it was then that the second phase of its construction, involving a further reduction of tariffs between members, was due to begin. De Gaulle made French acceptance conditional on agreement by the Five to the full inclusion of agriculture in the Market. He had his way, after a marathon session of ministers in Brussels, and the EEC embarked on its second phase. The question of the gradual supranational integration envisaged in the Treaty of Rome remained for settlement at the next stage, which was due three years later, so there was no need for de Gaulle to reveal his intentions too clearly.

Having shaped the economic structure of the EEC to his will, de Gaulle was encouraged to attempt the same with its political form. He instructed Fouchet to present his commission, which had more or less reached agreement on the text of the draft treaty of political union called for in the Godesberg declaration, with a revised plan more closely corresponding to de Gaulle's own views. This added economic affairs to the subjects to be discussed in the Union and eliminated all reference to coordination of defence policy with outside powers. The effect would be to increase the authority of the Political Union over the work of the EEC Commission in Brussels, and to eliminate any obligation to consult the Anglo-Saxons on defence before agreeing on a common attitude among the Six.

When Fouchet produced the revised plan on 18 January, it destroyed the balance of compromise already reached and provoked rival proposals from the other members, who realized of course that the General had been at work. In the next few months de Gaulle made a great personal effort to impose his views on the heads of government of the Six, but only with Adenauer was he entirely successful. A week before the foreign ministers of the Six were due to meet on 17 April to try and approve a text, Edward Heath, who headed the British team negotiating entry into the EEC, introduced a new complication by announcing that Britain was ready to accept the political obligations of the Treaty of Rome and wished to be associated with the discussions on political union.

The meeting in Paris on 17 April failed to reach agreement. Belgium and Holland did not wish to bring the Treaty into effect until Britain had joined the EEC and Italy was hesitant. There were also rival views on whether the text should refer to the possibility of a move later on towards political integration between the signatories. At the end of the day Ministers broke up without setting a date for another meeting. Subsequent efforts to repair the damage was unavailing, and it proved that de Gaulle's project for a political union of the Six was dead. The British had won the last battle without being present on the field. He had contributed to this result by stiffening the French attitude at the eleventh hour, but the repeated British interventions had also been a major factor. The General had this lesson of the strength of British influence fresh in his mind when, six weeks later, Harold Macmillan came to see him in the hope of clearing the way for British entry into the EEC.

By the time de Gaulle received Macmillan at the Château de Champs outside Paris on 2 and 3 June, the negotiations in Brussels had established that the British required very substantial concessions if they were to join the EEC, and that, if France were willing to make such concessions, the Five would do so too. It was plain by now that success or failure depended on whether Macmillan could come to a bilateral agreement with de Gaulle.

The talks ended with a session tête-à-tête between de Gaulle and Macmillan. When they emerged, de Gaulle announced that they had reached agreement and invited the British Premier to outline its content. Macmillan did so. First, he said, Commonwealth ties were now less important than those with Europe, which would mean that in future Europe would take priority in British policy. Second, Britain recognized that France had twenty million agricultural workers to Britain's four and a half million, and that EEC policies must take account of France's agricultural interests. Third (as mentioned in the previous chapter), Britain recognized that Europe needed a nuclear deterrent and that France was European. Anglo-French collaboration on nuclear weapons was possible.

De Gaulle then stated that he agreed and had nothing to add. He did not say a word to link his agreement with British entry into the EEC, but hopes were aroused on the British side by his attitude. Both parties, French and British, therefore took the line that the discussions at Champs had gone well.

If Macmillan had been able to press the negotiations in Brussels to a decision at once, this was the moment at which de Gaulle would have had reason to hesitate in blocking a successful outcome. Pompidou's government had lost their majority through MRP defections and were in danger of defeat in the Assembly. They might not have wanted to risk provoking a vote of censure by displaying open hostility to British entry into the EEC, which public opinion supported. But Macmillan had not reconciled either his own Conservative party or Britain's Commonwealth partners to the sacrifices in terms of tariff policy that would be required to satisfy the Five as well as the French, so he was unable to strike while the iron was hot. The summer holidays arrived without decisive progress having been made in Brussels. In November the Gaullists gained a sweeping victory in the premature parliamentary elections brought on for reasons of internal politics, which assured them a majority in Parliament for five years ahead and liberated de Gaulle from a major inhibition to saying No to the British. Almost certainly he would have said No anyway if it had come to the point, but he did not have to face making a choice at his moment of vulnerability.

Meanwhile de Gaulle had found a solution to the problem posed by the failure of his projected Treaty of Political Union among the Six. He had hoped to present this to French opinion as proof that Europe offered them prospects that would compensate for what had been sacrificed in North Africa. As an alternative he decided to dramatize the reconciliation with the Federal Republic. An exchange of ceremonial visits between him and Adenauer took place. In France from 2 to 8 July Adenauer was given a cordial welcome. The climax was a High Mass in the Cathedral at Reims, which the President of the Republic and the Chancellor attended side by side. In his speeches de Gaulle described Franco-German cooperation as the basis on which the unity of all Europe could ultimately be built.

His return visit from 4 to 9 September was a more constrained affair because the West Germans were aware that he was in a sense competing with President Kennedy. Most of them felt that the

American shield was their indispensable protection, however much they might favour Franco-German reconciliation. Moreover de Gaulle omitted Berlin from his itinerary, which not a few regretted. On balance, however, the exchange of visits had an excellent effect on public feeling in both countries.

In his dealings with the Germans, de Gaulle was in a hurry, since Adenauer would be obliged to give up the Chancellorship in the autumn of 1963. The General wanted to make use of Adenauer's influence while it was still strong, in order to advance Franco-German cooperation. Accordingly either during or soon after his visit to West Germany he raised with the Germans the question of nuclear defence in common. The offer he made was more restrictive than the agreement concluded in 1958 in the time of the Gaillard government. It is said to have envisaged no more than allowing West German Air Force officers to train with the *force de frappe* and to take part in its strategic planning, in return for a German contribution to the costs of research and development of nuclear weapons which would remain in French hands. As the *force de frappe* was not yet operational, this was more of a request for German financial aid than anything else. Whatever Adenauer's personal inclinations may have been, the West Germans knew they could not accept the offer without giving serious offence to Washington. So they declined it. For his part Adenauer urged on de Gaulle the conclusion of a Franco-German Treaty of Friendship and Cooperation, as a seal on the reconciliation of the two countries. De Gaulle had doubts about its utility, given German-American ties, but he did not reject the idea.

German-American ties were indeed strong, and the Americans were resolved to keep them so. On 4 July, while Adenauer was being fêted in Paris, Kennedy had marked Independence Day by proclaiming his own Grand Design, an Atlantic Community in which Europe and North America would stand as equal pillars sustaining NATO. What his proposal lacked in detail it made up for in popular appeal. It was an effective challenge to de Gaulle's European Europe. Kennedy was also openly critical of de Gaulle's nuclear policy and went so far as to describe it as 'unfriendly' in a press conference he gave on 27 June. If Britain had been the stumbling-block to the political union of the Six, America was the obstacle to Franco-German unity of the kind de Gaulle sought.

De Gaulle's efforts in Europe had progressed no further when, as a result of the Skybolt affair, he found himself invited to adhere to an agreement which Kennedy and Macmillan had worked out for their own purposes at Nassau without even consulting him. The Americans and the British, who had been doing their best to frustrate his aims in Europe, suddenly offered him a new version of tripartism. It must have seemed an ironic stroke of chance to de Gaulle, but, once he had read the Nassau agreement, he can have been in no doubt that he could not accept it. Kennedy himself made the whole transaction sound less precise by telling the press 'it will take a good many weeks, possibly months, to work this out. It isn't something to which the French or anyone else can give an answer of Yes or No.' In this the President proved to be mistaken.

De Gaulle then threw up the usual smokescreen of contradictory reports with which he liked to precede a dramatic move. He received the British and American ambassadors and gave them to understand that he was considering matters carefully. Various ministers made various forecasts of what he would do and how long he would take to make up his mind. But de Gaulle had a discouraging message for the British Prime Minister. 'Macmillan has let me down, and you can tell him so,' he said to his Ambassador, Geoffroy de Courcel. This was presumably a reference to his disappointed hopes that Macmillan, after the cancelling of Skybolt, would turn to the nuclear cooperation with France of which he had spoken at Champs.[5]

What nobody predicted was that de Gaulle would give a resounding answer to both Kennedy and Macmillan at his press conference at the Elysée Palace on 14 January, yet that was what he did. Before the large audience usual on such occasions he announced that Britain was unable at present to accept the obligations of membership of the EEC; that France rejected Kennedy's offer of Polaris missiles in a NATO force and would go her own way as a nuclear power; and that she would develop her special relationship with the Federal German Republic. He did not state in so many words either that France meant to veto further negotiations with Britain in Brussels or that she would sign a Treaty of Friendship and Cooperation with the Federal Republic, but both actions were implicit in his remarks and they were soon accomplished. Adenauer came to Paris on 21 January and the Treaty was signed the next day. Couve de Murville put a stop to the negotiations in Brussels, despite the remonstrances of the Five, on 29 January.

This was de Gaulle's most sensational press conference. The shock in Britain was profound. Until 14 January the government, though anxious, had thought it unlikely that de Gaulle would go so far as a unilateral veto. Sentiment towards the French changed, and ancestral prejudices revived. In the Foreign Office consideration was given to various reprisals ranging from a propaganda campaign against de Gaulle pillorying him for ingratitude towards the country which had sustained him in 1940, to a declaration that Britain no longer felt bound by her obligation under the Treaty of Paris of 23 October 1954 to maintain an army of at least five divisions on the Continent for the next fifty years. But the decision taken was to maintain the British application to join the EEC and to cultivate the Five in order to prevent the establishment of French hegemony on the Continent. The Americans endorsed this British policy and concentrated on maintaining the solidarity of NATO and the primacy of their own influence in Bonn against de Gaulle's inroads.

De Gaulle's double rebuff to the Anglo-Saxons was calmly received by French public opinion. More people favoured an entirely independent *force de frappe* than opposed it, so the Polaris offer had no appeal; and the veto in Brussels was seen as an interruption, justified by British obstinacy, of a negotiation that could be resumed later on. Public opinion polls showed that 44 per cent approved the 'interruption' and only 21 per cent did not; yet at the same time 43 per cent wanted Britain to join the EEC, and only 21 per cent were opposed. There was little conception in France of the depth of British resentment.

It is sometimes suggested that the General kept Britain out of the EEC as a reprisal for the humiliations he had suffered at her hands during the war. He certainly felt resentment at some of the treatment he had received, but it would have been out of character for him to allow such emotions to sway his judgement either way in a question of national importance. The most rational explanation seems the best, although de Gaulle never advanced it himself. It is that in de Gaulle's judgement the interests of France were best served by the exclusion of Britain, as he saw her in 1963. She was too formidable a rival for the leadership of Western Europe. A British-dominated English-speaking EEC was an unacceptable prospect.

Was there a price that would have persuaded him to think differently? Opinions differ among those who knew him best. If so, it was a nuclear price. But Macmillan judged that the Nassau arrangements were more in Britain's interest; and there is no certainty that de Gaulle would have accepted any price. France was a long way behind Britain in nuclear weaponry in 1962 and would have had to play second fiddle in any joint nuclear defence project. If de Gaulle had allowed Britain into the EEC, he might have been putting France in a weaker position than Britain both in the Common Market and in any nuclear arrangement between the two.

De Gaulle's veto was hurtful to British prestige, and its consequences were a heavy blow materially. At the end of the 1950s the GNP of Britain was still worth more than that of France, as it had been since the keeping of economic statistics began. In the early 1960s France took a lead which rapidly increased. On 28 January Macmillan noted sadly in his diary: 'All our policies at home and abroad are in ruins . . . French domination of Europe is the new and alarming feature.'[6]

According to de Gaulle's unsentimental philosophy, the great nations were competitors. A setback to Britain did not distress him. Sufficiently weakened she might even become an acceptable partner in the EEC, a partner no longer capable of sustaining a special relationship with the United States. The story in Paris at the time was that after the veto he had said: 'I will have her naked.' It became so current that at a later press conference he denied it. But even if the story was not literally true, it expressed a truth. French tactics after the veto in Brussels were indicative of a desire to undermine British positions systematically. An attack was opened on the use of sterling as a reserve currency. The strain on the British economy of sterling's special functions was described by French diplomats as one of the difficulties that would have to be overcome before Britain could assume the obligations of the Treaty of Rome. This campaign was evidently aimed not only at sterling but at the dollar, which was the lynchpin of the reserve currency system.

At the end of his dramatic month of January, the General turned to the Russians, who, as he knew, viewed France's *rapprochement* with the Federal Republic with deep suspicion. He tried to allay these feelings by summoning Vinogradov, the Soviet Ambassador, to the Elysée for a *'tour d'horizon'*. His gesture did not have the desired effect. A few days later the Soviet government circulated a note to powers involved in the victory over Nazi Germany warning that the Franco-German treaty might encourage the spirit of revanchism in the

Federal Republic. The Russians were as strongly opposed as the Americans to de Gaulle's enterprise in Germany, but at least they cannot have failed to understand after 14 January that the time of tripartism was over.

# 33 'The Great Quarrel'

De Gaulle's spectacular rejection of the Anglo-Americans on 14 January 1963 marked a turning-point in his conduct of foreign policy. Until then he had always appeared as the most resolute ally of the United States at moments of crisis, such as the collapse of the summit conference in 1960, the building of the Berlin Wall in 1961, and the confrontation over Cuba in 1962, however difficult he might be at intervening times. From the beginning of 1963 onwards, however, he became on more and more issues openly hostile to American policy. He had more freedom of manoeuvre thanks to the Algerian settlement, the electoral victory of the Gaullists and the cessation of Khrushchev's threats about Berlin and Germany. He used it to make manifest the independence of France.

For de Gaulle independence was meaningless unless exercised with vigour in pursuit of a distinctive policy. To understand the way he went to work it is necessary to remember the revealing misquotation from *Hamlet* with which he prefaced *Le Fil de l'Épée* – 'To be great is to sustain a great quarrel.' His great quarrel was with the Americans, with the tendency of that immense power automatically to dominate the conduct of any great enterprise in which it took part. He wanted to create space in Europe for France to play her independent part. His aim in the long run was to create a security system based on the European powers alone. The two poles of security were to be France with her nuclear strength and Russia with hers. Western Germany – Charlemagne's Germany – would be the great supporter of France, and would look to her, not to the United States, as the prime guarantor of her security. Ultimately the practice of this system would lead to reconciliation between Russians and Germans, and even perhaps – who could say? – to a kind of reunification of Germany.

He knew that the world thought France too weak to act in the role for which he had cast her. But such a belief was for him an example of the fatalism against which he used to warn his pupils at St Cyr, the clever cowardice that was the sin against the Holy Spirit. If France would turn her eyes to the heights and scale them with de Gaulle, she would become strong enough, in association with her German ally, to bear the burden of greatness. Of course she would welcome the support of her natural allies in the West, America and Britain. Their function would be to serve as buttresses of the great European edifice, outside but indispensable.

From 1963 onwards he drew his Atlantic and European policies together and directed his efforts towards making this grand design by degrees a reality. Inevitably the first stages involved much strife against American domination of Europe, because it was essential to begin by persuading the Germans to look primarily to France rather than to the United States for security. It was necessary to show that the American deterrent was no longer reliable for Europe. Those who favoured a federal Europe, the supranationalists, must also be frustrated.

De Gaulle was, however, most careful to take French public opinion along with him in his enterprise. He made the press conferences which he gave twice a year an important instrument to serve that purpose. Recognizing that the show of independence pleased the French but that they would be disturbed if they thought America and Britain were no longer friends, he repeatedly rejected at his press conferences the charge of anti-Americanism, even when criticizing American policies in detail. All the time in the years from 1963 onwards he had in mind the Presidential election that would take place in December 1965. Until then he kept France not only in the Atlantic Alliance but in NATO, and asserted that she was an ally, critical at times but basically friendly, of the United States. On these lines he pursued his 'great quarrel' from 14 January 1963 onwards; and his first move was the signature of the Franco-German Treaty a week later.

In his Memoirs, Couve de Murville, a man not given to exaggeration, describes the first six months of 1963 as the period of by far the most serious, although not the most spectacular, of the series of crises that occurred between France and the United States between 1961 and 1967. This, he says, was because the substance of it went right to the heart of America's relations with Europe.[1]

De Gaulle had indeed probed the heart of the matter at his press conference of 14 January by calling in question the reliability of the American deterrent as a protection for Western Europe. It was a repetition of what he had already said in private to Eisenhower and Kennedy. Since the Americans were now exposed to the Soviet deterrent: 'Nobody in the world, in particular nobody in America, can say where, when, how, or to what extent, American nuclear weapons would be used to defend Europe.' So France was going to construct, and if necessary use, her own deterrent, 'without, of course, refusing cooperation, technical or strategic, if that is wished by our allies'.[2] Those words indicated to the initiated that he had not forgotten Dean Rusk's warning about the consequences of independent targeting.

The message was addressed above all to the West Germans, the people in the front line; and when, a week later, they signed a treaty with France that called for coordination of defence and foreign policies and provided for regular meetings of the leaders who decided them, it was natural for the Americans to be alarmed. As Couve puts it, they feared that the Franco-German Treaty could lead to 'emancipation of Western Europe, or at least of the two signatories'.[3] The way the Americans put it was that they meant to prevent de Gaulle taking over from them in Bonn.

They went into vigorous action, backed by the British, and inspired a great deal of anti-de Gaulle comment in the American and European press. Some eminent Europeans shared their views, notably the 'Committee for the United States of Europe' headed by Jean Monnet. American disapproval of the Franco-German Treaty had considerable impact in Bonn, where Adenauer was beginning to lose his grip on his party as the date of his resignation drew nearer. Many leading figures in the CDU, notably the Foreign Minister, Gerhard Schroeder, refused to attach the same importance to the French connection as did the Chancellor. The problem of ratification of the treaty had to be faced, and it provoked an anxious debate. There was general agreement that it was impossible for the Bundestag to refuse to ratify a treaty which sealed the bond of reconciliation between the two great enemies, but the idea was produced by Jean Monnet and his allies of adding a rider reaffirming that nothing in the treaty prejudiced Bonn's loyalty to NATO or close relations between Europe and the United States. This, it was felt, would remedy one of the greatest faults in the treaty, which was that it made no reference to Bonn's other treaty commitments.

President Kennedy also invited the West Germans to join the multilateral force envisaged in the Nassau agreement, and now generally known as the MLF. This was intended to be a sea-borne force assigned to and manned by NATO and armed with nuclear weapons under American control. The benefit to Europeans was largely psychological or political. The Americans hoped that the MLF would give them a feeling of having some share in the Western deterrent. It was detached from the main American deterrent because it was under a different command and might conceivably be used without involving the main deterrent, but it was under firm American control, and policy decisions as to its use would rest with the President of the United States. The West Germans professed interest in this curious hybrid, and an experimental destroyer with a mixed NATO crew under American command was put to sea. On 8 April the Russians duly delivered a protest note on the MLF. The French also criticized it vigorously seeing it as a device for tying the Federal Republic to the American deterrent.

In May, after considerable delay, the ratification debate took place in the Bundestag in Bonn and resulted in the victory of the pro-American forces. The treaty was ratified on 16 May, but a proviso was duly added to the preamble to the effect that it was without prejudice to the Federal government's loyalty to NATO and to close relations between America and Europe. De Gaulle was displeased and spoke of treaties that lasted no longer than roses or young girls. Nevertheless the Assembly in Paris completed ratification without a preamble on 20 June. The next day the General withdrew the French Atlantic Fleet from NATO.

At this point President Kennedy embarked on a visit to Western Europe whose high point was his stay in the Federal Republic and West Berlin from 24 to 26 June. This was a calculated effort to outdo the success achieved by the General the previous September. On the whole Kennedy achieved his end. He brought with him all the prestige of the man who had forced the Russians to retreat from Cuba. Nothing could be more reassuring to the Germans than to hear such a champion declare '*Ich bin ein Berliner.*' These were his only words of German, but they outweighed de Gaulle's relative fluency. Nevertheless his victory was not conclusive. A few days after his departure de Gaulle appeared in Bonn, surrounded by senior ministers, for the first session of talks under the new treaty.

The crisis in Franco-American relations of which Couve spoke was not, however, only a matter of rivalry for influence in Germany. Nuclear proliferation was also involved. Kennedy attached the highest importance to preventing this and believed it was a subject on which Washington and Moscow had a common interest. If de Gaulle was determined to persist in building an independent French deterrent, that was bad enough, but it would be still worse if he encouraged similar aspirations in others and aided their fulfilment.

On 25 May, Kennedy raised the subject with Couve, who was on a visit to Washington. It would have been more natural for him to take it up directly with the General, but a meeting could not be arranged, and it would have been a difficult matter to handle by correspondence.

Couve assured the President that France had no intention of helping Germany over 'the production or possession of nuclear arms'. When questioned further, he also told the President that nuclear cooperation with Britain was not a practical possibility, although not to be ruled out in principle, and that aid to Israel under the agreement of 1957 that might have helped her to produce weapons-grade plutonium had been halted soon after de Gaulle's return to power.[4]

After the Bundestag had added its preamble to the Franco-German Treaty and Couve had given these assurances in Washington, some of the tension went out of American-French relations, and Kennedy tried in vain to persuade de Gaulle to authorize French participation in talks which the Americans and British were having with the Russians about a ban on nuclear tests in the atmosphere. When the test ban treaty was signed in Moscow on 25 July, the General promptly declared at a press conference that France would not adhere to it.

The test ban negotiation was intended by the Americans as a sign to any doves that might exist in Moscow that it was possible to do business with the West after Cuba. At a press conference on 29 July, de Gaulle gave a perfect illustration of the role of the candid friend of America which he was to play repeatedly from 1963 until 1968. He denied that he was anti-American and asserted that the American press distorted French policies. Fundamentally, he said, the two countries were friends. Having made these soothing observations, he then proceeded to create a new Franco-American difference of the first magnitude by making his first critical reference in public to the difficulties caused for other countries by the deficit in the American balance of payments. Many European countries, he said, had more dollars than they needed. This was the opening shot in a French campaign against the reserve currency system which had prevailed since the war and which gave the dollar – unlike other currencies, except sterling to a limited extent – the same status as gold for international settlements, fixing the price of gold at $35 an ounce. There was no immediate action to follow up the General's criticism, but the warning had been served on the Americans that in future they were liable to be challenged on the dollar no less than on nuclear policy and Germany.

In the autumn de Gaulle had to face an unwelcome change in the political climate in Germany. On 11 October his great friend and ally, Konrad Adenauer, was obliged to make way as Chancellor for a very different type of German, Ludwig Erhard, a Protestant and the principal architect of the German 'economic miracle'. Erhard's affinities were far more with Washington than with Paris. There would be no instinctive rapport between him and de Gaulle. Adenauer remained Chairman of the CDU party, a post of influence, but it was evident that a new era had arrived in Bonn.

The General could not claim victory in the campaign of 1963. His young rival in Washington was growing more formidable with experience. Then suddenly the prospects changed. President Kennedy was assassinated in Dallas on 22 November.

De Gaulle flew to Washington for the funeral and met the new President, Lyndon Johnson. As Couve de Murville says, contact between them was never really established.[5] There was a misunderstanding at their first private talk which complicated arrangements for future meetings. De Gaulle had been due to visit Kennedy in February 1964. Johnson urged him to maintain the visit, and told some State governors who saw him subsequently that de Gaulle had accepted. From them the news immediately leaked to the press. The General, who had not meant to commit himself and had thought his conversation with Johnson private, was irritated. He issued a denial of the story, which put Johnson in an embarrassing situation. The matter was never satisfactorily cleared up, and no visits were exchanged between the two men. Their only other meeting took place at Adenauer's funeral in Bonn in 1967. The state of relations between France and the United States in the intervening years was such that a meeting between them would only have dramatized their disagreements.

On his return to Paris de Gaulle predicted in private that a time of troubles was beginning for the United States due to social and racial conflicts. He did not accept the official version of the Kennedy killing.

He believed that the police and right-wing extremists were involved, people like the OAS in France, who had sought his own death. In all this he saw an additional reason for maintaining a policy of independence vis-à-vis Washington: 'We must deal with the United States as equals. Not equal in our resources of course . . . but equal as States.'[6]

From this point onwards, however, de Gaulle's 'great quarrel' was carried on in less dramatic circumstances, because he found himself dealing with a man whose tactics were to avoid him rather than confront him. 'I made it a rule for myself and the US government', said Johnson in his Memoirs, 'simply to ignore President de Gaulle's attitudes on our policies.'[7] He had none of Kennedy's attraction towards Europe, of which he knew little, and no desire to give new inspiration to his European allies. He was more concerned with keeping the Alliance on an even keel with as little commotion as possible.

The Atlantic Community quietly disappeared from the scene, and was followed in time by the MLF, both developments welcome to de Gaulle. But Johnson had a particularly good understanding with Erhard, who proved willing to retain vast amounts of dollars in Bonn's reserves in order to oblige Washington, and generally followed his lead in questions of defence and foreign affairs. De Gaulle therefore had to bide his time on the German front. He contrived to open 1964 with a move which was no more agreeable to the Americans than had been the signature of the Franco-German Treaty twelve months before. On 27 January it was announced in Paris and Peking that ambassadors would soon be exchanged between France and Red China.

At his press conference on 31 January 1964 de Gaulle explained recognition as a natural consequence of the stability and power of Communist China, which was such that no Asian problem could be settled without her voice being heard. No important material consequences flowed from the exchange of ambassadors between Paris and Peking. It was the gesture itself that mattered. It slightly reduced the polarization of the international world; China was beginning to emerge from isolation, and at the same time moving away from her Russian ally. France, for her part, was moving away from her American ally, and making the first moves in a cautious détente with Russia.

De Gaulle waited some months longer before bringing real pressure to bear on Erhard. His dealings with the new Chancellor had, however, been unproductive thus far. He was intractable even on EEC matters, such as the level of agricultural prices. It became urgent therefore to bring pressure on him. De Gaulle revealed his discontent privately to Adenauer and other CDU leaders and aired it in public at his press conference of 23 July 1964, in which he gave a strong hint that if the Franco-German Treaty proved to have nothing to contribute to building European Europe, he would lose interest in it. He added with pride that the first units of the *force de frappe* would become operational before the end of the year.

In this press conference de Gaulle also developed another theme that was to become increasingly dear to him, that of 'the break-up of the two-power world', as Walter Lippmann called it. It is worth quoting his words at some length:

It is clear that things have changed. The Western states of our old continent have remade their economy and are restoring their military forces. One of them, France, is becoming a nuclear power . . .

On the other hand the monolithic character of the totalitarian world is breaking up . . . The Empire of the Soviets, the last and greatest colonial power of our time, finds the domination it exerts over vast territories in Asia challenged by the Chinese, while the European satellites, which it conferred on itself by the use of force, gradually draw away. At the same time the Communist régime, despite the immense effect it has made in Russia during half a century . . . is proving to be a failure as far as living standards and human satisfaction and dignity are concerned, by comparison with the system in Western Europe, which combines the planned economy [*dirigisme*] with liberty. Finally, great aspirations and great difficulties are profoundly disturbing the states of the Third World.

From all these new facts, intertwined as they are, it follows that the division of the world between two camps led respectively by Washington and Moscow corresponds less and less to the true situation . . . It is apparent that Europe, provided that she desires it, is now called to play her own distinctive part.

No doubt Europe should maintain an alliance with America . . . as long as the Soviet menace lasts. But the reasons which made the alliance a matter of subordination for Europe are disappearing day by day. Europe should assume her share of responsibilities . . . an event that would suit the interests of the United States . . . For the multiplicity and complexity of her tasks already exceeds, perhaps dangerously, her resources and her capacity.[8]

The timing of these harsh remarks about the Communist system was surprising, since it came only a few weeks after the signature of an anodyne Soviet-GDR Treaty of Friendship which did not purport to terminate the Allies' rights in Berlin. Khrushchev's threat was thus finally lifted. But de Gaulle thought it natural to show that he could sting when he was seeking to impress.

Erhard tried to appease de Gaulle by agreeing during the autumn to an increased Common Market price for wheat, and advancing a plan for political and defence consultations among the Six. But on that important matter de Gaulle wished to give the lead himself. He turned down Erhard's plan. Difficulties continued into 1965.

De Gaulle did not wait until then to make another move against the dollar. His Finance Minister, Giscard d'Estaing, suggested to the International Monetary Fund at a meeting in Tokyo in September 1964 that the time had come to modify the Gold Exchange Standard, as the French called the reserve currency system. The Americans were hostile and nothing came of the proposal. Nor were the French any more successful in rallying support the following February when de Gaulle proposed at his press conference that the international community should put in hand preparations for an early return to the Gold Standard proper.

On 11 February 1965 the French government proceeded to announce its withdrawal from the system of the Gold Exchange Standard, but it acted alone. The political implications of the French initiative were obvious. If the dollar ceased to be treated as the equivalent of gold by Western countries, America's ability to finance her foreign policy might be called in question. France on the other hand would have benefited from an increase in the value of gold, for her reserves were by this time very great.

So many contentious issues had piled up by the time the American Secretary of State, Dean Rusk, came to Paris in December 1964 for the annual ministerial meeting of the NATO Council, that he could not cover them all in a single interview with de Gaulle. He had to ask for a second talk. At this, according to Rusk's telegram to Washington,[9] he proposed that 'the five powers which now have such [i.e. nuclear] weapons might in some way get together to limit their further spread'. China had just joined the nuclear club by exploding her first bomb on 16 October. The first step might be a talk between the Western Three, Rusk suggested, thus raising the ghost of tripartism. De Gaulle waved such ideas aside. The French would not give the bomb to anybody, he said, but other states were bound to get it. 'Trying to prevent the nuclear bomb was like the attempts to ban the crossbow in the Middle Ages, which had not succeeded either.'

On nuclear coordination – i.e. joint targeting – de Gaulle sounded more forthcoming: 'When France had created a real nuclear force by 1968 or 1969, and if by then we were still allies, as he hoped, we should certainly study together as to how to coordinate our nuclear forces between governments, he emphasized, and not within NATO.' Dean Rusk did not comment on this proviso, and it was agreed that Messmer and McNamara should keep in touch on the subject. The Americans were perhaps not quite so inflexibly loyal at this time to the rules of nuclear consultation within NATO as they professed to be to their other allies.

As to Southeast Asia, the Americans were considering at this stage whether to send their own ground forces into South Vietnam, but Rusk was not specific. He confined himself to saying that 'If Hanoi were to continue pressure, this would lead to trouble'. He added that 'he would like to hope for France's support of US efforts.' The General replied with a warning: 'He personally felt that our present course of action was not the right one. . . the United States could never achieve the upper hand in that part of the world. Everything there was different, even Communism.' France, he said 'preferred peace, whatever the consequences might be, and they would in any case be less bad than war'. He suggested that an international conference should try to work out a *modus vivendi*. Rusk of course was not convinced.

The episode was reminiscent of wartime days. De Gaulle had guessed what the Americans were planning to do and had advised them not to do it. This time, as in the past, his advice was ignored. On 7 February 1965 the US Air Force began bombing targets in North Vietnam, and on 8 March the first American military units landed in South Vietnam. In the following months the war steadily escalated: American soldiers began to die in the jungles where the French had long fought.

There was now a Labour government in Britain which had no intention either of pursuing the vetoed applications of its Tory predecessor or of making a grievance of it. When de Gaulle visited London for Churchill's funeral in January 1965, he had talked with the new Premier, Harold Wilson, and invited him to Paris. Wilson came for talks on 2 and 3 April, and a measure of Anglo-French détente was confirmed. The British remained generally loyal to American policies, although worried by President Johnson's direct intervention in Vietnam, but the hatchet was buried as far as the veto of 1963 was concerned. The French in return promised to provide support for sterling, which had been weakening since Labour took over, to the tune of $50 million if necessary.

There was one surprise for the British visitors. Couve de Murville opened the conversation with his British colleague, Michael Stewart, by asking if Britain intended to join the Common Market. The question was not included in the Foreign Office brief prepared for the new Minister,[10] so he had to improvise his answer, which was that the terms of entry were what mattered, but that the question was not engaging the government's attention at the moment.

The enquiry was perhaps designed to ensure that the British front would remain quiet during the battle that was approaching in Brussels. It had long been apparent that a conflict was inevitable before the end of the year because the Treaty of Rome provided that majority voting on such important matters as agricultural prices and tariffs, to which General de Gaulle was firmly opposed, should come into effect on 1 January 1966. Clearly France would have to take preventive action.

The area of the impending dispute was enlarged in March when the European Parliament in Strasbourg approved budget proposals which would secure to the EEC Commission resources of its own accruing automatically from customs revenues instead of being approved as in the past by member governments. The draft regulation governing the use of funds for the agricultural policy during the years 1966–70 was linked with the budget proposals.

France at once opposed this procedure and demanded that the agricultural regulation be fixed by 30 June, as previously foreseen in the EEC timetable, as a separate matter. In the debate which followed, the German President of the Commission, Walter Hallstein, an ardent supranationalist, resisted the French demands.

The time limit of 30 June came and went without agreement, and the French government took immediate action. On 1 July the Council of Ministers approved a decision to suspend French participation in the workings of the EEC in Brussels and recall their permanent representative. Until the situation was radically changed, France would confine her cooperation to dealing with routine matters. As conditions of her return to Brussels she demanded not only the fixing of the agricultural regulation and the abandonment of Hallstein's budget proposals but also the suppression of the provisions for the entry into force of majority voting on 1 January 1966. It soon became clear that the conflict could not be resolved before the presidential election in France in December.

De Gaulle had operated with tactical skill. He had made the inevitable dispute over majority voting seem as if it had been forced on him in defence of the interests of French agriculture. There was still a definite risk that the crisis in the Common Market would disturb French farmers, who in general did well out of it, and cost him votes. The danger was not one that can have greatly concerned him, however, for it was taken for granted that he would be easily victórious if he decided to stand for re-election. Public opinion polls all pointed to that conclusion. Naturally he had not yet declared his intentions.

With the election in mind, he delayed his usual summer press conference until 9 September. Even then he did not declare whether he would be a candidate or not; he merely promised to announce his decision within two months. But he spoke as if he expected to remain in control of affairs for many years to come, and was confident that all would go well. He said that France would remain 'the ally of her allies' as long as there was a danger to the West, but would leave the integrated structure of NATO by 1969 at the latest. He avoided any harsh criticism of American policy, while expressing hopes of détente with Russia. He also affirmed his determination to protect the interests of French agriculture in the EEC dispute and, without predicting its outcome, induced confidence by forecasting closer relations with Germany and the Six generally. His performance would have done well as an electioneering address.

When he announced on 4 November that he would stand for re-election, few were surprised and most expected him to win easily. But matters were to turn out otherwise.

# 34 CULTIVATING THE RUSSIANS

An understanding with the Russians had always been an essential aim of de Gaulle's foreign policy. To his way of thinking national interest was the strongest and most durable force in international affairs, and France had the same reasons for seeking good relations with Communist Russia as had impelled her to conclude an alliance with the Tsarist régime in the 1890s. He had applied that philosophy when he signed a treaty of friendship with the Soviet government in December 1944, and he approached the question from the same angle when he returned to power in 1958. Communism was another matter, and he contrived to oppose it vigorously in France, just as he had done in the years of the RPF. Khrushchev, however, seems to have had much the same opinion of him as Stalin: that he was basically a reactionary – that was how he was described in the postwar *Soviet Encyclopedia* – and that he was not 'realistic' because he did not recognize that after the fall of 1940 France was no longer the great power that had interested Russia before and between the two world wars. Moreover the Berlin crisis stood in the way of a rapprochement for a long time after 1958.

In consequence Franco-Russian relations made no real progress during the early years of de Gaulle's Presidency. When he took up his great quarrel in January 1963, therefore, conditions were by no means ideal for approaching Russia as he drew away from America. His first démarche to the Soviet Ambassador at the end of January was coolly received. The Russians were as doubtful as the Americans of what the Franco-German Treaty might portend. Was de Gaulle going to help the Germans to become a nuclear power? In the course of 1963, however, diplomatic exchanges allayed Russian suspicions to some extent.

When, in January 1964, France took an independent line by recognizing Red China, Russian interest in de Gaulle quickened as a result. If he acquired influence in Peking just as the Russians were losing theirs, he might prove a nuisance. De Gaulle showed his continuing interest by sending his Finance Minister, Giscard d'Estaing, to Moscow in January to open the negotiations for a new Franco-Russian commercial treaty. In February there came a gesture from the Russian side. The President of the Supreme Soviet, Nikolai Podgorny, came to Paris at the head of a parliamentary delegation. He was received by de Gaulle, to whom he suggested that there was no fundamental divergence of policy between the two states. The General replied more realistically that the substantial differences that existed, particularly over European questions, could better be taken calmly than contentiously.[1]

Calm prevailed between East and West during 1964 and the prospects for its continuance were improved when the anodyne Soviet–East German Treaty of Friendship was signed in June. Unlike the treaty which Khrushchev had threatened to conclude, it did not purport to terminate Allied rights in Berlin, and was a clear sign that this particular menace had been shelved indefinitely. An even more reassuring event took place on 15 October, when Khrushchev was voted out of power by his colleagues, being replaced as party chief by Leonid Brezhnev and as head of government by Alexei Kosygin.

The French found that it was easier to do business with the new men. On 30 October the new Franco-Soviet Treaty of Commerce was signed. In the course of the following three months the Foreign ministers of Bulgaria, Czechoslovakia and Hungary successively visited Paris to record the desire of their governments to follow the Soviet example and improve relations with France. In December a new Franco-Romanian Treaty of Commerce was concluded. Only Poland among Soviet allies hesitated to take up ministerial exchanges, perhaps because relations with France had been of such special importance to her in the past, perhaps because de Gaulle had himself fought with the Poles against the Russians. Franco-Polish relations remained a particularly sensitive area.

With Moscow, however, détente made further progress in the New Year. On the initiative of Kosygin, intergovernmental consultation began on questions of foreign policy.[2] Gromyko visited Paris from 26 to 30 April and was received by de Gaulle and Prime Minister Pompidou as well as having exhaustive discussions with Couve de Murville. The principal subject was of course Germany, on which nothing new was said on either side. But the abandonment of Khrushchev's menacing style made it possible to talk calmly, and the two sides were not far apart in their appraisal of the situation in Vietnam.

There were other discussions between Couve and Gromyko during the summer, and in his pre-electoral press conference in September de Gaulle stated that France attached great importance to the new trend in relations with Russia. True to his philosophy he referred to '*La Russie*' and not to '*L'Union Soviétique*'.

The Russians of course understood this distinction as clearly as anybody. In seeking closer relations with France, Brezhnev and Kosygin had their eyes open and had not forgotten what de Gaulle had said a few months before they came to power about Soviet colonialism and the gradual emancipation of the countries of Eastern Europe. Their interest in de Gaulle was as objective and as hard-headed as his own in them, and as firmly rooted in a philosophy. He believed that history was demonstrating once more the primacy of national interest over ideologies, and that the Fifth Republic could deal with the commissars as well as the Third Republic had with the Tsars. They believed in the law of divisions in the capitalist world and thought they could exploit it as between France and America. Each also knew what was in the mind of the other. It was a game of chess that both parties thought worth playing.

From 28 October to 2 November, shortly before the electoral campaign began in France, it was Couve's turn to go to Russia. He was received with every consideration, seeing Brezhnev and Kosygin as well as Gromyko. Evidently the Russians were hoping to resume the dialogue after the elections. The logical step was an exchange of visits at the highest level.

# 35 'The Peoples Rising to the Surface of Our Civilization'

In the non-aligned countries of the Third World, de Gaulle developed an active policy which he saw as a function of his attitude towards the Russians and Americans. It was essential to bring home to the new nations emerging from the disintegration of the European colonial empires that France was an independent and friendly force.

In 1963 the Algerian war was over and the generous terms of its settlement made it possible for France to seek a better understanding with states in the Third World who had sided with the rebels. Egypt had restored diplomatic relations with her in April 1963, for the first time since Suez, and other Arab States followed suit. In the autumn de Gaulle was able to make his first visit to an Islamic State outside Francophone Africa. In October he was the guest of the Shah of Iran, who had already been to see him in Paris more than once. The crowds that welcomed him showed extraordinary enthusiasm. Even at this distance from home his personality and his history had a meaning for the man in the street. He began to plan more voyages outside Europe and decided to concentrate in 1964 on Latin America, a part of the world to which he had previously been able to pay little attention.

He set the scene for these visits and expounded the philosophy of his dealing with the Third World at the press conference which he gave on 31 January 1964 by saying:

> Our policies are linked. The efforts we are making to construct a Europe that will be European have a connection with what we are doing to help the peoples rising to the surface of our civilization. Yes, from now onwards this cooperation is a great ambition for France.[1]

Before setting out for South America, de Gaulle made two important moves in African affairs. On 18 February he responded to an appeal by the President of Gabon, who was menaced by a coup d'état, by sending French troops to his aid in accordance with the terms of the security pact between the two governments. This was the first test of the reaction of the UN and the Third World to the use of French troops in a political role in Black Africa under Community arrangements, and the results were satisfactory. President M'Ba was saved and the UN was uncritical. A valuable precedent was created for French action to help friends in Africa.

Then on 13–15 March the General received Ben Bella, President of the new Algerian Republic, and reached agreement on a number of subjects disturbing relations between the two countries, in particular the presence of French troops in Algeria, for whom, except in Mers-el-Kebir and the Algerian Sahara, an accelerated timetable of withdrawal was prepared. It was agreed that economic and commercial difficulties should be the subject of further discussion. The success of these talks was helpful to the image of France in the Arab World.

De Gaulle's tour of Mexico from 16 to 19 March was a considerable act of stoicism. He was suffering from prostate trouble and knew an operation was imminent. Nevertheless he carried out an exhausting programme, including a visit to the University of Mexico, although it was the scene of anti-government disturbances at the time, and the police, barred by local tradition from the campus, could not be present to ensure his security. Mobbed by friendly students, he must have suffered physically from their attentions and the efforts of his bodyguards to protect him in the mêlée.[2] He remained imperturbable and made a speech which was received with enthusiasm, as were all his appearances in Mexico. It was a satisfactory prelude to the autumn visit to South America.

Back from Mexico he kept his impending operation secret and gave a radio and TV address to the nation on 16 April. It was an account of his stewardship in social and economic affairs since his return to power, and painted an impressive picture of progress. The papers were full of the speech the next day, just as he was entering hospital, and it offset fears and hopes that his strength might be failing. The operation was a success and he was back at the Elysée by the end of the month.

His second visit to Latin America followed in the autumn. From 20 September to 16 October he visited ten countries of South America in a blaze of enthusiasm and publicity which was a surprise to almost everybody. The theme of his speeches was the same as in Mexico. France had always striven for liberty and the independence of nations.

Her influence had played a part in the liberation of Latin America. They were all part of the Latin world and all opposed to hegemony and domination, both words which evoked United States policy towards Latin America. They should develop economic, technical and cultural cooperation.

The tour was an extraordinary affair, even if its practical consequences were slight. France lacked the resources, economic and technical, to give aid on a scale anywhere near what Latin America required, and there were definite limits to her capacities as a trading partner. The General's visit was more of a twenty-six-day wonder than the occasion of a lasting change in relations between France and Latin America. But he attached great importance to the 'wonderful', the symbolic side of it all. He wanted to affirm the existence of France, and to encourage the countries he visited to affirm their own existence in face of the superpowers. In those terms he made his mark in South America.

There were no spectacular visits in 1965, but France strengthened her position in the Third World by economic and diplomatic means. In the Middle East a gradual shift of emphasis was perceptible away from the former preferential relationship with Israel and towards a better understanding with the Arab countries. As soon as he had come to power de Gaulle had severed some of the extraordinarily close ties in defence and atomic collaboration which had been created between Israel and successive French governments in the period from 1956 to 1958; but, as long as the war in Algeria continued, relations had been close and, when the Prime Minister of Israel, David Ben-Gurion, made an official visit to France in 1961, the General had spoken publicly of '*Israël notre ami, Israël notre allié*'. After the Algerian settlement the climate of these relations grew cooler. Diplomatic relations between France and the Arab States were restored, and, although France continued to be Israel's principal arms supplier, there were no ministerial visits from France to Israel.[3]

In July 1965 France created a precedent which was of much importance to the oil-owning countries of the Third World. An agreement was reached with the Algerians which gave them full ownership of Saharan oil, while preserving valuable rights of association and purchase to France. This was a concession which caused anxiety to American and British oil companies, which were still maintaining rights of ownership in many parts of the Third World.

By the summer of 1965, however, American anxieties were centred on another matter, the consequences of sending troops into the Vietnam war. France had condemned both that action and the American military intervention in April in a civil war in the Dominican Republic. The latter was soon over, but no end was in sight in Vietnam. On 20 June the Vice-President of the United States, Hubert Humphrey, visited de Gaulle in order to discuss Franco-American differences, but no rapprochement was possible. The General had warned Dean Rusk where he expected American policy in Vietnam to lead, and he knew that the great majority of the new countries in Asia and Africa shared his disapproval. It was a situation which added to the stresses on America and might have consequences for his plans for a European Europe after the elections. As he had told his press conference in January 1964, all his policies were linked.

# 36 The Home Front, 1959–65

If the development of de Gaulle's foreign policy attracted most attention abroad, it was the substantial changes he introduced at home that were of chief concern to the French voter. Some account of how these had functioned from 1959 onwards is therefore needed in order to complete the scene for the electoral campaign of November and December 1965.

The new political system produced by and large the results that de Gaulle expected. His purpose was to give France the governmental stability she had lacked since the great Revolution of 1789. In this he was remarkably successful. From 1959 to 1965 there were only three governments under two Prime Ministers, as compared with the twenty-one that the twelve years of the Fourth Republic had seen come and go, before de Gaulle became Prime Minister of the twenty-second and last. Some Ministers, notably the Foreign Minister, Couve de Murville, and André Malraux, in charge of cultural affairs, remained at their posts unchanged throughout, and beyond, the seven years of the General's first term as President.

The institutions of the Fifth Republic as operated by de Gaulle made the Presidency the fountainhead of authority to an even greater degree than the text of the Constitution laid down.

It soon became customary under the Fifth Republic to use the phrase 'the reserved domain' to describe the area in which the President personally directed national policy without necessarily consulting ministers. This domain consisted of foreign and French Community affairs, defence and finance. But, as de Gaulle pointed out in his *Memoirs of Hope*, no reserved domain exists in the Constitution. The phrase came into use to describe de Gaulle's practice rather than a constitutional provision. In fact, as he also points out, he concerned himself directly with other matters, such as educational policy, when he saw fit.

The drama of the Generals' Putsch in April 1961 gave de Gaulle the chance to test an important piece of constitutional machinery. He invoked the special powers conferred on him by Article 16 to govern in an emergency and kept them in force until October. In fact the crisis was so quickly brought under control that he hardly needed them, but the precedent of calling on them had been created. Likewise the procedure of the referendum was applied on Algerian questions in 1961 and 1962.

There was a change in the political atmosphere in March 1962 when the Evian accords were signed and the ceasefire was proclaimed in Algeria. As long as the war continued, there had been a tacit agreement on all sides not to push internal disputes too far. Georges Pompidou, who took over as Prime Minister on 17 April 1962 from Michel Debré, never a friend of Algerian independence, had to face a different situation. De Gaulle had frequently predicted in private that once he had solved the problem the political parties lacked the courage to face, they would try to overthrow him. So it proved in the course of 1962.

In May the members of the MRP who had joined Pompidou's government the month before resigned in protest at the uncompromising hostility to European integration which de Gaulle expressed at his press conference of 15 May. Their withdrawal posed a threat to the government's hold on the Assembly which crystallized when the General decided later in the summer to seek approval by referendum of a major constitutional amendment.

This he did as a consequence of the attempt on his life at Petit Clamart on 22 August from which he so narrowly escaped. He is said to have told a friend afterwards that this was the first time in his life that he felt fear. If so, it was not for his personal safety so much as for the effect on his refashioned Republic if he were suddenly removed from the scene so early in its life. After the meeting of the Council of Ministers on 29 August he announced that he meant to propose a modification of the Constitution 'designed to ensure the continuity of the State'. This proved to be a provision that in future the President should be elected not by a college of notables but by universal suffrage. It was clearly a means of strengthening the authority of the Presidency after de Gaulle, with his unique prestige, had left it. He proposed to submit the change not to Parliament but to a referendum.

The timing of de Gaulle's proposal was determined by the Petit Clamart affair, but its substance was the fruit of prolonged reflection.

He had told the pretender to the throne, the Comte de Paris, 'I am certain that monarchy is the régime that suits our country . . . but how to do it?' His conclusion had been that the restoration of the monarchy was a political impossibility, and that the best that could be done to give the French the strong personal direction which he thought suited to their temperament was to reinforce the prestige of the Presidency by establishing the link of direct election between the holder and the mass of the people.[1]

There was an immediate outcry from the Assembly, and de Gaulle agreed that a special session should be convened to debate the change. When it was held on 5 October a motion of censure on the government secured a majority. On 10 October de Gaulle dissolved Parliament and ordered elections to be held on 18 and 25 November.

On 28 October, 77.25 per cent of the electorate took part in the referendum, and 61.7 per cent of them voted for the General's proposal. This was a decisive enough margin, and yet it left him less than satisfied. It was smaller than in previous consultations and fell short of being a majority of the total electorate. Popular confidence in him seemed to be on the ebb for the first time since his return to power. He delayed his return from Colombey to Paris for twenty-four hours, and perhaps considered resignation.

His decision, however, was to stay in office and intervene personally in the parliamentary elections in the hope of winning more support. In a broadcast to the nation on 7 November he endorsed the UNR and their small ally, the more leftist UDT (*Union Démocratique du Travail*). His direct backing proved effective and the elections resulted in a triumph for the UNR/UDT and their associates, the Independent Republicans, which exceeded all expectations. Of the 465 seats in the new Assembly they secured respectively 233, a majority in itself, and 35. Five years of assured control of Parliament lay ahead of the Gaullists.

Nevertheless the elections marked a change in de Gaulle's standing in the country. By his direct intervention he had identified himself with a group of political parties more closely than ever before. De Gaulle thus became a more controversial figure, the leader of a majority as well as a heroic personality.

Constitutional revision continued to be discussed, and in a speech in the Assembly on 24 April 1964, François Mitterrand envisaged the establishment of a presidential régime with separation of powers as in the United States.[2] Nothing came of the debate, but it provided evidence of a change of heart among the Opposition. The stance adopted by Mitterrand and others amounted to an acknowledgement that there were merits in de Gaulle's system and that it should not automatically be rejected in favour of a return to the past if his opponents came back to power.

De Gaulle made as much difference to the economic as to the political life of the nation. At the end of 1958, in order to give reality to the EEC, France had to begin dismantling the protective wall behind which her industry and agriculture had sheltered for so long, and to live on terms of freer competition with their neighbours. The Fourth Republic had accepted the commitment by signing the Treaty of Rome, but had done little to prepare for meeting it. That task was left to de Gaulle, and he carried it out with the help of experts such as Antoine Pinay and Jacques Rueff, by means of devaluation and reduced social benefits.

The preparatory measures were harsh, but the opportunities thereby created were considerable. With the Assembly under control and ministers free of the obligations and inhibitions which membership of it would have imposed, Debré, and Pompidou after him, were able to carry out a considerable programme of modernization and renewal. They did not extend the area of nationalization, which remained as de Gaulle's two governments of 1944-6 had defined it, but their administrations had a strong *dirigiste* tendency. The General was never a friend of *laissez-faire* capitalism. An important part of the funds for industrial and agricultural investment came from the nationalized banking sector and was therefore ultimately under State control. The national planning organization, known simply as *Le Plan*, founded by de Gaulle after the war and fostered by the Fourth Republic, was given a new impulse to match the challenge of the Common Market. Increased funds were placed at its disposal and a higher rate of expansion set, 5.5 per cent per year, in a revised interim plan for 1959-61. The following plan set a rate of 24 per cent for growth in the period 1962-5.

Up to the end of 1962 targets were very nearly achieved, but in 1963 the economy ran into rougher waters. A rise in prices led to more insistent wage demands, and the number of strikes, minimal as long as the Algerian crisis lasted, began to increase. On 1 March the coalminers started a strike. De Gaulle, acting against the advice of his

Prime Minister, made an attempt to break it by having call-up notices issued to strikers subject to military service. This proved to be a serious mistake. The strike went on, and working-class opinion swung swiftly and sharply against the General. The only period of his ten years as President during which his popularity rating fell below 50 per cent began in March 1963 and lasted until November of that year. In April, when the strike ended, there were as many people against him as for him. The General, always a pragmatist as to ways and means, learnt his lesson and never again used a military call-up as a social weapon.

Overheating of the economy and general restlessness continued throughout the summer of 1963, and the Assembly passed a law on 27 July requiring public servants in future to give notice of their intention to strike. Then on 12 September the 'stabilization plan' for controlling inflation by means of credit and price controls was announced. The Finance Minister, Giscard d'Estaing, would have preferred to leave the cure to market forces, but he was overruled by de Gaulle. Stabilization proved only a partial success. Expansion was more difficult once it was imposed. France was still making substantial progress, however, and her rate of growth exceeded that of Britain or the United States, although it was nothing exceptional within the still booming Common Market. Reserves continued to accumulate, and in 1964 much external debt was paid off before the date of maturity.

Distribution of this increased wealth was a different question. In this respect the Fifth Republic was not revolutionary. Living standards went up for all, but the real gains accrued in the main to those who were already well off. Direct taxation was light by West European standards. From 1963 onwards the parties of the left and the trade union leadership became increasingly vocal on the score of unequal distribution, and strikes persisted. The General began to talk at his press conferences of the need for an incomes policy, but said that the difficulties were such that decisive action would have to be postponed until after the presidential election.

De Gaulle took a more personal interest in social than in strictly economic measures, notably in government aid to private education and in the promotion of his ideas of 'worker participation'. Under the Fourth Republic, State help for extracurricular activities had been granted to religious schools, but the question remained controversial. De Gaulle saw to it that the position of the religious schools was protected.

'Worker participation' was more difficult to promote. The word described his long-held, but cloudy, idea that a more harmonious society could be created if the work force were given an interest in either the profits or the direction of the enterprise employing them, or in both. An ordinance of 7 January 1959 launched a scheme relating to profits, but it was optional and had little impact. The idea of *intéressement*, or *participation* as he sometimes called it, was to continue to haunt de Gaulle. He could not find a way to give it practical effect, and he received no encouragement either from trade union leaders or from Pompidou, who regarded the notion with all the scepticism of a hardened banker. De Gaulle approached the problem from a different background. He knew what it was like to be the commanding officer of a first-class regiment. He dreamt at times of a France that would be equally loyal to its chief.

The administration of justice was a supremely difficult problem. De Gaulle did not establish an independent judiciary, nor did he leave the repression of crime exclusively to the regular police forces. The conditions of the Algerian war would have made it difficult for him to do so even if he had wished. But in fact de Gaulle was as much a believer in *raison d'état* as a necessary element in justice as the kings of France had been.

Under the Fourth Republic leniency towards the 'counter-terrorist' activities of the settlers in Algeria had become as automatic as the severity, and even torture, used against the rebels. There was no immediate change when de Gaulle took over. It only came when the settlers turned against him. After Barricades Week he was incensed by the mildness shown by military courts in France towards offenders brought before them, and he took steps to prevent a recurrence in the wake of the Generals' Putsch in April 1961. He set up a special tribunal, with military and civilian members selected by him, to try the main offenders. But when the tribunal, after condemning General Jouhaud to death, merely imposed a life sentence on the equally guilty Salan, de Gaulle replaced the special tribunal by an even more special Military Court of Justice, whose duty was evidently to return the verdicts that the State required. The first President he selected for it, General de Larminat, a Gaullist since 1940, committed suicide rather than serve. This tragedy was a measure of the anguish felt by officers required to condemn their peers for *raison d'état*. This was the court which tried and condemned the conspirators of Petit Clamart. Soon afterwards a new State Security Court with less sweeping powers was set up and continued in existence until 1981, when it was dissolved by President Mitterrand.

The police was not the only force charged with pursuing offenders under the Fifth Republic. Special groups, known colloquially as '*les barbouzes*' – 'the Beards' – were set up with governmental blessing to hunt OAS conspirators in Algeria and later in Europe. The most spectacular coup of the *barbouzes* was to capture the OAS leader, Colonel Argoud, in Munich in February 1963 and deposit him bound and gagged in the boot of a car outside police headquarters in Paris. Separate from the *barbouzes* were the groups known as *Service d'action civique*, which had in the past guarded meetings of the RPF from disruption by Communists and which now performed various protective functions as required. Just how operations were directed was a closely-guarded secret. Three men who had been close to the General in the days of the RPF, Roger Frey, Minister of the Interior since April 1961, Jacques Foccart, special adviser on Africa at the Elysée, and Olivier Guichard, were all said to be involved.

There was undoubtedly an element of the 'police state' in the Fifth Republic's methods of dealing with political crime and punishment, but this was in a long French tradition. De Gaulle did not invent it, although it was certainly with his approval that the Free French movement developed a tendency from its early days in London to conform to that tradition.

Matters sometimes escaped control. An example of this caused a major scandal in October 1965 as the presidential election campaign was impending. Ben Barka, a Moroccan political refugee of left-wing persuasion living in Paris, disappeared mysteriously. It transpired that he had been delivered with the help of members both of the French police and of the intelligence service, the *Service de Documentation Extérieure et de Contre-Espionnage* (SDECE), to Moroccan security officers, including their chief, Colonel Oufkir. It had to be assumed that the Moroccans had murdered him and decamped. The question which exercised opinion was how high up the affair had gone on the French side. At a press conference de Gaulle declared that investigation had shown Ben Barka's kidnapping to be a 'subaltern affair'. Nevertheless, the head of SDECE was replaced and the whole organization was put under stricter discipline. A few Frenchmen and a Moroccan implicated in the Ben Barka affair were sent to prison and Colonel Oufkir was condemned *in absentia.*

So there were warts on the picture the Fifth Republic presented to the voters in the autumn of 1965. Nevertheless the main outlines were impressive. If there were blemishes on the administration of justice and the distribution of wealth, it remained true that France was at peace and more prosperous than ever before. The achievement was de Gaulle's. He could justly claim that it was due to his guidance that France had since 1958 'espoused her century' as he put it. He had modernized the polity and the economy. Above all he had revived the morale and the self-respect of the French. His resolute assertions of the grandeur of France gave them a better opinion of themselves and their capacities, whether or not they were Gaullists.

When the General entered the electoral lists on 4 November, two other important candidates had already declared themselves. François Mitterrand had been chosen in September as the representative of the United Left. He was neither a Socialist nor a Communist but leader of a small group known as the Convention of Republican Institutions. It seemed that he had been given the task of opposing de Gaulle because it was too hopeless to attract the chiefs of the major formations. The only other serious contestant was Jean Lecanuet, who represented the Opposition centre parties.

It was taken as a foregone conclusion from the outset that, if there was a second round, it would be fought between de Gaulle and Mitterrand; but few thought it would be necessary. Public opinion polls in the first week of November gave 66 per cent of the vote to de Gaulle and only 23 per cent to the candidate of the Left.[3] In this situation de Gaulle made the pardonable error of thinking that it would be good tactics to hold aloof from the campaign and rely on the state of public opinion to carry him to victory.

It was the unforeseen power of television which upset his calculations. In normal times television, under the usages of the Fifth Republic, was subject to firm government control. De Gaulle had a virtual monopoly, among politicians, of its use. He was the régime's regular spokesman. He attached little importance to the power of the press in forming opinion but much to that of radio and television, in which he used his privilege to the full. It was a rare event even for a minister to expound policy on television. Pompidou himself only did so for the first time in October 1965. As for the Opposition, they were almost totally excluded.

But the law governing the use of television during a presidential election changed all this. It accorded to each candidate the right of two hours' time on the screen to state his case during the two weeks of the official campaign which immediately preceded the polling date. This period began on 19 November. Mitterrand, Lecanuet and the rest used their allotted time to the full while the General ignored most of his, confining himself to two brief interventions. This proved to be a grave tactical error.

The unaccustomed sight and sound of Opposition politicians attacking de Gaulle had an explosive effect on the voting public. It was the novelty rather than the substance of their criticisms and promises that gave them force. In fact both Mitterrand and Lecanuet campaigned with restraint and a certain respect for the General. Neither of them called the Constitution as such in question, although Mitterrand was critical of the extent of the President's reserved powers and the arbitrary use de Gaulle had made of them. It was apparent that everybody realized that the new institutions had by and large proved their worth and come to stay. As a result de Gaulle's warning that a vote against him was a vote for a return to the old and disastrous ways of the Third and Fourth Republics did not carry conviction with all. Mitterrand and Lecanuet began to win votes at a great rate. Opinion polls before 19 November still gave 61 per cent to de Gaulle against 24 per cent to Mitterrand, but a dramatic change followed. By 1 December de Gaulle was down to 46.5 per cent, Mitterrand up to 27 per cent and Lecanuet to 20 per cent.[4] The General had lost 15 per cent of his support in the ten days since television had been thrown open to the Opposition.

The first round took place on 5 December. De Gaulle won 43.7 per cent of the votes against 32.2 per cent for Mitterrand, and 15.9 per cent for Lecanuet. The race was even closer than the polls had predicted.

De Gaulle had a moment of discouragement and considered resignation. Then he rallied and resolved to change tactics and come down into the political arena for the second round against Mitterrand. He spoke twice to the nation on television and gave three televised interviews to a well-disposed journalist, Michel Droit. In these interviews he tried to unbend and give his fellow citizens a less

Olympian version of himself. It was painfully obvious that he had no talent for the task, but some voters may have been impressed, or touched, by the effort he made. He also offered a comprehensive defence of his policies at home and abroad. Significantly, he rejected at some length the charge of anti-Americanism, saying that France would always be the ally of the United States if the freedom of the world were in danger. In his final words on 17 December he reverted to the simple theme that the voters must choose between a return to 'the régime of the past' and a continuation of the new Republic. It was his argument of earlier years: 'Me or Chaos.'

On 19 December he was re-elected President with 54.5 per cent of the vote. Compared with his performances in earlier years, it was a poor result. On the other hand, judged by the margins normally achieved in American presidential elections, it was a handsome victory. The lesson of the elections of 1962 was reinforced. De Gaulle was no longer the nation's Man of Destiny, but he was still the choice of the majority.

# 37  De Gaulle Makes Haste

General de Gaulle began his second term of office as President of the French Republic on 8 January 1966. He knew that he was in the last phase of his career and that, at seventy-five years of age, he could not count on being able to serve out the whole of his new mandate. Yet his greatest task in foreign policy, the establishment of France's independent position in the world, was still incomplete. Decisive action had to be taken soon. During 1966 those who were close to him began to notice that he was inhabited by an increasing sense of urgency.

First, however, there were matters closer to home which required attention. De Gaulle invited Georges Pompidou to continue as Prime Minister, but recalled Michel Debré as Economic and Finance Minister in place of Giscard d'Estaing, who left the government. This amounted to a change of policy. Debré was more *dirigiste* than Giscard, whose liberalism and personal independence as the leader of the group of Independent Republicans had marked him out as a political personality in his own right. Debré soon announced a set of measures designed to give a fresh impulse to the economy, beginning with price and credit controls.

Then the continuing crisis in the Common Market had to be settled. Once de Gaulle was back in power, the Five accepted the need for a compromise which would save face all round but give France the essence of what she wanted. An agreement concluded at Luxemburg on 29 January effectively ruled out the use of majority voting in matters of importance as long as France continued to be opposed to it, and provided for the prompt completion of the agricultural price structure and financial regulation for the period up to the end of 1969. All risk of France finding her hands tied by the EEC just as she was about to release them from NATO was thus removed.

Having cleared the decks for action, he turned to NATO. He used his press conference of 21 February to obscure his intentions. France would, he said, withdraw progressively from the integrated structure of NATO, but she would do so in a manner that would not incommode her allies, and she would remain a member of the Atlantic Alliance. His audience was left with the impression that he was thinking in terms of a long-drawn-out process. De Gaulle therefore achieved tactical surprise when on 7 March he wrote to President Johnson stating that France, while remaining a member of the Atlantic Alliance, was withdrawing from NATO as soon as possible.

The text of the letter, the fruit of many years' reflection, was so important that it deserves quoting in full:

Dear Mr President,
Our Atlantic Alliance will complete its first period in three years' time. I wish to tell you that France is aware of the extent to which the defensive solidarity thus established between fifteen free peoples of the West contributes to their security, and, in particular, of the vital role played in this respect by the United States of America. Accordingly it is the present intention of France to remain, when the moment comes, a party to the treaty signed on 4 April 1949. This means that, unless the events of the next three years should change the very basis of relations between East and West, France would remain resolved in and after 1969, just as she is now resolved, to fight at the side of her allies, in case one of them should be the object of an aggression which had not been provoked.

At the same time France considers that the changes brought about since 1949, or now in the process of being brought about, in Europe, Asia and elsewhere, as well as the development of her own position and her own forces, no longer justify, as far as she is concerned, the military arrangements made after the conclusion of the Alliance, whether by multilateral agreement or by bilateral accords between the French and American governments.

France therefore intends to recover the full use on her own territory of her own sovereignty, encroached on in the existing situation by the permanent presence of allied military elements and by the use made of her skies; to cease participating in integrated commands, and no longer to place her forces at the disposition of NATO.

It goes without saying that France, in applying these decisions, is prepared to lay down the practical measures required in conjunction with allied governments, and in particular with that of the United States. She is moreover ready to reach agreement with them as to the military facilities to be mutually accorded in the case of a conflict in which she would engage herself at their side, as well as regarding the conditions of cooperation between her forces and theirs in the hypothesis of combined action, notably in Germany.

On all these matters, my dear President, my government will accordingly

establish contact with yours. But, in accordance with the spirit of friendly frankness appropriate to relations between our two countries, and may I add, to those between yourself and me, I have thought it proper to begin by indicating to you the reasons, the purpose and the limits of the modification which France, for her part, considers she must make in the structure of our alliance, without altering its basis.
Charles de Gaulle.[1]

The purpose of this finely tuned communication was to reconcile President Johnson to what he was losing by calling his attention to how much he would retain if he accepted de Gaulle's decision gracefully.

It worked. Johnson had already had time to bow to the inevitable, and to tell his allies of his decision, before, three days later, the French government sent its note about the modalities of withdrawal to the NATO governments. The essence of these was that all NATO and American forces should leave France, and all agreements placing facilities in France at their disposal should be terminated, while French forces in Germany would no longer be assigned to NATO. At the same time the French government offered to negotiate liaison arrangements with major NATO commands and to discuss conditions in which French forces in Germany would cooperate with NATO forces in case of war.

General de Gaulle accompanied the notes to Britain, Italy and Germany with letters of his own to the three heads of government. They were on the same lines, modified as he thought appropriate, as his letter to President Johnson. To Wilson he spoke of the dangers of the war in Vietnam, where the British Premier had recently taken an unsuccessful peace initiative; to Erhard he expressed willingness to reach an agreement for the continued stationing of French forces in Germany.

President Johnson sent a reply to de Gaulle arguing the case for integration in modern conditions, but that was a formality. The NATO powers had little choice but to try and minimize the damage to the Alliance by retaining as much cooperation with France as possible. It was agreed that French troops in Germany would cease to be under NATO command on 1 July 1966, while NATO would evacuate French territory by 1 April 1967. French liaison officers were appointed to the more important NATO establishments.

The break was, however, not quite complete. It was agreed that the *force de frappe* should continue to benefit from the NATO system of early warning against air attack. Without it the French nuclear force would have lost much of its military credibility, if not its political utility. De Gaulle made it clear that he would also like to keep the headquarters of the North Atlantic Treaty Council in Paris, since he considered it part of the Atlantic Alliance rather than of the integrated military organization of NATO. But the Americans did not want to make him a present of such an important symbol of the unity of the Alliance. The Council moved to Belgium, along with NATO military headquarters, although France remained a member.

Public opinion took the General's decision calmly. Since NATO chose not to make a drama of it, there was no proof critics could advance that Western solidarity had been seriously affected. Socialists and centrists put down a motion of censure, but when debated in the Assembly on 20 April it obtained only 137 of the 244 votes needed to carry it.

The only real difficulty that arose was between Bonn and Paris. The West Germans were sensitive to the fact that French forces in Germany, once they left NATO, would have no juridical title to be there and no agreed functions to perform. They proposed a new Franco-German agreement on the matter. De Gaulle was irritated and wrote to Erhard, pointing out that he was perfectly prepared to withdraw his forces if the Germans did not desire their presence. A certain amount of friction followed which affected personal relations between de Gaulle and Erhard, and deadlock ensued on the legal questions. But the French troops stayed where they were.

By the time he announced the withdrawal of France from NATO, de Gaulle knew that he was to make a State visit to Russia during the summer. The step he had taken towards independence was obviously calculated to ensure a warm welcome from his hosts, and to increase the interest everywhere aroused by the occasion. The eyes of the world were upon him when he arrived in Moscow on 20 June.

Of all his spectacular and intriguing journeys abroad this was probably the occasion to which he attached the greatest political importance. France under his leadership had become the most considerable and the most independent power in Western Europe. Now it was his business to begin the process, which would necessarily be lengthy, of persuading the Russians that they could build a system of European security jointly with France which would conform better to their interests than any system constructed by negotiation with the United States. If he or those that followed him in office were successful in the task, then a 'European Europe' would become a reality.

De Gaulle was received with marks of consideration unprecedented for a Westerner. Encouraged by the authorities, exceptionally large and enthusiastic crowds received him in all the major cities he visited. The Russians did not fail to impress on him that his favourite phrase 'Europe from the Atlantic to the Urals' – which he did not use while in the Soviet Union – was without meaning for them. They took him beyond the Urals to visit the Science Centre at Novosibirsk, in Siberia, and the rocket launching site at Baikonur in Soviet Central Asia, previously unseen by Westerners.

Ample time, however, was reserved for talks in the Kremlin between de Gaulle and the Soviet collective leadership of Brezhnev, Kosygin and Podgorny. These covered all major subjects of common interest except China, a topic which the Russians did not mention.[2]

Most of the discussion centred on the German problem. The Russians repeated their familiar demands: signature of a peace treaty based on recognition of the two existing German States and Poland's existing western frontier; renunciation of nuclear weapons by the two German States; and a special status for West Berlin. The two German States were to be free to remain members respectively of NATO and the Warsaw Pact after conclusion of the peace treaty, if they so wished. De Gaulle's reply had more novelty to it. He argued that the threat to peace arose from the fact that Germany had become an area of conflict between the two superpowers. If that situation could be terminated, Germany could be allowed to achieve her natural destiny, which would involve some sort of reunification. Of course the new Germany would have to accept existing frontiers and renounce nuclear weapons. On those points France agreed with Russia. But France would not recognize the East German State, which was an artificial creation. If the European States could work out a solution of the German problem between themselves, there would be no reason for the United States, which also had rights in Germany, to reject it.

De Gaulle's solution implied liquidation of the power blocs, NATO and the Warsaw Pact, and surrender by the Russians of their hold on East Germany. He was trying to persuade them that acceptance of some kind of German reunification was a price worth paying in order to secure withdrawal of American forces from Europe. De Gaulle urged that Moscow should adopt a less hostile attitude towards Bonn. France had accepted reconciliation with the Germans. If the Russians moved the same way, détente in Europe would be possible. Thereafter the Continent would be sustained by two pillars of comparable strength: Russia to the east, and a Franco-German alliance, in which France alone would have nuclear arms, to the west.

Brezhnev showed no sign of departing from the established Russian plan but was attracted by de Gaulle's idea of 'Europeanizing' the German problem. He suggested the holding of a European security conference, in which the United States would not take part.

The high point of the talks was reached when, after hearing a full exposé of Soviet foreign policy from Brezhnev, de Gaulle leaned back in his chair and said: 'Well, I conclude that the aims of the Soviet government are peaceful.'[3] The French participants had the impression that this statement lightened the atmosphere. Brezhnev smiled with pleasure. It was on the basis of the common interest of the two sides in peace and security in Europe that agreement was reached to hold regular Franco-Russian political consultations in future, as well as exchanges on practical collaboration in commercial, cultural and scientific matters. A permanent Franco-Soviet commission was set up. A joint communiqué, issued on 30 June, noted agreement on the pursuit of European security, on Vietnam, and on future cooperation, and pledged the two governments to pursue détente together. The new relationship was given symbolic expression by the agreement to establish a 'hot line' for crisis communication between the Elysée and the Kremlin, like that installed between Moscow and Washington after the Cuba crisis.

The Moscow communiqué revealed more accord on procedure than on substance, on which there were still profound differences, as Couve de Murville noted,[4] but the talks left both de Gaulle and the Soviet leaders willing to pursue a closer relationship. Their aims were not the same and they knew it. While each hoped that the course of events would gradually force the other in the desired direction, there had not been the slightest sign of Russian movement towards de Gaulle's thesis on Germany.

During the summer months de Gaulle rode the crest of a wave of popularity in France. Not since the days of the Algerian settlement had he enjoyed such support, and public opinion polls indicated that his foreign policy was the cause. He had taken care to justify his moves to the public in advance, and now he reaped his reward. The French were proud of his reception in Russia and not sorry to see American forces packing up for departure not back home but to Belgium.

The most anxious spectators of de Gaulle's voyage to Moscow had been his allies in Bonn. He was able to give them a fairly reassuring account when he came to see Chancellor Erhard on 21 July, for he had stood firm on the question of recognizing East Germany and had urged the Russians to modify their hostility to the Bonn government. But he made no more progress towards European Europe than he had in Moscow. Erhard was firmly in the American camp on matters of foreign and defence policy. The General did not hide his dissatisfaction from Adenauer and other critics of Erhard in his own party, the CDU, where a feeling was growing that a new leadership and a coalition government with the second party in the State, the Social Democrats (SPD), might be better suited to the times.

The one subject on which de Gaulle had reached an agreement of substance with the Russians was that the Americans should withdraw from Vietnam before negotiations on a peace settlement began. He reverted to Vietnam when visiting Cambodia in the course of a world tour in late summer.

The main event of his tour was a speech on 1 September to 80,000 Cambodians assembled to greet him in a stadium in Phnom Penh, in which he made his sharpest public condemnation yet of American intervention. It was, he said, 'more and more condemned by numerous peoples in Europe, Africa, and Latin America, and, to sum it up, ever more menacing to world peace'. He called on the Americans to commit themselves, even before peace negotiations began, to the complete withdrawal of their forces. He made this appeal, he said, in the interests of the American people themselves and in the name of the friendship which France had always felt towards them. It was in fact a proposal he had made privately to President Johnson in a letter of 5 February in response to the resumption of American bombing of North Vietnam.

This was a speech which made a considerable stir in the world and was much resented in Washington. But, as had sometimes been the case during the war, de Gaulle's position aroused more sympathy among Americans in general than it did in government circles. After eighteen months of unproductive war in Vietnam, disquiet was widespread in the United States.

At his press conference on 28 October de Gaulle defended himself once more against the charge of anti-Americanism. France, he said, pursued the policies she did, not to hurt her American friends but because she thought they were right. 'Regarding what we say and do about Vietnam, Europe, NATO, currency, I sincerely believe it would be to their advantage to take the same line themselves.'[5] No doubt de Gaulle believed what he said, even if he was thinking more of the advantages that would ensue to his own policy rather than to America, for whom every change he advocated would involve a reduction of power and influence.

As he had done before, de Gaulle followed up his disclaimer of anti-Americanism by another thrust at an American position. He complained that Erhard was not applying the Franco-German Treaty, which called for common foreign and defence policies, but the pro-American preamble added to it by the Bundestag. He argued that a solution of the German problem could only be found after détente had been established and that Bonn had missed chances of contributing to the process by ignoring the French connection. Erhard was already in difficulties with his Cabinet, and de Gaulle's complaints added to them. The Chancellor had to resign on 8 November, and a coalition was formed of the two major parties, the CDU and the SPD, with Kurt Kiesinger of the CDU as Chancellor and Willy Brandt, who had come to fame as the SPD Mayor of Berlin, as Foreign Minister and Vice-Chancellor.

The new men were known to be eager to cultivate closer relations with France, and they soon gave proof of it. The terms of stationing of French forces in Germany, now that they were no longer in NATO, had never been settled with the Erhard government. Within a few weeks an exchange of letters between Brandt and Couve de Murville did what was necessary. On 13 January 1967 Kiesinger and Brandt came to Paris and the conversations went well. The General held out to Kiesinger the prospect of a joint negotiation of the German problem with the Russians when the time was ripe. There is a story that he summed up by saying: 'When you and I fly to Moscow together, that will be the day!'

This was a moment of hope for de Gaulle. He instructed Couve to tell the Soviet Ambassador, Valerian Zorin, that the Germans had changed for the better. It was an echo of his appeal last June to Brezhnev to be less suspicious of Bonn's intentions. And yet he had reason to be suspicious himself of the intentions at least of the SPD. Willy Brandt had written an article in the American magazine *Foreign Affairs* which showed interest in the idea of a direct German approach to Moscow. That would be as unwelcome as direct American-Russian negotiations.

Simultaneously with these developments, another question which had lain dormant since 1963, that of Britain's application to join the EEC, showed signs of becoming active once more. The Labour government, which had won an increased majority in the elections of March 1966, was still at grips with economic difficulties. Inevitably the swifter expansion of the EEC made it seem an attractive haven to some of those in Britain who had earlier been unenthusiastic about entry. The Prime Minister, Harold Wilson, decided to carry out a reconnaissance in the capitals of the Six jointly with the Foreign Secretary, George Brown, who had long been an advocate of British membership of the EEC, in order to see whether conditions were right for a new application. They found encouragement everywhere except in Paris, which they visited on 24 and 25 January 1967. The General spoke of difficulties, and his advisers laid stress on the problems posed by the weakness of sterling. Clearly he did not welcome the British enterprise; but Wilson and Brown, encouraged by Washington, so the French believed, had already more or less decided to make their application. Only a point-blank warning of another veto might have stopped them, and the General had not gone as far as that. On 10 May the British government made formal application for full membership of the EEC.

The timing of the British announcement complicated arrangements for the summit meeting of the Six which was due to convene in Rome at the end of the month to celebrate the tenth anniversary of the conclusion of the Treaty of Rome. De Gaulle had been trying to encourage the launching at this meeting of a new proposal for political and defence consultation among the Six, a resurrection of the Fouchet Plan. As soon as British candidature for the EEC became a live issue once more, the chances of agreement on a new proposal that excluded Britain became more remote. It was a repetition of what happened in 1961.

The General made it clear at a press conference on 16 May that, even though there were signs that Britain was perhaps evolving away from America and towards Europe, he was convinced that a great deal more time must elapse before negotiations for her entry into the EEC could begin. The British held to their intentions, however, and the summit of the Six was reduced to a mainly ceremonial occasion. No progress towards a European Europe was registered. The meeting did, however, decide to refer the British application to the Council of Ministers of the Six for study. It was as if the British had appeared off-shore deliberately in order to hinder the General's projects in Europe.

Meanwhile more urgent reasons for dissatisfaction had appeared at home. In the parliamentary elections of March 1967 the UNR/UDT did badly, losing forty-three seats. Even with the support of the Independent Republicans led by Giscard d'Estaing and minor allies, the Gaullists could muster a majority of only a few seats in the new Assembly. De Gaulle had said after the presidential elections in 1965 that the majority which had returned him to power must in the national interest grow larger and more solid – the frankest admission he ever made that he had come to accept that he was a majority rather than a purely national leader. But it was the opposite that had happened.

The result was a painful shock to the Gaullists. It was largely an expression of growing disquiet at rising prices and a faltering economy. Fear of unemployment had set in for the first time under the Fifth Republic and dispelled some of the popularity which de Gaulle had won in 1966. He himself was partly responsible for this, since his determination to keep the franc strong and gold reserves high – as an instrument of his foreign policy – had involved caution in approving plans for expansion.

The new government, again under Pompidou, promptly decided to reduce its parliamentary problems by asking the Assembly for powers under Article 38 of the Constitution to legislate by ordinance until 31 October 1967 in the social and economic domain in order to adapt the country to the requirements of the final phase of the Common Market, which was due to take effect on 1 July 1968. This was a sweeping demand which suggested a lack of respect for the parliamentary process, and the government survived a vote of censure on 18 May by only eight votes before its request was finally granted on 11 June. More power was thus concentrated in de Gaulle's hands, and he bore more direct responsibility in the eyes of the workers for continuing unemployment. The outlook on the labour front was more uncertain in the summer of 1967 than ever before under the Fifth Republic, and some of the General's supporters, notably Giscard, who had been out of the government since the presidential election, were unhappy about the methods he was using to deal with the situation.

De Gaulle did not, however, allow domestic problems to distract him from foreign affairs. The 'great quarrel' had to be pursued. But before he could make the move he was planning, which was a spectacular visit to the New World, a sudden war in the Middle East produced consequences which put him at odds with the Russians as well as the Americans.

# 38 THE SIX-DAY WAR

By the spring of 1967 tension was once more increasing in the Middle East. Israel was still hemmed in by hostile Arab states, as she had been ever since coming into existence nineteen years earlier, and the violence of frontier clashes intensified in 1966 with the advent of a new and more belligerent Syrian government. Early in 1967 this situation began to breed rumours of another war. Anxieties were sharpened when, early in May, the Soviet military attaché in Damascus passed on to the Syrians intelligence reports that Israeli forces were massing on their borders and that an attack was planned for 17 May. The reports were baseless, but the Syrians were alarmed and appealed to President Nasser to take action in order to reduce Israeli pressure on them. In response, Nasser, who had also received the Soviet intelligence reports, strengthened Egyptian forces in Sinai. On 17 May he went further and demanded the withdrawal of the UN Emergency Force in Sinai. U Thant, Secretary-General of the United Nations, failed to consult the Security Council and complied with Nasser's request on his own initiative. As the UN garrisons handed over to the Egyptians, Israel strengthened her forces on the Sinai border and decreed partial mobilization.

Nasser had done more than enough to relieve Israeli pressure on Syria, if that had been his sole purpose, but he did not draw a halt there. Instead on 22 May, while on a visit to Sinai, he proclaimed the closure of the Straits of Tiran to Israeli shipping. This act transformed the situation. Either the Straits would have to be reopened or Israel would be under semi-blockade indefinitely. Nasser had put the port of Eilat, Israel's gateway to the Indian Ocean, in the situation with which Khrushchev had threatened the Allies in Berlin. Without firing a shot, he had cut its access to the outside world.

The threat of war was now imminent. The Israeli government sent its Foreign Minister to Washington to see if the Americans meant to take action to open the Straits of Tiran, which Eisenhower had proclaimed an international waterway in 1957, and instructed him to consult General de Gaulle en route. Meanwhile President Johnson issued a statement condemning Nasser's act as illegal and sent messages to de Gaulle and Wilson seeking their views on invoking the Tripartite Declaration of 1950, which threatened any aggressor in the Middle East with military action, or organizing an naval force to keep the Straits open.

De Gaulle was being consulted urgently by the Russians as well at this point. He had to make his mind up in a fast-moving situation on which his views were, as usual, different from anybody else's. Later on he revealed, partly or wholly, the factors which he took into consideration.

First came his conviction that the trouble in the Middle East was a byproduct of the war in Vietnam and the tension it bred between the two superpowers. He expressed this view in a statement on 21 June, when the Six-Day War was over. He was not precise about the causal connection, perhaps because he did not wish to suggest specifically that the Russians were trying to involve the Americans in difficulties in the Middle East in order to put them under more strain in Vietnam. It was a tempting tactic for the Russians to adopt, since they were under increasing pressure themselves. They had to provide a greater proportion of North Vietnam's growing needs as China sank deeper into her Cultural Revolution. The question was whether the Russians wished to push the Arabs to the point of war with Israel or not.

Secondly, de Gaulle had to take account of the need to maintain the good relations with the Arab States that had been restored since the Algerian War. Thirdly, it was his view that Israel, surrounded as she was by enemies who were militarily her inferior, was under a permanent temptation to attack them. In 1960, when he received Ben-Gurion in Paris, he spoke in public of Israel as France's friend and ally, but in private conversation with Ben-Gurion he revealed that he still regarded the Israelis as having aggressive intentions. 'What are your dreams for the real borders of Israel?' he asked. 'Tell me. I will not repeat it to anyone else.' Ben-Gurion replied that he had larger visions in the past but would now be content with the existing borders, 'and please God the Arabs should sign a peace treaty with us on the basis of the *status quo*'.[1]

It seems from what he says in his Memoirs that de Gaulle was not convinced and continued to suspect Israel of expansionist plans. If so, however, he kept his views to himself at the time. The French Jewish community remained pro-Gaullist, as they had been ever since the war, and France continued to be the main supplier of arms to Israel. The flow was abundant, the supplies of excellent quality. The highest level was reached in the last two weeks of May 1967 when $40m worth were sent to Israel, much of it in El Al planes with seats removed.

Thus France was giving much more help to Israel than any other power at the moment when de Gaulle was deciding what line to take with the Anglo-Saxons, the Russians and Israel's Foreign Minister, Abba Eban. French public opinion was also on the Israeli side. The Left, apart from the Communists, were automatically sympathetic; the Right were still in the main anti-Arab because of Algeria.

From de Gaulle's viewpoint the objection to President Johnson's ideas was obvious. Invoking the Tripartite Declaration would mean a commitment to military action in the Middle East without the Russians. The naval plan could lead the same way. Given the state of relations between the superpowers a confrontation could result. He thought the best approach was to involve the Russians in a joint action. He accordingly proposed four-power consultations in messages sent on 24 May.

Some of the ideas he would have put forward were revealed in the statement issued by the Council of Ministers later in the day to the effect that whichever side launched hostilities in the Middle East would be the guilty party in the eyes of the French government. This was the advice which de Gaulle gave Eban very firmly when receiving him after the Council meeting. He urged that the four Great Powers be left to solve the problem. Eban argued that Egypt had already committed an act of war, but de Gaulle would not accept this. He replied that, given time, France could 'concert the action of the Four Powers to enable ships to pass through the Straits'. Israel must be patient and 'not imagine she was strong enough to solve all her problems alone. She should not undertake never to act but she should allow a respite for international consultation.' The Arab forces for their part were not strong enough, he said, to threaten the security of Israel. *'Ne faites pas la guerre'* were his last words to Eban, as they had been his first.[2] Eban realized that 'France was disengaging herself from any responsibility for helping us if we chose resistance,' and so reported to his government.

Then came disappointment for de Gaulle. Britain accepted his proposal for four-power consultations, and the United States, though more reserved, was ready to consider talks in a UN framework. The Russian reply, however, was entirely negative. It stated that in Moscow's view there was no crisis to overcome. Israel must refrain from aggression, that was all. When an effort was made to discuss the Middle Eastern situation in the Security Council, the Russians raised enough votes to block it.

When President Johnson received Eban on 26 May, his message was not dissimilar from de Gaulle's. He needed time to find a way of opening the Straits, and asked the Israelis to give it to him. His trouble was that Congress was chary of giving him authority for any new overseas enterprise because of the consequences of the American intervention in Vietnam. It was not Johnson himself but his Ambassador to the UN, Arthur Goldberg, who made this damaging admission to Eban.[3] Vietnam was destroying the American President's credit with Congress. There was a link, as de Gaulle had diagnosed, between Vietnam and the Middle East. The superpowers had to think of every move they made in the Arab-Israel dispute, in the light of their commitments in Southeast Asia.

A lull followed President Johnson's request to the Israelis for time. During it the voice of Cairo became increasingly bellicose. Nasser proclaimed on 29 May that the Arabs had succeeded in restoring the situation to what it had been before 1956, and that their next step would be to cancel out the effects of 1948. Heikal, the editor of *Al Ahram*, Nasser's preferred spokesman, wrote that war was inevitable. The news from Israel was of a public impatient with its government's hesitations and eager to strike back.

Seeing the dangers increase, de Gaulle took the steps he judged necessary to keep France uncommitted to either side if war broke out. On 31 May he ordered the suspension of the supply of arms to Israel and on 2 June issued a statement calling for a four-power solution and repeating 'the country which is first to use arms will have neither our support nor our aid'. De Gaulle received the Israel Ambassador, Walter Eytan, and explained that the embargo would last as long as there was uncertainty whether or not Israel meant to go to war. If it became clear that she would not open hostilities, the embargo would be lifted. Eytan argued that the embargo increased the pressure on Israel to fight while she was still strong. De Gaulle remained unmoved and told him 'war would be a disaster for Israel even if she won', because Arab hatred and rejection would increase in strength. On 4 June the Israeli Cabinet had to consider the situation in the light of the cessation of French arms and supplies and the continued failure of Anglo-American efforts to ensure free passage through the Straits of Tiran. It was decided that Israel could wait no longer.

On the morning of 5 June the Israel Air Force struck at Egyptian bases and, despite all that Nasser had said about Arab preparedness, achieved complete surprise. De Gaulle, as a connoisseur of the art, must have appreciated the performance technically but he at once issued a statement condemning Israel for aggression.

The powerful Egyptian Air Force was almost totally destroyed on the ground. It was a stroke which decided the war. By 10 June Israel had defeated the armies of Egypt, Jordan and Syria and occupied Sinai up to the Suez Canal, Jerusalem and the West Bank of the Jordan, and the Golan Heights in Syria. A ceasefire followed.

The reaction in France to de Gaulle's 'volte-face' on the Arab-Israel conflict, for that is how it was seen, was critical. Opinion polls showed that French sympathies were overwhelmingly on Israel's side and that de Gaulle's course of action aroused as much disapproval as support.[4] In the past his foreign policy initiatives had been well received. The Six-Day War provided the first exception. The General seemed for once to be supporting Goliath against David, and that did not correspond with the world's idea of him.

It was the Russians who had played the principal part in frustrating de Gaulle's proposal for four-power talks, but they made a point of consulting him as ostentatiously as possible after the war. Kosygin visited Paris on his way to and from the special session of the United Nations which soon followed, but there was no agreement between them on what to do. The Russians still opposed four-power talks and seemed concerned only with securing French support for their tactics in the United Nations. De Gaulle made no commitments to Kosygin and discussed the situation in pessimistic vein with Harold Wilson, who came to see him on 19 June. The Prime Minister gathered that Kosygin's visit had not been a success. He had talked of meeting President Johnson in the United States, not a prospect to please de Gaulle. As Harold Wilson put it in his book, *The Chariot of Israel*:

'General de Gaulle felt he had been spurned, and if this was so it was a sad ending to all his hopes about Franco-Soviet relations.'[5] On 23 June the Premier sent a private telegram of his impressions to President Johnson:

. . . I think that the talk with Kosygin and the Middle East situation as a whole have forced him to face up to the realities of France's lack of effective influence in world affairs and to ask himself what his foreign policy has so far achieved. In his heart I believe he realizes that it has led him to something of a dead end. But he is too old and I think physically too weary, to work out a new approach.

De Gaulle told the Premier that the United States was now the greatest power in the world and that the only course for France, and Britain, 'was to disengage and to make it clear that America's quarrels are not our quarrels and their wars will not be our wars.' He thought that events in the Middle East had increased the danger of general war and was determined to keep France uncommitted.[6]

No doubt de Gaulle was both disappointed in the Russians and worried about American intentions in Vietnam and elsewhere. But contrary to Harold Wilson's expectations he had a new approach in mind and he was soon to undertake it without regard for either American or Russian susceptibilities. He meant to try more openly than before to stir up difficulties within their own camps for the two superpowers who were ignoring his voice.

This chapter cannot be concluded without a reference to de Gaulle's famous description of the Jews at his press conference of 27 November 1967 as 'an élite people, self-confident and dominating'. The word 'dominating' caused an outcry in the Western world, and was regarded as an injustice even by some members of the General's family.[7] De Gaulle did not withdraw it but invited the Chief Rabbi to the Elysée and assured him he had meant no slight on the Jewish people. This was a gesture of appeasement without precedent or sequel during the General's decade as President, but it did not assuage the critics. In his family circle de Gaulle insisted that he had done no more than repeat what his father Henri had told his children long ago. In fact he was echoing Charles Maurras's description of the Jews long before the Nazi era. 'Dominating' was his favourite adjective for them, and it must have lodged in the tenacious memory of de Gaulle, so long a reader of *L'Action Française*.

In terms of public relations there was a price which de Gaulle had to pay for his abandonement of the Israeli cause. An influential section of the French and American press turned against him permanently after the Six-Day War, and he forfeited the long-standing sympathy of French Jewry. Arab goodwill, however, increased. He had achieved that aim at least, and it was not without material importance for France.

# 39 The Solitary Exercise of Power

A month after his melancholy conversation with Harold Wilson, de Gaulle was sailing up the St Lawrence to begin a state visit to Canada which is likely long to remain unique in the annals of such events. For it was the guest's undeclared intention to do his best to disrupt the political cohesion of the host state during his stay. His justification for such extraordinary conduct lay in his reading of the history of Canada.

1967 was the centenary of the establishment of the Confederation of Canada, and to mark the event heads of the principal states closely connected with Canada, among them of course the President of the French Republic, were invited to visit the country during the summer. De Gaulle, however, thought further back than 1867; he had not forgotten that Canada had been founded by French settlers whom Louis XV had been obliged to surrender to British rule in 1763 after losing the Seven Years War. In the more liberal climate of the twentieth century, the French of Canada, mostly concentrated in the province of Quebec, had begun to demand equality with English-speaking Canadians, and on his visits to Canada since 1944 de Gaulle had seen this demand grow and generate in its turn a minority movement in favour of complete independence. He records in his *Mémoires d'Espoir*, written in 1969–70, that he wondered after his visit of 1960 whether it would not be necessary one day to divide Canada into French-speaking and English-speaking States in order to remedy the 'historic injustice' of 1763.[1] In the provincial elections of 1966 a party, *L'Union Nationale*, had come to power in Quebec whose programme seemed to make such a division a real possibility. Its slogan was 'Equality or Independence' and its leader, Daniel Johnson, was threatening to take what his party wanted if its demands were not met at the inter-provincial conference due in November 1967.

De Gaulle naturally hoped that the outcome of this situation would be full independence for Quebec and decided he would only go to Canada in 1967 if his visit would be conducive to that end. 'If I go', he said to his Secretary-General, Etienne Burin des Roziers, 'I expect it will only be to light the powder barrel.'[2] At first, in the autumn of 1966, he declined the Canadian government's invitation although it was supported by Daniel Johnson, saying that the time would not be ripe. There was, indeed, no certainty of a crisis in 1967, for the attitude of the English-speaking provinces was fairly conciliatory. De Gaulle's refusal was not, however, final. Perhaps, indeed, it was a purely tactical move, of the kind he had so often made in the past in order to mislead the adversary. In March a study had been launched by his staff into the delicate question of how to travel to Canada so as to make it natural to visit Quebec before Ottawa, where state visits normally began. It was decided that it would be necessary to make the journey by sea and approach up the St Lawrence if Quebec were to be the first port of call, while the General's official refusal still stood.[3] Only on 20 May did he receive Daniel Johnson and accept his renewed and pressing invitation to visit Quebec in July.

Such was the complicated background to the voyage which brought de Gaulle to the landing-stage at Quebec on 23 July. His intentions were firm in his own mind but held even more closely secret than usual. There is no proof that even Daniel Johnson knew how far he meant to go. But all was revealed once he was ashore. He made it clear from the outset that his aim was to make an irreversible change in the state of Quebec, to push the movement for independence beyond the point of no return. The language of his speech at the State Dinner in Quebec on the day of his arrival could be interpreted in no other way. He saluted the appearance in Quebec 'of a people who intend to dispose of themselves and take their destiny in hand in all domains'. There is no talk here of equality, the first of the two alternatives in Daniel Johnson's campaign slogan.

He drove the point home the next day, 24 July, on the terrace of the Hôtel de Ville of Montreal, with his cry of *Vive le Québec Libre* which made a world-wide sensation. There was some speculation at the time that this might have been an unpremeditated reaction to the immense enthusiasm of the crowd. But de Gaulle was well accustomed to enthusiastic crowds, and he was hardly saying in substance more than he had in Quebec. He surely knew what he was doing.

Ottawa was shocked. Public opinion instinctively condemned the General's act even in France. The question for the government in Ottawa was, however, how to react; and the answer had to be produced swiftly. Those who understood the history of Canada could see that there was a case for taking the matter calmly, because a protest would seem to condemn the behaviour of the people of Quebec as well as the General. But here another and more deadly passage in de Gaulle's words from the terrace had its effect. This had come right at the beginning: 'I will tell you a secret which you won't pass on. This evening here, and all along my route today, I found myself in an atmosphere of the same kind as that of the Liberation.' To suggest that the French population of Canada were in a condition in any way resembling that of the French people under the Nazi occupation had implications which could not fail to be deeply wounding to English-speaking Canadians. The remark was resented in America and Britain too. Perhaps it had not been prepared in advance; conceivably the enthusiasm of the crowds during the day had reminded de Gaulle of what he had felt during his immortal march down the Champs Elysées on 26 August 1944, and he was trying to convey no more than that. But he alienated many who would have understood 'Vive le Québec Libre'.

De Gaulle's mission in the New World was accomplished with his words at the Hôtel de Ville. Repetition of his theme might detract from its effect rather than add to it. So when the Canadian Cabinet met on 25 July and after a whole day's discussion issued a statement describing some of his declarations as 'unacceptable', this was a sufficient pretext for him to cancel his visit to Ottawa and return to France the next day. He knew that he was flying back to a hostile reception. Opinion in France had been in no way prepared for what he had done. It came as an even greater shock than his volte-face upon the outbreak of the Six-Day War. The French press was disturbed and mostly critical, while that of the English-speaking world roundly condemned him. The Times had been particularly severe, speaking in its editorial of his 'erratic decline' and treating him as already a victim of the shipwreck of old age. But he was unrepentant. His resolve was to justify his action to the French people without delay and to carry his project forward in association with Daniel Johnson as soon as possible.

He set the tone as he landed, before dawn on 27 July at Orly Airport. His Ministers had been summoned and were waiting in the VIP lounge.

None of them, not even Pompidou, had been forewarned of what he intended to say in Montreal, and not all of them approved. The General entered the lounge from his plane full of enthusiasm. '*C'était magnifique, Messieurs les Ministres ... magnifique.*'[4] The task of explanation was begun. His Ministers knew the line to take.

On 31 July the Council of Ministers met and the General gave them an account of his voyage and its implications. The communiqué issued after the meeting laid more stress on the future than the past. 'General de Gaulle emphasized to the French Canadians and their government that France meant to help them to attain the goals of liberation which they had set themselves.'

It was a definite engagement for the future, but the reaction of the French people was unfavourable. Public opinion polls in early August showed that 45 per cent disapproved of his position on Quebec and only 18 per cent approved.[5]

Despite all the enthusiasm of Quebec's welcome to de Gaulle, a similar feeling had its influence there. Second thoughts suggested certain questions. Why this sudden overwhelming display of French concern after two centuries of neglect? In whose interest had the General been acting, that of Quebec or that of France?

This mood of scepticism affected even Daniel Johnson. His pledge to the voters had been 'Equality or Independence', in that order. The interprovincial conference on Quebec's demands was due in November. He preferred to await its outcome despite de Gaulle's urgings that nothing decisive could be expected from such a meeting. In reply to a secret letter from de Gaulle in early September encouraging him to proceed to 'solutions' Johnson wrote saying that Quebec was not yet economically strong enough to take the risk.[6]

De Gaulle put his cards on the table at his press conference of 27 November. For Quebec to become free, he said, there were two conditions. The first was the end of the existing Canadian Federation: 'This will lead in my view to Quebec acceding to the rank of a sovereign State, in control of its own destinies, as are so many other peoples and states around the world.' The second condition was the solidarity of the French community on the two sides of the Atlantic. He quoted Paul Valéry: 'French Canada affirms our [France's] presence on the American continent.' The mission of independent Quebec would be, he said, to cooperate with the rest of Canada in developing resources and 'standing up to American encroachment'.

This declaration coincided with the opening of the interprovincial conference at Toronto and created something of a sensation. But the conference was no more conclusive than de Gaulle expected, and Johnson continued to hesitate. They had agreed to meet every six months, alternately in Paris and Montreal, but Johnson fell ill, and had to delay his visit to Paris. Then came the upheaval of May 1968 in Paris which caused further delay. In September Johnson died of a heart attack. No more was ever heard of the formidable programme de Gaulle had announced at his press conference. It was stillborn.

There was no simple answer to the questions of the *Québecois* about de Gaulle's motives. He would have said that the interests of Quebec and France naturally coincided. But, no less naturally, he set his enterprise in Quebec in the framework of his own French foreign policy. When he cried '*Vive le Québec Libre*', he was addressing his words to Washington as well as to Ottawa. By his criterion Canada was not truly a sovereign state, because it did not perform the essential task of sovereignty, defence of the national territory. Canada was in his eyes a self-governing American protectorate, and this fact explains the way he treated the Ottawa government in 1967. He was urging the French of Canada to declare their independence of the economically dominant United States at least as much as of Ottawa. De Gaulle might have described his foray in Canada as a blow struck against the Great Power that was encroaching on European territory where the leading role belonged to France.

De Gaulle's dreams were not fulfilled. But, for all that, he marked Quebec and Canada profoundly; and the terrace from which he cried '*Vive le Québec Libre*' is regarded both by the citizens of Montreal and by tourists with all the respect that is due to the scene of a great historical event. Whether it is an event that will have a future remains to be seen.

De Gaulle had planned to visit the Russian sphere of influence as well as the American during the summer of 1967. He had accepted an invitation to visit Poland, but it was postponed because of the Middle Eastern war. Its purpose in the General's eyes was probably changed by this fact. He might have been more considerate of Russian susceptibilities while in Poland had he not been irritated by Moscow's refusal to cooperate with him before and after the Arab/Israel conflict. When he finally made his visit from 6 to 12 September, he had no hesitation in encouraging the Poles to be themselves. He appealed systematically to the historical ties between Poland and France, and made several references to the fact that he had fought for Poland. He did not go so far as to mention the enemy, but everybody knew it had been the Red Army. He also praised the national spirit of the people and their loyalty to their traditional faith.

None of this was calculated to ring pleasantly in Russian ears. Still less was his condemnation before the Diet of 'the confrontation of two blocs lining up face to face their rival forces and pacts. On the contrary, let a policy and deliberate practice of détente, entente and cooperation be established between us all from the Atlantic to the Urals.'[7] Here was a revival of the formula he had avoided in Moscow, and he linked it with a new concept of a Europe not just divided in two but in three: East, Centre, and West. Poland was manifestly in the Centre, with Russia in the East, no closer to her than France in the West. Of course he emphasized French recognition of Poland's western frontiers, but he had little else to say that the Russians would have endorsed. His major speeches contained not a single reference to the existence of the Soviet Union.

De Gaulle knew perfectly well what he was doing. His most provocative speech was made in Gdansk on 10 September.

You are a great nation. You don't need the advice of France. But . . . we hope you will perhaps look a little further and think rather bigger than you have been allowed to do till now. The obstacles which you think insurmountable today, you will without any doubt surmount them. You know what I mean.[8]

The General did not normally give personal guidance to his press spokesman, who was Roger Vaurs on this voyage. That was Couve's task. But after speaking at Gdansk, he himself told Vaurs to ensure that what he had said was given maximum circulation.

The Polish communist leaders were made more than a little nervous by de Gaulle's tactics. Gomulka had had his troubles with the Russians in 1956 and earlier. In reply to de Gaulle he emphasized before the Diet Poland's unshakeable loyalty to the Soviet alliance. But, when taking leave of him at the airport, he spoke rather differently. One of de Gaulle's party recalls him saying approximately, 'I think we are developing along the lines you desire. But do not expect too much of us and give us time. We have to take account of realities.'

De Gaulle's behaviour in Poland attracted less attention than it merited, because people's capacity for surprise had been more or less exhausted by his earlier performances over the Six-Day War and Quebec. It showed, however, that he was no more respectful of the Soviet position in Eastern Europe than of the American in the West; and it left its mark on the Polish people.

De Gaulle also demonstrated France's detachment from both superpowers when civil war broke out in Nigeria during the summer. In varying degrees the British, Americans and Russians, as well as most Islamic states, gave support to the Nigerian government. But de Gaulle's sympathies were from the first on the side of the Biafran rebels. There were many reasons for this. Nigeria had taken a lead in condemning French nuclear tests in the Sahara and had expelled the French Ambassador; the Federation was a large English-speaking complex which might easily come to dominate its smaller French-speaking neighbours if it achieved stability and success. There was no reason why France should wish Nigeria well. The Ibo tribe, on the other hand, who had set up Biafra, were Christians, unlike the other peoples of Nigeria, had important oil deposits in their territory and were on good terms with their French-speaking neighbour, the Ivory Coast. It seemed preferable that Biafra should succeed in breaking away from Nigeria. France did not recognize the rebels but made her sympathies known. Arms were sent to the Ibos not directly from France but through French-speaking neighbours. There was no quick victory for either side. The war took root, and France found herself involved on the side of the rebels, in disagreement with all the Great Powers. In the judgement of Harold Wilson, it was French intervention alone which kept the war going beyond the summer of 1968.[9]

In November, after the devaluation of the pound sterling, de Gaulle took the opportunity to disagree with France's five partners in the EEC by declaring at his press conference that it was obvious that Britain as she was could not enter the Common Market as it was. 'A very great and very profound mutation' on Britain's part was still needed, and negotiations would be pointless. Perhaps a commercial agreement could be made instead. This time de Gaulle had vetoed negotiations before they began instead of delaying for eighteen months.

French nuclear policy also made the headlines in November when the Chief of the General Staff, General Ailleret, wrote an article which appeared in the authoritative *Revue de la Défense Nationale*, stating that the French nuclear defence system should be '*tous azimuts*', capable of covering all points of the compass. The pen was Ailleret's but the inspiration came from de Gaulle.

The timing of the article was probably prompted by de Gaulle's knowledge that French nuclear forces would become fully operational in 1968. They were still many years away from being able to include America in their targeting plans, but the General wanted for political reasons to make the point that they would be entitled to do so when they had the capacity. It was a function of national independence even between allies. After all, had not Dean Rusk warned long ago that the Americans would target France if she tried to use nuclear weapons outside an agreed plan?[10] Sauce for the goose was sauce for the gander.

The proclamation of '*tous azimuts*' caused surprise, and added to the impression of a man acting alone without much consideration for the views of others which de Gaulle had repeatedly given the French public during 1967. The shocks in the field of foreign affairs were of a piece with government by ordinance instead of normal legislative process over a wide range of domestic affairs. An arbitrary spirit seemed to have taken over the government of the Fifth Republic. Giscard d'Estaing in a statement on 17 August spoke of a growing fear that 'if the solitary exercise of power became the rule, it would not prepare France to chart her future course in conditions of calm, free exchange of ideas, and national consensus'. It was a prophetic remark and the phrase, 'the solitary exercise of power', was much repeated by critics of de Gaulle.

# 40 YOUTH REBELS: MAY 1968

All that happened to France in 1968 has to be considered in the light of the events of May which nearly swept de Gaulle from the scene and cast a long shadow over the rest of his career, even after he had succeeded in dominating the immediate crisis at the last minute of the eleventh hour.

There were plenty of indications beforehand that there was something rotten in the state of France. The malaise created in 1967 by the exercise of government by decree and the General's arbitrary decisions over Israel and Quebec persisted in the New Year. A Western ambassador reported home an indefinable feeling that de Gaulle might be riding for a fall. So he was. But nobody foresaw that the barricades of the University of Paris would be the obstacle at which he came to grief.

De Gaulle, indeed, seemed detached from domestic anxieties. He had lost some of his taste for direct contact with the people and the 'bain des foules'. Not since April 1966 had he made one of those four-day provincial tours which had been a feature of his first term as President. He was absorbed in the solitary exercise of power and was encouraged by indications that some of his aims in foreign policy might be coming closer to fulfilment. America was evidently in dire straits and a wind of change was rising even behind the Iron Curtain.

In America the wind of change had reached gale force by March with the success of the New Year offensive of the Communist armies in Vietnam and signs on the international exchanges of loss of confidence in the dollar. President Johnson showed that he had at last abandoned hopes of gaining a military victory when he refused General Westmoreland's demand for an increase of 200,000 men in his expeditionary force of half a million. On 3 March he called a halt to the bombing of North Vietnam, save in the frontier zone with the South, and declared his readiness to send representatives to any meeting organ-

342

ized to discuss means of ending the war; on the last day of the month he accepted the political consequences of his failure by announcing that he would not be a candidate for re-election to the Presidency in November.

De Gaulle issued a statement on 9 April praising Johnson for 'an act of reason and courage' in stopping the bombing. Shortly thereafter the Hanoi government showed its appreciation of French policy by choosing Paris as the site for the peace talks proposed by the American President. Thus France was cast in the kind of mediatory role for which de Gaulle believed her to be particularly qualified in a matter which was of importance to the whole world. It was a mark of trust from the belligerents which was bound to raise her prestige and that of her President, and which conformed with the position of national independence to which de Gaulle was attaching increased importance. Independence rather than grandeur in the traditional sense was by now his principal objective.

There was progress on the monetary front as well in March, when governments and central banks agreed on the creation of a two-tier market in gold. Official transactions were to continue at the established price of $35 an ounce, but a private market was authorized on which the price would be free. This made France's vast gold reserves, 'the General's second *force de frappe*' as Gaullists called it, seem even more imposing.

None of this, however, had much impact on public opinion in France, which was more concerned with the weaknesses of the economy. Unemployment reached 450,000 in January, a very high figure for France, and prices continued to rise. There were demonstrations, strikes and some violence. Demonstrations took place not only in industry but in the universities. These were particularly violent at Nanterre, a new suburban campus of the University of Paris, where student discontents were given a political focus by the leadership of Daniel Cohn-Bendit, a German Jewish votary of the New Left, whose doctrine it was that the real revolutionary force in modern society was the students and not the workers. Shock waves spreading from the Cultural Revolution in China and the constant student demonstrations in America against the Vietnam war had spread to France and brought recruits to the New Left which regarded orthodox Communism of the Moscow brand as a reactionary force.

A good deal of combustible material lay about in the French universities as a result of the conditions in which they had expanded

343

under the Fifth Republic. The government had spent money lavishly on national education at all levels, and Pompidou, as a former teacher, was particularly proud of the results. Since 1958 the number of university students had risen from 175,000 to 530,000.[1] Such figures were quoted with pride by ministers, but they referred less frequently to the immense administrative problems which had followed. Teaching staff increased quickly to cope with the flood and its quality deteriorated. Instructors were overburdened and less accessible to students than in the past, while lecture facilities were overcrowded. The university became more impersonal, and the number of young left-wing teachers increased. The demand rapidly spread for junior teachers and students to have a voice in the government of universities, previously the monopoly of senior professors.

The situation was made more difficult by the effects of the long-standing principle of French education that any student who was successful in the standard school-leaving examination, the Bacca-lauréat, had a right to enter a university. There was no separate entrance examination. Certain specialist Faculties, such as Law and Medicine, had entrance examinations and controlled the number of their students, but in the Faculty of Letters anybody with a Bacca-lauréat had the right to a place. This right was exercised by many thousands who had no intention of working at the university but wanted to enjoy the use of its subsidized restaurants and other facilities for a year. It was at the end of the first year that there was an examination which had to be passed. These students naturally contributed to an atmosphere of restlessness. The authorities were in fact about to introduce a university entrance examination when the May explosion took place.

Another transformation was wrought by the growing numbers of women students. Students began to demand the right for co-residential accommodation.

The two chief demands of French students at the beginning of 1968 were *mixité*, or cohabitation, and *cogestion*, or joint administration. The New Left devoted itself to trying to add a political orientation to these essentially social demands, and they were particularly successful at Nanterre, where police had to be called in to curb violent demonstrations in January.

This was the beginning of a movement which it proved impossible to bring under control in the following months. The authorities were uncertain whether to be firm or flexible, and alternated between the two attitudes without success in either. On 22 March students at Nanterre seized the administrative building of the university. They were soon forced out, but the event gave birth to the Movement of 22 March, aimed at nothing less than the overthrow of the government. After more clashes in late April, the university authorities suspended courses at Nanterre on 2 May. This proved to be a grave tactical error, because Cohn-Bendit and his allies immediately moved to the traditional university centre of the Sorbonne in the Latin Quarter, which was much more in the public eye than Nanterre. On 3 May students rioted in the Latin Quarter, and on 4 May the Sorbonne was closed, an event which made newspaper headlines.

Fortunately for the government, the orthodox Communist party was bitterly opposed to the Movement of 22 March because of its pro-Chinese sentiments. In an article entitled 'Unmask the false revolutionaries' published in the Communist newspaper *L'Humanité* on 3 May, Georges Marchais denounced Cohn-Bendit as an anarchist and urged trade unionists to reject his proposals for the creation of a common front between students and workers. His orders were obeyed but did not check the growth of trouble in the universities. Nightly riots and clashes with the police in the Latin Quarter followed the closure of the Sorbonne.

As the crisis unfolded stage by stage de Gaulle found himself confronted by a problem different from any that had previously faced him in his long career. There was evidently a challenge being mounted in the University of Paris to the authority of the State: it was posed, however, not by outright rebels, as it had been in Algeria, but by students who confined themselves to marches and demonstrations. He had known how to deal with the risings of 1960 and 1961 in Algeria: he had taken emergency powers, gone on television to appeal to all good citizens to rally to his support, prepared the Army and the police for action, and very quickly he had triumphed. But the threat now before him was amorphous. As he said repeatedly to his intimates it was '*insaisissable*', impossible to grasp.

By an unlucky chance Pompidou had left on 2 May for an official visit to Iran and Afghanistan. To recall him would have been to advertise to the whole world that France, which had seemed so stable, was suddenly in crisis. De Gaulle could not do that. In the days that followed he tried to handle matters along with Louis Joxe, the interim

Prime Minister, Fouchet, the Minister of the Interior, Messmer, Minister of Defence, and Peyrefitte, Minister of Education. From the outset he was for treating the students with a heavy hand. He told a delegation of members of the Assembly: 'We must not allow the enemies of the University to establish themselves inside it. We must not tolerate violence in the streets.'

But his ministers constantly pleaded for restraint. Most of them had been at the university and had some sympathy with the students. This was indeed the predominant feeling in Parisian society in the early days, and police reports tended to play down the seriousness of the disturbances. Only when the trade unions began to play a part on 13 May did the bourgeoisie begin to feel real anxiety. Until then they did not take Cohn-Bendit very seriously and spoke with understanding of the high spirits of the students, on edge at the approach of the examination season. Things might calm down from one day to the next, it was widely believed.

De Gaulle allowed himself to be persuaded to exercise restraint and to reopen the Nanterre campus on 9 May, but he rejected advice to do the same with the Sorbonne 'until the return of calm'. There was, however, no return. On the night of 10/11 May the students threw up barricades, in the old revolutionary tradition of Paris, and tried to create a fortified zone under their control in the Latin Quarter. It took the police a night's hard fighting to clear the streets, and hundreds of students were arrested. By this time the trouble had spread to provincial universities, imitative as ever of the Sorbonne.

At this point, on 11 May, Pompidou returned full of confidence in his ability to restore peace at the cost of a few concessions. He begged the General to give him a free hand and leave for Romania on 14 May, as had been planned. De Gaulle, eager to make the trip, allowed himself to be persuaded. Pompidou at once proclaimed the reopening of the Sorbonne and the release of students under arrest. But it was too late for concessions. The trade unions had called a general twenty-four-hour strike on 13 May, the tenth anniversary of the Algiers rising which had brought de Gaulle back to power, and the students joined in on a grand scale. Hundreds of thousands marched through the streets from the Place de la République, and for the first time in the history of the Fifth Republic, demands were made for the General's resignation. Placards carried in the demonstration proclaimed 'De Gaulle to the Museum' and 'Ten Years is Enough'. The authorities were powerless to intervene. That evening students occupied the Sorbonne building and made it their headquarters. Celebrations went on all night, and young orators in crowded lecture-halls spoke passionately of 'the need to change society'.

De Gaulle kept his own counsel and departed for Romania on 14 May, as planned. As subsequent events showed, however, he had already made two decisions. Since Pompidou had failed to fulfil his promise and restore order, he would have to change his Prime Minister and introduce sweeping reforms. There was now no other way of regaining his ascendancy over the French.

In his absence matters deteriorated dramatically. The Communist-led *Confédération Générale du Travail* (CGT), the country's biggest union, did not take the side of the rebellious students, but it called for more strikes of indefinite duration, and the other trade union organizations followed suit. They had little choice. The spirit of rebellion had spread to the younger workers, and they had to give it scope or risk losing control. On 14 May workers occupied the Sud-Aviation factory at Nantes without consulting their unions,[2] and their example was soon followed elsewhere. Pompidou told the Assembly that France was facing a crisis of civilization, not of government: 'It is the problem of youth itself that is posed, its place in society, its rights and duties, its moral equilibrium.' It was a sound analysis, but de Gaulle may have felt, when he heard of it, that such sweeping judgements were in the domain of the President of the Republic rather than the Prime Minister.

On 16 June at Craiova in Romania he talked at length to Couve de Murville of the reforms he proposed to introduce, and, finding Couve sympathetic, told him in confidence that he would be Prime Minister of the government charged with carrying out the programme.[3]

De Gaulle returned on 18 May to a situation bordering on chaos, from a visit which had been completely overshadowed by events in France. Before leaving he had let it be known that he intended to speak to the nation on 24 May. The question now was whether he should bring the date forward, as many of his advisers urged him to do. But what was the point? The situation could not yet be grasped unless he ordered the use of force against thousands of disorderly students. He decided it was better to allow it to develop further. He made a comment, however, for immediate publication. It was 'Reform, yes. A shambles, no'. (*'La réforme, oui; la chienlit, non.'*) It was the crude second part of the phrase that drew attention, but the first was also significant.

His words did nothing to improve matters, and by 20 May ten million workers were on strike. The operation was, however, selective. Factories, airlines and public transport were at a standstill, but television and food and drink supplies were maintained. Lorries rolled into the great market of Les Halles in the middle of Paris every day, and many restaurants stayed open. In Paris and the provinces the citizens were able to listen to radio commentators describing the evening's demonstrations in the Latin Quarter while they dined peaceably at home. This contributed to a certain atmosphere of dreamlike unreality which surrounded these extraordinary days and nights. Cause and effect seemed to have been disconnected. People wondered whether they would wake up to find that nothing had changed, or everything.

Unending debates, to which the public were admitted, went on in the lecture halls of the Latin Quarter about the need to remake civilization and morality. Some of the slogans painted by the young rebels on the walls of the now very dirty Sorbonne caught the world's imagination. One was, indeed, '*L'imagination au pouvoir*'. The most popular of all was 'Make love, not war'. Both demonstrating students and striking workers remained on the whole remarkably good-humoured, and there was little violence. Men were not dying in this novel revolution. In a radical departure from French tradition, there was only one death, seemingly accidental, in the riots of May. This was due in no small measure to the government's policy of restraint. If police and troops had been ordered to clear the Sorbonne, the dream of May might in a few minutes have turned into a nightmare.

De Gaulle was by now in a state of grief and incredulity. He knew that grave damage was being done to the image and the economy of his beloved France with every day that passed, and he was astonished to discover that among the student rebels the children of the well-to-do figured in large numbers. But what could he do? His instinct told him that the mass of the people were not afraid of what was happening, and it was part of his philosophy that the French could only be spurred to a united effort by fear of dire consequences if they did not pull together. The situation was still unripe, *insaisissable*. In fact it was still so on 24 May. A political crisis would have been created two days earlier if the Opposition parties, who were demanding fresh elections, had been able to muster the votes in the Assembly to pass a vote of censure on the government, but Pompidou survived by eleven votes.

On the same date the trade unions made a new move which did not point in the direction of an immediate intensification of the crisis either. They rejected the idea of calling a general strike of unlimited duration aimed at forcing the government to resign, and declared instead their willingness to negotiate with the government and the employers' organization, *Le Patronat*, for wage increases and improvements in working conditions. Thus they definitely separated themselves from the revolutionary wing of the student rebellion, and remained faithful to the directions of the Communist leader, Georges Marchais. The government had been hoping for a return to the normal strike pattern, and Pompidou promptly agreed to early negotiations, announcing that he himself would lead the government team. These negotiations were impending when de Gaulle finally appeared on television to address the nation on the evening of 24 May, and in consequence tension was eased. It seemed that the country would soon be back at work and, if that happened, the New Left would lose all hope of achieving revolutionary aims.

Extraordinarily enough, de Gaulle for once in his career made matters worse rather than better. Very possibly he felt deflated by the way in which Pompidou had upstaged him by arranging negotiations for the very next morning which, if successful, would mean that he himself need never have spoken at all. Showing none of the fire and resolution he had always displayed in past crises, he declared that current events in the university and elsewhere demonstrated the need for 'a mutation of society'. A reform of the economy according more participation to workers was indispensable, as was university reform. He was ready to undertake the task if the nation wished. The draft of a law on the subject would be submitted to a referendum in June. If it was rejected, he would retire; if it was approved, he would, in conjunction with the administration and with the help of all men of goodwill, 'change, wherever necessary, narrow out-of-date structures and open a wider way forward to the new blood of France'.

In manner and in matter his speech was a complete failure. He had made no reference to the political crisis and no acknowledgement that his own responsibility as President for the last ten years was engaged in what had happened in the university and in the factories. It was as if he were offering his services to clear up a mess made by others. Still worse he had appeared old, tired and depressed, a spent force.

That night the demonstrators emerged *en masse* from the Latin Quarter for the first time, invaded the business area on the other side of the river and made a vain attempt to burn down the Stock Exchange. The police erected precautionary barricades on the approaches to the Elysée. They were not tested by the rioters but it was clear that de Gaulle's appeal had been followed by escalation, not détente. Suddenly it became a real and imminent possibility that he was finished, and might give up without even a referendum.

It was obvious that Pompidou would make swift and sweeping concessions in the negotiations which opened on 25 May, and so it proved. Early in the morning of 27 May at the Ministry of Social Affairs in the rue de Grenelle, agreement was reached on a protocol of proposals including generous increases in pay, pensions and family allowances, marginal social benefits, and a rise of 35 per cent in the minimum wage. Pompidou had not even waited to have the cost calculated by his experts before accepting it. The trade union negotiators stipulated that they would have to submit the proposals to the strikers before they could give their final assent. The Secretary-General of the CGT, Georges Séguy, hurried to a meeting of 12,000 strikers in the Renault factory at Billancourt on the outskirts of Paris. They heard him out and then, to his astonishment, voted unanimously to continue the strike. The accords of Grenelle seemed to be a dead letter. Pompidou had not found a way out of the crisis after all. Even if he had been successful, his fate would not have been changed.

Now the crisis intensified. De Gaulle's lacklustre performance and the failure of the Grenelle accords between them stimulated all the contending parties to prepare for a decisive moment. On the evening of 27 May the UNEF, the students' union, called a meeting at Charléty Stadium. The Communists boycotted it, but André Barjonet, a former leader of the CGT, was there. He had just resigned in order to challenge the party's view that a revolutionary situation did not exist in France. On the contrary, he asserted, power was theirs if they had the courage to seize it promptly. He received an ovation. So did Pierre Mendès-France, the only parliamentarian of mark to be present. He remained silent but seemed by being there to give tacit approval to Barjonet's thesis.

The next to enter the lists was François Mitterrand, who announced at a press conference on 28 May that he would be a candidate for the Presidency if the General withdrew before or after a referendum, and called for the resignation of Pompidou and the formation of a provisional government as soon as de Gaulle left the scene. Seeing that de Gaulle's will to power seemed in doubt and that the rest of the opposition was staking its claims, the Communist Party decided to assert its own position. The trade union organization they controlled, the CGT, called for mass demonstrations throughout the country on the following day, 29 May, in support of a demand for the formation of 'a popular government of democratic union with Communist participation'. The CGT also broke off the contact which it had maintained since the beginning of the crisis with the non-Communist trade unionists of the CFDT.[4] The rumour spread that the Communists might be preparing a *coup d'état* for the morrow. Waldeck Rochet, their parliamentary leader, probably expressed their real sentiments, however – although at such times almost any words are open to rival interpretations – when he approached Jacques Vendroux, the General's brother-in-law, in the corridors of the Assembly on the afternoon of the 28th and said 'Tell him not to go'. Nevertheless it was impossible for the government to rely on Communist good intentions, and tank units were ordered to move closer to Paris.

These gathering clouds brought opportunity as well as danger to de Gaulle. The call for revolution at Charléty, Mitterrand's avowal of his candidature for the succession, the menacing Communist activity, made the situation easier for him to seize. These were open rivals against whom he could react. His own followers had been preparing a counter-demonstration in his favour for several days past, with his own approval. It ws fixed for 30 May. The demonstrators were to meet in the Place de la Concorde and march up the Champs Elysées to the Arc de Triomphe. The intention was to evoke the huge demonstration of 26 August 1944. Now his supporters would also have the threat of illegal action from the Left to denounce. It would impart the stimulus of fear that had hitherto been lacking.

The trouble was that de Gaulle himself gave no sign. He remained silent and hidden in the Elysée. No doubt he was horrified by the thought of how much had already been lost. His inertia made some Gaullists begin to think and say that the time had come for Pompidou to take charge.

Pompidou went to see de Gaulle on the evening of the 28th after dinner and told him that plans had been made to reply to force with force, subject to de Gaulle's approval, but that he expected tomorrow's demonstrations would be orderly and would provoke a reaction in favour of the government. De Gaulle replied gloomily that he was too optimistic and had been all through the crisis.

De Gaulle was left to pass a sleepless night, wrestling with his problems. The Communists had committed themselves for the first time in the crisis to a clear demand for political power while leaving unsaid how it was to be achieved; and they would be marching in the afternoon from the Place de la Bastille to the Gare St Lazare, which was close to the Elysée. It would take only ten minutes for an excited crowd to charge the Elysée. If the General was there at the time he would be in danger of capture, unless he brought in troops and police beforehand and authorized them to open fire on the attackers. So far the government had managed to avoid firing a single shot at the demonstrators. The charm of the bloodless revolution now risked being broken.

In this situation the argument in favour of following de Gaulle's traditional tactics of withdrawal was obviously very strong. This was the course on which he decided, as he told his son-in-law General Boissieu early in the morning. He had summoned Boissieu overnight from his command at Mulhouse on the Rhine, an appeal to the family which was typical of his habits in a crisis.

What de Gaulle had apparently not done, however, during his sleepless hours was to decide where he should go and for what purpose. His mood seems to have been similar to that of early January 1946 when he was contemplating resignation and retired to Antibes with his brother-in-law, Jacques Vendroux, and their wives, to reflect. That venture had indeed ended in resignation and the General was thinking of it once more early in the morning of 29 May. When Boissieu arrived, de Gaulle unfolded to him a number of alternative courses of action,[5] and after discussion resolved to withdraw from Paris without announcing any decision about resignation. One destination which he considered and rejected was Brest.

It happened to be Wednesday, the day of the regular weekly Cabinet meeting. Soon after 9 a.m., the General, looking very weary, received his Secretary-General, Bernard Tricot, and said, 'Cancel to-day's Council of Ministers. I'm too tired and it will show if I try to preside.' Then he completed his preparations for departure. About 11 a.m. he again summoned Tricot, and told him to inform Pompidou that he was leaving for Colombey for twenty-four hours rest. Pompidou was immediately alarmed and demanded to see him at once. At this point the

General came on the line, said he could not receive him as he was departing at once, and reassured him as to his intentions. But he finished with a sudden change of tone: 'I am old, you are young. It's you who are the future.' His final words were '*Au revoir. Je vous embrasse.*'[6]

Pompidou feared he was departing for good. It was the fear, or the hope, of many as the news spread in Paris that he had disappeared from the Elysée. During the early afternoon Pompidou met majority party leaders and discussed what to do. As they were debating, Tricot was announced. He told them that the helicopters in which the General and his party, including his wife and son-in-law, had departed had not arrived at Colombey but disappeared.

Pompidou sent a message to the State radio and television service, the ORTF, warning them that he might wish to speak to the nation that evening. At this point Tricot intervened. He feared that Pompidou's anxiety might cause him to proclaim an interim government, whereas he himself remained convinced that the General would return. When informed by the ORTF of Pompidou's message, he said, 'You must play for time. If the Prime Minister calls you again, get in touch with me before doing anything else.'[7] He let it be understood that nobody was to speak on television without the General's authority, and that he was the proper channel for conveying that authority. This he did, as he has confirmed to me, without Ministerial authority. It was an expert reading of the balance of power as between the President's Secretary-General and the Prime Minister under the constitution of the Fifth Republic.

Two events, however, contributed to easing tension. The Communist demonstration began at 3 p.m. in a most orderly fashion, and de Gaulle's helicopter was traced to Baden-Baden, where he had landed at French military headquarters and was with General Massu, Commander of French forces in Germany. His son Philippe arrived there too, brought from France with his family in an Air Force plane. His daughter Elisabeth and her children were already safe at Mulhouse on the German frontier.

What had happened *en route*? It seems that while making for Colombey, de Gaulle had given orders to his pilot to change course, break radio contact, and head for Baden-Baden at tree-top level. Why he had done so remains even today a matter of disagreement. His order may have been part of a carefully laid plan to create the right conditions for a spectacular and triumphant return to Paris. But, if we are to judge from what de Gaulle himself said to General Massu at Baden-Baden, and on a number of subsequent occasions, it seems more likely that he was assailed in his helicopter by his familiar demons of despair. Before leaving Paris, he had spoken to Pompidou as if he were really in two minds about his intentions. Now the balance tilted in favour of departure and he spoke the decisive words to his pilot. It is also conceivable that he had made up his mind in Paris as to what he was going to do and had deliberately made appointments he had no intention of keeping, as he had done on the morning of his departure from Bordeaux on 17 June 1940. But, if that is so, he had completely misled a man who knew him as well as Bernard Tricot. The probability is that his decision was made at the last moment.

When he arrived at Baden-Baden at about 2 p.m. de Gaulle seemed to his host and loyal supporter, General Jacques Massu, to be in a state of profound depression. His first words were: 'C'est foutu, Massu'. The two men talked together for two hours. Massu made a record of their conversation which he afterward kept secret at the request of Pompidou, when President, and of Valéry Giscard d'Estaing after him. But it is no secret that the General talked of resigning and spoke of his deep discouragement. He did not speak as if he meant to return to France. It was in fact Massu who did most of the talking and urged him to go back to France as soon as possible. He summoned his officers in order to show that there were still plenty of young Frenchmen who respected the President of the Republic and were loyal to him. The crisis of youth in France had, in the judgement of Massu, produced no repercussions among his young soldiers. There was no discussion of using the Army to crush a possible coup d'état in France.

Perhaps Massu also told de Gaulle of his conversation the day before with the Russian Commander-in-Chief in East Germany, who had paid him a protocol visit arranged before the troubles began. 'Why doesn't the Army get rid of your Maoist students in Paris?' General Kochevoi had demanded during lunch. 'That's what we'd do in Russia. My son came home once and started complaining about his school to my wife. She said to him: "Don't dare talk like that, you don't know how lucky you are. If you try and start any trouble, I'll wring your neck for you!"' Kochevoi, a squat massive figure who seemed almost as broad as he was tall, nodded his head and took a swig of brandy. 'And quite right too!' he added. This was Kochevoi's message to the French, cleared no doubt with his political advisers.[8]

De Gaulle departed in far better spirits than he had arrived, and, as Massu had hoped, he departed for France. After dinner at Colombey an hour or two later with his Naval ADC, Captain Flohic, he revealed what he would have done if he had decided not to come back. 'I had told Kiesinger I was in Germany. I should have stayed there for a while and then gone on to Ireland, the country of my maternal ancestors, the MacCartans, then much further away. Anyway I should not have stayed in France.'[9]

De Gaulle had been through another cruel test of spiritual agony, one of many that had scarred him since the days after his failure at Dakar when he had thought of suicide. He came nearer to breaking-point on 29 May 1968 than at any other time. But he did not break. He paid his tribute to Massu at a luncheon he gave in his honour the following 8 November. Turning to Madame Massu, he said: 'It was Providence that placed your husband in my path on 29 May. It had considerable consequences then and there and perhaps incalculable consequences for the future. He said to me, "You cannot go away."' Later de Gaulle added: 'It was the 29th of May which changed the mind of France and my own, for I was ready to go.'[10] This was the second time that Massu had played a vital part in de Gaulle's career. On his first visit to Algiers after taking office in 1958 de Gaulle had said 'you were the flood and the dam', meaning that he had headed the Public Safety Committee on 13 May, but afterwards imposed restraint. In May 1968 Massu was a dam once more, this time against the temptations to depart.

On 30 May de Gaulle returned to Paris and the final triumph of his career. The tactics were modified at the eleventh hour. He had intended to broadcast to the nation in the evening, but Foccart persuaded him to speak before the demonstration on the Champs Elysées began. The choice of a broadcast instead of a television appearance was made in order to recall not the melancholy affair of 24 May but his wartime speeches on the BBC.

His conversation with Pompidou was not without difficulty. The Prime Minister resented not having been taken more fully into his confidence the day before, and was embarrassed at having indulged in speculation with party leaders on the afternoon of the 29th about the possibility of de Gaulle resigning. He offered to resign, but the General rejected the idea. He yielded, however, to Pompidou's insistence that he should postpone the referendum and instead dissolve Parliament and call fresh elections.

At 4.30 pm de Gaulle announced his intentions in a broadcast of less than five minutes, and appealed to the nation for support against 'the Communist conspiracy'. At 6 pm the demonstration on the Champs Elysées began. It was a fine evening and the crowd was far larger than expected. The Communist demands and de Gaulle's disappearance had roused their fears. His return and his fighting words had created a sense of drama. A million people rallied to de Gaulle's support.

The following days and weeks proved that de Gaulle had turned the tide. The Communists made no challenge. Strikers accepted the Grenelle accords and went back to work; students went on holiday. The elections held on 23 and 30 June resulted in a landslide victory for the Gaullists. With 293 seats the Union of Democrats for the Fifth Republic, or UDR, the new name of the Gaullist party, had an absolute majority.

The crisis of the régime was over. But how had it arisen? Why was it that student unrest, so widespread in 1968, had graver consequences in France than elsewhere?

It had arisen because the General, 'feeling the approach of the eternal cold', had made too much haste for the previous eighteen months in pursuing his Grand Design and paid too little attention to domestic discontents. When disaster overtook the State, he put most of the blame in his private thoughts on Georges Pompidou, feeling that his Prime Minister had been chiefly responsible for the government's neglect of his ideas on participation which could have prevented the alienation of the working class. Perhaps there was some truth in the diagnosis, but a good part of the responsibility for May 1968 lay with his solitary exercise of power.

As to the unique effects in France of the restlessness of 1968, much of the explanation must lie in the event that was unique to France, the success of the rebellious students in triggering off an explosion of discontent among the workers. The trade unions then went their own way and, because of Communist policy, refused to make common cause with the students. Had they united their efforts, de Gaulle would almost certainly have had to choose between using naked force against them or resigning. The current of contestation had run from the Sorbonne to the provinces and the factories. De Gaulle himself took a gloomy pride in observing, when things were going downhill: 'Naturally it had to happen here. Paris is still the intellectual capital of the world.'

The events of May did not radically change the condition of the workers in France, but they did change that of the students. Apart from the revolutionary aims of a minority, the students who took part in the disturbances were demanding *cogestion* and *mixité*. They only achieved a little of the first, but they won and kept the second in full. By degrees this change had its effect on the values of French society. The events of May were part of a sexual rather than a political revolution, a revolution of permissiveness that has won the day since then in most parts of the Western world.

For de Gaulle himself the month of May was a tragedy. The two years of suffering to which his wife referred when he died began in this month of May and did not cease.[11]

# 41 DECLINE

De Gaulle had survived, but he was under no illusion that the success of June had cancelled out the disaster of May. In any case it was Pompidou's success rather than his. He still felt that he needed a personal victory in a referendum on a programme of reforms such as he had announced on 24 May if he was to restore some of his lost prestige. He aspired to 'a vast social mutation' as he put it in his election address of 29 June. It would, however, clearly require months of preparation, before a programme could be put to the voters.

The announcement on 10 July that Couve de Murville was to be Prime Minister came as a general surprise, but the General tried to mollify Pompidou by sending him a cordial letter saying that he was being placed 'in the reserve of the Republic' for a period of well-earned rest. The inference that Pompidou could look forward to being the next President was widely drawn when the letter was published. Pompidou's personal relations with de Gaulle were now, however, a good deal less friendly than was generally imagined.

Couve de Murville's Foreign Minister was Michel Debré. The General's instructions to him were clear:

You know my thinking. And I know how much importance you attach to our independence. You've always fought against supranationality. Its supporters will try to exploit our present difficulties. It will be hard going. I need someone who will stand firm. France needs him. America will try to make use of our situation. You're the man who can stand up to their diplomacy.[1]

But it was the Russians who struck a heavy blow at European Europe when they occupied Czechoslovakia on 21 August and overthrew Dubcek's liberalizing government. De Gaulle condemned the act but he knew that there was nothing France or the West could do about it except mark their disapproval. It was a major setback to his policy of détente. He discussed the question at Colombey with Couve and Debré and they agreed that, nevertheless, there was no alternative policy France could adopt. Since the Russians were not yet ready for détente, France must be patient and vigilant, without changing her ultimate aims. He summed up the effect of the Soviet action in the press conference he gave on 9 September. It was, he said, 'nothing but the expression of Soviet hegemony. It presents us with the spectacle of the maintenance of the Eastern bloc, and, in consequence, of the Western bloc.' France and all Europe had hoped for 'something quite different, far better' from 'the great Russian people'. But it was too late to divide Europe for ever into two opposing blocs. That was why France would persevere in her policy of working towards 'the independence of peoples and the liberty of man ... for détente, entente, and cooperation, that is for peace'.[2] Such were the final words of what was destined to be de Gaulle's last press conference.

Diplomatic exchanges with the Soviet government continued after the occupation of Prague, as provided for in the understandings of 1966, but the spirit was gone from them. Prudence required an effort to seek rather closer contact with the Americans and British, and de Gaulle turned towards them both. They, for their part, had both sent new ambassadors to Paris; Sargent Shriver, a brother-in-law of the Kennedys, for the United States; and Christopher Soames, son-in-law of Winston Churchill, for Britain. These dynastic envoys appealed to the General's taste, and he gave them both a cordial welcome.

It was some consolation to him at a time when so much was going ill that France had at last succeeded in solving the mystery of the bomb. She achieved her first two thermonuclear explosions, both in the megaton range hitherto inaccessible to her, in a series of tests carried out in the South Pacific during August.[3] De Gaulle knew that the Americans would have observed this and would be reflecting on the fact that France, whatever her other problems might be, was now a fully fledged member of the nuclear club.

As far as Britain was concerned, Debré was urging the General to reconsider his attitude. His thesis was that the Five now regarded France as vulnerable to 'blackmail' in order to make her agree to the entry of Britain into the Common Market. The ideal opportunity, Debré argued, would present itself at the end of 1969 when the existing financial regulation governing agriculture ran out and had to be replaced by the definitive and permanent regulation. At that point the Five could refuse to give France the kind of permanent regulation her agricultural interests required unless she accepted Britain as a fellow member. There was to be a summit meeting at the Hague at that time, and there France might well be faced with the invidious choice of backing down over the British application or breaking up the Common Market. The former course would be humiliating, the latter expensive. Germany, exposed to Anglo-Saxon pressure, would doubtless let France down, as she had done over the ratification of the Franco-German Treaty in 1963. It would be better, in his view, to seize the initiative before then and open a bilateral negotiation with Britain aimed at agreeing on modification of the economic clauses of the Treaty of Rome and creation of a common front over the terms of political cooperation in Europe, on which Britain shared the French opinion that national sovereignty must be preserved. De Gaulle listened and promised to reflect on what Debré had said.[4] Shortly afterwards, early in November 1968 he sent a message to Christopher Soames that he would like to have a long talk with him early in the New Year about European prospects. This was the genesis of what was later to become famous, or notorious, as 'l'Affaire Soames'.

In November a new financial crisis arose. The parity of the franc had been suspect since May, and France had exhausted her line of credit with the IMF in defending it. The full Customs Union of the EEC had come into effect on 1 July and was imposing a considerable strain. A new alignment of currency values was foreseen, and speculators began to sell francs and buy German marks and gold. It became clear that France urgently needed more international support. Finance ministers and governors of central banks of the Group of Ten met in Bonn on 20 November. The French Finance Minister, Ortoli, undertook that, if a loan was forthcoming, his government would be willing to devalue as part of a general adjustment of currencies. The German Finance Minister, Franz-Josef Strauss, refused, however, to value the German mark upwards as part of the transaction. When the meetings ended on Friday 22 November, the only change foreseen was the devaluation of the franc. Ortoli returned to Paris to seek his government's approval, and central banks agreed on a new loan to France.

Agreement seemed to have been reached, but de Gaulle, who in any case detested the idea of devaluation, was deeply unhappy that, because of German obstinacy, the only change to be made was that in the value of the franc. It would be a painful admission of weakness, after all the proud boasts that had been made before May of the strength of the French currency. He resolved to try and find a way out at the last minute. On Saturday morning he urgently summoned from Brussels Raymond Barre, the Vice-President of the Commission of the three European communities (EEC, Euratom, and the European Coal and Steel Community). Barre, a Frenchman, was in charge of financial matters in the Commission, and had been invited to attend as an observer the meetings of the Ten in Bonn. He was therefore completely informed about the positions of the governments and bankers concerned. The General explained the problem to him. Would France still receive the international loan, which was indispensable for the support of the franc, if he decided after all not to devalue? Barre was able to tell him that the answer was yes.

This was the vital piece of information which the General needed. He decided that if the loan was forthcoming, heavy cuts in proposed government spending would do the rest of the work of defending the franc at its present value. On the evening of 23 November, as all the world was waiting to hear what the new rate of exchange would be, the General sprang a tactical surprise in his old style. A communiqué was issued from the Elysée:

The President of the Republic makes it known that after a meeting of the Council of Ministers today 23 November the following decision has been taken:
The existing parity of the franc will be maintained.

The decision was popular with the general public, who took the same uncomplicated view of currency values as did de Gaulle himself, but French exporters were worried. Governments and bankers among the rest of the Group of Ten had mixed feelings too. The loan had not been tied to devaluation, but it had been made on the assumption that it would take place. There were also raised eyebrows at the extent to which Raymond Barre, an international civil servant at the time, had put himself and his knowledge at the disposal of his government. It was felt that de Gaulle had sailed very close to the wind, but since he was de Gaulle nobody challenged what he had done − except the faraway Japanese. The experts knew that he had only postponed the inevitable.

One last arbitrary gesture followed in the field of foreign affairs. At Christmas, as a reprisal for heavy guerrilla raids mounted from

Lebanese territory, Israeli commandos descended on Beirut airport and destroyed many of the planes of Lebanon's national airline. Without consulting the Council of Ministers, de Gaulle promptly announced an embargo on the sale of military aircraft to Israel. It was not a popular act, and did nothing to improve his prospects in the approaching referendum.

In the New Year Pompidou, who knew that a referendum was in the offing, began to assert his claim to be recognized as heir apparent. He told journalists in Rome on 17 January that if the President were to retire, he would be a candidate for the succession. It was a statement that immediately led to speculation that Pompidou knew that de Gaulle had plans to retire soon, and obliged the General to issue a reply. This he did on 22 January, when it was announced in a communiqué that he had 'the duty and the intention' to carry out his mandate to its end, which was 8 January 1973. Undaunted, Pompidou returned to the charge during a visit to Geneva. There he referred before a distinguished audience to the possibility that he might, 'if God willed, have a national destiny'. By then de Gaulle had changed the situation by announcing, on 2 February while on a visit to Quimper in Brittany, that a referendum on participation would be held in the spring. He did not say that he would stake his own future on the result, but the likelihood of his doing so was immediately apparent. As it proved, the curtain had been raised on the last act.

# 42   THE SOAMES AFFAIR

On 4 February 1969 General de Gaulle received the British Ambassador, Sir Christopher Soames, for the *déjeuner intime* arranged the previous November. The only others present were Madame de Gaulle and Lady Soames. According to plan the two men had a long discussion beforehand on the future of relations between France and Britain.[1]

De Gaulle said that he believed there could be much closer cooperation. It might be possible to change the Treaty of Rome so as to make economic collaboration easier for Britain. Political and defence cooperation, which were not subjects for the EEC, would need to be concerted in regular meetings between the four great European powers, France, Britain, Germany and Italy. When Soames asked how this arrangement would fit in with NATO, the General replied that NATO would continue for a time, but that in the longer run Europe would have to organize its own defence. The Americans would remain allies of course, but not present in Europe.

These matters would need to be discussed between the countries concerned, said the General, but he thought it would be useful to begin with secret bilateral talks between Britain and France. If progress was made, others could be informed by mutual agreement. If this idea appealed to the British government, they had only to propose conversations. France would accept. The Ambassador promised to inform his government and obtain their reply.

The General had been talking informally, but the potential importance of what he had said was evident. It seemed as if the May crisis and the Russian occupation of Czechoslovakia might have inclined him to open the doors of Europe to Britain after all. It was not clear whether he was inviting her to join the existing EEC or a looser group, and his ideas about NATO were different from Britain's. But there was material for a serious discussion. On the other hand the Foreign Office also saw reason for suspicion. The General had talked of changing the Treaty of Rome. Britain had stated in her application to join the EEC that she was prepared to accept the Treaty as it was. He had also suggested secret talks on British initiative. If the talks leaked to the Five, might they not regard Britain as a traitor to the EEC? And what would the Americans think of talks that foresaw the break-up of NATO?

The Foreign Office had, therefore, to consider whether de Gaulle was setting a trap for Britain; and the consideration had to be urgent, because the Prime Minister, Harold Wilson, was due to go to Bonn on 10 February for talks with the German Chancellor. A decision had to be taken before then whether to tell the Germans of de Gaulle's approach. If the Prime Minister did not do so, and Kiesinger subsequently found out from the French, Britain might have put herself in a false position.

The presence of this element of urgency was fortuitous. De Gaulle had offered Soames a choice of 10 January or 4 February for the luncheon. Soames had chosen the later date because he knew that Debré and his junior Minister, Jean Lipkowski, were urging the General to change his attitude towards the British role in Europe and he wanted to allow more time for their influence to have an effect. If he had chosen the January date, more unhurried consideration could have been given to the General's proposals and a different course might have been taken by the British government.

It was of course vital that there should be no mistake about what the General's proposals were. He had spoken impromptu, and there was no full-length French record of what he had said. Soames, therefore, gave a copy of the report he had sent to London to Bernard Tricot at the Elysée and asked for the General to confirm or correct it.[2] When he called at the Quai d'Orsay a couple of days later Debré returned the report to him and confirmed its accuracy. Debré would have preferred the General to put forward his ideas in a more formal manner than in a private lunch, but he welcomed the initiative, which he had been urging, and began at once to select the French team for the talks which he assumed would soon begin.

Not everybody was so sanguine. When the General had telephoned Couve de Murville immediately after his lunch with Soames to tell him what he had done, Couve replied that he expected the German Foreign Office had already heard about it from the

British.[3] In this he was mistaken, but his remark was prophetic all the same.

Meanwhile anxious consultations proceeded in London, and Soames was instructed not to come home to take part in them in order not to risk putting the press on the trail. An account of the General's proposals was also sent to ambassadors in EEC capitals other than Bonn with a warning that they might – or might not – later receive instructions to deliver it urgently and at a high level to the governments to which they were accredited. The Foreign Office was taking every precaution against being trapped.

The Prime Minister himself was tempted to accept de Gaulle's offer and mention in confidence to Kiesinger that he was doing so, without dramatizing it. This was also the course Soames favoured. But the Foreign Secretary, Michael Stewart, and his officials, were eager to tell all to the Five and to the Americans. It was a vivid illustration of the depth of distrust of the General which existed by then in the Foreign Office, once so Francophile.

The decision was still open when the Prime Minister's party left for Bonn on 10 February. Soames had received no instructions to give any kind of reply to the French. It would have been possible, for instance, to tell them that the UK accepted their proposal for talks but not for secrecy, and to suggest jointly informing the countries concerned. But the Foreign Office rejected that idea because it would enable the French to give the Five their own version of the General's initiative while London still awaited their reply.

In the event the Prime Minister accepted the advice of the Foreign Office. He mentioned the matter briefly to Kiesinger in their tête-à-tête talk and later gave a detailed account. Instructions were sent to the forewarned ambassadors to take the same action urgently. One or two of them took dramatic as well as urgent action, and went beyond their instructions by describing the General as a traitor to the EEC. Only when this action was complete did the Foreign Office send instructions to Soames. These were to accept the General's offer of talks but to say that as the UK could not agree to them being secret, it had already informed the Five. Inevitably the French were furious and reproachful, and all idea of talks was dead from that moment on. De Gaulle himself was perhaps the most angry of all.

Strangely enough the story did not leak to the press for nearly a fortnight. The French spent that time mending their fences with the

Five. Then a brief reference appeared in *Le Figaro* to exaggerated and inaccurate reports circulating in certain capitals about proposals made by General de Gaulle to the British Ambassador in Paris.

The British reply was extraordinary. The Foreign Office was not content with giving its version of the proposals, or refusing to comment at all on the grounds that the talk was confidential. Instead it took the unprecedented step of issuing the full text of Soames's account of his discussion with the General, and describing it as an agreed record. Such treatment of the text of a confidential diplomatic exchange with a foreign Head of State is perhaps without precedent in British history. It was accompanied by guidance to the press to the effect that de Gaulle seemed to be contemplating the break-up of both the EEC and NATO, whereas it was British policy to strengthen both organizations.

A few days later the Quai d'Orsay retaliated with a note criticizing various aspects of British behaviour in this matter and denying the assertion that there was an agreed record. In doing this, they were taking refuge in semantics. They had said that Soames's record was correct, and both Debré and Tricot are willing to confirm this today. That was the important point. The fact that the text had not been agreed in the sense of being jointly signed before dispatch altered nothing of substance.

The question remains whether de Gaulle was in fact setting a trap for the British. It hardly seems likely that he was setting one of the kind imagined by the Foreign Office, but a series of conversations on Europe and NATO with the French at that time would certainly have presented pitfalls for the British. The picture the General outlined to Soames was that of a European Europe to be attained by stages. Given Britain's close ties with the United States in defence policy, progress could not have been great. Moreover de Gaulle had an ulterior motive in making his proposal, which was to ease the pressure of the Five on him to open negotiations on the British application to enter the EEC. The British were, therefore, probably wise to refuse the kind of diversion that the General's proposal represented – and refuse it they did, despite their nominal acceptance.

The press made a feast of *l'Affaire Soames*, as it was called, and Anglo-French relations sank to a nadir. Soames's mission seemed to be in ruins and he thought seriously of resigning. It was fortunate that he did not do so, because the departure of an ambassador would have added much to the harm done by the affair. Soames's presence in Paris after the General had left the scene made it easier for the real Anglo-French negotiation to begin.

The General remained by all accounts deeply angered by the way the British had treated him. He spoke of the 'Soames Affair' to intimates after his retirement to Colombey as an example of Anglo-Saxon unscrupulousness. Perhaps he remembered, though, that in his book *La France et son Armée* he had described the French Monarchy, with a hint of approval, as 'having few scruples about the means it employed'.[4] In his Memoirs he rated among Britain's advantages the possession of 'the finest diplomacy in the world'. It is not necessary to assume that he changed his mind as a result of the Soames Affair.

# 43 RENUNCIATION

On 19 February 1969, two days before the Soames Affair appeared in the press, the Council of Ministers announced that 27 April had been chosen as the date of the referendum on regionalization and the reform of the Senate. The General had had last-minute doubts before committing himself to the date. Two days previously he had summoned Roger Frey, now the Minister of State in charge of relations between government and Parliament, and asked if he thought it was too late for him to postpone the referendum without losing face. Frey asked for a few hours to reflect; de Gaulle gave him ten minutes, and read *Le Monde* while waiting. Then Frey told him he believed postponement, after what he had said at Quimper, would cost him prestige. He had never yet shown fear. That quality was part of the image he should bequeath to the France of the future. So it was too late to retreat. 'It's the answer I was expecting from you,'[1] replied the General. There were others who favoured delay, but it was Frey's advice which prevailed. De Gaulle committed himself.

Before he could begin his campaign, there was a very important visitor to welcome. The new President of the United States, Richard Nixon, came to Paris on an official visit on 28 February, only five weeks after taking office. He was accompanied by his foreign affairs adviser, Henry Kissinger. It was a hopeful moment in relations between France and the United States. De Gaulle had known and admired Nixon when he was Eisenhower's Vice-President. During Nixon's years in the political wilderness between 1962 and 1968 he had not forgotten, and had received him with cordiality when he visited Europe and was neglected elsewhere. There was every chance, therefore, that de Gaulle would have a better understanding with Nixon than with Lyndon Johnson. Nixon's evaluation of the General emerges clearly from his Memoirs, where he says: 'The high point of this trip personally and substantively was my series of meetings with de Gaulle.'[2]

One of the subjects discussed at greatest length with de Gaulle by Nixon and Kissinger was China, which was still in the throes of the Cultural Revolution. Nixon said he intended to work towards more normal relations with Peking. De Gaulle advised him to recognize Peking of his own free will before the growth of China's power left America with no choice. If the Americans leaned towards China, it might also have a salutary effect on the Russians, who were in an aggressive mood, as the occupation of Czechoslovakia had shown.[3]

On Vietnam de Gaulle asked why the Americans did not pull out. Kissinger replied: 'A sudden withdrawal might give us a credibility problem – in the Middle East for instance.' 'How odd,' was the reply. 'It is precisely in the Middle East that I thought your enemies had the credibility problem.'[4] For Nixon and Kissinger, however, withdrawal from Vietnam did not raise questions of principle. It was a matter of timing and tactics. This was a welcome change from the language of Johnson and Dean Rusk.

On Germany and on the nuclear deterrent the American visitors understood that France had her own policy, just as they had theirs, and did not make an issue of it. As they were taking leave, however, Kissinger asked how France proposed to prevent Germany becoming the strongest state in Europe. 'By making war on her,' replied the General. It was a pleasantry which contained a truth. De Gaulle never conceived of relations with Germany as relations between equals. Lost wars had already demoted the Germans.

Kissinger had the advantage, for the purposes of understanding the General, of being himself a European by birth. He could feel for the sensitivities of yesterday's superpowers more easily than Americans born and bred in the United States. The philosophy of national independence and a 'European Europe' was comprehensible to Kissinger, and he thought it could even be in the interest of the United States if centres of decision existed elsewhere which could relieve it of some burdens. Thus he could describe the foreign policy of the Fifth Republic as 'prickly' but 'serious and consistent', at times 'steadier and more perceptive than our own'.[5]

What impressed Kissinger even more than the General's policy was his willpower. He spoke of de Gaulle 'exuding raw willpower' like Mao Tse-tung. These were the two who exuded the quality more than any other statesmen he met. The impression remained with him. On British television in 1980 Kissinger ranked de Gaulle along with the two Chinese leaders, Mao Tse-tung and Chou En-lai, above all the other statesmen with whom he ever had dealings.

It was ironical that Nixon and Kissinger should come to power just as de Gaulle was about to leave it. De Gaulle accepted Nixon's invitation to visit the United States in 1970, and Nixon repeated it after the General's retirement. But it did not take place.

Had de Gaulle won his referendum, it is not impossible that an era of easier relations between him and the Americans would at last have dawned. The Nixon administration was preparing to adopt many of the policies the General had long been pressing on Washington – notably withdrawal from Vietnam, recognition of Peking, renewal of contact with the Arabs, and abandonment of the Gold Exchange Standard – and it had more understanding for his vision of Europe. By 1970 it was also clear that the new Chancellor of the Federal Republic, Willy Brandt, was not interested in going to Moscow with de Gaulle and meant to do so alone. Paris and Washington were both going to have to adjust to a less dependent client.

When de Gaulle's American guests had departed and he returned to the referendum campaign, he had need of all the willpower which Kissinger perceived in him. His ministers, including Couve de Murville, his Premier, had no stomach for the battle. Most of them did not believe in participation and felt that in any case whatever reform the General insisted on could be passed through the Assembly by the massive majority won the previous June. A referendum could easily be lost. To ministers and to the party faithful in general there seemed no sense in running an unnecessary risk. If the referendum could not be averted, their hope was that at least de Gaulle would not stake his own future on its outcome. He had done so last year, but not when reviving the project at Quimper on 2 February.

There was also unhappiness about the form which de Gaulle chose to give to the referendum. He wished it to demand a single answer to two questions the link between which was unclear to the general public: regional and Senate reform. The proposal for regionalization entailed restoring to the ancient provinces of pre-Revolutionary France some of the functions they had lost after 1789, when the centralizing spirit of the Republic had created the Departmental structure. There was to be an Assembly in each region partly elected and partly nominated by professional organizations, trade unions and other such groups, and a local administration funded by the central government. The reform of the Senate involved converting it into an advisory instead of a legislative chamber and incorporating in it the non-elected Economic and Social Council and representatives of the regions.

Neither of these was a new idea, and the second chamber had been repeatedly modified in the past. As to regionalization, it had been one of Charles Maurras's favourite proposals. He had seen it as a way of restoring power to 'the real country', as he called it, at the expense of the 'official country' of the Jacobins. Here de Gaulle's inveterate tendency to regard reform as to some extent the restoration of a previously existing state of affairs was once more evident. In the political climate of 1969 regionalization might well be popular with the public none the less, but Senate reform, which was vigorously opposed by the Senate itself, was likely to be unpopular. To most people, moreover, the two questions were unconnected.

It was also asked why de Gaulle had chosen these two questions to be the subject of a referendum, when others equally relevant to the general concept of participation were referred to Parliament. The Assembly had already passed the law on university reform, and was to receive a bill on arrangements for participation in industry and commerce. But no very clear answer was offered. De Gaulle simply asserted that 'in his soul and conscience' the two reforms were linked. On 10 April he put paid to any lingering hopes that he might not stake his fate on the result. In a televised interview with the journalist Michel Droit he not only insisted on the holding of the referendum, but also stated firmly that, if the verdict went against him, he would retire.

It was now clear what was at stake, and opinion polls showed that the issue was doubtful. All Opposition forces, including the trade unions, were calling on their supporters to vote No. On 14 April Giscard d'Estaing, whose party had representatives in the government, announced that he too would vote No. This decision tended to swing a few per cent of the vote against de Gaulle, just as it was becoming apparent that a few per cent one way or the other would probably make the difference between victory and defeat.

De Gaulle had set the electorate a very difficult question. If they had been asked whether they wanted him to remain as President, they would have said Yes. Public opinion polls made that clear: 53 per cent were satisfied with him, and only 33 per cent dissatisfied. But he was asking a public in a conservative mood to approve a radical reform. As usual, he warned them that the choice was between 'Progress and Upheaval', but this threat carried less conviction than on previous occasions, since Pompidou had declared that he would be a candidate if the Presidency fell vacant. To some it seemed that the question posed by the referendum was 'De Gaulle or Pompidou'.

As the date of decision approached, de Gaulle realized that unless a miracle happened, the vote would go against him. He said so to those around him. On 24 April they made an effort to produce the miracle. Unbeknown to the General, Foccart telephoned Pompidou and suggested he should declare that, if de Gaulle withdrew, he would not after all be a candidate for the succession. Pompidou refused. In a sense de Gaulle had chosen the fate which befell him. He alone had prevented his Presidency continuing until its natural term of life, or his own, ran out. He did not wish to remain in office merely to preside over the administration of current affairs. He felt he must have a Grand Design to pursue in mystical communion with the French people. If that was not possible, he preferred to depart and so to leave intact for future generations the image of a Frenchman who had wanted great power only for great purposes, who had been ambitious for his nation and not for himself.

In the referendum on Sunday 27 April, 52.41 per cent of the votes were cast against the draft law. In the early hours of 28 April, de Gaulle, who had left the Elysée for Colombey the previous Friday, issued a communiqué:

I am ceasing to exercise my functions as President of the Republic. This decision takes effect at midday today.

At midday accordingly Alain Poher, President of the Senate, a member of the Democratic Centre, an Opposition party, became interim President of the Republic. In the afternoon he drove in an open car, with a more modest motorcycle escort than de Gaulle's, to the Elysée and set in motion the machinery for the election of a new President of the Republic by universal suffrage. France remained quiet. The institutions of the Fifth Republic proved capable of functioning in the absence of their creator. The value of his legacy to France began to appear, while Le Connétable himself remained silent at Colombey. Of the flood of personal letters that he received, the most moving, so he told André Malraux,[6] came from Lady Churchill, to whom he wrote every year on the anniversary of her husband's death.

# 44  LAST DAYS

Two days after de Gaulle's renunciation of power, Bernard Tricot came to Colombey to hand over various personal papers to him. The General told him he was planning to visit Ireland. It was a country which had always interested him, he said. His uncle Charles had written a history of the Celts, and there was Irish blood in the family. His decision meant that he would be absent from France during the impending campaign for the election of his successor. Pompidou was to be the candidate of the Union for the Fifth Republic, the man of whom he had said in his family circle on 24 April 'he has betrayed me'. De Gaulle decided that he could not actively support him, but he sent him a letter a few days after his retirement, which he asked him not to make public. In it he stated that Pompidou would have done better not to announce his availability while de Gaulle was still in office, but was now entitled to expect his support for his candidacy; and that he did in fact approve it, although he would not participate in the electoral campaign. Pompidou thus benefited from the private certainty that the General would not say or do anything to spoil his chances in the election. The letter was only published after Pompidou's death.

For de Gaulle his withdrawal from France was a political abstention: for the Irish it was a political event. France had often sustained Irish nationalism against Britain in the past, and the ferment created by the Revolution of 1789 had been at the origin of the rising of 1798 which had marked the rebirth in Ireland of the long dormant spirit of rebellion against the Crown. The events of May in France had played a part in stimulating fresh hopes of change in Northern Ireland, where a Civil Rights Movement had begun among the Catholics in 1968. At first it had been non-violent, but it had been met by repression at the hands of the Northern Irish Government, and on 19 April 1969 there had been bloody clashes in Londonderry between Catholics and

Protestants. Thus it was at a moment of high tension in Ireland that de Gaulle's visit to the Republic was announced to the Dublin government, whose policy was to prevent the troubles in the North complicating their relations with Britain. Consequently the visit of a world statesman best known to Irish public opinion for his habit of thwarting the British government was a considerable complication, the more so since a general election was due in the Republic on 18 June. But he had to be welcomed, and the Prime Minister, Mr Lynch, was at Cork Airport when the General landed there on 10 May.

He remained in the southwest in peaceable seclusion until 15 June, when Georges Pompidou duly defeated the interim President Alain Poher and became the second President of the Fifth Republic. De Gaulle sent him a telegram of congratulations. Then, before returning to France, he paid a brief visit to Dublin, where he received at the French Embassy his MacCartan kinsmen from County Down, some thirty of them, and was the guest of President de Valera. The Irish authorities, with an eye on the North, treated him as circumspectly as if he had been an explosive package. All went calmly until the farewell luncheon given in his honour at Dublin Castle by the Prime Minister, still in uncertainty as to the result of his own election the day before, on 19 June. There de Gaulle ended his speech by offering a toast to '*l'Irlande tout entière*'.[1] It can hardly have been by inadvertence that he used a phrase evoking a united Ireland. In the highly charged atmosphere of the hour it might have had repercussions as potent as his cry '*Vive le Québec libre*'. Possibly, however, the Irish authorities had not forgotten that incident. There was a technical failure in the General's microphone just as he reached the words of his toast, and they did not carry to those beyond earshot. Had he gone so far the night before, in the privacy of the dinner offered him by de Valera, as to say '*Vive l'Irlande libre*'? Some diplomats believed so.

At Colombey his main task was writing his *Memoirs of Hope*, narrating the story of his time in office from 1958 to 1969. He wrote for posterity and he wrote in haste. He also resumed the keeping of a diary and read once again the great classic writers: 'Aeschylus, Shakespeare, "Les Mémoires d'Outre-Tombe", a little Claudel . . . you can add Sophocles' was the list he gave to André Malraux.[2] He received few visitors outside his family circle and no members of Pompidou's government.

Pompidou's policies he regarded as in no way inherited from his own. He saw him as devoted to the arts of compromise and the interests of conservatism. When at the Hague summit of the Six late in 1969 Pompidou made a speech indicating that France might accept British entry into the EEC, de Gaulle heard the news on the radio and shook his head with a sardonic smile. '*Ce pauvre Pompidou*', he murmured. He could see him yielding to the British and their allies as readily as he had done to the students and the strikers in May 1968. 'He won't dare to let them in while you are here' a friend suggested. 'I am not immortal, you know,' was the reply.[3]

'*Ce pauvre Pompidou*' was a phrase that came to his lips without difficulty. '*Ce pauvre Pompidou*', he said on another occasion, 'his health is bad' – '*Il n'a pas la santé.*' Pompidou was indeed already affected by the malady that was to cause his death in 1974.

De Gaulle scrupulously refrained from intervening in any way in the course of French politics. Nonetheless his presence in Colombey was never forgotten by government or opposition in Paris. He was still a guardian of the national interest who might speak out if he saw a reason – still if necessary, *Le Connétable*. The need, however, did not arise. Even if Pompidou had gone his own way at the last, the words de Gaulle had used in his farewell radio address on 25 April were proving true. 'The army of those who support me . . . have in their hands, whatever may happen, the future of the nation.'

Everything to do with France remained of concern to him. One of his relaxations was to watch international rugby on television, but he could not bear to see France losing. If that was happening, he would retire to another room. His wife would call him back if things went better.[4]

On 11 December 1969 André Malraux came to lunch at Colombey. De Gaulle began their conversation by saying 'This time, perhaps it's all over'.[5] He was still not quite sure, not quite reconciled to the idea that France would never need him again. That at least was his morning mood. By the time darkness had fallen and Malraux departed, he had become Nietzschean. At the front door the two men looked up at the falling snow and the first stars, which were visible in a patch of clear sky. 'They confirm to me the insignificance of things', said de Gaulle.[6] Malraux drove away, and they never met again.

In the summer of 1970 de Gaulle paid a visit to Spain, like Ireland a country he had never seen before. In 1971 he planned to go further afield. He had accepted Mao Tse-tung's invitation to visit China.

On 9 November 1970, thirteen days short of his eightieth birthday, he was as active as ever at Colombey. He worked in his study at the second volume of his Memoirs. The first, covering the period up to the grant of independence to Algeria in 1962, had been published in the autumn. Two chapters of the second were now prepared in draft.

His day's work ended, he dealt with private correspondence. He sent a brief letter to his cousin, Henri Maillot, a lifelong friend. They had played on the beach together when Charles was eight and Henri was four, and had been in trouble with Charles's father for returning home late. Considering his father's reproaches unjust, Charles had deserted the family supper table and shared the small Henri's meal in the nursery instead. Was it the first of those withdrawals which he had so often practised in later life as a means to an end? Henri Maillot had for many years been mayor of his village of Lambersart. Charles referred in his letter to 'your heavy charge of mayor of Lambersart'. It was only half a joke. Charles was always respectful of the public service at whatever level. He sent the letter to the post.

His day's work finished, de Gaulle played patience before dinner. There his father's fate, which ran in the family, overtook him. A blood-vessel ruptured. He exclaimed suddenly in pain and fell forward over the table. Soon he was dead, with no more pain.

# 45 THE ACHIEVEMENT AND THE LEGACY

De Gaulle is both a historical and a legendary personality. Because of the heroic stature he acquired relatively early in his political career, he was able to imbue his historical achievements with symbolic significance. This duality is an essential feature.

To become a hero it is not enough to have heroic qualities; one must also live in times fit for heroes. One must suffer great misfortune and be called on to overcome it. De Gaulle had that chance thrust upon him in 1940 when France sustained the most overwhelming military defeat in her national history. He proved to possess the capacities necessary to rise to the challenge. These were not so much his patriotism and his ambition. Many shared these, and his intelligence and energy as well, but accepted Marshal Pétain's lead to surrender. What made de Gaulle different were rather his rebellious streak and his artistic temperament. He had shown his talent for 'ignoring the requirements of a false discipline', as he put it in *Le Fil de l'Épée*, by rejecting orthodox theories at the Senior War School during the years 1922–4, by the lectures calling for reform in the training of the military élite which he had given in 1927 under Pétain's protection, and by his sustained campaign for the unpopular plan for a professional mechanized army which he had pursued from 1934 to 1938. With this he combined the artist's flair for creating the right occasion to make an impression with his unorthodox views. His lectures which Pétain had compelled the teaching staff of the Senior War School to attend were an example. He loved to stand alone.

The evidence of those who knew him well indicates that de Gaulle was a far more sensitive man in private than he allowed himself to appear in public. It confirms his own account of how acutely he suffered at the humiliations France and her Army underwent in May and June 1940. He never foresaw the fall of France. He was confident in his own star and expected to rise to fame as a victorious General, then a Minister of War and then a national leader. The road events obliged him to follow was wholly unexpected and infinitely more painful to him. That anguish explains much of his conduct.

It is possible indeed to describe de Gaulle's career as little more than a series of failures, and he sometimes diverted himself in moments of gloom by doing so. He had missed his chances of distinction in the First World War by being captured; he was graded in the second class at the Senior War School; his campaign for *L'Armée de Métier* did not save France from disaster; as ruler of France he lost the greater part of the overseas patrimony for which he cared so passionately, from Syria to Algeria; his ideas of European Europe fell on deaf ears; French youth held him up to mockery in 1968; and public opinion rejected him in 1969.

All this is true, and yet his achievements for France were immense. To be valued at their true worth, however, their symbolic as well as their purely material significance must be taken into account.

In the summer of 1940 the armed forces of Free France hardly weighed a feather in the balance. On 31 July they numbered only 7,000 disorganized men from many different broken units. Politically the movement's importance lay only in the figure of de Gaulle himself, who had been given personal recognition by the British government as the leader of the Free French. But de Gaulle knew how to give the maximum symbolic weight to every gesture he made. He very quickly developed the habit of speaking and writing in the name of France, and the BBC gave wide circulation to his words.

The initial importance of de Gaulle's appeals to the French in June 1940 lay in the hope he brought. This steadied British opinion and encouraged some French patriots by suggesting that France was not completely deserting the cause of freedom; but the real France manifestly chose Pétain, and it was his government at Vichy that the political realists like Roosevelt and Stalin recognized. Equally a matter of symbolism was the issue at Brazzaville on 27 October 1940 of de Gaulle's manifesto assuming the powers of governing France and making himself an absolute, if temporary, ruler. The immediate impact of this astonishing initiative was still further diminished by British censorship imposed because of fears of driving Pétain into Hitler's arms. If the British had been consulted, they would certainly have advised de Gaulle not to make his proclamation, but, despite his total dependence on their support, he did not consult them. He accepted the risk of being laughed off the stage for burlesquing reality and carried his gesture off with success. Only a born actor, and a political artist, could have managed it in the circumstances. De Gaulle issuing his manifesto at Brazzaville recalls the schoolboy calling on his parents disguised as General Faidherbe, the man who never surrendered to the Germans in 1870. By the extraordinary device of making himself a sovereign with retrospective effect to the date of Reynaud's resignation, he was able to maintain and impose by degrees the fiction that the real France had never surrendered. He gave France an alibi for her fall.

On 26 August 1944 when he walked down the Champs Elysées to the wild applause of the Parisians, de Gaulle was acting again, playing the part, long and carefully prepared, of the Liberator, with General Leclerc's Armoured Division in the supporting role. He had no real power at all except that which the French people gave him, by the enthusiasm with which they hailed his performance, but because they turned to him with such acclaim, the Allies had no alternative but to recognize his authority over them. Thanks to de Gaulle, and of course to the support which the British government as well as the French people gave him, French history books did not have to record that the German occupation régime was followed by an Anglo-American military government. Churchill's diplomacy at Yalta could not have succeeded in persuading Roosevelt and Stalin to accept France as an occupying power in Germany with the same status as the Big Three who had actually defeated her if France herself had been under occupation at the time; nor would France have been accepted by the United Nations as a permanent member of the Security Council along with the four powers who had convened the San Francisco Conference.

In France from the summer of 1944 until the autumn of 1945 de Gaulle held real power for the first time and proved that he could govern. His most widely criticized decision inside France was probably the rejection of the tempting argument of the ex-Vichyites that all Frenchmen had been doing their best for their country in different ways during the war, and that acts performed in obedience to Pétain's orders should incur no punishment. De Gaulle had to be severe with the Vichyites after liberation because there was no other way of saving France from bearing responsibility before the world in the post-war era for their collaboration with the fascists. In opting for severity, de

Gaulle was also obeying the dictates of his character. He had shown as an instructor at St Cyr and as a battalion commander that he believed in being hard, and he applied his creed in his treatment of Pétain and Laval, just as he had with Noguès, Boisson, Peyrouton and other Vichy proconsuls.

The elections of October 1945 suddenly deprived de Gaulle of power. He could probably have prevented this happening by organizing his own political party in time, for he was still immensely popular, but he did not make the attempt, apparently because he had grown into the part he had been playing of personifying France, and took for an immutable reality what had been in fact the product of a most exceptional combination of chances, whose effect could of its nature only be temporary. When he was called on to pay the price he did so, and resisted the temptation of mounting a military coup d'état. That was an act of intelligence which wrote another salutary page into the history of France.

De Gaulle was then disappointed in his hopes of being recalled to power by the people, and had to adjust himself to living with the Fourth Republic. It was inconceivable that he could ever support a régime that had so much in common with the Third Republic that had in his estimation failed France in 1940. The majority of the Constituent Assembly that made the Fourth Republic had, like the Bourbons of the Restoration, learned nothing and forgotten nothing. They devised a Constitution which put all effective power once more into the hands of the elected Assembly and deprived the Presidency of the prerogatives it had enjoyed in the provisional government.

The choice before him in 1947 was opposition or silence. He decided on opposition within the law and when the *Rassemblement* failed to bring him back to office he resigned himself in 1955 to waiting, and hoping, in silence for the course of events to lead the French people to appeal to him once more.

His return to power in 1958 was the most dubious event of his career. His investiture was legitimate on the face of it, but it only took place because the French Army was threatening a coup d'état if parliament did not make him Prime Minister. His followers played a part in bringing about this state of affairs and he knew that they were doing so. He used his influence not to frustrate the coup but to postpone and exploit it. On the other hand powerful forces were involved in the coup who owed no allegiance to de Gaulle and would have tried to overthrow the Fourth Republic even if he had supported it. The crisis of May 1958 represented the last chance of returning to power that he was likely to have, and he took it, because he still believed he could achieve much for France that nobody else could do.

From 1958 to 1969 his career was less heroic, as he recognized himself in his *Memoirs of Hope*, and not all his goals were attained. But his successes were considerable. His settlement in Algeria was the work of a statesman, the more remarkable in that the French Army had not lost the war. In liberating France from the colonial burden he performed a great service to her which no other man would have had the courage and prestige to carry out at that time. He also endowed the country with a new Constitution which has given her more stability than she has enjoyed in any period comparable in length since 1789. At the same time he made the launching of the EEC possible in 1959 and created an atmosphere of confidence which enabled the French economy to compete on equal terms with its neighbours. And the reconciliation with Germany, symbolized by the High Mass jointly attended with Dr Adenauer at Reims Cathedral, was a truly historic event.

In Britain and America de Gaulle is often reproached with ingratitude and hostility to the two powers who saved the West, including France. It is impossible to acquit him of frequently opposing their policies, but it can be argued that he did so only for practical and never for emotional reasons. His mission was to restore the greatness of France and time and again he found American or British greatness in his way. Britain, he believed, wanted France as an ally in Europe but not really an equal; the United States of its very nature exercised a domination of any alliance it joined, unless it was resisted. There was bound to be friction. De Gaulle had to strive to give France a greater place in the world than the Anglo-Saxons wanted to accord her. Hence his vain effort to build a European Europe under French leadership and his more successful opposition to British plans for the EEC and American purposes all over the world. It was not ingratitude, but '*la nature des choses*' that was the cause. He was no more anti-American than he was pro-Russian.

De Gaulle's call for an end of the 'policy of the rival blocs' was not heeded; and yet it expressed a universal desire that continues to be felt. There can be no doubt that it has a future; and that the fact that de Gaulle was the first to formulate it is held to the credit of France in many parts of the world.

The way in which de Gaulle mastered the crisis of 1968 at the last added another chapter to his legend. It was no small matter either to have written a virtually bloodless revolution into the history of France. That was due to the advice of his ministers more than de Gaulle's own judgement; but he had the judgement to take their advice.

Nothing became him more than the manner in which he departed in 1969. His followers were in control of Parliament until 1973, and he was under no obligation to put his own position at risk. But he rightly considered that the electoral victory of June 1968 had been due to a reflex of conservatism, not to a recognition of the need for reform which the events of May had brought home to him. So he staked his future on proposals for change although the country was not truly in the mood for it. By so doing he proved once more that he was not interested in holding on to political power for its own sake but only if he could use it for greater purposes than day-to-day administration. He acted like a jealous lover who becomes more demanding when he feels that his hold on his mistress is weakening. In consequence he himself was rejected, but the unselfishness of his act gave new strength to the institutions that had been menaced the year before. He made his legacy to France more secure by departing as he did, and by dying not at the Elysée but in the solitude of Colombey. The last image he bequeathed to the French was not that of the President but of the hero who had so often been alone.

President Nixon records in his memoirs that after the funeral ceremony at Notre Dame, President Pompidou said to him 'Enfin seuls'.[1] Nixon took him to mean that he had suffered a loss comparable to Nixon's when Eisenhower died. Possibly, however, Pompidou, who had been very conscious of the General's watchful eye directed upon him from his retreat at Colombey, was simply expressing relief. In that case his remark would have been an example of the kind of truth in doubtful taste that sometimes escapes mourners at funerals.

Whatever Pompidou may have said, the legendary de Gaulle continues to exist, and those who guide the destinies of France must still take account of the changes he wrought in the national spirit.

In the presidential campaign of 1981, for instance, none of the candidates campaigned on a programme of breaking with the Gaullist past. On the contrary they vied with one another in trying to suggest that part at least of the General's mantle had fallen on their shoulders.

President Giscard d'Estaing, who had voted against de Gaulle in 1969, still asserted a right to the support of the Gaullist movement and described the choice before the electors as one between order and confusion, an echo of the General's famous formula '*Moi ou le chaos*': François Mitterrand did not focus attention on his years of opposition to de Gaulle and used phrases from the General's vocabulary in his speeches, declaring that France needed grandeur, and that he was a free man who would not take directions from Washington, Moscow or Bonn; even Georges Marchais, the Communist, reminded the electors that his party had been in de Gaulle's governments from 1944 to 1946, and that they favoured keeping the independent French nuclear deterrent.

In office since May 1981, President Mitterrand's Socialist government is adhering to the main lines of de Gaulle's foreign and defence policies. The basis of them is national independence. France remains in the Atlantic Alliance but takes a very different view from the United States of, for example, the situation in Central America. She cooperates with NATO in Germany but is strengthening the independent French deterrent. Even in home affairs some of de Gaulle's ideas are considered respectable. The new régime has already introduced a measure of regionalization, different in detail but similar in concept to the proposal which the General put forward in the lost referendum of 1969, and, although it possesses an ample majority in the Assembly, it has also employed the Gaullian tactic of legislating by decree in order to gain time.

Most striking of all is the fact that a coalition of Socialists and Communists is governing France under the Constitution created by de Gaulle. President Mitterrand has stated his intention of serving out the seven-year term laid down in the Constitution and he told me in December 1981 that the government found it a workable instrument and had no early plans for changing it, despite its imperfections.

There seems, in fact, to be more of a consensus today in France about the method by which the country should be governed than at any time since 1789. This is a situation which can quickly change, and assumptions for the future are not yet warranted. At this stage, however, de Gaulle's Constitution of 1958 appears to have hopes of surviving the present supremely important test of its capacity to meet the needs of alternating left-wing and liberal or right-wing governments. Perhaps de Gaulle was right in believing that a strong

Presidential system would suit the national temperament. If it should prove that he has indeed endowed France with durable institutions, he will have done more than any other statesman to restore the cohesion and stability which she lost in 1789. That would be the richest jewel in his legacy.

In all the phases of his career de Gaulle was an artist, who observed himself in action. He described in his journal how he felt that he split into two persons at the moment of going into action for the first time in August 1914, one leading a bayonet charge, the other anxiously watching him.[2] He kept this habit of watching himself and of recording what he saw when he thought it sufficiently important. As a result he won fame as a writer as well as a man of action.

His masterpiece was his *Memoirs of War*. This work did not purport to be a general history of the war, as was for example the comparable book by Churchill *The Second World War*. It was the story of what de Gaulle himself had done in the cause of France, and of so little relative importance were the other characters and the events narrated that its three volumes were published without an index. De Gaulle took Caesar's Commentaries as a model and was concerned, like Caesar, to portray himself as the hero of a great enterprise, a man who knew what he wanted and achieved it in the end despite temporary and local setbacks. He glosses over indecision and failure.

De Gaulle's war memoirs are in fact a history of his feelings almost as much as of events. His passion for France, his ambition to serve her, his grief at her fall in 1940, his sense of the immensity of his self-imposed task of keeping France in the war, his joy in his triumphs of 1944, his irritations at the attitude of the politicians after the war, his recurrent wrath at the selfishness, as he saw it, of his allies. All this and much more is powerfully described. De Gaulle meant his work to be part of his legacy to France, and it is.

In *Le Fil de l'Épée* he had presented '*le jeu divin du héros,*' the divine and heroic game which the man of character must play, as the supreme object of life. In his War Memoirs he tells how he played that game himself in exile and won it against all the odds. His *Memoirs of Hope*, of which only the first volume was completed before his death, did not make the same appeal to his feelings and became progressively less attractive to him as it went on, as he told André Malraux at their last meeting in December 1969.[3] His Memoirs from 1962 onwards could only have been a record of what he had hoped but failed to achieve. But death overtook him when he had played the divine game of the hero to the end and narrated to the end the part of the game he had won.

Oliver Harvey, one of my predecessors as British Minister in Paris, wrote in his diary as the Allied armies were dissolving at the end of May 1940: 'Will the next few days bring out some Frenchman of destiny?'[4] To a student of France it must seem that the emergence of de Gaulle in 1940 corresponded to a law of historical and artistic necessity. France has to produce a heroic figure in moments of national crisis because she is France. Joan of Arc and Napoleon were de Gaulle's spiritual ancestors.

De Gaulle had to exist so that France could continue to be France; and in responding to his country's greatest crisis, he made himself the greatest of Frenchmen. His supreme legacy to the French is, I believe, renewed confidence that their country will always be capable of producing what is necessary for France to go on being France. The story of de Gaulle is a guarantee of continuity for the land he loved and a lasting assurance for others who love her.

# BIBLIOGRAPHY AND SOURCES

## I ARCHIVES AND LIBRARIES

The French Foreign Ministry Library and Archives, Paris
Guerre, 1939–45. CNF Fonds de Londres, 1941–43
CFLN. Fonds d'Alger, 1943–44
AE. Fonds de Vichy. Relations Franco-Britanniques 1940–43
The Charles de Gaulle Institute Library, Paris
The Public Record Office, Kew (Prime Minister's Papers (PREM/3) Cabinet Papers. Foreign Office Papers.)
The National Archives, Washington, D.C. (State Department files and boxes)
The State Department Archives, Washington, D.C. (Material released under Freedom of Information Act)
The Seeley Mudd Library and Dulles papers, Princeton, N.J.
The Churchill College Archive Centre, Cambridge

## II PRINTED WORKS

This list includes all books quoted in references and others which are valuable for background

THE WORKS OF CHARLES DE GAULLE.
*La Discorde chez L'Ennemi* (Berger-Levrault, Paris, 1924)
*Le Fil de L'Épée* (Berger-Levrault, Paris, 1932)
*Vers l'Armée de Métier* (Berger-Levrault, Paris, 1934)
*La France et son Armée* (Plon, Paris, 1938)
*Mémoires de Guerre:*
    *L'Appel, 1940–42* (Plon, Paris, 1954)
    *L'Unité, 1942–44* (Plon, Paris, 1956)
    *Le Salut, 1944–46* (Plon, Paris, 1959)
*Mémoires d'Espoir* (Plon, Paris, 1970)

*Le Renouveau, 1958–62* (Plon, Paris, 1970)
*Discours et Messages:*
    Vols. I–V (Plon, Paris, 1970)
*Articles et Ecrits* (Plon, Paris, 1975)
*Lettres, Notes et Carnets:*
    Vol. I 1905–18 (Plon, Paris, 1980)
    Vol. II 1919–40 (Plon, Paris, 1980)
    Vol. III 1940–41 (Plon, Paris, 1981)

BIOGRAPHIES
G. Cattaui, *Charles de Gaulle* (Fayard, Paris, 1960)
P.M. de la Gorce, *De Gaulle Entre Deux Mondes* (Fayard, Paris, 1964)
J. Lacouture, *De Gaulle* (Editions du Seuil, Paris, 1969)
A. Crawley, *De Gaulle* (Collins, London, 1969)
B. Crozier, *De Gaulle*: Vol. I *The Warrior*, Vol. II *The Statesman*. (Eyre Methuen, London, 1973)

GENERAL (IN FRENCH)
H. Alphand, *L'Etonnement d'Etre* (Fayard, Paris, 1977)
R. Aron, *Charles de Gaulle* (Perrin, Paris, 1964)
J. Auburtin, *Colonel de Gaulle* (Plon, Paris, 1965)
M. and S. Bromberger, *Les 13 Complots du 13 Mai* (Fayard, Paris, 1959)
R. Cassin, *Les Hommes Partis de Rien* (Plon, Paris, 1974)
Gen. Catroux, *Dans la Bataille de Méditerranée* (Julliard, Paris, 1949)
M. Couve de Murville, *Une Politique Etrangère 1958–1969* (Plon, Paris, 1971)
M. Debré, *Français, Choisissons l'Espoir* (Albin Michel, Paris, 1979)
Admiral Docteur, *La Grande Enigme de la Guerre: Darlan* (Eds de la Couronne, Paris, 1949)
F. Flohic, *Souvenirs d'Outre-Gaulle* (Plon, Paris, 1979)
O. Guichard, *Mon Général* (Grasset, Paris, 1980)
N. Gun, *Pétain, Laval, de Gaulle. Les Secrets des Archives Américaines* (Albin Michel, Paris, 1979)
S. and I. Hoffman, *De Gaulle: Artiste de la Politique* (Seuil, Paris, 1973)
L. Joxe, *Victoires sur la Nuit* (Flammarion, Paris, 1981)
M. Jullian, *L'Homme de '40* (Laffont, Paris, 1980)
    *Madame de Gaulle* (Stock, Paris, 1982)
P.-O. Lapie, *De Léon Blum à de Gaulle* (Fayard, Paris, 1971)
P. Lefranc, *Avec Qui Vous Savez* (Plon, Paris, 1979)
A. Malraux, *Les Chênes qu'on Abat* (Gallimard, Paris, 1971)
Gen. J. Massu, *Le Torrent et la Digue* (Plon, Paris, 1972)
C. Mauriac, *Un Autre de Gaulle* (Hachette, Paris, 1971)
J. Mauriac, *La Mort du Général de Gaulle* (Grasset, Paris, 1972)

DE GAULLE

F. Mitterrand, *Le Coup d'Etat Permanent* (Plon, Paris, 1964)
L. Nachin, *Charles de Gaulle, Général de France* (Colbert, Paris, 1944)
H. Noguères, *Histoire de la Résistance en France*, Vols I–V (Laffont, Paris, 1967)
Col. Passy, *Souvenirs*, Vols I and II (Raoul Solar, Monte Carlo, 1947)
A. Peyrefitte, *Le Mal Français* (Plon, Paris, 1976)
G. Pompidou, *Pour Rétablir une Vérité* (Flammarion, Paris, 1982)
P. Reynaud, *La France a Sauvé l'Europe*, Vols I and II (Flammarion, Paris, 1947)
A. and P. Rouanet, *Les Trois Derniers Chagrins du Général de Gaulle* (Grasset, Paris, 1980)
Maj.-Gen. Sir E. Spears, *Pétain et de Gaulle: Deux Hommes qui Sauvèrent la France* (Presses de la Cité, Paris, 1966)
L. Terrenoire, *De Gaulle, 1947–54. Pourquoi L'Echec?* (Plon, Paris, 1981)
J.-R. Tournoux, *Pétain et de Gaulle* (Plon, Paris, 1964)
 *Pétain et la France* (Plon, Paris, 1980)
 *La Tragédie du Général* (Plon, Paris-Match, 1967)
 *Le Mois de Mai du Général* (Plon, Paris, 1969)
B. Tricot, *Les Sentiers de la Paix* (Plon, Paris 1972)
J. Vendroux, *Cette Chance que j'ai eue* (Plon, Paris, 1974)
 *Ces Grandes Années que j'ai vécues* (Plon, Paris, 1975)
A.J. Voituriez, *L'Affaire Darlan*, Présentation F. Broche (J.C. Lattès, Paris, 1980)

GENERAL (IN ENGLISH)
D. Ben-Gurion, *Israel* (New English Library, London, 1972)
W. Churchill, *The Second World War*, Vols I to VI (Cassell, London, 1948–54)
Count Ciano, *Diary 1939–43* (Heinemann, London, 1947)
 *Diplomatic Papers* (Odhams, London, 1948)
A. Eban, *An Autobiography* (Weidenfeld and Nicolson, London, 1978)
A. Eden, *The Reckoning* (Cassell, London, 1965)
Gen. Eisenhower, *Crusade in Europe* (Heinemann, London, 1948)
M.R.D. Foot, *S.O.E. in France* (H.M. Stationery Office, London, 1966)
Lord Gladwyn, *De Gaulle's Europe* (Secker and Warburg, London, 1969)
D. Grinnell-Milne, *The Triumph of Integrity* (Bodley Head, London, 1961)
A. Grosser, *The Western Alliance* (Translated from the French) (Macmillan, London, 1980)
A. Horne, *A Savage War of Peace* (Macmillan, London, 1977)
O. Harvey, *Diplomatic Diaries 1937–40* (Collins, London, 1970)
L.B. Johnson, *The Vantage Point* (Holt, Reinhart and Winston, New York, 1971)
F. Kersaudy, *Churchill and de Gaulle* (Collins, London, 1981)

H. Kissinger, *The White House Years* (Weidenfeld and Nicolson, London, 1979)

H. Macmillan, *At the End of the Day* (Macmillan, London, 1973)
*The Blast of War* (Macmillan, London, 1967)

R. Murphy, *Diplomat Among Warriors* (Doubleday, New York, 1964)

J. Newhouse, *De Gaulle and the Anglo-Saxons* (André Deutsch, London, 1978)

R. Nixon, *Memoirs* (Sidgwick and Jackson, London, 1978)

R. Sherwood, *The White House Papers of Harry L. Hopkins* (Eyre and Spottiswoode, London, 1948)

Mary Soames, *Clementine Churchill* (Cassell, London, 1979)

Maj.-Gen. Sir E. Spears, *Assignment to Catastrophe* (Heinemann, London, 1954)

H.S. Truman, *Year of Decisions, 1945* (Hodder and Stoughton, London, 1955)

Sir H. Wilson, *Chariot of Israel* (Weidenfeld and Nicolson and Michael Joseph, London, 1981)
*The Labour Government 1964–70* (Weidenfeld and Nicolson and Michael Joseph, London, 1971)

COLLECTIONS AND ARTICLES

'L'Entourage de de Gaulle' (G. Pilleul), prepared under the direction of L'Institut Charles de Gaulle (Plon, Paris, 1979)

'Les Français et de Gaulle' (J. Charlot), a study of IFOP public opinion polls on de Gaulle (Plon, Paris, 1971)

'De Gaulle – Churchill' (Article by Geoffroy de Courcel, *Revue de la France Libre*, No. 226, 1979)

'Le Role d'Aléxis Leger dans les Rapports Anglo-Franco-Americains' (R. Mengin, Contrepoint No. 31–32. 1979–80)

# NOTES

## 1 The End and the Beginning
1 J. Mauriac, *Mort du Général de Gaulle*, p. 163
2 C. de Gaulle, *L'Appel*, p. 1
3 Ibid.
4 Ibid.
5 Ibid., p. 4
6 G. Cattaui, *Charles de Gaulle*, p. 14
7 Author's interview with Geneviève de Gaulle (Madame Anthonioz), 9.4.81
8 J.-R. Tournoux, *Pétain et de Gaulle*, p. 25
9 G. Cattaui, op. cit., p. 21

## 2 Schooldays
1 J.-R. Tournoux, *Pétain et de Gaulle*, p. 27
2 G. Cattaui, op. cit., p. 20
3 C. de Gaulle, *L'Appel*, p. 2
4 J.-R. Tournoux, *Pétain et de Gaulle*, p. 39
5 Ibid.
6 G. Cattaui, op. cit., p. 24
7 Ibid., p. 23
8 C. de Gaulle, *Lettres, Notes et Carnets 1940–41* (Complément), p. 397
9 J.-R. Tournoux, *Pétain et de Gaulle*, p. 40
10 Ibid.
11 C. de Gaulle, *Lettres, Notes et Carnets 1905–18*, p. 36
12 J.-R. Tournoux, *Pétain et de Gaulle*, p. 41

## 3 The Young Writer
1 C. de Gaulle, *Articles et Ecrits*, p. 30
2 G. Cattaui, op. cit., p. 26

## 4 The Young Officer
1 C. de Gaulle, *L'Appel*, p. 2

2  C. de Gaulle, *Lettres . . . 1905–18*, p. 52
3  G. Cattaui, op. cit., p. 28
4  J.-R. Tournoux, *Pétain et de Gaulle*, p. 49
5  G. Cattaui, op. cit., p. 30
6  C. de Gaulle, *Lettres . . . 1905–18*, p. 78

## 5  The Great War, 1914–18

1  C. de Gaulle, *Lettres . . . 1905–18*, p. 80.
2  Ibid., p. 88
3  J.-R. Tournoux, *Pétain et de Gaulle*, pp. 53–4
4  C. de Gaulle, *Lettres . . . 1905–18*, pp. 94–6
5  Ibid., pp. 97–107
6  Ibid., p. 80
7  Ibid., pp. 273–4
8  G. Cattaui, op. cit., p. 33
9  The first part of de Gaulle's letter to General Boud'hors is to be found in *Lettres . . . 1905–18*, pp. 526–9; the second in *Lettres . . . 1940–41* (Complément), pp. 401–7
10  C. de Gaulle, *Lettres . . . 1905–18*, pp. 336–7
11  Ibid., p. 320

## 6  Building a Career

1  C. de Gaulle, *Lettres . . . 1919–40*, p. 30
2  Ibid., p. 31
3  M. Jullian, *Madame de Gaulle*, p. 54
4  C. de Gaulle, *Lettres . . . 1919–40*, p. 44
5  J. Vendroux, *Cette Chance que j'ai eue*
6  J.-R. Tournoux, *La Tragédie du Général* (Annexe), p. 514
7  J.-R. Tournoux, *Pétain et de Gaulle*, p. 98
8  'The man at the top does not bother with trifles.'
9  J.-R. Tournoux, *Pétain et de Gaulle*, p. 90
10  Ibid., p. 88

## 7  Under a Cloud

1  The society was 'Le Cercle Fustel de Coulanges', named after the eminent French historian
2  J.-R. Tournoux, *Pétain et de Gaulle*, p. 119
3  Ibid., p. 125
4  Ibid., pp. 134–5
5  J. Lacouture, *De Gaulle*, p. 44
6  C. de Gaulle, *Lettres . . . 1919–40*, p. 357

**8 The Approaching War**
1  C. de Gaulle, *Le Fil de L'Épée*, p. 63
2  C. de Gaulle, *Vers L'Armée de Metier*, pp. 188–90
3  Ibid., p. 218
4  Ibid., pp. 248–9
5  *Hamlet*, Act IV, Scene 4
6  C. de Gaulle, *Lettres . . . 1919–40*, p. 393
7  J.-R. Tournoux, *Pétain et de Gaulle*, p. 159
8  L. Nachin, *Charles de Gaulle, Général de France*
9  J. Lacouture, *De Gaulle*, p. 60
10  C. de Gaulle, *Lettres . . . 1919–40*, p. 457

**9 Disaster**
1  L. Nachin, *Charles de Gaulle, Général de France*
2  C. de Gaulle, *Lettres . . . 1919–40*, pp. 473–4
3  O. Guichard, *Mon Général*, p. 59
4  J. Lacouture, *De Gaulle*, p. 64
5  G. Cattaui, *Charles de Gaulle*, p. 85
6  M. Jullian, *L'Homme de '40*, p. 80
7  C. de Gaulle, *L'Appel*, p. 31
8  C. de Gaulle, *Lettres . . . 1919–40*, p. 500
9  Ibid., pp. 495–7
10  Author's interview with Admiral de Gaulle, 16.12.81

**10 De Gaulle Refuses to Despair of the Republic**
1  P. Reynaud, *La France a sauvé l'Europe*, Vol. II, p. 264
2  C. de Gaulle, *L'Appel*, p. 44
3  Ibid.
4  General Spears, *Assignment to Catastrophe*, Vol. II, p. 120. Churchill asserts in his *Second World War* that de Gaulle made this remark at the end of their interview on 16 June, but it fits better with the war situation and the subject of discussion on 9 June. Moreover Spears was writing from notes made at the time
5  R. Murphy, *Diplomat Among Warriors*, p. 42
6  C. de Gaulle, *L'Appel*, p. 53
7  W. Churchill, *The Second World War*, p. 138
8  Ibid., p. 140
9  Ibid.
10  Ibid., p. 198
11  C. de Gaulle, *L'Appel*, p. 56
12  W. Churchill, *The Second World War*, p. 160
13  Ibid., p. 161

14  P. Reynaud, *La France a sauvé l'Europe*, pp. 320–1
15  C. de Gaulle, *L'Appel*, p. 57
16  General Spears, *Assignment . . .*, Vol. II, pp. 218–19
17  C. de Gaulle, *L'Appel*, p. 58
18  J. Auburtin, *Colonel de Gaulle*
19  P. Reynaud, *La France . . .*, pp 352–6
20  C. de Gaulle, *L'Appel*, p. 59
21  Ibid., p. 60
22  F. Kersaudy, *Churchill and de Gaulle*, p. 66
23  C. de Gaulle, *L'Appel*, p. 65
24  General Spears, *Assignment . . .*, Vol. II, p. 293
25  General Spears, *Deux Hommes qui sauvèrent la France*, pp. 162–3
26  C. de Gaulle, *L'Appel*, p. 67
27  Churchill College Archive Centre, SPRS 2/18
28  C. de Gaulle, *L'Appel*, p. 67

11  **De Gaulle Assumes France**
 1  C. de Gaulle, *L'Appel*, p. 71
 2  O. Harvey, *Diplomatic Diaries 1937–1940*, p. 375

12  **The Darkest Hours**
 1  W. Churchill, *The Second World War* (henceforth *SWW*), Vol. II, pp.
    109–11. See also War Cabinet Memorandum WP (40) 70 of 26.5.40
    (FO 371/24946)
 2  Author's interview with Sir John Colville, 17.7.80
 3  Ciano, *Diary 1939–43*, p. 274
 4  R. Sherwood, *The White House Papers of Harry L. Hopkins*, p. 150
 5  General Spears, *Deux Hommes . . .*
 6  Author's interview with Lady Soames, 8.7.80; see also Lady Soames,
    *Clementine Churchill*, p. 290
 7  C. de Gaulle, *L'Appel*, p. 88
 8  R. Cassin, *Les Hommes Partis de Rien*, p. 77
 9  C. de Gaulle, *L'Appel*, p. 80
10  J.-R. Tournoux, *Pétain et de Gaulle*, p. 228
11  Ibid., p. 210
12  Quai d'Orsay. Guerre 1939/45. Fonds de Londres 1940/43. Relations
    CNF-Agence Juive

13  **To Africa and Back**
 1  J.-R. Tournoux, *Pétain et de Gaulle*, p. 234
 2  General Catroux, *Dans la Bataille de Mediterranée*. See also G. Cattaui,
    *Charles de Gaulle*, p. 136

3 C. de Gaulle, *L'Appel*, p. 113
4 R. Murphy, *Diplomat . . .*, p. 76
5 *Fonds de Vichy. Relations Franco–Britanniques*, Quai d'Orsay
6 Ibid.
7 C. de Gaulle, *L'Appel*, p. 118
8 D. Grinnell-Milne, *The Triumph of Integrity*, p. 162
9 C. de Gaulle, *L'Appel*, p. 303
10 Ibid.

### 14 The Widening War

1 J.-R. Tournoux, *Pétain et la France*, p. 195
2 See de Gaulle's telegram of 2 November 1940 to Churchill, *L'Appel*, pp. 309–10
3 M. R. D. Foot, *SOE in France*, pp. 22–3
4 C. de Gaulle, *L'Appel*, p. 126
5 Ibid., p. 70
6 Ibid., pp. 141–2
7 W. Churchill, *SWW*, Vol. III, p. 289
8 State Department file 711, 51/158. Minute of 21.5.41 by Mr Hull. (US National Archives)
9 C. de Gaulle, *L'Appel*, Annexe, pp. 412–13
10 N. Gun, *Pétain, Laval, de Gaulle. Secrets des Archives Américaines*, pp. 236–9
11 General Catroux, *Dans la Bataille de Mediterranée*, pp. 136–7
12 C. de Gaulle, *L'Appel*, Annexe, pp. 425–6
13 Ibid., pp. 431–2
14 Ibid., pp. 486–8

### 15 Crisis with Churchill

1 *Chicago Daily News*, 27.8.41
2 PREM 3/120/1. Minute of 27.8.41 to PM
3 PREM 3/120/5. PM's telegram of 27.8.41 to Minister of State
4 Ibid. PM's Minute of 30.8.41 to FO and Morton
5 Ibid. PM's Minute of 1.9.41 to Mr Eden
6 Ibid. 2.9.41
7 PREM 3/120/4 contains the British records (a diluted version was made for circulation to officials), and de Gaulle's, which he sent to the PM on 15.9. According to de Gaulle's account, Churchill had said HMG wanted to treat Free France as the whole of France and thought the formation of a Committee would help to make this possible. On Churchill's instructions Morton wrote back to de Gaulle stating that this part of his record was not correct. De Gaulle's account also omits Churchill's reference to his suspected 'Fascist' views. But Churchill did use the word and restored it to

the War Cabinet record with his own hand when a prudent secretary tried to replace it by 'authoritarian'.

8   Interview with Sir John Colville
9   PREM 3/120/4
10  Admiral Muselier, *De Gaulle contre le Gaullisme*
11  F. Kersaudy, *Churchill and de Gaulle*, pp. 164–5
12  PREM 3/120/2, 3, and 4 contains the story of these manoeuvres
13  PREM 3/120/4 contains the PM's directive
14  F. Kersaudy, *Churchill and de Gaulle*, p. 166
15  PREM 3/120/4. PM's Minute of 26.9.41 to A. Eden
16  PREM 3/120/4
17  J.-R. Tournoux, *Pétain et de Gaulle*, p. 209
18  C. de Gaulle, *L'Appel*, pp. 224–5

## 16  Dealings with the Russians and Americans

1   Quai d'Orsay, *Fonds de Londres, Relations CNF–URSS*, p. 220
2   State Department file, 711. 51/7–444 contains an interesting review of this subject which Murphy sent to Mr Hull on 4.7.44 when about to leave Africa
3   PREM 3/120 contains a copy which de Gaulle sent Churchill a month later.
4   C. de Gaulle, *L'Appel*, Annexe, p. 494
5   The sequence of events can be worked out by collating the secret account which Admiral Muselier gave the United States Consul in the islands, Mr Pasquet (State Dept. file 851..00/48, despatch of 26.12.41) with the Quai d'Orsay archive (*Guerre 1939–45, Fonds de Londres*) and the messages in the annexe to *Le Salut* (pp. 486 *et seq.*)
6   C. de Gaulle, *L'Appel*, Annexe, p. 503
7   State Department file 851A/00/48. Mr Hull's Minute of 11.1.42 to the President
8   See Mr Pasquet's despatch of 26.12.41, note 5
9   C. de Gaulle, *L'Appel*, p. 223
10  C. de Gaulle, *L'Unité*, p. 7

## 17  France: Resistance Grows and Turns to de Gaulle

1   H. Noguères, *Histoire de la Résistance en France*, Vol. I, p. 442
2   C. de Gaulle, *L'Appel*, p. 633
3   M. R. D. Foot, *S.O.E. in France*, p. 231
4   Ibid. The text of Moulin's original report is at Appendix E., pp. 489 *et seq.*
5   Ibid., p. 181
6   J. Lacouture, *De Gaulle*, p. 95

7  O. Guichard, *Mon Général*, pp. 139–47
8  These exchanges are to be found in PREM 3/120/7
9  J.-R. Tournoux, *Pétain et de Gaulle*, p. 282 (footnote)
10  PREM 3/120/4
11  C. de Gaulle, *L'Appel*, pp. 602–3
12  F. Kersaudy, *Churchill and de Gaulle*, p. 187 (footnote)
13  PREM 3/120/10A
14  C. de Gaulle, *L'Appel*, pp. 604–7
15  J.-R. Tournoux, *Pétain et de Gaulle*, p. 281
16  Mrs Peregrine Worsthorne told me this

18  **'The Mutes of the British Seraglio'**
 1  Colonel Passy, *Souvenirs*, Vol. I, p. 236
 2  Quai d'Orsay, *Guerre 1939–45, Fonds de Londres* (1211 CM)
 3  C. de Gaulle, *L'Unité*, p. 360
 4  Ibid., p. 33
 5  N. Gun, *Les Secrets des Archives Américaines*, pp. 386–7

19  **Operation Torch Lights a Political Blaze**
 1  W. Churchill, *SWW*, Vol. IV, p. 543
 2  J. Lacouture, *De Gaulle*, p. 108
 3  C. de Gaulle, *L'Unité*, pp. 42–3
 4  J.-R. Tournoux, *Pétain et la France*, p. 411
 5  Ibid., p. 413
 6  R. Murphy, *Diplomat Among Warriors*, p. 129
 7  W. Churchill, *SWW*, Vol. IV, p. 567
 8  C. de Gaulle, *L'Unité*, p. 51
 9  W. Churchill, *SWW*, Vol. IV, p. 570
10  Quai d'Orsay, *Guerre 1939–45, Fonds d'Alger, Papiers Massigli* 1463
11  L. Joxe, *Victoires sur la Nuit*, p. 65
12  C. de Gaulle, *L'Unité*, p. 67
13  N. Gun, *Les Secrets . . .*, pp. 234–5.
14  H. Macmillan, *The Blast of War*, pp. 228–9
15  C. de Gaulle, *L'Unité*, p. 67
16  See R. Murphy, *Diplomat . . .*, p. 169, and A.-J. Voituriez, *L'Affaire Darlan* (Présentation F. Broche), pp. 234–9
17  Admiral Docteur, *La Grande Enigme de la Guerre: Darlan*, p. 252
18  N. Gun, *Les Secrets . . .*, p. 339
19  C. de Gaulle, *L'Unité*, pp. 79–81
20  Author's interview with M. Gaston Palewski, 1.7.80
21  R. Murphy, *Diplomat . . .*, pp. 174–7
22  C. de Gaulle, *L'Unité*, p. 461
23  H. Macmillan, *The Blast of War*, p. 313

24 General Cochet's account is among papers in Box 13, Office of European Affairs, State Department, 1940–4
See also N. Gun, *Les Secrets* . . ., p. 278

**20 De Gaulle in North Africa: Conflict with Roosevelt**
1 N. Gun, *Les Secrets* . . ., pp. 394–5 (Not Roosevelt's original words. Re-translated from the French translation)
2 C. de Gaulle, *L'Unité*, pp. 103–4
3 W. Churchill, *SWW*, Vol. V, pp. 154–5
4 H. Macmillan, *The Blast of War*, p. 312
5 Quai d'Orsay, *Fonds d'Alger, Papiers Massigli*, Vol. 1463
6 Ibid.
7 H. Macmillan, *The Blast of War*, pp. 345–6
8 C. de Gaulle, *L'Unité*, p. 496
9 N. Gun, *Les Secrets* . . ., p. 350
10 Ibid., p. 347
11 F. Kersaudy, *Churchill and de Gaulle*, p. 289
12 W. Churchill, *SWW*, Vol. V, p. 157
13 Quai d'Orsay, *Fonds d'Alger, Papiers Massigli* 1464
14 C. de Gaulle, *L'Unité*, p. 115
15 H. Macmillan, *The Blast of War*, pp. 346–7
16 Quai d'Orsay, *Fonds d'Alger, Papiers Massigli*, Vol. 1464. Report of 8.7.43 from Massigli to Couve
17 *New York Times*, 17.7.43

**21 Towards Liberation**
1 Author's interview with President Mitterrand, 19.12.81
2 C. de Gaulle, *L'Unité*, p. 198
3 N. Gun, *Les Secrets* . . ., pp. 417–18
4 Author's interview with Lady Soames, 8.7.80
5 State Department file 711 . . 51/341A, minute of 5.1.44
6 N. Gun, *Les Secrets* . . .
7 State Department file 711 . . 41. Reports of the Stettinius Mission to London March–May 1944
See also OEA 1940–4. Box 13

**22 Triumph**
1 C. de Gaulle, *L'Unité*, p. 223
2 Ibid., p. 224
3 Quai d'Orsay, *Papiers Massigli*, 1465
4 Ibid.
5 C. de Gaulle, *L'Unité*, p. 229

6 Ibid., p. 230
7 OEA 1940–4. H. Freeman Matthews' Minute of 15.6.44 to Mr Hull (US National Archives)
8 OEA 1940–4. Papers of Mr Dunn and Mr Matthews. Telegram of Mr Eden of 16.6.44 (US National Archives)
9 C. de Gaulle, *L'Unité*, p. 232
10 Ibid., p. 240
11 C. de Gaulle, *L'Unité*, p. 241
12 Ibid., p. 283
13 Ibid., pp. 293–4
14 N. Gun, *Les Secrets . . .*, p. 358
15 Ibid., p. 400 and footnote
   See also C. de Gaulle, *L'Unité*, p. 297
16 C. de Gaulle, *L'Unité*, p. 306
17 Ibid., pp. 311 *et seq.*
18 Ibid., p. 315
19 Ibid., p. 320
20 General Eisenhower, *Crusade in Europe*, pp. 326–7


23 **On to Victory**
1 C. Mauriac, *Un Autre de Gaulle*, p. 39
2 'Français, si vous saviez', broadcast on French TV in 1973, and on the BBC in 1980
3 C. Mauriac, *Un Autre de Gaulle*, p. 23
4 Ibid., p. 47
5 Ibid., p. 60
6 J.-R. Tournoux, *Pétain et de Gaulle*, p. 329
7 C. de Gaulle, *Le Salut*, pp. 52–4
8 Ibid., pp. 60–79
9 N. Gun. *Les Secrets . . .*, p. 413
10 Author's interview with Sir John Balfour, British Chargé d'Affaires in Moscow during de Gaulle's visit, 27.1.81
11 Ibid.
12 C. de Gaulle, *Le Salut*, p. 83
13 Ibid., pp. 175–6
14 Ibid., p. 176
15 Ibid., pp. 172–5


24 **Discord and Departure**
1 A. Horne, *A Savage War of Peace*, p. 27

2 C. de Gaulle, *Le Salut*, p. 194
3 H. S. Truman, *Year of Decisions*, p. 160
4 Ibid.
5 Ibid., p. 156
6 G. Pilleul, 'L'Entourage de de Gaulle', p. 356
7 O. Guichard, *Mon Général*, p. 185
8 C. de Gaulle, *Le Salut*, p. 250
9 Ibid., p. 38
10 C. Mauriac, *Un Autre de Gaulle*, pp. 52 and 86
11 Ibid., p. 61
12 C. de Gaulle, *Le Salut*, p. 204
13 Ibid., p. 205
14 Ibid., p. 230

## 25 In Opposition

1 J. Lacouture, *De Gaulle*, pp. 148–9
2 State Department file 33174 (US National Archives)
3 PREM 3/121/5. Sir A. Cadogan's minute of 18.6.45 to PM
4 C. Mauriac, *Un Autre de Gaulle*, p. 253
5 J.-R. Tournoux, *La Tragédie du Général*, p. 37
6 Ibid., p. 38

## 26 The Rally of the French People 1947–53

1 J. Charlot, *Les Français et de Gaulle* (A study of IFOP opinion polls), pp. 35–6
2 Author's interview with M. Jacques Foccart, 24.4.81
3 Author's interview with Lady Soames, 8.7.80. There is some doubt about the date of the letter, but none that it was sent
4 J.-R. Tournoux, *La Tragédie du Général*, p. 547
5 Ibid., p. 129
6 Author's interview with Geneviève de Gaulle (Madame Anthonioz), 9.4.81
7 Ibid.
8 J.-R. Tournoux, *La Tragédie du Général*, p. 276

## 27 Withdrawal

1 L. Terrenoire, *De Gaulle 1947–54. Pourquoi l'Echec?*, pp. 269–70
2 O. Guichard, *Mon Général*, p. 304
3 L. Terrenoire, op. cit., pp. 269–70
4 J.-R. Tournoux, *La Tragédie . . .*, p. 179
5 Author's interview with Baron de Courcel
6 C. de Gaulle, *Le Salut*, p. 290

7 B. Crozier, *De Gaulle, The Statesman*, p. 551 (footnote)
  See also A. Grosser, *The Western Alliance*, pp. 172–3
8 J. Vendroux, *Cette Chance que j'ai eue*, p. 433

## 28 Return to Power

1 M. and S. Bromberger, *Les 13 Complots du 13 mai*, pp. 44–5
2 Ibid.
3 B. Crozier, *De Gaulle, The Statesman*, p. 460
4 M. and S. Bromberger, *Les 13 . . .*
5 J. Massu, *Le Torrent et la Digue*, p. 123
6 C. de Gaulle, *Mémoires d'Espoir*, pp. 25–6
7 J. Massu, *Le Torrent et la Digue*
8 M. and S. Bromberger, *Les 13 . . .*
9 J. Massu, *Le Torrent et la Digue*
10 C. de Gaulle, *Le Renouveau*, p. 30
11 P.-O. Lapie, *De Léon Blum à de Gaulle*, p. 841

## 29 The Birth of the Fifth Republic

1 A. Horne, *A Savage War of Peace*, p. 309
2 Ibid., p. 307
3 C. de Gaulle, *Le Renouveau*, p. 39

## 30 Algeria, 1959–62

1 A. Horne, *A Savage War . . .*, pp. 337–9
2 C. de Gaulle, *Discours et Messages*, Vol. III, pp. 162–6
3 A. Horne, *A Savage War . . .*, pp. 411–14
4 Ibid., pp. 447–8
5 Author's interview with Louis Joxe, 11.12.81
6 The late Jacques de Beaumarchais, who had conducted secret negotiations with the Chinese on recognition while Director of Political Affairs at the Quai d'Orsay, and was later French Ambassador to Britain, told me this

## 31 The Time for Tripartism

1 C. de Gaulle, *Mémoires d'Espoir*, p. 214
2 Author's interview with M. Couve de Murville, 8.4.81
3 No fewer than six successive versions of Dulles's speaking notes for his first meeting with de Gaulle, all in turn discarded, are to be found among the papers in the Dulles collection at Princeton
4 State Department record of conversation between General de Gaulle and Mr Dulles on 5 July 1958, released to me under the Freedom of Information Act

5 Author's interview with Geneviève de Gaulle (Madame Anthonioz), 9.4.81
6 This account of the de Gaulle-Adenauer conversations is drawn from *Mémoires d'Espoir*, pp. 184–90
7 A. Grosser, *The Western Alliance*, p. 187
8 State Department record of conversation between General de Gaulle and Mr Dulles of 15.12.58, released to me under Freedom of Information Act
9 Ibid.
10 State Department incoming telegram No. DULTE 8 of 6.2.59 from Paris, for President from Secretary of State, released to me under Freedom of Information Act
11 C. de Gaulle, *Le Renouveau*, p. 226
12 J.-R. Tournoux, *La Tragédie du Général*, pp. 364–5
13 J. Newhouse, *De Gaulle and the Anglo-Saxons*, p. 117
14 Private information
15 Private information
16 J. Newhouse, *De Gaulle and the Anglo-Saxons*, pp. 160–61
17 Ibid., p. 163
18 Author's interview with Geoffroy de Courcel
19 Private information
20 Private information
21 H. Alphand, *L'Etonnement d'Être*, p. 368n
See also J. Newhouse, *De Gaulle and the Anglo-Saxons*, p. 185, for the same threat in slightly different words
22 J. Newhouse, *De Gaulle and . . .*, pp. 231–2

32 **Europe for the Europeans**
1 C. de Gaulle, *Mémoires d'Espoir*, p. 177
2 Ibid., p. 182
3 A. Peyrefitte, *Le Mal Français*, p. 53
4 C. de Gaulle, *Mémoires d'Espoir*, p. 200
5 Information from Baron de Courcel
6 H. Macmillan, *The End of the Day*, p. 367

33 **'The Great Quarrel'**
1 M. Couve de Murville, *Une Politique Etrangère*, p. 106
2 C. de Gaulle, *Discours et Messages*, Vol. IV, pp. 73–6
3 M. Couve de Murville, *Une Politique Etrangère*, p. 106
4 Ibid., pp. 97–8
5 Ibid., p. 121
6 J.-R. Tournoux, *La Tragédie du Général*, pp. 459–60
7 L. B. Johnson, *The Vantage Point*, pp. 23–4

8  C. de Gaulle, *Discours et Messages*, Vol. IV, pp. 226–7
9  Telegram S/520 of 16.12.64 from US Delegation to NATO Ministerial Meeting, Paris, to State Department, released to me under Freedom of Information Act
10 I remember because I had prepared the brief

## 34  Cultivating the Russians
1  M. Couve de Murville, *Une Politique Etrangère*, p. 199
2  Ibid., p. 204

## 35  'The Peoples Rising to the Surface of Our Civilization'
1  C. de Gaulle, *Discours et Messages*, Vol. IV, p. 174
2  Author's interview with Roger Vaurs, press spokesman on the tour, now French Ambassador to Belgium, 4.7.81
3  Author's interview with Walter Eytan, Israel Ambassador to France at the time, 21.5.81

## 36  The Home Front 1959–65
1  O. Guichard, *Mon Général*, p. 403
2  C. de Gaulle, *Discours et Messages, 1962–65*, p. 166 (footnote)
3  J. Charlot, 'Les Français et de Gaulle' (IFOP), p. 228
4  Ibid.

## 37  De Gaulle Makes Haste
1  I have translated from the French text as given in 'L'Entourage de de Gaulle', by G. Pilleul, pp. 384–5
2  In the account here given I have drawn extensively on *Une Politique Etrangère* by M. Couve de Murville, pp. 219–21
3  Private information
4  Couve de Murville, *Une Politique Etrangère*, p. 221
5  C. de Gaulle, *Discours et Messages*, Vol. V, p. 99

## 38  The Six-Day War
1  D. Ben-Gurion, *Israel*, p. 803
2  A. Eban, *An Autobiography*, pp. 343–4
3  Ibid., p. 360
4  J. Charlot, *Les Français et de Gaulle . . .*, pp. 86–7
5  Sir H. Wilson, *The Chariot of Israel*, p. 357
6  Ibid., pp. 357–61
7  P. Lefranc, *Avec Qui Vous Savez*, pp. 253–4

39 **The Solitary Exercise of Power**
  1 C. de Gaulle, *Mémoirs d'Espoir*, p. 255
  2 A. and P. Rouanet, *Les Trois . . .*, p. 50
  3 Ibid., pp. 69–70
  4 Ibid., p. 135
  5 J. Charlot, *Les Français et de Gaulle . . .*, p. 87
  6 A. and P. Rouanet, *Les Trois . . .*, p. 185
  7 C. de Gaulle, *Discours et Messages*, Vol. V, pp. 212–13
  8 A. and P. Rouanet, *Les Trois . . .*, p. 164
  9 H. Wilson, *The Labour Government 1964–70*, p. 560
 10 See Chapter 31, n. 21

40 **Youth Rebels: May 1968**
  1 This was the figure quoted by M. Pompidou speaking in the National Assembly on 14 May 1968
  2 A. and P. Rouanet, *Les Trois . . .*, p. 238
  3 Ibid., p. 239
  4 The then Secretary-General of the CFDT, the late Eugène Descamps, told me this
  5 A. and P. Rouanet, *Les Trois . . .*, pp. 320–21
  6 G. Pompidou, *Pour Rétablir une Vérité*, pp. 249–51
  7 Author's interview with Bernard Tricot
  8 Author's interview with General Massu, 15.12.81
  9 F. Flohic, *Souvenirs d'Outre Gaulle*, p. 182
 10 F. Flohic, *Souvenirs . . .*, pp. 104–5
 11 J. Mauriac, *Mort du Général de Gaulle*, p. 162

41 **Decline**
  1 M. Debré, *Français, Choisissons L'Espoir*, p. 132
  2 de Gaulle, *Discours et Messages,* Vol. V, pp. 334–5
  3 A. Peyrefitte, *Le Mal Français*, p. 85
  4 M. Debré, *Français . . .*, p: 139

42 **The Soames Affair**
  1 I was involved in the Soames Affair from the beginning, and much of this chapter is based on my recollections
  2 This was done at my suggestion. I remembered reading of an occasion in the 1840s when Guizot had disavowed ideas attributed to him by the British Ambassador in a report to the Foreign Office, and had reproached the Ambassador for not clearing his despatch with Guizot himself
  3 Interview with M. Couve de Murville
  4 C. de Gaulle, *La France et Son Armée*, p. 53

### 43 Renunciation

1 Author's interview with M. Roger Frey, 23.4.81
2 R. Nixon, *Memoirs*, p. 371
3 Ibid., pp. 371–4
4 H. Kissinger, *The White House Years*, Vol. I, p. 110
5 Ibid.
6 A. Malraux, *Les Chênes qu'on Abat*, p. 98

### 44 Last Days

1 F. Flohic, *Souvenirs d'Outre-Gaulle*, pp. 223–4
2 A. Malraux, *Les Chênes qu'on Abat*, pp. 189–90
3 Author's interview with M. Pierre-Louis Blanc, who assisted the General with his Memoirs during 1969–79
4 Ibid.
5 A. Malraux, *Les Chênes qu'on Abat*, p. 21
6 Ibid., p. 229

### 45 The Achievement and the Legacy

1 R. Nixon, *Memoirs*, p. 386
2 C. de Gaulle, *Lettres . . ., 1905–18*, p. 88
3 A. Malraux, *Les Chênes qu'on Abat*, pp. 192–3
4 O. Harvey, *Diplomatic Diaries 1937–40*, p. 375

# INDEX

Abbas, Ferhat, 242, 254
Abyssinia, 91
Acheson, Dean, 272
Adenauer, Konrad: Franco-German accord (1958) cancelled by de Gaulle, 260; visits de Gaulle at Colombey, 261–3; Franco-German entente, 262–3, 281–2; West Germany stays in NATO, 262; Berlin, 265, 266, 268, 271; loses support over Berlin Wall, 271; supports de Gaulle on EEC, 277, 277–8, 279; Franco-German Treaty of Friendship, 282, 283, 289; succeeded as Chancellor by Erhard, 292; private talks with de Gaulle, 294, 322; funeral, 292
Africa, in Second World War, 57–8; French West and Equatorial Africa, 79–86, 137, 156–7; Roosevelt's policy towards, 87–8, 117, 156–7; East Africa, 90, 91; Madagascar, 123–4, 130–1, 131–2; North Africa, see North Africa
Africa, post-war policy of France in (see also Algeria), 166, 239, 240–1, 245, 246, 302–3
Africa, see also Egypt; Nigeria
Aiglon, L' (Rostand), 7–8
Ailleret, General Charles, 340
Alexander, A.V., 105–6, 107, 116
Algeria: French post-war policy in, 166; nationalist riots in, 200; failure of Mendès-France to carry reforms, 224; armed rebellion in, 225, 226–7; settlers plan revolt, 227; de Gaulle returns to power, 228–37; de Gaulle's reception in Algeria, 238–9, 241–2; FLN form provisional government, 244; French military success, 245; de Gaulle proclaims self-determination, 245–6; insurrection by settlers, 246–8; FLN solidarity broken briefly, 249–50; opposition to war in France, 250–1; new referendum, 'no' by settlers, 251–2; desperate settlers form OAS, 252; attempted coup by army officers, 252–3; peace talks with FLN and ceasefire (1962), 252, 253–6, 307; exodus of settlers, 256; independence recognized (1962), 256;

de Gaulle's achievement, 256–8, 381; agreement on faster withdrawal of French troops (1964), 303; agreement on Sahara oil (1965), 304; de Gaulle's legal measures against rebel officers, 311–12
Algiers, American capture of, 135
Algiers Committee, see CFLN
Ali, Rashid, 92, 94, 95
ALN (Armée de la libération nationale), 245
Anfa, see Casablanca
Anglo-French Union, proposed, 63–4
Anne de Gaulle Foundation, 220
Anvil, Operation, 176
Ardennes offensive, 192–3
Argenlieu, Captain Thierry d', 75
Argoud, Colonel Antoine, 247, 312
Aron, Raymond, 72
Astier de la Vigerie, Emmanuel d', 139
Astier de la Vigerie, General François d', 139–40, 141, 154
Astier de la Vigerie, Henri d', 139, 141
Atlantic Alliance, 259, 260, 288, 317, 319
Atlantic Charter, 100
Atlantic Community, 282, 293
Attlee, C.R., 171–2, 205
Auburtin, Jean, 42, 61
Auphan, Admiral, 182
Auriol, Vincent, 211, 218, 233, 236

Badoglio, Marshal Pietro, 161
Balfour, Sir John, 191
barbouzes, les, 312
Barjonet, André, 350
Barre, Raymond, 361
Bastien-Thiry, Colonel Jean-Marie, 258
Baudet, Philippe, 156
Baudouin, Paul, 49, 60, 61, 83, 87
Bayeux, de Gaulle acclaimed at (1944), 172
BBC, Free French broadcasts on, 67–8, 69, 75, 88
BCRA (Bureau Central de renseignements et d'action), 125, 153–4, 156
Beaverbrook, Lord, 59

405